EVERY SCREEN ON THE PLANET

EVERY SCREEN ON THE PLANET

The War Over TikTok

EMILY BAKER-WHITE

W. W. NORTON & COMPANY
Independent Publishers Since 1923

Copyright © 2025 by Emily Baker-White

All rights reserved
Printed in the United States of America
First Edition

For information about permission to reproduce selections from this book, write to Permissions, W. W. Norton & Company, Inc., 500 Fifth Avenue, New York, NY 10110

For information about special discounts for bulk purchases, please contact W. W. Norton Special Sales at specialsales@wwnorton.com or 800-233-4830

Manufacturing by Lakeside Book Company
Book design by Lovedog Studio
Production manager: Lauren Abbate

ISBN 978-1-324-08666-6

W. W. Norton & Company, Inc.
500 Fifth Avenue, New York, NY 10110
www.wwnorton.com

W. W. Norton & Company Ltd.
15 Carlisle Street, London W1D 3BS

10 9 8 7 6 5 4 3 2 1

For Adam and Jigsy

CONTENTS

Introduction — 1

ACT I

Chapter 1	INFORMATION LOOKING FOR PEOPLE	9
Chapter 2	THE MORAL CHAMPION	14
Chapter 3	"VERY SIMILAR TO RUNNING A COUNTRY"	21
Chapter 4	THREE WAYS TO MAKE MONEY ON THE INTERNET	29
Chapter 5	MANUFACTURING HYPE	35
Chapter 6	A GUY NAMED JORGE	46
Chapter 7	CONTENT MODERATION	54
Chapter 8	RECTIFICATION	61
Chapter 9	EXPRESSION AS A USER RIGHT	66
Chapter 10	THE FIFTH ESTATE	77

ACT II

Chapter 11	LEVERAGE	87
Chapter 12	TO INFINITY AND BEYOND	96
Chapter 13	"BRO GET KPOP STAN ON THIS"	108
Chapter 14	GALWAN VALLEY	118
Chapter 15	AMERICAN PUPPET	125
Chapter 16	KEY MONEY	131
Chapter 17	TIKTOK GLOBAL	138

ACT III

Chapter 18	DRIVER CARRIES NO CASH	147
Chapter 19	THE CORPORATE GROUP	154
Chapter 20	DISAPPEARANCES	158
Chapter 21	OWNERSHIP AND CONTROL	168
Chapter 22	THE TIKTOK TAPES	178
Chapter 23	INTERNAL AUDIT AND RISK CONTROL	184
Chapter 24	THE MISGUIDED EFFORT	192

ACT IV

Chapter 25	WARTIME	203
Chapter 26	SELL OR ELSE	209
Chapter 27	SHOUTIME	216
Chapter 28	LOYALTY TESTS	226
Chapter 29	"NO INSULT TO BYTEDANCE . . ."	236
Chapter 30	ENSHITTIFICATION	244
Chapter 31	"LOL HEY GUYS"	250
Chapter 32	PAFACAA	258

ACT V

Chapter 33	THE PIVOT	269
Chapter 34	A SENSE OF CRISIS	273
Chapter 35	CONTINGENCY PLANS	282
Chapter 36	THE TIKTOK PRESIDENT	289
Chapter 37	DEFENSIVE DEMOCRACY	294
Chapter 38	PER CURIAM	304
Chapter 39	THE FLICKER	315
Chapter 40	TWO DADDIES NOW	321

Epilogue	329
Acknowledgments	331
Notes	332

INTRODUCTION

THE NOTE ARRIVED SOMETIME AROUND MIDNIGHT, WITH no letterhead and no address line. Slipped by an unknown person under the hotel room doors of tech luminaries from around the world, it posed a challenge: register your objections by 8 a.m., or the following ideas will be attributed to you.

When global tech founders and leaders descended on the 2014 World Internet Conference in Wuzhen, China, they didn't know what to expect. Representatives from Apple, Facebook, and Microsoft were ferried into the town's pristine tourist zone on traditional black-awning boats alongside Chinese tech moguls like Alibaba's Jack Ma and Tencent's Pony Ma. Chinese state media characterized the conference (a state-sponsored affair) as an opportunity for their government to challenge the digital dominance of the United States. For the most part, though, the gathering was a standard tech conference—until its final night, when its participants received the piece of paper.

Purporting to speak for the conference goers, the paper was titled "Wuzhen Declaration," and it endorsed an idea championed by Chinese autocrat Xi Jinping: cyber sovereignty. The concept was simple—the web should be carved up into countries just like the physical world, and each government should be free to control its own domain.

Atop the declaration was a short cover sheet, which gave recipients an email address to which they could send any objections or proposed revisions. A group of them sprung into action: in China, "cyber sovereignty" meant letting the government surveil, censor, and propagandize its people, who did not enjoy the right to free speech or a free press. Global executives didn't want to be seen condoning such an authoritarian stance.

The Chinese government had hoped to produce a document that would challenge American and European ideals of an open internet. But without the buy-in of foreign executives, the statement was useless. Defeated but proud, and ever-controlling of their messaging, the conference organizers pretended the paper had never existed in the first place.

The 2014 Wuzhen gambit was soon lost to history, but it was a sign of tensions to come. It's difficult to remember now, but the 2014 internet was an optimistic place. Social media use was surging; it seemed that the dreams of early digital pioneers were becoming reality. That the internet would be a place where anyone on earth could express themselves freely, a place where discourse and commerce flowed beyond the constraints of geography.

This unenclosed frontier was a threat to governments. And their efforts to control it would shape the next decade of international competition.

~

THE WUZHEN CONFERENCE is remembered as a geopolitical project, but it had a simpler mission, too: showcasing a wildly impressive crop of up-and-coming Chinese entrepreneurs. Just hours before conference goers received the piece of paper, they had heard from Zhang Yiming, a founder whose product would, in just a few short years, give China exactly the sort of soft power it sought, without the inconvenience of joint statements or the buy-in of any other governments. Yiming's creation would become so beloved by citizens around the world that it would ignite a new cold war, resetting the balance of digital power between the US and China.

Yiming wasn't a conference headliner, though a dramatic orchestral theme still played as he approached the stage. He was short and slight; his shoulders barely reaching above the laptop protruding from the lectern. His presentation laid out plans for a futuristic marvel: a company that, through machine learning, aimed to eliminate the feeling "I wish I had known." It was wild to think that a computer might someday identify our desires better than we could. The idea challenged basic ideas of human agency and self-determination. Would we really be willing to cede our own curiosity to this man's machines?

Yiming's company was called ByteDance, and it was fueled by a central algorithm that profiled users, determined their interests, and fed them news and entertainment that it thought they would like. Its secret sauce was attention, as much of it as possible: if an app could hold users' focus for long enough, it could track their decisions and actions, and use those decisions and actions to predict what they wanted to see next, before they even knew to look for it.

ByteDance would eventually build an app called TikTok: a frictionless feed of short, entertaining videos trained meticulously on people's interests, personalities, and senses of humor. By 2021, TikTok would overtake Google as the most visited website in the world. By 2024, it would amass a following of more than a billion users, nearly the size of Islam.

TikTok would collect a daily census of this worldwide population, noting who they were talking to, what thoughts they were broadcasting to fellow users, what they were paying attention to, and what city or town they were in at any given moment. The app's algorithm would then make billions of decisions each day about what information to show people, creating a unique, custom experience for all who developed a relationship with it.

As a business, ByteDance was an extraordinary success. It had a flywheel effect: the more you used its apps, the better they learned your preferences, which led them to serve you things you liked, which led you to use them more, which led them to get even better. By the time it launched TikTok, ByteDance was the most valuable startup in the world. It had hundreds of millions of users in China, but Yiming wanted more. He wanted ByteDance to have a presence on every screen on the planet.

When Yiming went global, he began competing with companies that openly cast themselves as engines of democracy and self-determination. Facebook said it was about connecting people. Google's slogan was "Don't Be Evil." But TikTok—the first major internet speech platform that wasn't American—introduced itself as pure entertainment. If he wanted to play both sides, Yiming could take no position on the knotty problems raised by the piece of paper in Wuzhen.

The rise of China as an economic and technological superpower has been endlessly discussed in the US. But until the late 2010s, its arrival in Silicon Valley hadn't really set in yet. American tech giants embraced the idea that they were tied to a moral arc that bent toward online openness. TikTok's rise clearly wasn't tied to that arc, though, and its skeptics claimed it was tied to a conflicting one.

In the years between the 2014 Wuzhen Conference and TikTok's launch, Xi Jinping fully realized his project of fragmenting the internet—at least in China. Three years after the Wuzhen resolution went unadopted, a project that began as an effort to build consensus ended in conscription. The Chinese government passed a law saying that any Chinese company or person could be forced to spy for the state and then deny that they'd done so.

Yiming was neither a cheerleader for nor a member of the Chinese Communist Party. ByteDance was a haven for brilliant, often liberal Chinese engineers, and was routinely the target of government crackdowns for insufficiently toeing the party line. But politicians in the US, Europe, and elsewhere took the Chinese government at its word: Yiming and his staff, as Chinese nationals, might at any moment be forced to act as (unwilling) spies, gathering data or covertly seeding propaganda to advance China's geopolitical ends.

Around the world, lawmakers began asking questions about how much TikTok was subject to Chinese government control. The company ducked and dodged, trying to claim the platform wasn't controlled by people in China. But it was, and its own employees knew it.

The public was shocked to learn that details of their private lives were subject to capture by Chinese ByteDance staff. Whistleblowers came forward to correct the record, throwing ByteDance into a panic. Members of the company's internal audit team were let go for using location data to track journalists (including me). This was in many ways precisely the kind of spying that made people fear Chinese control of the app, and led to a criminal investigation.

The White House negotiated with ByteDance, asking it to wall off

TikTok's US business, and to grant the US government unprecedented control over its operations. During those negotiations, ByteDance invested more than $2 billion to build a system that purported to keep Americans' data in the US. The system, known as "Project Texas," was a novel attempt to divorce ownership from control. When its shortcomings came to light, American legislators sprang into action, determined to strip the Chinese government of its power over TikTok by forcing ByteDance to sell it off. But in targeting a foreign government's capacity to warp and distort discourse, they ultimately granted that same corrosive ability to their own.

As governments jousted over control over TikTok, and investors circled around a potential fire sale, the app's users continued to give ByteDance their greatest asset—their attention—for free. Across 150 countries, people formed relationships on and to the app, often spending more time with it than they spent with their family and friends. The jury might be out on whether TikTok could know us better than ourselves, but it came to know us better than just about anybody else.

This is a book about a tug-of-war between the world's two most powerful governments, and the team of transactional technologists caught between them. It is about how a private internet platform became a titan of soft power, at a moment when China threatened to overtake the US in cultural and economic influence across the world. It is about how supplanting intentional human choice has strained an increasingly fragile democratic project. And it is about how world leaders sought to harness a machine that could shape the personal realities of more than a billion people.

It's inevitable that strongmen would come for a tool that could seize and hold so much human attention. This is the story of what happened when they did.

ACT I

Chapter 1

INFORMATION LOOKING FOR PEOPLE

On a sunny May day in 2019, four young women in jeans and sneakers roamed the streets of the ritzy River North neighborhood of Chicago, looking for people to interview about a new phone app called TopBuzz. The women were employees of the Beijing-based tech giant ByteDance, which made TopBuzz, though nobody was supposed to know that. Their boss had told them to pose as college students working on a school project.

The women were in Chicago to learn, to *feel* American society so they could better build technology for it. As they enjoyed a Lake Michigan boat cruise and posed for photos under The Bean, their boss encouraged them to talk to as many Americans as possible, to figure out what motivated them, interested them, and kept them engaged.

Their app, TopBuzz, aimed to be a one-stop shop for everything on the internet. Bright yellow moulding bordered a personalized "bottomless feed" of posts scraped from thousands of websites: articles from *USA Today* and Agence France-Presse (AFP) abutted celebrity gossip, posts from meme sites like *Cheezburger* and *Bored Panda*, and online communities like GirlsAskGuys and Quora. Between the news, gossip, and community chatter were posts by accounts with names like Buzz Fire and PlayBuzz, which reposted popular material from elsewhere on the internet, like popular photos from Instagram and videos from YouTube.

Machine learning models categorized each article, blog post, and other piece of content by topic and theme, and then targeted them to people who might not be actively looking for them, but would click when they saw them. TopBuzz used your behavior to tailor your feed: every second you spent in the app was an opportunity, a clue about what might better draw you in and hold your attention next time. Even when you didn't click, perhaps you paused before scrolling past a certain topic or type of post, or there was a pattern in the last posts you viewed before you closed the app.

By spring 2019, TopBuzz had amassed more than 40 million American users—in the US, it was roughly 60 percent the size of Twitter. But because TopBuzz was run from China, the people working on it often didn't understand the news they were curating. Employees with limited English and minimal context about American daily life were ripping and republishing American news—but first, they were feeding it through a censorship filter: TopBuzz strictly forbade publishing articles that might displease the Chinese government.

In some cases, TopBuzz employees were allowed to green-light articles on US-China relations, if—as one China-based staffer described it—the angle of the story was not critical of the Chinese Communist Party. But in other cases, news about China was disallowed entirely. An automated "Leader Sensitive" flag excluded articles that mentioned, for example, the 2019 Hong Kong protests, the Chinese autocrat Xi Jinping, and even the children's book character Winnie-the-Pooh, whom some said resembles Xi.

Curators at TopBuzz also had the ability to "sticky" or "pin" certain articles or videos at the top of users' feeds—a useful feature in breaking news scenarios. Infrequently, however, employees said they were ordered to "pin" specific posts, and would have to submit screenshots back to the company to show that they had done so—or, at least, that's what former staffers told me. One recalled employees posting panda videos and promoting Chinese tourism in the app, while another remembered staff "stickying" a stilted video of a white man talking about why he was glad he had moved his startup to China.

At the helm of TopBuzz's US operations was a Chinese tech veteran in his thirties named Wang Xinyuan. Wang was an extrovert, well put together and personable, with a love for travel and an easy smile. He was the boss who had encouraged his young staffers to strike up conversation with locals in Chicago under the guise of being college students. In addition to his Beijing-based team, Wang also managed a small team of American staffers who acted as "cultural translators," helping their Chinese colleagues run a news app in a foreign country.

TopBuzz's team struggled with some of its practices. Americans pushed back when the company censored news (LGBTQ-themed videos were often blocked) and they balked when it republished scraped articles under made-up bylines without authors' permission. One staffer said the fake bylines "sounded like stripper names."

Chinese staffers also criticized the company's censorious policies, though unlike the Americans, they worried they might face consequences for speaking out. One particularly outspoken Chinese employee told friends she believed the Chinese government wouldn't let her travel to the US because of her anti-government speech. Another similarly vocal Chinese employee didn't show up for work one day, leading American colleagues to worry that he might have been "disappeared" by the government.

As Wang and his staffers interviewed their way across Chicago, they were joined by a few of Wang's American reports—members of the company's "cultural translation" project. The group rented cars and drove to Indianapolis. On the highway, the Chinese staffers marveled at billboards about Christianity and abortion. One asked a colleague why the government allowed homeless people to live on the streets.

The US team often struggled to convey to their Chinese colleagues what was and wasn't culturally appropriate. For a while, the company hosted a Q&A feature inside TopBuzz, where Chinese staff wrote questions for American users, often on topics like race, policing, and guns. US staffers were horrified by the questions, which they sometimes saw as racist. One American remembered seeing the question: "Why are Black people always so loud?"

In Indianapolis, Wang and his team descended on a lively craft beer hall with its tables arranged in a big square. Wang sidled up to a group of blue-collar workers, buying them drinks and trying to make friends. After he sat down with the group, his American staff watched with alarm as Wang began telling jokes about Asians and referring to himself as a "yellow man." By the end of the night, his new friends seemed to warm to the performance.

The next day, the TopBuzz group met up with executives from their parent company, ByteDance, in an aging office building on the north side of the city. The ByteDance leaders had flown in to observe a session at IndyFocus, a local market research firm where the company had rented a two-way mirror lab for the day.

The lights were dimmed. The observer section of the lab was like a cross between a small movie theater and a college lecture hall. On the other side of the mirror was a small, drab conference room dotted with concealed cameras, where IndyFocus interviewers would talk to TopBuzz users one-on-one. The ByteDance group sipped on bottles of Perrier and nibbled on sandwiches as they watched the interviews through the mirror. Monitors powered by the hidden cameras showed close-ups of the interviewees' facial expressions and phone screens. One American staffer munched on popcorn.

At the end of each interview, the jet-lagged observers would come out, thank the interviewees, and hand them a "swag bag" containing TopBuzz merch. There were two types of swag bag: one featuring a blue hat with white lettering, and another featuring a red hat with white lettering, which resembled then-President Donald Trump's signature MAGA hat.

In the observer room, after each interviewee filtered through, one employee was asked to guess their political leanings. Based on the staffer's guesses, likely Democrats were given blue hats, and likely Republicans were given red ones—a surprisingly low-tech form of inference for such a tech-focused company.

ByteDance shuttered TopBuzz in 2020, and later denied that it had ever ordered employees to push pro-China videos to its users. Some Americans who worked for TopBuzz, though, eventually came to feel a deep discomfort about their time there. They looked back in disbelief: a Chinese news app, run largely by people who didn't even understand the news they were curating, had accumulated more than half a Twitter's worth of US users and served them a personalized news feed of often misappropriated, censored news.

The next morning, Wang and his staff flew home. Sitting in an airport café with staff, Wang watched a TV news segment about the thirtieth anniversary of the Tiananmen Square massacre, expressing disbelief: he just couldn't believe people were talking openly about it. A colleague asked why he was so surprised. In asking their question, they said the words "Tiananmen Square."

Wang quickly shushed them. (The colleague couldn't tell if he was joking.) He said: "You never know who's listening."

Chapter 2

THE MORAL CHAMPION

ByteDance was a more than $10 billion company in China by the time it launched TopBuzz. Its signature product was a news app called Jinri Toutiao ("Today's Headlines" in English).

The app had a buttery-smooth user experience, and offered Chinese readers a personalized feed of news and entertainment years before Apple News launched in the US. It took a maximalist approach to collecting data, and was run by a culturally fluent and savvy team. Helmed by a culturally competent staff, the algorithm's power was formidable: it catapulted ByteDance to Tech Giant status within just a few years of its founding.

Toutiao was the brainchild of ByteDance's founder and CEO, Zhang Yiming: a techno-optimist obsessed with the idea of creating technology that would know us better than we knew ourselves. Yiming (as he preferred to be called) was a slight, bespectacled introvert. Some colleagues described him as cold, but nearly all agreed that he was humble and reasonable, and that he had excelled at building a company based on data, mathematics, and rationality.

Yiming grew up in modest privilege, as an only child to upper-middle-class public servants. His father worked for the municipal Science and Technology Commission before changing careers to open an electronics factory. In high school, he developed a deep love for science and computers, and he attended Nankai University, a renowned public research university in the Tianjin region of China similar to elite US state schools like the University of Virginia and UC Berkeley.

Yiming was deeply rationalistic: he viewed his human experience as a set of inputs, and tried to optimize the best outputs that those inputs could produce. In college, he didn't join any student clubs, and largely set his studies above friendship, dating, and the other defining escapades of university life. He embraced an extreme approach to self-discipline, almost always refraining from watching movies and playing cards or video games with his classmates. He was proud of this abstention, so much so that he even gave himself a nickname for it: the "moral champion."

Yiming married his college girlfriend, whom he met on the Nankai campus by offering to fix her computer. His grades were good, but not exceptional, and he had a largely flat affect: he rarely got visibly excited, but almost never showed anger. On the rare occasions that he consumed works of popular culture, he did so through a cerebral lens. According to a now-deleted social media post republished by the Chinese-language blog 老郭种树, he once watched a *Twilight* movie with members of his family only to dissect it later on social media, studying its psychological effects on its audience. "Satisfying the psychological needs of users is user experience," he allegedly posted.

Yiming believed his particular psychological needs were different from most people's. "A small number of elites pursue efficiency and realize self-awareness, and they live in reality," he told *Caijing* magazine. He thought most people, though, would fall prey to vice to some degree, whether that meant drinking, gambling, or some other form of indulgence. He didn't expect other people to eschew these temptations in the way that he had—in fact, he would later come to see Jinri Toutiao, his flagship creation, as something of a vice itself.

For a person who called himself a moral champion for his abstemious behavior, Yiming was unusually fixated on the mechanics of temptation and indulgence. As he sought to perfect the art of delaying gratification in his own life, he began exploring how apps could learn from their interactions with humans, and eventually simulate the same type of reward center that he sought to control. When he read David Kirkpatrick's *The Facebook Effect*, an admiring 2010 narrative about Facebook connecting communities around the globe, he allegedly said on social media that it reminded him of studying the properties of dopamine.

After college, Yiming cycled through engineering jobs at tech companies. One of them was Microsoft, where he quickly learned that he didn't like feeling like a cog in the wheels of a larger organization. After Microsoft, he joined Fanfou, China's first Twitter competitor, and first experienced working on social media. This was more like it: he loved the pace, the excitement, and the real time user engagement of the microblogging platform. But in 2009, his time there was abruptly cut short.

In summer 2009, ethnic clashes broke out in Urumqi, a city in the northwestern Chinese province of Xinjiang. Uyghur Muslim factory workers in the city had been accused of sexual aggression toward coworkers who were Han Chinese, the country's dominant ethnic group. Protests over the accusations grew into a series of riots that killed nearly two hundred people, resulting in a brutal government crackdown against the Uyghur community.

At the time, social media apps were viewed as largely liberal institutions: in a series of uprisings across the Middle East, Twitter and Facebook had helped anti-government protestors document and publicize democratic movements. Fearing the same types of public accountability from its own apps, the Chinese government took an unprecedented step: it shut down internet access across Xinjiang, and shut down platforms where citizens were discussing the riots nationwide.

The government announced a series of blocks and outages on Facebook, YouTube, and Twitter, and on a spate of similar Chinese platforms, including Fanfou. This was one of the first times—but far from the last—that Yiming would find himself frustrated with the Chinese government's suppression of online speech. In a now-deleted blog post, he voiced support for Google, another target of the crackdown. "Go out and wear a T-shirt supporting Google," he wrote. "If you block the internet, I'll write what I want to say on my clothes."

When Fanfou closed in 2009, Yiming took a calculated risk: at age twenty-six, with his college roommate, Liang Rubo, he founded his first startup. The product was a real estate search engine called Jiujiufang (or, in English, "99 Rooms"), which claimed it could help you buy a house from the palm of your hand. Smartphones were just beginning to take off in China, but Yiming saw how they would change our relationship to computers. Unlike many of its competitors, Jiujiufang embraced a design that it called "vertical search"—vertical because it was optimized for the vertical orientation of mobile phones, rather than the horizontal orientation of computer monitors.

Jiujiufang was a success—by 2011, it had more than six million monthly active users. But after just three years, Yiming was ready to move on from search engines. Search was inefficient: it required a user's full attention, and people were inherently lazy. The ideal system would give them the information they wanted without them having to ask for it.

Yiming believed tech was undergoing a shift: one from "people looking for information" to "information looking for people." So he, Rubo, and a few other engineers from Jiujiufang struck out to form a new venture, called ByteDance, that would be centered on building apps that predicted what you wanted to see, and served it to you without prompting.

Their first app was painfully simple: named "Hilarious goofy pics," it loaded a stream of, well, goofy pics. Similarly simple creations included "Inspirational quotes," "I'm a foodie" (for food pictures), and "Real Beauties—Every day 100 beautiful girls." Of these initial apps, the most successful was a comedy app called Neihan Duanzi, or "Implied Jokes," which would load an endless stream of funny memes. Users could upvote them or downvote them, then, based on their up or down vote, another post would load. The more votes a user made, the better the app would be able to infer their sense of humor.

Using this same underlying theory, the team also began training an algorithm to predict which news articles they would most want to read—the algorithm that would eventually undergird ByteDance's first true breakthrough product, Jinri Toutiao.

The predictive aspect of this project—when compared to the user-prompted "99 Rooms" search engine—was key to Yiming. He believed that algorithms could do a better job of identifying things for people than people could themselves, and that, accordingly, recommendations would supplant search as the primary way that we would find and consume information. Yiming was early to this idea, but it was one that would later fuel apps from Facebook to Baidu to Spotify, and even influence how mainstream newspapers presented information. (Today, even the *New York Times* engages in personalization on its home page.)

Toutiao began collecting the stuff that recommendation engines run on: clues, as many as possible, about users' habits, networks, and preferences—both stated and revealed. By 2013, these signals included users' browsing habits, their comments, the amount of time they spent reading specific articles, and the articles they chose to forward to others. The platform also offered an integration with Weibo, a Chinese social media platform similar to Twitter. Where users opted in, the integration would give Toutiao access to all the user's posts, comments, likes, and other data from Weibo—a rich source of data, especially about new Toutiao users who hadn't yet given the algorithm other meaningful information about their interests.

Toutiao was a near-instant success. By late 2013, when Yiming was just thirty, it had amassed more than 60 million users. In its early days, the app developed a reputation for trafficking in lowbrow news. It kept people coming back for more, but they were coming back for celebrity gossip and tawdry photos, rather than rigorous, reported news. To Yiming, this wasn't troubling: "Users need some indulgence," he said in an interview, "whether these things are religion, novels, love, or Jinri Toutiao.... I don't think there is much difference between playing Texas Hold'em and drinking red wine and watching gossip and videos."

Perhaps unsurprisingly, the Chinese Communist Party was not wild about Yiming's dream of a fully automated, personalized news curator— though it wasn't the celebrity gossip they were most worried about. In China, the government tightly controlled the media, and required it to promote certain narratives and suppress others. If an algorithm was in charge of serving people news, then how was ByteDance to ensure that it was sufficiently "promoting national unity," or distributing enough government propaganda?

Yiming argued that the lack of human editors was a good thing. "If Toutiao has an editor-in-chief, he will inevitably choose content according to his own preferences, but what we do is not choose," he told *Cai-*

jing. He acknowledged that some human interference would always be necessary when anyone could post to an app. "Violations of laws and regulations require intervention," he said, "but we do not interfere with user preferences or the diversity of content that is tolerated by society and the law."

In a basic sense, Yiming thought people were just getting in their own way. ByteDance's central creation, its algorithm, was essentially just a prediction machine—it took reams of data about how a person had acted in the past, and used that data to predict how they would act in the future—and Yiming believed it would do a better job showing people news they were interested in than any person ever could.

The story of ByteDance is in large part the story of its algorithm, the same one that Yiming first built to power Toutiao and would eventually power dozens of other ByteDance apps, too. In the early 2010s, ByteDance rose to power alongside companies like YouTube, Facebook, and Twitter to define the modern recommendations engine. But what would make Yiming unique was his insistence that his code could not only come to know Chinese consumers better than they knew themselves, but that it could extend that predictive power to every country and culture across the globe.

In 2014, Yiming went on a trip for Chinese tech founders to Silicon Valley organized by a Chinese startup incubator called GeekPark. The group visited the tech campuses of Google, Facebook, Yahoo, Tesla, and other renowned American startups, engaging in panel discussions and Q&As with some of the world's most prominent technologists. In a blog post about the trip, Yiming wrote admiringly about a new era of sharing, where the internet allowed people to share everything from houses (Airbnb) to cars (Uber) to design (Pinterest) and ideas (Twitter).

"Some people may say they are not willing to share what they own with others, nor will they share their private data—but these are just current views," he wrote. "We are still in the early days of the sharing era, and as time goes by more and more people will join in, which will lead to the reconstruction of business and social resources and the accelerated collapse of traditional boundaries. Technology and the Internet have no boundaries."

Technology and the internet did have boundaries—or at least they would, soon. And though he didn't know it yet, Yiming would spend the next decade of his life finding, moving, crossing, and forcing the world to define them.

Chapter 3

"VERY SIMILAR TO RUNNING A COUNTRY"

In October 2016, a buttoned-down audience filed into the swanky Dogpatch, San Francisco, event venue The Pearl for the venture capital firm Greylock Partners' annual #ProductSF conference. The agenda was filled with inscrutable, jargony panels: talks on things like "The Journey of the Pivot" and "Secrets Every PM Should Know." One panel stood out, though, for being less focused on products and more on a vision for the future, in which platforms would operate like countries, competing to lure the world's most powerful companies and institutions to their shores. The presenter was a Chinese hippie in sneakers, jeans, a long-sleeved T-shirt and a scarf, somehow suave in a sea of button-down shirts and business-speak.

Alex Zhu was thirty-seven years old, with an angular chin and shiny dark hair falling just above his shoulders. He was thin, almost gaunt, with a soft voice and a face brushed with the slightest hint of facial hair. His startup, Musical.ly, was virtually unknown to members of the crowd, unless they happened to have a child between the ages of eight and sixteen. Musical.ly was an app that let users record themselves lip-synching and dancing to clips of music. It was irrelevant, even "cringe," to older teens. If you could drive a car or buy a beer, you had outgrown it. Few people over twenty-five had even heard of it. But to young American teens and tweens, it was the center of the world.

By fall 2016, Musical.ly boasted approximately 50 million monthly active users, many of them under the age of thirteen. By one estimate, nearly half the teens and preteens in the US were on the app, which led to strange media coverage, such as an ABC news anchor featuring a video made by her nine-year-old daughter, or a local Denver station interviewing a class of third graders. A *New York Times* article asked: "Who's Too Young for an App?"

Entrepreneur and internet personality Gary Vaynerchuk declared it "no question the youngest social network we've ever seen." Youth-oriented apps like Instagram and Snapchat had courted child users in the past, but they mostly marketed their apps to adults and older teens.

Though Musical.ly had offices in Los Angeles, Alex and his team primarily ran the company from their headquarters in Shanghai. To ensure that they understood the needs of their users—teens and tweens halfway around the world—the team stayed in constant communication with groups of the app's most avid devotees via the Chinese texting platform WeChat. The Musical.ly team hosted daily WeChat threads with "musers," asking them for product feedback and feature suggestions, but also just chatting about nothing. Sometimes, these conversations were "just to talk, to understand what they think, making jokes, to be immersed in the American teen culture," Alex said.

Onstage at the Greylock Partners conference, venture capitalist Josh Elman asked Alex how he thought about building a community of users, especially when competitors like Instagram and Snapchat were trying to lure the app's young stars away. Alex's answer was that he wasn't just building an app, he was building a new society—one with its own government, laws, and incentives. "The way I look at it, building a community is very similar to running a country, running an economy," he said.

As Alex saw it, Musical.ly offered a wide-open frontier, new land to be settled. Alex compared his platform to the colonial United States, and his competitors—Facebook, Instagram, YouTube—to countries in Europe. "The economy in Europe is already very developed, and in your country, there is no population, you know, there aren't so many things going on," he analogized to Elman. "There is no economy. How can you attract those people to come in?"

Alex then answered his own question: people move to colonies for opportunity, for upward mobility, for the American Dream. And that dream—or its illusion, at least—was something he could engineer. He told Elman that his new colony would distribute "a majority of the wealth . . . to a small percent of people, to make sure those people then get rich"—and to make sure that everyone else *saw* them get rich.

The lucky few would "become role models for other people living in [metaphorical] Europe," he said, inspiring them, too, to come to his new Musical.ly land. "You have to give the opportunity to average people, and make sure they get satisfaction. Make sure they are a middle class, coming up."

Elman asked Alex about what role his Chinese-ness played in the development of Musical.ly. "Talking about centralized economies and more capitalistic economies, you have this really unique vantage point in that you live in China," Elman said. He asked how Zhu's Chinese team was able to so intimately understand the desires of teenagers in the United States.

Alex responded that many Chinese people followed US discourse quite closely: "A lot of Chinese people know American culture very well. Like, today, if you go to social media in China, many people talk about the presidential election, the debates," Alex said.

"Really?" Elman asked.

"Yeah, people talk about the US presidential debate more than the Chinese one, because"—here, Alex's voice betrayed a little nervousness—"there is no Chinese one."

Elman, and the crowd, laughed uncomfortably.

Alex's presentation was compelling—so much so that his charisma normalized behaviors that, from another speaker, might have raised eyebrows. Toward the end of the conversation, during Q&A, Alex offered a more direct answer to the question about how he came to understand Musical.ly's American teen audience: he'd posed as a teen himself, asking others what they thought of the app, and trying to make them feel like their posts were reaching people.

"I personally registered a lot of fake accounts, and used this fake identity to talk with the users on the platform, comment on their videos, and see why they post these videos, and just try to understand, try to get empathy."

~

ALEX ZHU WAS born around 1979 in Anhui, China, four years before ByteDance founder Zhang Yiming. Like Yiming, he attended a prestigious college—Zhejiang University—but unlike the "moral champion" Yiming, Alex's passion was for the arts: he loved design, music, and other forms of creative expression.

Alex traveled extensively in his twenties, exploring and photographing destinations from Italy and Holland to Tahoe and Yosemite to the deserts of Inner Mongolia. Unlike Yiming, he embraced drinking and smoking, appearing to live life to its fullest. He wore his hair long—sometimes nearly down to his waist—and dressed in loose, artsy clothing. "He totally looks like a poet," Elman later told *Bloomberg*. "Like an ancient Chinese painter sitting by the side of a river, you know, doing one of those giant scroll paintings."

Perhaps unbeknownst to Elman, Alex actually *was* a poet, and since his college days, he had used the internet as a personal canvas for his creative output. By 2002, he had registered the domain www.keepsilence.com, a website that would serve as his personal blog throughout his twenties. On the site, he recommended music to his readers, from rock and folk songs to classical and Buddhist compositions. He also republished the works of writers he liked, especially the poet Haizi, and posted his own writing—sometimes prose, but mostly poetry.

Throughout his twenties, Alex wrote about classic themes of love and death, addiction and religion. "If my delicate life were trampled into dirt by careless horses' hooves the moment it began, then my eternally unbound soul would scatter its final fragrance on the lift of a gentle breeze. But I do know this well: the Master of Heaven will show mercy to his last child on earth. He has allowed me to bloom in silence, to sing in silence, and even to resist in silence."

He also tackled more abstract themes—one poem was titled "about the century and the motherland."

As Alex aged, so did his writing. On the blogHi domain, in his late twenties, he began writing more about psychology and how the human brain processes information. (This blog, unlike the original keepsilence.com, was written in English.) In one 2005 blog post, he explored the cognition science behind human memory. In another, a comment on a short story published in *Salon*, he wrote: "Be always *curious* about our miraculous world. Everything around us contains tremendous information, but we are just ignoring it."

This passage revealed another parallel between Alex and Yiming: both were obsessive about learning through observing the people around them—something Alex would do intently for nearly a decade in the United States before he launched Musical.ly.

Between 2004 and 2007, and again from 2011 to 2015, Alex had a fun job at a boring company: he was a "solution manager" and then a user experience (UX) designer—and eventually the resident "futurist"—at the German software conglomerate SAP, which makes software for businesses, like the platforms used to manage supply chains and track expenses. His job was to figure out new features for SAP to build, and to make SAP's tools easier for their users to understand—so that they would intuitively know what each button and function and product would do, and why they would want to use it. And, as an antidote to the tedium of corporate life, he also started a Twitter account under the handle @bullshitting.

SAP allowed Alex to exercise his creativity and his artistic talent. But in the end, the work was just too corporate to keep him engaged. He told Elman at The Pearl: the company just "wasn't sexy enough." He wanted to build something for regular people, rather than businesses.

"I want to be a sexy man," he quipped.

So in 2013, Alex left SAP and teamed up with a friend, Louis (Luyu) Yang. The two would-be founders had overlapped as product managers at a Shanghai insurance company called eBaoTech several years before. At first, their dream was to build an education platform called Cicada, where people could upload short videos teaching others something—how to tie a fisherman's knot, or care for a tulip bulb, or play a song on guitar. But the idea was a bust. The way Alex tells it, the barriers to entry were simply too high: creators had to invest considerable time and effort into producing educational videos, and people watching the videos had to devote their undivided attention to them.

Alex and Yang analyzed Cicada's failure, asking what they could have done differently. What they decided was that they should have made it frictionless: "If you want to build a new UGC [user-generated content] platform or social network, the content needs to be extremely light, meaning the content creation and content consumption have to be within seconds, rather than minutes or hours," Alex said.

In 2014, Alex and Yang started Musical.ly, initially rolling out the service in both China and the United States. Chinese young people didn't take to it, but it exploded in the US. Alex would later tell *The Economist* that this was because American teens had more free time than their Chinese peers did, and because they often had more freedom to make videos just for fun.

Musical.ly was one of the first apps made for kids who had never known life before the internet. Facebook, Instagram, and YouTube had offered millennial teens an exciting new addition to their existing, offline social lives. But Musical.ly users were true digital natives: phones and computers and tablets had always been there, and were used as much for school as for entertainment and pleasure. Of course, their devices would also help them individuate, key to how they made friends and developed their style, culture, and community for the first time.

Today, Gen Z nods to their digital nativeness with an observation they call the "Millennial Pause." When people born in the 1980s or early 1990s make videos, there is often a second or two of dead air at the beginning. The creator is looking, perhaps, for confirmation that their phone is now recording—or just taking a moment to compose themself. After all, the video is a public performance, a publication of a purposefully made recording.

Gen Z doesn't feel the performance. There is no delineation between physical presence and digital presence. To them, there is just presence, with nearly every facet of it distributed both online and in the physical world. To frictionlessly record and post a video is simply to exist.

Long before Alex started Musical.ly, he began thinking about how a new era of digital sharing would change people's social lives. In January 2012, on a new blog that he called *The Passion of Sisyphus*, he published a short story called "Social Network, Big Data," told from the perspective of an internet anthropologist, set two hundred years in the future.

The anthropologist studied what he called "the first wave of social network users" and described conducting research "entirely within" social networks. He talked about the effect on social media companies when people passed away and reflected on the permanence that the internet affords dead people, whose "lifestyles and thoughts" become "digital fossils that record the bygone eras."

Describing his work in what he called "microhistory," the character talked about studying in detail the social media profiles of the dead, looking for clues in selfies and other postings, anything that might provide a window into an individual's understanding of and response to the world. "Then, I use pattern recognition tools to analyze his or her contacts . . . observing the formation, intensity, and eventual cooling off of each interpersonal relationship."

Alex was playful and empathetic in his depiction—from the future—of modern digital life. Of social media's early users, his anthropologist character said: "Their knowledge system was surprisingly simple, yet they kept a passionate interest in all social events at all times, always expressing their opinions. Their technology was primitive, which is precisely what makes us envy the almost idyllic lifestyle of that era."

Alex's blog post was fanciful, the stuff of run-of-the-mill science fiction. But the extent to which our world came to resemble it in just a dozen years suggested it had real value. The account had a nostalgic note to it, mourning "the beautiful landscapes, vibrant cities, and various plants and animals that were wiped out" and suggesting that "people of that era were happy because of their ignorance." But there was a dystopian cast to it, too. In this futuristic world, the people of 2012 had "their thoughts and privacy ... completely stored in [a] lunar data center," from which they were "thoroughly scrutinized by their descendants." And perhaps the darkest part was the narrator's description of what life would be like two hundred years from now, when everyone lives in "nutrient tanks," and are called "informational beings."

Chapter 4

THREE WAYS TO MAKE MONEY ON THE INTERNET

As Alex Zhu tells it, he had the idea for Musical.ly in 2014 while riding the Caltrain from SAP's Silicon Valley offices to his home in San Francisco. He saw a group of teens—some listening to music, others snapping photos and videos for social media—and thought, why not combine the two?

Alex was not the only entrepreneur to have this idea. At the time, the web's preeminent destination for teen short videos was Vine, a platform owned by Twitter that allowed users to make videos that were six seconds or shorter. Because it gave people such a small window in which to make an impact, Vine's videos skewed toward stunts and other raucous, silly behavior that quickly grabbed a viewer's attention.

Soon, several other startups emerged to compete with Vine, specializing in a particular genre that was popular among teens and preteens: lip-synching and dance routines set to popular music. One such competitor was Flipagram, a slideshow app that let users make picture and video collages and set them to clips of music. Another was Dubsmash, an app that let people lip-sync over audio clips and dub their own audio over video clips.

Initially, Flipagram—which would later become ByteDance's first entry into short video in the US—showed massive potential. It boasted stars like Britney Spears and Macklemore as early adopters, and in early 2014, the acclaimed Sequoia Capital partner Michael Moritz, along with fellow venture capital heavyweights Kleiner Perkins and Index Ventures, poured $70 million into the slideshow app. "It looked to us like a monster," said John Doerr of Kleiner Perkins. "On the order of an Instagram."

Doerr's prediction did not materialize, because Flipagram wasn't a replacement for Instagram—it was just an add-on. Flipagram was a tool for making slick videos, but not a destination for watching them. Teens would use it to prepare polished, cohesive "stories" that they would then post on Instagram and Snapchat. This gave Flipagram free advertising (the slideshows contained a visible watermark) but also cabined its ambitions: this was not an Alex Zhu–style conquest of a new land, not the creation of a new society; it was just a tool to help people navigate their existing land and society a little bit more smoothly.

Flipagram was founded by Farhad Mohit, a graduate of the Wharton School of Business and a serial founder coming off of a string of failed ventures. Mohit was older than Alex, and more focused on the business side of social media. He was a programmer by training, but saw himself as something of a hybrid between an engineer and a businessperson. As he told a local tech blog in 1999, "I . . . saw myself as the ideal person to bridge this gap between the techies and the suits."

Long before he ever thought of Flipagram, Mohit made his Silicon Valley fortune. At Wharton in the mid-1990s, he and a classmate had founded Bizrate, a website where customers could review vendors they had hired, and Shopzilla, a related shopping comparison app. In 2005, they sold the websites to the E.W. Scripps Company for $525 million. Mohit was rich for life—two years later, he bought a 14,000-square-foot Bel Air mansion that is now valued at $38 million.

But Mohit was also still in his thirties, and hooked on the feeling of building companies from scratch. So he tried out several other ideas. There was Gripe, an attempt to integrate consumer complaints about businesses into social networks, and Cheers, which, as he put it, was "the 'like button' for the world around you." Before them, there had been DotSpots, a platform that would "allow ordinary people, or what we call the 'wisdom of crowds,'" to append user-generated content to works of journalism. Mohit later acknowledged on LinkedIn: "This didn't work out as planned :)."

As an editing tool, Flipagram was a success. Tens of millions of people, mostly teens, had seized on it as a way to make their Snapchat and Instagram stories cooler. But Mohit wanted people to use Flipagram *instead* of Instagram, to like and engage with one another's posts directly on the app—because that's where money was.

On a Wharton podcast in 2009, talking about DotSpots, he laid out the stakes: "There's only three ways to make money on the Internet. One is: sell subscriptions. We're not selling subscriptions. Two is: sell software. We're not selling software. Three is some form of selling advertisements. Today, we're not selling advertisements. You know why? We don't have anybody using the damn system. So if we never get anyone to use the system, it's pointless for me to sit here and explain to you how we make money from it."

What was true for DotSpots was also true for Flipagram. Mohit could charge for use of Flipagram's services by charging for each slideshow a user made, or perhaps with a monthly subscription fee. (Eventually he did try a version of this, charging users to remove the Flipagram watermark from their slideshows, for $1.99 per post.) But the real money in early 2010s Silicon Valley was in advertising, which meant Mohit was chasing eyeballs—attention—and the goal was ubiquity. He began telling people that Flipagram had evolved from a tool into a network, and the company tried desperately to attract and retain creators to make videos and slideshows exclusively for the app. But when they weren't on Instagram, Flipagram users were starting to spend more and more time on another app: Alex Zhu's Musical.ly.

In August 2015, Musical.ly announced that it had raised a $16+ million funding round, mostly from Chinese and Chinese American investors. Alex had pitched Silicon Valley's top firms, too, but had faced skepticism: no Chinese app had yet been able to break through to American audiences. Still, Musical.ly was starting to see cracks in the ceiling, because it had developed its own, distinctive style.

When teens recorded a Musical.ly post, music would play as they recorded, but they could pause it and slow it down, often to half or a quarter of its normal speed. This allowed them to film intricate, precise movements that they'd never be able to pull off at full tempo—but that looked very cool when stitched back together in a fifteen-second clip. They also began to experiment with "tutting," an elaborate, angular style of movement, often done just with the arms, that grew out of the 1970s/80s Electric Boogaloo form of California hip-hop dance. The app became flooded with challenges and competitions, in which users snaked their fingers and hands across screens in routines that were tightly synched to popular music.

Tempo manipulation and tutting differentiated videos made on Musical.ly from those on other platforms. It was no longer just another video platform competing with Vine and Flipagram; instead, it was something with a language of its own. And while Flipagram, like Instagram and Facebook, sought out celebrity users as evidence of their success and free advertising for the service, Musical.ly—true to Alex's theory that building a social platform was like building a new society—focused on minting new stars entirely.

Ariel Martin, who began using Musical.ly at age fourteen, landed herself on *Time* and *Forbes* lists of the internet's most influential creators for the distinctive hand motions in her Musical.ly posts. She made how-to videos for other young dancers, teaching them how to record videos that would look precise and striking when played at full speed. Lisa and Lena Mantler, a pair of thirteen-year-old identical twins from Germany, became known for their tightly synchronized, bubblegum pop–style dances, gaining nearly 30 million followers on the platform. Jacob Sartorius, a teen musician who first posted on Vine, became so popular on Musical.ly that he launched national and international tours, and two of his songs broke into the *Billboard* Hot 100.

All of these platforms—Flipagram, Musical.ly, Vine, and Dubsmash—were competing for the same primary audience: teens and tweens. To win them, an app would need to establish that it was where the cool kids were. Platforms competed fiercely for users like Martin, Sartorius, and the Mantlers, who had built devoted followings. They offered them money, free promotion, and other perks, all with the ultimate goal of signing them to exclusive contracts, which would lock them and their fans to a specific app, making it the one where they would spend their time.

By building its own community from scratch, Musical.ly had made what Mohit at Flipagram had tried to, but couldn't: a digital destination that threatened Facebook and Instagram. And Mohit knew it. In August 2016, after laying off staff, the company hired a banker to shop it around to potential acquirers. By that point, it was bleeding money and users, and VCs were worried about recouping their investments. Meanwhile, Mohit had two small children at home, and had promised his wife that he wouldn't sink more of his own money into the company.

Many of Flipagram's top prospects passed on the opportunity to buy it, but a few gave it some thought. The most exciting prospect was Snap, the corporate owner of Snapchat, which was considered "cool" by Flipagram's users, and which had first popularized the twenty-four-hour "stories" that Flipagram was famous for making in the first place. But by late 2016, a Snap deal had failed to emerge. Demoralized, Mohit's team began negotiating with another potential acquirer—a company from China known for a news aggregator called Jinri Toutiao, which was just starting to put down roots in the US under the name TopBuzz.

In May 2016, Musical.ly announced that it had raised another funding round—this time, for $133 million, at a valuation that made the company worth more than $550 million. Just under two months later, the company launched a second app, called Live.ly, that would allow Musical.ly users to make and watch livestreams. And that summer, amidst the launch of the Live.ly platform, Alex began hearing from Mark Zuckerberg.

In 2014 and 2015, as the market for teen lip-synching video apps had exploded, Facebook announced that it would begin a "pivot to video" that would promote short videos in its News Feed.

"With the launch of auto-play and the surge in mobile use, it's also important to focus on posting videos that grab people from the first frame of video," said a Facebook blog post. "Shorter, timely video content tends to do well in News Feed. Keep in mind that auto-play videos play silently in News Feed until someone taps to hear sound, so videos that catch people's attention even without sound often find success."

As Facebook announced this product shift, Zuckerberg began devoting much of his personal time and energy to studying China and the

Chinese app market. Facebook had been banned by the Chinese government in 2009 along with Twitter, Fanfou, and other apps, but Zuckerberg was hopeful that he could find a way back into the most populous country in the world.

He studied Mandarin, becoming proficient enough in the language to give speeches and host Q&A sessions at Beijing's renowned Tsinghua University. He posted a picture of himself in March 2016 jogging through Tiananmen Square—on a day when the air pollution was so severe that the air smelled of smoke and locals wore masks outdoors. (The incident was described in the *New York Times* as Zuckerberg's "Smog Jog.") In a bizarre request, Zuckerberg even asked China's authoritarian leader, Xi Jinping, to choose a name for his firstborn child. Xi declined, saying the choice was "too much responsibility."

In August, Zuckerberg invited Alex to Facebook's headquarters in Menlo Park. Though the talks were serious, Facebook was wary about just how young Musical.ly's users really were. Collecting information about children under thirteen was illegal under federal law. Still, illegal or not, hooking preteens was good for business: young people spent a huge amount of time on social media, and data about their developing commercial habits was valuable to advertisers.

Facebook also hoped that acquiring Musical.ly might help its other apps become cool again. By this point, the company's internal research showed that its namesake app had lost popularity with young users. Teens' views of Instagram, which Facebook had bought in 2012, were better, but still not as strong as the company would have liked. So in September, Zuckerberg sent a team to meet with both Alex and his cofounder, Louis Yang, at Musical.ly's headquarters in Shanghai. But by then, he was not the only bidder knocking on Alex and Yang's door.

Chapter 5

MANUFACTURING HYPE

STARTUPS ONLY END THREE WAYS. MOST SIMPLY FAIL: THEY raise some money, pursue a business plan, but fail to make the economics work, so they shut down. Luckier ones survive: they raise some money, then make some money, and if they're profitable or promising enough, they drive toward an "exit."

There are two types of "exits"—acquisition by a larger company or an initial public offering (IPO). But IPOs are only available to the very largest firms, so most founders and investors chase payouts through acquisition, which is how they turn their stake in a startup into cash.

"Exits" are the ultimate goal of successful startups, but they often aren't as rosy as they appear. If a company is acquired for less money than investors put into it, then founders usually take home nothing. The story might still be an exit (better than most founders ever achieve), but an exit does not equal a profit.

By late 2016, Farhad Mohit, founder of Flipagram, was considering even the least appealing exits for his startup. Investors wanted to broker a deal, any deal, that would save them from total loss. Sequoia Capital, a firm that had invested in both ByteDance and Flipagram, had introduced Zhang Yiming to Mohit, hopeful that it could at least recoup its stake in the struggling slideshow app.

In January, Yiming pulled the trigger. Flipagram's cash reserves had become critically low; according to one office rumor, Mohit had put down the company card during a meal with ByteDance execs, only to have it declined. Author Matthew Brennan reported that the purchase price had been a meager $50 million—$20 million less than the company's Series A fundraise.

Flipagram employees were relieved when they heard the company had sold. Upon acquisition, Mohit said that Flipagram would continue to operate independently from ByteDance. The Chinese tech giant offered its new staff a show of goodwill—it sent Flipagram's L.A.-based staff shirts emblazoned with 666, a good luck symbol in Chinese culture that often means "smooth," "awesome," or "cool," without realizing that in the US, the number was associated with the devil. The employees laughed. Yeah, the shirts were weird, but at least their employer had enough money to send them free swag.

The Flipagram acquisition was the first in a series of moves Yiming would make to enter the US market. In 2018, Yiming had announced that he had two main goals for the coming years: first, an aggressive pivot into short video apps, and second, a global expansion that would make ByteDance's apps as important to people beyond China as they were to those within it. By 2020, he said, he wanted more than half of the company's users to be foreigners.

Within China, Yiming pivoted hard to the short video market. ByteDance was, if anything, late to the trend—in 2014, some three years before, Yiming had said he couldn't ride the subway through Beijing without being bombarded by ads for new apps serving users feeds of short videos.

As early as 2011, Yiming had recognized that plummeting TV watch time, especially among young people, was an opportunity for web-based video—and he reasoned that online ads could be worth much more than TV ads, because they could be more precisely targeted to likely purchasers.

Yiming worried that ByteDance was both too small and too late to compete with other Chinese short video apps. But in 2016, it launched not one but three new apps that would try anyway. Each was targeted to a different segment of the market: Huoshan (or "Volcano Video" in English) targeted low-income, rural users, as Kuaishou had done. It grew by paying people cash for videos they posted on the app—the payments were small for ByteDance, but significant for the cash-strapped creators receiving them. The second app, known as Xigua or "Watermelon

Video," was a YouTube clone focused on longer videos. The third was a short video platform called A.me.

A.me was modeled after Musical.ly, but Musical.ly hadn't done well in China. Alex Zhu had believed this was because Chinese preteens were studying while their peers in the US were socializing (a belief that was validated by studies comparing Chinese and American students' study time). Still, ByteDance hoped that A.me could capture the attention of a demographic that his other apps couldn't: digital native, wealthy, cosmopolitan teens.

Following the Musical.ly playbook, A.me obsessively courted its earliest adopters. A.me "talent managers"—who felt like peers and friends to A.me's young creators—added them to group chats with ByteDance project managers and engineers. Just as the Musical.ly team had done in their WeChats, the ByteDance staffers encouraged their young users to make feedback requests and report bugs, and even to download and play around in test versions of the app. The company even paid for the young stars to travel to Beijing for meetups and events.

Like Alex Zhu had done with Musical.ly's young "musers," ByteDance's talent managers became personal friends with the app's earliest users. In the Chinese press, ByteDance was panned for cloning Musical.ly, but A.me's users didn't care; the app suited their needs.

A few months after the launch of A.me, ByteDance asked its creators' chat to weigh in on a key strategic question: in December 2016, ByteDance decided to change A.me's name, and the company wanted suggestions: What should the new name be? The chat members considered several options—Huangke 晃客 ("Rocker" or "Shaker") and Shanka 闪咖 ("Flash Mobber") were among them—but they settled on Douyin, or "Shaking Sound," which reflected their focus on music and dance. When the company updated the app, changing its name from A.me to Douyin, it publicly credited several users from the chat with creating its new moniker.

To Yiming, the success of A.me—now Douyin—was important, but it was just one piece of the puzzle. ByteDance was also preparing to launch internationalized versions of its short video apps, just as it had launched TopBuzz as an internationalized version of Toutiao. Yiming was obsessed with out-expanding his competitors. He might not have been first to short video in China, but he could still be first to it abroad, and specifically, in the United States.

In mid-2017, ByteDance launched a clone of Douyin in Japan, Korea, Indonesia, and Thailand, luring celebrities to the app by throwing lavish parties that featured popular actors, singers, and models. These countries were a sensible place to start: most of Douyin's fiercest competitors had not yet launched across Asia, so ByteDance began on an open playing field. And it worked: within a year, Korean pop supergroup BLACKPINK joined the platform, bringing millions of devoted fans along with them—and by 2019, the even bigger group, BTS, would join.

Back in the US, despite Mohit's claim that Flipagram would continue to operate independently, ByteDance quickly seized the reins in LA's Flipagram office. A new manager named Peggie Li transferred over to Flipagram from TopBuzz, and served as the primary manager of the startup's L.A. office. She was young—in her late twenties—but experienced in video entertainment, with prior stints in Hollywood and at a studio that made YouTube videos. ByteDance also added some support staff to Flipagram, to fill out an office that had been plagued by layoffs as its cash reserves had run low. Maybe the new owners would help turn the place around, thought staffers.

Still, there were signs that ByteDance's management approach would strain its new American employees. Li told her reports that they would need to move onto ByteDance's employee goal system, under which they received evaluations every two months. She told them to set goals with the assumption that they would only meet 60 percent of them, and had a demanding, intense demeanor that frightened some of her staff.

The transition was especially tough for Flipagram's community team, a handful of cheerful twentysomething talent managers whose job was to woo creators to the platform. Li told them that they would be evaluated based in part on how many views their creators received, but they quickly found out that those view counts weren't fully accurate. Flipagram, like ByteDance's Chinese app, Huoshan, had started to pay some creators based on the number of views they garnered. But the creators were often paid for fewer views than the app claimed they had received. This led to awkward conversations. The talent managers didn't understand which views were real any better than their creators did.

Soon, though, the community team encountered a bigger problem: they started receiving a rash of complaints from victims of impersonation.

On all social media platforms, some degree of impersonation is inevitable. Someone steals someone else's content and reposts it as their own. Or they sit on the username of a famous person or brand, confusing fans. Usually platforms respond by setting up systems to report and take down accounts engaged in impersonation.

But this was different: impersonation complaints had spiked dramatically and stayed high. The claims came from all sorts of people: well-known influencers from other platforms, parents of children, and even some of the creators that Flipagram staff were trying to recruit. Their claims shared parallel facts: each victim had discovered an account on Flipagram that was a mirror image of an account they maintained on another platform, like Instagram, YouTube, or Musical.ly.

Flipagram's young talent managers were flummoxed. They consulted a back-end system to look at the email addresses linked to the mirror accounts, in the hopes of identifying the impersonators. To their horror, the addresses for the mirror accounts all shared a common format: they contained a string of numbers and the word "orange"—and ended in @bytedance.com. The fakes were coming from inside the house.

Unbeknownst to most of its US employees, ByteDance had assigned a team in China to scrape more than ten thousand videos each day from US-based social media platforms, including Instagram, Snapchat, and Musical.ly. The company would then use the scraped posts to train its For You algorithm (which had become exceptionally good at predicting Chinese users' tastes, but less good at capturing virality in the US)—and to create fake accounts impersonating people on Flipagram.

When US employees found out about the scheme, they were furious. Their employer had falsely represented that a whole slew of people (in some cases, children!) had chosen to join their platform and agreed to their terms of service when those people didn't even know the platform existed. The talent managers' bosses told them to respond to the mountain of complaints by offering to turn over the impersonating accounts to their rightful owners. But they were not to reveal that it had been ByteDance itself doing the impersonating. Instead, they would say the offending accounts were created by "fans."

Some US staffers pushed back on the scraping project, but ByteDance employees in China did not see the problem. Norms and laws about intellectual property and web scraping were different in China, and some Chinese staff argued that the fake accounts gave the company valuable information about which content users most wanted to see. They also said the scraped videos gave users examples of successful posts that they should emulate. But the fake accounts gave Flipagram another benefit: they made it look more popular than it really was.

Ultimately, the social media startup business is about manufacturing hype. People join new apps when their friends, or people they admire, are also on those apps. Nobody has time to keep up with yet another app—so for people to download and embrace a new platform en masse, it has to seem necessary, inevitable, like you'll miss out on something important if you're not there.

This hurdle is a variation of the classic "cold start problem": at the beginning of every business's life, it needs its first ten, then its first hundred, then its first thousand customers. How will it find and recruit those initial buyers? Platforms that rely on user-generated content have a compounded version of this problem, because the product *is* the users: their posts, their likes and comments, their interactions.

Misleading your customers is a bad look. But ByteDance was hardly the only tech giant using fake accounts to get ahead. Alex Zhu had solved Musical.ly's cold start problem in part by posing as fictional teens to make other teens feel loved and accepted by their peers. Perhaps Flipagram's fake accounts—like Alex's—were a necessary evil, a helpful tool to jumpstart a flywheel of authentic engagement.

There was a problem with this theory, though: Flipagram wasn't new.

It already had many hundreds of real, human creators. Every time a user was shown a post from a fake account, that meant they'd see one fewer post from a real one—a reality that directly hurt creators who were paid per view. And at a moment when they were already losing momentum to Musical.ly, it pained Flipagram's talent managers to watch their actual creators struggle to gain traction.

In the end, Flipagram turned out to be something of a social media Ponzi scheme—lots of people joined, but they joined in part because they were falsely told everybody else was already there. When they got there, the vibes were off—the app was missing dopamine. Flipagram's failure made Musical.ly's success all the clearer: Alex had created a new, distinct place online where people would want to spend time.

It would be years before ByteDance could claim to have built a place like that in the United States. So Yiming—who had begun his foray into video apps by trying to clone Musical.ly—did the next best thing: to the absolute shock of the Flipagram team, he announced that ByteDance would be spending nearly $1 billion to acquire Musical.ly.

For Yiming, the acquisition process was a very different beast the second time around. While Flipagram had been desperate to sell, poet-founder Alex Zhu had spent months entertaining not just Zuckerberg, but also other suitors including Apple, Disney, and Kuaishou. Alex was in the 1 percent of founders who truly made it: unlike Mohit, constrained by Flipagram's dire finances, Alex didn't have to sell to anyone—and with the world's top tech companies in chase, he wouldn't take a deal he didn't like.

Alex's choices *were* constrained, however, by one of his board members: Cheetah Mobile CEO Sheng Fu. As an early investor in Musical.ly, Cheetah Mobile, a Chinese maker of smartphone games, owned 17 percent of the company, and Sheng's board directorship came with a vote of veto power over any deal *he* didn't like.

Just as Sequoia had furthered its own interests by matchmaking Yiming and Mohit, Sheng had his own set of priorities for any potential Musical.ly deal. Under his freewheeling leadership, Cheetah Mobile's apps would eventually be booted from the Google App Store for engaging in click fraud, and Sheng himself would be charged with insider trading and fined more than $500,000 by the SEC. But for the moment, he was eager to condition any sale of Musical.ly on some extra upside for him.

As Cheetah's CEO, Sheng had arranged for the company to invest in a Europe-focused news aggregator called News Republic, and to build a fledgling livestreaming app called Live.me. Sheng wanted to offload the investments as a bundle, he said, so he would only approve the sale of Musical.ly if the buyer invested in the other two apps as well.

The prospect of acquiring unnecessary apps turned Kuaishou's CEO away, and fears of violating federal laws against collecting data from children caused Facebook to waffle. But Yiming took the bundle, acquiring News Republic (which, after all, could fit in nicely with Toutiao and TopBuzz) and agreeing to make a $50M investment in Live.me. For Alex, the deal was a once-in-a-lifetime payday: he had brought his company to acquisition at a purchase price close to the "unicorn" level of a billion-dollar valuation. For Yiming, buying Musical.ly and Live.me was a way to circumvent the near-impossible task of persuading millions of American teens to migrate to an unknown Chinese app.

Right from the start, the plan was to merge Musical.ly into ByteDance's domestic juggernaut, the app its users had renamed "Shaking Sound" or Douyin. Just a day after the deal closed, the ByteDance VP who had led the negotiations, Liu Zhen, told the press: "In the future, Douyin and Musical.ly will leverage their technology and content advantages to jointly create the world's largest short video social entertainment platform."

Just as it had with Flipagram, ByteDance quickly started making changes to Musical.ly, integrating its systems into the ByteDance back end. It kept Flipagram around, too, but stripped it of its more advanced editing tools, and lowered the video resolution, optimizing the app for regions of the world where internet connections were weaker. Flipagram would become an anglicized version of Huoshan, the app ByteDance had targeted at low-income, rural Chinese communities—and Musical.ly would become the equivalent of Douyin.

By early 2018, the transformation was complete. Flipagram was rebranded as Vigo Video, which shared Huoshan's logo. ByteDance stripped away the bright orange branding in Flipagram's L.A. office on Santa Monica Boulevard, replacing it with an awkward, temporary red sign that said ByteDance. Then, it moved Musical.ly's US staff into the building, where the staffs of the two acquired companies—still bitter rivals—began working across the open-plan office from one another.

The vibes between teams were awkward, to say the least. Under ByteDance, Flipagram had pilfered videos from Musical.ly and impersonated their users. Meanwhile, according to one former Flipagram employee, Musical.ly had coded an autocorrect feature that changed mentions of Flipagram on the Musical.ly app to "lol."

Despite the fact that they were all now ByteDance employees, the teams were told to continue competing directly with one another. Each cohort kept courting the same influencers, hawking the same exclusive contracts that would forbid them from working with the other, and hosting events where staffers for the other app were decidedly not invited.

ByteDance also began aggressively advertising both Flipagram and Musical.ly on YouTube and Facebook. Most of the ads featured typical Musical.ly and Flipagram fare: skits of young teens dancing to pop music. But a few of them took a different tack: a slew of Musical.ly ads that ran on Facebook in spring 2018 paired a reel of popular video from the platform with provocative language about the current president of the United States: "Donald Trump doesn't use musical.ly. Join now."

Toward the end of the summer 2018, the Musical.ly staff was tapped by ByteDance HQ to help plan the biggest event yet: an August 1 launch party that would mark a rechristening of Musical.ly, a merging of it into ByteDance's internationalized version of Douyin. Because Douyin was unknown in the US, ByteDance had the opportunity to define it to millions of people for the first time.

Before the launch party, ByteDance had lined up top US creators, whom it would pay tens of thousands of dollars per post to direct their fans to follow them on the Douyin clone. Some contracts specifically required the creators to make posts advertising the new Musical.ly on their Instagram stories (complete with a new Douyin watermark), and promised to reward creators with "verified" status in exchange for posts.

The party itself was held at the celebrity-studded NeueHouse Hollywood, a ritzy club and coworking space. The Douyin logo—a cheerful, almost bouncing, music-note-shaped lowercase *d*—was emblazoned on the walls, people posed in photobooths wearing headgear in the shape of clocks, and waitresses wore minidresses with translucent aprons that shimmered back and forth between Douyin's teal and hot-pink shades. Custom cocktails like the #ForYouFizz and the #Trendy-Tini flowed freely from an open bar, though many guests were underage. In a sea of sequins, stage lights, and exposed midriffs, hundreds of young performers filmed themselves and each other, "making content" as they edited snippets of the night's energy to share with fans.

Projected on the walls was Douyin's first-ever English language slogan—the hashtag #MakeEverySecondCount. The night featured a series of influencer performances, with a lineup that went out of its way to highlight ByteDance's international appeal. Alongside Aruban Musical.ly stars Jayden and Gilmher Croes were a Korean influencer known as Sister Yell and a Taiwanese prankster duo known as the Huang Brothers.

After the influencers, and as the clock approached midnight, Alex Zhu—who had, like Yiming, flown into town for the event—took the stage to announce Musical.ly's official transformation. Alex's voice was raspy, and he hyper-enunciated each sentence into the microphone, working to break through the crowd's side chatter. He described the app as a "twin" of Musical.ly, and told attendees that it was the most-downloaded app in the world in 2018.

"Now, the world is your stage," he thundered. "You can reach a new global audience that you could not have reached before. People in Taiwan, people in Korea, people in China." The audience let out some whoops. One audience member yelled "my dream!" to giggles from his side of the crowd.

When the clock struck midnight, an update hit the iPhone and Android app stores, replacing the Musical.ly app with a new app on millions of phones—not just for attendees of the party, but for everyone who had ever downloaded the app.

"The new name of the new platform will be TikTok!" Alex was in full performance mode. Drawing on the energy of the thrilling young creators and the ebullient staff and likely also his own enormous payday, Alex began chanting into the microphone:

"Tick!

"Tock!

"Tick!

"Tock!"

Chapter 6

A GUY NAMED JORGE

WHEN YOU FIRST OPEN TIKTOK, THE APP DOESN'T KNOW that much about you yet. It knows your approximate location, your language preferences, and whether you've showed up in any of its other users' contact lists—but your interests are still largely a mystery. So it shows you a preselected set of popular videos, and watches you react, recording how long each video holds your attention, and whether you like, comment, share, or text the video to a friend.

Some people carefully perform their initial interactions, knowing the machine is watching. Through their swipes, likes, and texts, they try to express their preferences to it, to create the feed they want, or the feed they think they should want. They do this especially at the beginning, because they know that the algorithm has only a handful of data points, and that it will rely on them more heavily than when it has many thousands down the road.

In late 2018, ByteDance hired a small team of content curators in Mexico City to introduce TikTok to the Latin world. Among them was a twentysomething-year-old named Jorge Reyes, who would select cooking tutorials, dance routines, soccer highlights, and other short clips to promote to the app's Spanish-speaking users. Because he chose many of the first videos featured on Latin American TikTok, Jorge's tastes and instincts shaped the For You algorithm, eventually determining what hundreds of millions of future users would see.

Jorge Reyes was one of four initial Mexican content operators that ByteDance hired to curate the TikTok feed for Latin America and Spain. Like the TopBuzz team in New York, his cohort in Mexico City was based out of a WeWork, and reported to a team in China. Also like the

TopBuzz team, their job was in large part to be "cultural translators": young, educated, "cool" Spanish speakers who could act as teachers to the team back in China, helping them learn which videos would resonate with Latin urban youth.

Jorge and his cohort also had another student, though, one even more important than their colleagues in Beijing. Initially, the For You algorithm was bad at recommending videos outside of China. It would push posts that were, for example, only two seconds long, or so blurry you couldn't make out what was happening. To fix this problem, ByteDance relied on local teams like Jorge's: every time they removed a bad video or boosted a good one, they gave the For You algorithm another data point to learn from about what its next recommendation should be.

The bluntest instrument Jorge could use to boost a video was a lever known as "heating," an override of the normal recommendations system that ensured a video would receive a certain number of views. Employees could choose how many views they wanted the video to accrue—5,000; 50,000; 100,000; 500,000; 1,000,000; or even 5,000,000. Once they made their selection, the video would immediately be shown to users until it hit its mark. Some of those people would engage with the post, sharing it out to their followers, some portion of whom would share it again, catapulting lucky creators to what could feel like instant virality.

Heating was an open secret within ByteDance, but one the company really didn't want its users to know about. If people knew that TikTok staffers were simply picking winners to blast out on the For You page, then Alex Zhu's grand theory of a "middle class, coming up" would fall flat. It was much better if aspiring creators believed in the opaque, meritocratic magic of the algorithm.

The algorithm, though, wasn't actually meritocratic or magical. Algorithms are equations—big math problems whose variables are a pile of preferences, incentives, and weights—but they're written by humans. They encode the biases, both overt and implicit, of their creators. A former FTC commissioner named Maureen Ohlhausen once suggested that people thinking about algorithms replace the word "algorithm" with the words "a guy named Bob." "Is it ok for a guy named Bob to collect confidential price strategy information from all the participants in a market, and then tell everybody how they should price?" she asked in a 2017 speech. "If it isn't ok for a guy named Bob to do it, then it probably isn't ok for an algorithm to do it either."

Ohlhausen was right: algorithms were just tools programmed by their human creators, and the decisions they made about how to price products or target people with news deserved the same scrutiny as other human judgment.

In TikTok's case, at least for Latin American users, the algorithm actually *was*, in part, a guy named Jorge, both in the literal cases where Jorge heated videos, but also in a more systemic way. ByteDance's For You algorithm, like all algorithms, was just a big jumble of preferences. And the preferences of those early curators, each expressed as an override to the existing system, had helped train and retrain the For You page. Each heated video, each deleted one, brought the algorithm ever closer to curators' own subjective judgments about which videos the platform should reward.

One of Jorge's other big tasks as an early curator was broadening TikTok's appeal. Upon acquiring Musical.ly, ByteDance had claimed that it would become "the world's largest short video social entertainment platform." The company's goal for TikTok looked less like Musical.ly and more like Cicada, the app Alex Zhu had first tried to build: one where everyone from bored investment bankers to gardening grandmas would tune in to learn how to tie a fisherman's knot, or care for a tulip bulb, or play a song on the guitar.

When Jorge joined TikTok in 2018, it was nowhere close to being that platform. Videos of teens lip-synching and dancing were so pervasive on the app that if a person did literally anything else in their video, it would be labeled as "diverse." Jorge told me that "Only 12 percent of videos were initially labeled as 'diverse.'" Jorge was charged with reversing these numbers, by coaxing new types of creators into making videos, and making sure that when they did, those videos did well.

Heating was one tool Jorge could use to reward "diverse" videos, but there were others, too. Curators could promote hashtags related to current events, movies, songs, and other pop culture that would encourage users to post about them. (Jorge recalled promoting the Luis Fonsi song "Despacito.") Curators could also arrange the order of posts on hashtag-specific pages. They could add an "official" label that would show users that TikTok, the company, had endorsed certain videos. And then there was the Discover page—a tab that would show users a seemingly random selection of videos to help them explore new content. Jorge and his colleagues could choose and rank the videos on that page, too.

In deciding what types of videos to promote, Jorge and his team also received help from data science teams back in China, which sent them weekly reports about the topics that were performing best in each market, whether it was soccer in Colombia, or cooking videos in Spain. There were certain topics they were forbidden from pushing: politics, religion, and anything that might be considered "vulgar" for younger users. But aside from these restrictions, Jorge's team was told to go forth and try things, aiming to maximize diversity of topics and user satisfaction.

The manual curation tools that Jorge and his colleagues used were a key part of TikTok's early rise across the world, but the people who made and watched videos on TikTok didn't know heating was a thing. Heating served multiple purposes for the company, but among the most important of them was the ability to woo celebrities, brands, and creators from other platforms. If Jorge could convince a YouTuber to give TikTok a try, he could immediately heat the person's first posts and give them a first-tier slot placement on a hashtag page—the instant engagement would convince the YouTuber that the app was worth their time. Jorge wouldn't reveal that the creator's instant success had been manufactured.

At the beginning, Jorge and other TikTok employees did make regular people into stars, and they loved doing it. But as the field became more crowded, the chances of becoming a breakout star necessarily decreased, and before long, the days of picking individual winners were over. ByteDance began making deals with marketing agencies, promising them payment in cash if they could deliver a consistent stream of new users. But even that couldn't scale quickly enough. So they adopted an idea from the competition.

Kuaishou, the platform popular with rural communities, which the Chinese government had partially acquired in 2016, had created an app called Kwai for international markets. To spur downloads, Kwai had offered a small cash payment if a user referred a friend. Especially for users in less-wealthy communities, the payments could be significant, and Kwai's downloads surged. In 2019, ByteDance launched TikTok Rewards, also known as TikTok Bonus: a program where people would receive points, redeemable for cash, for referring new users to TikTok.

The downloads that TikTok gained through this program were, to put it gently, not always authentic. Sure, there were the people who received a referral from a friend, watched some funny videos, and referred the app on to others. But there were also scaled operations—such as agencies and entrepreneurial click-farmers, which set up systems to generate referral cash at scale. At TikTok, employees anticipated abuse within the program. Still, even if the referred accounts weren't real people, they looked good in both internal and external metrics. Inflated numbers helped the platform look stronger in the battle for app store ratings and hype.

The TikTok Bonus program was only the beginning. Over the course of its first year, ByteDance invested enormous sums to drive downloads, spending almost $1 billion—another Musical.ly!—to market TikTok and its other apps. To most US users, TikTok was an unfamiliar upstart, but it came with the budget of a tech giant, spending more on promotion alone than the annual budget of most major US metropolitan police forces, nearly ten times the average value of an IPO.

The blitz amounted to an ad spend of nearly three million dollars per day. The lion's share of the spending went to platforms that would become TikTok's direct competitors: Facebook, Instagram, YouTube, and Snapchat.

The ads featured clickbaity videos that led users directly to a download page. They took user-generated posts that had performed well on TikTok and juxtaposed them with text and links instructing users to download the app. Some featured young teens—and even celebrities—who had posted videos not realizing they might later be used as ads. The ads became so ubiquitous online that the company faced diminishing returns: complaints started popping up on Reddit: "I got TikTok ads like 45 fucking times a day," said one user. "Only thing I'm seeing all day," said another.

The ads reflected the same strategy that had led Zhang Yiming to buy Musical.ly in the first place. He believed in the strength of ByteDance's technology, but knew it would be unusually hard to convince people to download a strange app they'd never heard of, especially once they learned it was Chinese. So he backed up a truck full of money, "acquiring" new users with advertising to build on the substantial user bases he had bought with the purchase of Flipagram and Musical.ly.

Driving downloads was a necessary part of the puzzle, but it wasn't the same thing as getting new users to stick around. The ads gave TikTok name recognition and an early brand identity. But converting someone who just downloaded the app into a regular user was another enormous task—and it's one that fell largely to regional curators like Jorge Reyes.

ByteDance's challenge—like Facebook's, and Google's, and Twitter's—was to achieve universality. There was nothing inherently Chinese about personalized news or video recommendations, the same way there was nothing inherently Californian about search engines or microblogging. As Alex Zhu had said at TikTok's launch, a global TikTok could give influencers a worldwide audience, potentially multiplying their popularity by the company's many markets around the world.

But teams like Jorge's quickly learned that virality wasn't universal. After acquiring Flipagram, ByteDance managers in China had tried cross-populating the app with viral videos from Douyin and Huoshan, and vice versa. These videos were known hits, meant to raise the overall quality of videos on each platform. Instead, they flopped. No matter how popular a video was on Huoshan or Douyin, it might not resonate with Flipagram's users. The company tried to prioritize content that was "not too Chinese," but they found that humor, memes, and internet culture were unusually tricky to translate.

One way ByteDance tried to engage with foreign users was by showing them content familiar to them. Back in 2017, Yiming had approached Jonah Peretti, the founder of BuzzFeed, about licensing the American company's corpus of entertaining viral videos. "I asked what kind of content and he said it didn't matter, he just needed tens of thousands of videos each day," Peretti later wrote. "He just needed raw tonnage of content so the AI could create a personalized experience and get the flywheel going."

In 2019, TikTok was among the most downloaded apps in the world. Yiming's billion-dollar ad bet had paid off, and an influx of new users gave the company something that fake accounts never could: a flywheel of new data about US and Mexican and Brazilian culture. A stream of videos, posts, and comments from new users fortified the For You algorithm, giving it the predictive strength across the Americas that it had previously lacked.

TikTok—like Musical.ly—also began to emerge as its own, distinct experience. Its main competitors—Facebook, Instagram, YouTube, and Snap—were apps where you could choose your own adventure: they were driven by friend requests, search queries, likes, comments, shares, and other expressed preferences. They used your vacation photos and your fundraising birthday posts to infer other things about you, but for the most part, they still kept the user in the driver's seat.

TikTok, by contrast, was just a thing that happened to you. You would open the app and the show would begin, driving your viewing experience on autopilot. Sure, you could like and comment, and sometimes you did, but you didn't have to—because TikTok ran on your revealed preferences, rather than your expressed ones: it knew that you always lingered on videos about bisexuality, or alcoholism, or divorce, even if you never liked or shared or commented on them.

Connie Chan, a partner at the renowned investment firm Andreessen Horowitz, described TikTok as "the first mainstream consumer app where artificial intelligence IS the product." The app, she said, "never presents a list of recommendations to the user (like Netflix and YouTube do), and never asks the user to explicitly express intent—the platform infers and decides entirely what the user should watch."

Chan suggested that TikTok could use this editorial power to "optimize the video feed for happiness," apparently without concern that it might choose to instead optimize the feed for other things—like the desire to spend more time on TikTok, or more money on the products advertised there. "In fact," she said, "the entire vibe of the platform is largely under TikTok's control, because they, not users, decide which videos to display."

Chapter 7

CONTENT MODERATION

There comes a time in every tech platform's life when executives realize they need a content policy. This moment is usually preceded by the words, "Oh shit."

Executives often resist forming content policy teams. Developing and enforcing rules about what people can say on your app is thankless work that annoys creators. Companies don't want to be the arbiters of taste, or decorum, or truth. Plus, making and enforcing policies is expensive.

First, a company has to hire experts in platform governance and online discourse. Those people, often known as Trust and Safety (T&S) employees, create and publish external-facing rules, and then craft internal guidelines to apply those rules to the nearly unlimited array of situations that will arise when hundreds of millions of people start doing things on a platform.

Then, the company hires thousands of content moderators, gives them the guidelines, and tells them to get to work evaluating millions of posts, videos, and comments every day. Invariably, they will make mistakes in difficult borderline cases. The company will have to either tell its content moderators to err on the side of taking too much down, and be criticized for censorship; or go the other way, and be criticized for platforming porn bots or terrorists. No matter what they do, people will be mad at them.

As the platform swells to millions, even billions of posts every day, human moderation becomes impossible. At this point, the company hires another team—this time, of engineers—to build and maintain custom machine learning models trained to mimic human moderators.

They'll have human moderators spot-check the machines' work, but most posts will never be reviewed by human eyes.

As new threats arise, the T&S team will revise the rules and guidelines and the engineers will rebuild and retrain the machines. Often, these teams will be at odds. Every time the T&S folks want to tweak the app, they'll have to check with the engineers, and vice versa, adding levels of bureaucracy that many startups take great pains to avoid. God help you if you want to release a new product or feature—now, half the company will have to vet the thing before you ship.

The "oh shit" moments, then, have to be pretty bad—so bad that despite all the downsides of creating content policies, *not* doing so seems worse. But that's a lesson every major tech company in the world has learned.

In the 1990s and early 2000s, when young, tech-curious writers like Alex Zhu began setting up the world's first blogs, there was no such thing as content policy. The internet had unlocked a newfound ability for any random person to pay a small amount of money for a website, and then publish their thoughts for all to see. There was no editorial board to review your article, no booker to invite you on TV. For a glorious, chaotic season, there were no gatekeepers: there was simply so much unenclosed space online that anyone could swing their fists how they liked without colliding with anyone else's nose.

But collisions came. People started using the internet to violate one another's rights, and even to commit crimes. They started ripping off, publishing, and sharing others' work without permission. A certain cohort of millennials will recall discovering pop music in the early aughts largely through Napster and LimeWire, apps where one person could upload songs, movies, games, and other media that they had bought, and then thousands of others could download them without paying.

In unrestricted chat rooms, adults groomed and exposed themselves to children, and trafficked drugs, weapons, endangered animals, and even people. Some recruited for terrorist groups and exchanged pictures and videos depicting child sexual abuse, and lawmakers quickly saw that they would need to step in. But in the US, at least, there were restrictions on what lawmakers could do.

The First Amendment to the US Constitution says that, in general, people and companies can say what they want, both in person and online, without fear of government intervention. The government can't ban people from holding a Nazi march on a town street, nor can it stop people from being Nazis online.

That does not mean, though, that everyone on the internet has to allow Nazis to post on their websites. The *government* might not be allowed to stop people from speaking in public, but *private companies* can decide they don't want certain speech on their patch of turf. Each website, like each bar, restaurant, and shop on the town strip, can set its own rules of decorum. A posh steakhouse can say "no jeans," while the surf shop down the street can allow bikinis.

Congress codified this understanding when it passed the Telecommunications Act of 1996. The law was largely an effort to crack down on online porn, but would become better known for twenty-six words buried on page 101 of a 128-page document. Known as Section 230, those twenty-six words created a carveout that said a website owner couldn't be held responsible for what other people said on the owner's site. If you were harmed by someone else's online speech, you should sue the person who spoke, not the company whose tools they used to publish their comment.

Like many pieces of legislation, Section 230 was about setting up a system of incentives. Lawmakers thought content moderation was a good thing, and wanted to protect companies' right to do it. Companies would want to ban spam, hate speech, harassment, and bullying not because they were illegal, but because they were bad for business. In large part, Section 230 was designed to let the free market work.

Section 230's co-author, California Republican Congressman Christopher Cox, said the rule was important for two reasons: first, to provide a safe harbor for companies that wanted to moderate content, but would do it imperfectly; and second, to "establish as the policy of the United States that we do not wish to have content regulation by the Federal Government of what is on the Internet"—a policy that was largely required by the First Amendment anyway.

Not every government, though, shared Congressman Cox's view, and no other country had a First Amendment. So around the world, governments began banning online speech they didn't like. Some countries were brazen, barring criticism of the dominant regime, while others banned only the most offensive hate speech. Germany and France outlawed swastikas and Holocaust denial, and Spain made it a crime to "provok[e] discrimination" on the basis of race, religion, gender, family status, sexual orientation, or disability. India made it a crime to send online messages that the government deemed "inflammatory."

But no country was more aggressive than China, where for more than a quarter century, the Chinese Communist Party has aimed to control what people can and cannot say online, creating a Big Brother–style panopticon that chills dissent and bends discourse to its will. Known as the Great Firewall, the effort has cost billions and employed thousands to spread propaganda and censor dissent.

In 1997, the Chinese Ministry of Public Security forbade citizens from using the internet to "harm the prosperity and interests of the state" or "undermin[e] national unity." This was content moderation on the scale of mass society: the government began experimenting with bans on American newspapers and search engines like Google and AltaVista. By the early 2000s, it also began scanning blogs for banned keywords: if the titles of Chinese blogs contained words like "democracy," "freedom," or "human rights," their authors would receive a message: "Prohibited language in text, please delete."

Chinese authors, though, often did not delete—they just creatively rephrased. Using a set of euphemisms, misspelled words, and superfluous punctuation, they created an "algospeak" that would convey their meaning without alerting the regime. Dissidents were aided by free speech activists and two US-funded tools, called FreeGate and The Circumventor, which enabled Chinese people to browse the web through un-Firewalled American computers.

The early Great Firewall was clumsy. While it clearly chilled some speech, it failed to chill much more. Pro-democracy agitators used irony and memes to evade detection, and were always a step ahead of the government. Just like platforms, the Chinese government had locked itself into a never-ending, ever-losing game of whack-a-mole. They would simply never be able to enforce their rules in every case.

Still, the new era of sharing that Zhang Yiming had predicted in 2014 was an enormous boon to autocrats. Every conversation that moved from IRL ("in real life") to a social platform could now be surveilled. Democratic nations made use of this opportunity as well as authoritarian ones—US and UK officials monitored activists and journalists, too—but it was game-changing in places like China, where neither laws nor norms curtailed the government's right to spy on its people.

When Facebook, YouTube, and Twitter first launched, they were not banned in China. Twitter, in fact, was popular enough to spur the creation of several homegrown Chinese copycat apps, including Fanfou, where Yiming first worked on social media. By the late 2000s, the government was toying with full blocks on American platforms; it took them offline for the twentieth anniversary of the Tiananmen Square massacre. But it was ultimately the crackdown following civil unrest in Urumqi in 2009—the one that took down Fanfou—that ended Chinese access to American social media.

The Urumqi crackdown sent a clear message to aspiring social media companies: to survive in China, platforms would have to become part of the Great Firewall. So that's what they did.

A month after the Urumqi crackdowns, a new microblogging platform emerged from the Chinese tech giant Sina: an app called Weibo. Weibo would become the dominant Twitter equivalent in China for years to come—people would turn to it to experience breaking news, sports, and other events together in real time. They would share freely, revealing all manner of details about their lives: who their friends were, what they thought about current events, their favorite restaurants and family haunts and current locations. Sure, this kind of open discourse could threaten the government's control. But if harnessed, it could also enhance it.

In a way that it had not before, the CCP developed intimate partnerships with Weibo and other platforms. It sent them orders multiple times each day specifying which narratives they should censor. The directives touched nearly every aspect of Chinese life—platforms were told, for example, to remove mentions of a serial killer shot by police, remove coverage of food safety issues on website front pages, and even refrain from speculating that an Achilles injury might affect the chances of a Chinese hurdler's Olympic victory.

The government also used platforms to spread propaganda—a strategy that grew more sophisticated and widespread over time. By the early 2020s, Chinese authorities had begun ordering "comment flooding" campaigns, aiming to bury inconvenient facts in mountains of irrelevant, unrelated posts. A directive for one 2022 Weibo campaign, ordered by a local government to bury reports of people suffering in COVID lockdowns, read as follows:

> Notice: All internet commentary personnel are to open a campaign of comment flooding on this Weibo Super Topic in accordance with work practices from the autonomous prefecture's training session for internet commentary personnel. Group leaders, please implement the following tasks:
>
> 1. All internet commentary organizational work units must carry out comment flooding work at the relevant times, and must not finish it behind or ahead of schedule. The time period in question is from 8 pm to 10 pm tonight!
>
> 2. Comment flooding must be carried out in accordance with procedure. At the same time, take steps to protect yourself, and do not touch on the pandemic situation, pandemic volunteers, pandemic prevention policies, etc.
>
> 3. There are no subject matter restrictions. Content may include domestic life, daily parenting, cooking, or personal moods. All

internet commentary personnel should post once per hour (twice in total), but not in rapid succession! Repeat: not in rapid succession!

4. All personnel should keep their work confidential and avoid posting this notice to Weibo in the course of their comment-flooding activities. If any such posts are discovered, relevant work units will be held responsible!

The Chinese government largely gave up on the idea of eradicating dissent from the internet. Instead, it learned not to fear the open web, but to embrace it as a battlefield, even beyond China's physical borders. By adopting tactics like comment flooding—and armies of troll accounts—it could pursue critics not only in China, but anywhere on earth.

Chapter 8

RECTIFICATION

In the 2010s, when "content flooding" and other techniques were still years away, China struggled to stamp out dissent. The Great Firewall was often surpassed by citizen ironists, satirists, and memesters. Back then, the memesters' favorite arena was the ByteDance platform Neihan Duanzi. Roughly translated to "Implied Jokes," the app never achieved the popularity of Jinri Toutiao (the news aggregator), but it found a devoted following in young, working-class men, who used it as a place to make jokes about women, admire sports cars, and chat about dude stuff.

People who used Neihan Duanzi used it heavily, making the app part of their social identity. It sat in the Alex Zhu sweet spot: the content was light, but users' affinity for it was strong. The most popular memes became inside jokes, and Duanzi fans, known as *duanyou*, communicated using coded signs and signals. Millions of Chinese became *duanyou*, and many signaled their affiliation publicly, by affixing the Duanzi logo to their cars and motorcycles. When they met on the road, they signaled to one another with a distinctive rhythmic honk of the horn. It was as if Barstool Sports fans had begun greeting each other with the Insane Clown Posse's distinctive "whoop whoop."

Duanyou even began to hold in-person meetups and charity events, which were generally the purview of government-controlled civil society groups. They chanted nonsense slogans together, like: "Sky king covers earth tiger, stewed chicken with mushrooms!" They were chaotic and whimsical and free—and though their camaraderie was far removed from liberal or pro-democracy views, they began to show signs that they could organize.

The power to organize was the promise of the social internet, and also the reason for the internet blackouts in Urumqi in 2009. But since then, the web had become unquestionably more social, and online movements began to draw scrutiny. In the US, groups like anti-vaxxers, so-called "incels," and conspiracy theorists began to pull people away from reliable, mainstream sources of news.

In China, the same shift was afoot, but the stakes were different. Newspapers and social groups were both tightly controlled by the state, and readers' shift to platforms represented a threat to that control. Duanzi was hardly political, but it was subversive because it provided an unsanctioned source of silliness and camaraderie—a subversiveness that would later lead to its downfall.

In June 2017, Chinese regulators began a nearly yearlong "rectification" campaign to curb platforms' growing power over discourse. That power, they believed, should be reserved for the party. And to reclaim it, they were ready to take on the titans of Chinese tech.

The rectification campaign hit the entire industry, but ByteDance seemed to have a special place in regulators' crosshairs. The campaign began with a three-part opinion feature in the CCP's *People's Daily* devoted to highlighting the harms of algorithmically curated news. Before it came for Neihan Duanzi, the government was coming for ByteDance's crown jewel: Jinri Toutiao.

The *People's Daily* series disputed the popular news aggregator's mission. Machine-curated news incentivized clickbait and punished nuance, its authors said. Personalization could lead users to "only see what we want to see and hear what we want to hear," the pieces argued, and IP theft meant reporters of original news often saw their work copied without their permission or compensation. "No matter how good the communication channel is, there must be a 'gatekeeper,'" they insisted.

Zhang Yiming was not a fan of human gatekeepers. He had argued to *Caijing* magazine months before that Toutiao did not need—and should not have—human editors. Editorial discretion, he believed, would inject bias into the app and detract from the user experience. But the Cyberspace Administration of China (CAC) disagreed.

In June, the regulator enacted new rules requiring news apps and websites like Toutiao to "service the people and socialism" and "play the role of supervising public opinion." It also established a permitting system for companies running news aggregation sites—one that would require them to employ full-time editors.

In December 2017, the CAC accused Toutiao of distributing pornography and clickbait, and claimed it was operating without a permit. It temporarily removed the app from Chinese app stores, and required ByteDance to pull down six sections of the app for twenty-four hours.

ByteDance promptly announced that it would hire 2,000 more content moderators, and that it would give priority to applicants who were members of the Communist Party. It also added a new section to the app titled "New Era"—a reference to Xi and his policy agenda—and filled it with propaganda.

Stuffing Toutiao with propaganda contravened ByteDance's central value proposition. Toutiao worked because it could figure out what users wanted to see and show it to them. Showing them something else was inherently inefficient—it made the app less appealing. But Yiming was in no position to fight back.

Three months later, in March 2018, China's state-run TV station, CCTV, ran a segment condemning "lowbrow" apps popular with poor, rural communities. One was Kuaishou, the short video app whose ads had first inspired Yiming to enter the video market. The other was Huoshan, the app ByteDance had built to compete with Kuaishou.

The apps had both promoted videos—similar to American TV shows like *Teen Mom* or *16 and Pregnant*—that depicted teen mothers, which the State Administration of Radio, Film, and Television (SARFT) said promoted the wrong messages about teen sex. The government hauled executives from the companies in for investigatory interviews, and demanded that they remove content that was "vulgar, violent, bloody, pornographic, and harmful." Then, again, it temporarily removed the apps from China's app stores.

In a response posted to Huoshan's Weibo account, ByteDance quickly apologized for promoting the videos. "Thanks to CCTV's supervision,

Huoshan Video feels deeply responsible and will immediately conduct a comprehensive inspection of the platform's content, review rules, and product mechanisms," the post said.

The following week, on Monday, April 9, SARFT began its final swipe at ByteDance, ordering app stores to remove Toutiao from the app store for three weeks. Yiming didn't immediately respond. ByteDance had issued a statement after the Huoshan rebuke—what more was left to say?

The next day, Tuesday, April 10, SARFT struck again—this time fatally—against Neihan Duanzi. The beloved joke and meme app "exhibited severe problems such as improper orientation and vulgar themes, sparking strong public backlash," the regulator wrote. It was to be permanently shuttered, effective immediately.

The news of Neihan Duanzi's death traveled quickly across the Chinese internet. It was true that there had been a lot of vulgar memes and jokes on the app. But vulgarity was everywhere online, and some people wondered whether the government had targeted Duanzi less for its tawdry humor, and more for the community it had built. After all, its magic had been its ability to unite millions of people around something the government could neither understand nor control.

The Duanzi community did not go quietly. On the evening of April 11, thousands of *duanyou* surrounded the offices of SARFT in downtown Beijing and rhythmically honked their horns in protest against the shuttering of the app. In other cities, *duanyou* spilled into the streets to block roads and sing songs in solidarity. Online, they rushed to find one another on other platforms, and many turned to Douyin—the short video app that Alex Zhu had deemed TikTok's "twin"—where some now joked that "*duanyou*" would become "*douyou*." But their efforts were thwarted: the same day, ByteDance announced that it was suspending the livestreaming and commenting features on Douyin—where *duanyou* had gone to register their complaints—to facilitate a "system upgrade."

On Wednesday, at around 4 a.m., Yiming spoke. In a lengthy public letter posted to his personal WeChat account, he apologized to regulators and the public, saying he had been up all night, wracked with guilt. Of Neihan Duanzi, he said, "Our product took the wrong path, and content appeared that was incommensurate with socialist core values, that did not properly implement public opinion guidance—and I am personally responsible for the punishments we have received."

In the letter, Yiming also promised to rebuild ByteDance as a different place. "All along, we have placed excessive emphasis on the role of technology, and we have not acknowledged that technology must be led by the socialist core value system, broadcasting positive energy, suiting the demands of the era, and respecting common convention," he wrote. "We must make a renewed effort to sort out our vision of the future. We say, we want to make a global platform for creation and conversation. This demands that we must ensure that the content of 'creation' and 'conversations' are positive, healthy and beneficial, that they can offer positive energy to the era, and to the people."

Yiming announced that ByteDance would nearly double the size of its content moderation team, again, from 6,000 to 10,000 people. It would establish a "rectification committee," establish a blocklist system to permanently ban violating actors, and launch new features to combat user addiction, vulgarity, and "rumor."

Yiming's apology contradicted the statements he had made about wanting to keep Toutiao free from bias—and the statements he'd made about most people needing a bit of indulgence. The apology went against Yiming's yearslong business philosophy that algorithms could be taught to understand human desires better than humans themselves. But Yiming was no fool. Unlike many other tech CEOs, he didn't need to be seen as powerful or commanding or even brilliant. He may have been furious at the government's shuttering of Neihan Duanzi, his first successful ByteDance app. But he knew there was nothing to be gained by showing it. If he wanted to keep running ByteDance, this was just what he would have to do.

Chapter 9

EXPRESSION AS A USER RIGHT

ONCE EVERY FIVE YEARS, SENIOR MEMBERS OF THE CHInese Communist Party gather in Beijing for the National Party Congress—China's most important political gathering. The Congress is a spectacle: it's like what would happen if the Democratic and Republican National Conventions merged and replaced the US presidential election. The event is held in a massive government building facing onto Tiananmen Square, and is attended by thousands of delegates. It was first established in 1921, but did not become a regular event until the 1990s.

The 19th National Party Congress, held in fall 2017, was unusual in several respects. First, members amended the CCP's constitution with a new doctrine called Xi Jinping Thought. The amendment marked the first time in decades that a politician was referenced directly in the document, putting Xi on a par with Mao himself. Then, Xi defied tradition by declining to name a successor, and party members appeared to endorse the idea that he would serve an unlimited term as China's ruler for life.

These actions came on the heels of a new suite of new national security laws, passed several months before, that redefined—at least in writing—the relationship between the country's private and public sectors. In a sweeping expansion of power, lawmakers instituted a new national intelligence law that said Chinese individuals and businesses, including those abroad, would be required to hand over information to intelligence agencies without a warrant, a subpoena, or any due process, and to then conceal the fact that they had done so.

This law would eventually devastate China's tech companies' international ambitions. It made Chinese firms radioactive to foreign governments. Now, according to the CCP, entrusting your data to ByteDance or Baidu or Alibaba or Huawei was the equivalent of giving it to the Chinese military—a fact that effectively ended business between those companies and government contractors in the US, India, Europe, Australia, and other Chinese adversaries. "The Intelligence law seems calculated to drive wedges of mistrust between U.S. or foreign citizens or firms and their Chinese partners," wrote one commentator in the blog *Lawfare*.

At the National Party Congress, lawmakers also added another new provision to China's constitution codifying the country's Belt and Road Initiative, an international development strategy focused on expanding the export of Chinese goods and services around the world. In its decisions, the Communist Party was embracing two central dictates: (1) Chinese companies owed absolute fealty to the government, and (2) those same companies should set out to become an indispensable part of economies around the world. It wouldn't be easy to comply with both.

During rectification, the Chinese government never remarked on ByteDance's international apps. It didn't say whether it expected TikTok, TopBuzz, or Vigo Video (the zombie remnant of Flipagram) to "service the people and Socialism" or "play the role of supervising public opinion." Some Chinese ByteDancers believed overseas platforms weren't subject to the same censorship requirements as domestic Chinese apps. But Yiming and Alex Zhu were initially silent about what TikTok's content policies should be—a silence that made the app's first forays into US content moderation a disaster.

ByteDance's first office of US content moderators was a crop of twentysomething contractors who worked out of a warehouse on LA's Santa Monica Boulevard. The rules they enforced were vague, ever-changing, and strange: Until at least 2019, they prohibited recommending videos depicting, among other things, people with "obvious beer belly" or "ugly facial looks." Videos that depicted rural fields, "slums," "construction sites," or "dilapidated housing" met the same fate, as did a variety of disfavored animals, including mice, spiders, lizards, and snakes, which, according to one training document, could "cause an uncomfortable viewing experience."

When moderators saw videos that depicted any of the above sights (and many more), they flagged violations in ByteDance's Byzantine internal content classification system. Some videos (those depicting graphic violence or child abuse, for example) were removed entirely from the platform. But many more were just given a flag, meaning they could stay, but they wouldn't be recommended by the powerful For You feed.

Women and girls in swimsuits were recommendable as long as the swimsuit was "in context"—meaning a pool or other body of water was in view. For non-swimwear, moderators had to apply the "one-third" rule for cleavage, flagging any video in which more than two-thirds of a woman's breasts were exposed by her outfit. And then there was the rule of "jiggle" for dancing: if moderators could see a woman's boobs or butt jiggling, the video would be flagged.

Life as an early ByteDance moderator meant spending a lot of time trying to decide what constituted "jiggle." Moderators received a free lunch each day, which they ordered through Grubhub, and their quotas were manageable. Oversight was minimal—their boss was often absent from the office, especially on the later shifts—and when he wasn't around, the workers would have occasional Nerf gun battles, and sometimes sneak a session on a Nintendo Switch.

For the most part, ByteDance's contract moderators didn't take their jobs too seriously. After all, they sat at the bottom of the totem pole: they neither made the rules nor had substantial power over them. But they played a critical role in helping the rest of ByteDance understand the people it was building technology for.

The L.A. team made weekly presentations for their colleagues in China, educating them about American internet culture. In an October 2019 presentation, the moderators steered their colleagues to Urban Dictionary instead of Google, using the abbreviation "asf" as an example: if you Googled the term, the first result would be the Apache Software Foundation, but if you put it into Urban Dictionary, you'd get "a more insightful and culturally relevant answer"—"A wrong way of abbreviating the words 'as fuck.'"

In the same presentation, L.A. moderators explained Halloween (which is not widely celebrated in China) to their colleagues. They wrote: "Traditions include costume dress up, visits to pumpkin patches, pumpkin carving, decorating haunted houses, getting lost in corn mazes and indulging in LOTS of pumpkin flavored treats!"

After a roundup of popular Halloween costumes and trending hashtags, another slide began with the title "Getchya' Facts Straight," which was written in a font made to look like it was dripping in some kind of spooky goo.

"What are MEMES? (pronounced 'Meem,' not 'me-me')" the slide asked. It then provided an answer—"memes can be a photo, a video, a person, an animal, a fictional character, an event, a song, a belief, an action, a GIF, a symbol, a word or anything else that interacts with culture and is shared on the internet"—that seemed to encompass virtually everything.

Between Nerf wars and meme presentations, TikTok moderators struggled with one of the hardest parts of their job: guessing TikTokers' ages. People didn't have to give their age when they signed up on TikTok, so staff had no definitive source of truth. Moderators were told to flag accounts based on how old users looked, with two types of flags: one for children who looked under fourteen, and another for those who looked like they were between fourteen and sixteen.

Not all fourteen- (or sixteen)-year-olds look alike—a problem that was highlighted by one of TikTok's most famous users. Danielle Cohn, a dancer with a very young-looking face, had accrued more than 10 million followers on Musical.ly, and then moved with her mother to L.A. to become a full-time social media star. Cohn's style was sometimes racy: she filmed videos in swimwear and lingerie, and even once posted photos of herself lying next to a wax statue of Playboy magnate Hugh Hefner. She also began facing bullies online: on Instagram, harassers made "hate pages" dedicated to criticizing her body, her outfits, and her dancing, and commenters called her a bitch and a ho.

Cohn represented publicly that she had been born in 2004 and had begun posting on Musical.ly at age thirteen—an assertion backed up by her mother, who became her talent manager. But her father eventually spoke out against her stardom, saying he feared for her safety. He shared a picture of her birth certificate online, which revealed she had been born in 2006, not 2004.

For TikTok, Cohn's age had legal ramifications: the company was not supposed to allow users younger than thirteen. She became the subject of conversations among moderators, some of whom argued that her account should be taken down. But it wasn't.

Early ByteDance staffers from across the world faced variations of the Danielle Cohn problem. Brazilian staffers described struggling to permaban a particularly determined sex worker, and staffers across the Middle East described persistent problems with solicitation. Local content teams tried to persuade their colleagues to deemphasize racy or scandalous videos, especially when they involved children. The videos might get clicks in the short term, staffers argued, but they were bad for TikTok's brand, and bad for the kids in the videos.

Meanwhile, back in L.A., the company implemented a rule that moderators called "the N-word pass." As one former moderator described it to me, "if you looked like you had some Black in you, we would let it slide." But figuring out whether any given user was part-Black was tricky, especially for the moderators on the overnight shift—a team of Malaysian nationals based in Kuala Lumpur. So in late 2019, the company opted to ban use of the word altogether.

Other topics were beyond discussion. On TikTok, just like TopBuzz, videos that touched on the Tiananmen Square massacre, Tibet, and the 2019 protests in Hong Kong were flatly prohibited. Even mentions of Winnie-the-Pooh and Peppa Pig, the animated children's characters, were forbidden—both had been banned by the Chinese government, Winnie because some people said he bore a resemblance to Xi, and Peppa because she became popular with an antiestablishment Chinese internet subculture.

Moderators did not know who within ByteDance had made the decision to censor these topics. But they assumed the bans could not be changed; after all, as several said to me, they knew it was a Chinese company.

Despite moderators' instincts, it actually wasn't inevitable that TikTok would engage in censorship. The person ultimately in charge of making US content policy was a Beijing-based policy manager named Yue Fu, who ran a team that made policies for TikTok's non-China markets. Fu's team was composed of content policy experts poached largely from US tech giants, and its goal was to make policies that would make sense to US audiences. The team didn't want to censor criticisms of the CCP. But actually implementing a shift away from censorship would take both time and buy-in from executives across the company.

US-based teams weren't the only ones feeling their way forward in the post-rectification era. In June 2019, a lynch mob in the mountainous eastern Indian state of Jharkhand captured twenty-four-year-old Tabrez Ansari, a Muslim man, tied him to a pole, and brutally beat him, forcing him to repeat religious Hindu phrases as they did so. He died four days later.

After the lynching, young Muslim Indians took to TikTok to decry the violence. Members of a group of celebrity stunt men who had become popular on the platform, known as Team 07, were among those to speak out. Hasnain Khan, Faisal Shaikh, and Shadan Farooqui, each of whom had millions of followers on TikTok, made posts condemning the incident specifically and Islamophobia broadly.

Then, their TikTok accounts went offline.

Romesh Solanki, a Hindu nationalist and member of the far-right Shiv Sena party, had tweeted at the Mumbai Police about the posts and then gone to the police station to complain. "When someone so famous makes a statement like this, it's not good for the country, especially with the ongoing situation of communal strife," he told the *Hindustan Times*. A statement from TikTok confirmed the takedowns, professing "a zero-tolerance policy towards content that has any negative impact on its users or the country it operates in."

TikTok never specified why or how it decided that the young men's posts had a negative impact on its Indian population. The posts themselves were quite tame—the most controversial language in them had been the statement: "You may have killed that innocent Tabrez Ansari, but tomorrow if his son takes revenge, do not say that all Muslims are terrorists."

In spring 2019, TikTok's head of operations in India reiterated its opposition to content with a "negative impact" on its users. In an interview with *Bloomberg*, he declared that the platform was a place "where people come to have fun rather than creating any political strife." When asked whether the platform would allow users to post videos or comments criticizing Indian Prime Minister Narendra Modi, he said no.

At ByteDance, censorship of political speech was the norm. American Trust and Safety employees wanted a mandate from leadership that TikTok would be free from censorship and propaganda. Indian lobbyists just wanted to keep the company in Modi's good graces. But soon, an incident in Europe would force TikTok's hand.

In September 2019, TikTok experienced its first brushes with investigative journalism. Content moderators using a set of censorious moderation guidelines leaked internal documents to the German publication *Netzpolitik* and the British newspaper *The Guardian*. *The Guardian*'s headline was explosive: "Revealed: how TikTok censors videos that do not please Beijing." By censoring mentions of Tiananmen Square, Tibetan independence, and the Falun Gong, TikTok was "advancing Chinese foreign policy aims abroad," the article said—just as the CCP's Belt and Road Initiative instructed it to do.

The publication asked ByteDance why it was censoring criticism of the Chinese government in other areas of the world, setting off—for the first time—a panic in the US and Europe about whether ByteDance was intentionally trying to warp foreign civic discourse.

Inside ByteDance, the leaks caused pandemonium. Yue Fu's team began issuing new rules, as fast as possible, to the company's contract moderators around the world. The company told *The Guardian* that the guidelines they were reporting on were no longer in use. It had new guidelines that did not "reference specific countries or issues," a company spokesperson said. "Today," the spokesperson continued, "we take localized approaches, including local moderators, local content and moderation policies, local refinement of global policies, and more."

Upon first blush, the idea of localized content moderation was appealing. It avoided the American exceptionalism of platforms like Google and Facebook, which had long expected their users from Indonesia to Kenya to Argentina to accept a set of rules (or a restaurant dress code, to return to the metaphor) that were a far cry from their regional norms. Rather than imposing its own cultural expectations on other countries, ByteDance was instead saying it wanted to learn from its foreign users, to meet them where they were.

It would be easy to read the company's statement as a commitment to building culturally sensitive content policies. But there is also a simpler explanation for why ByteDance decided to localize its policies: it had to, because of where it came from.

If ByteDance had created just one global set of content policies, as Google and Facebook had, those policies would have had to be approved by the Chinese government. The *Guardian* story showed that exporting China's censorious, propagandizing dictates was untenable—people in countries with speech protections simply wouldn't stand for it. So ByteDance would need, at minimum, two sets of rules.

It could've stopped there. But how, then, would it explain the divide? How would it decide which countries should get which rule system? Where would India fall, or Russia, Saudi Arabia, South Africa, or Venezuela?

The intellectually clean way out of this mess was a full embrace of cultural relativism—each country would get a content policy informed by its cultural and political environment. But cultural relativism has an ugly downside: it requires malleable views on human rights issues like religious freedom and the rights of ethnic minorities and women.

The early TikTok moderators in L.A. experienced this ugly downside up close, when they were tasked with enforcing a set of rules that they nicknamed "the Muslim tag." Enforced only in Muslim-majority countries in the Middle East and North Africa, the tag was applied to videos depicting alcohol consumption, people with tattoos, videos of dogs, and references to pigs. It flagged any discussion or depiction of same-sex love or romance, from Pride parades and hand-holding to more overt public displays of affection. It also enforced different standards of modesty for women—in American and European markets, shorts estimated to be less than three inches long received a flag, but in majority-Muslim countries, at least for a time, the line was drawn at anything above the knee.

Beyond the Muslim tag, ByteDance's cultural relativism also raised a critical question about how it would handle speech on another topic: elections. In the years since 2016, American T&S departments had come to see election interference as one of the single worst things that could happen to a platform, right alongside child sexual abuse, livestreaming mass shooters, and other atrocities. For several years, the biggest story in Silicon Valley had been the revelation that a powerful, Russian government–linked group had clandestinely used Facebook, Twitter, and other platforms to warp American discourse to help elect Donald Trump. The companies—and more than ever, the constitutional lawyers, human rights experts, and social scientists they had employed to build out their content policies—were determined to never let it happen again.

Earlier in 2019, before the *Guardian* story, Zhang Yiming and Alex Zhu had started thinking about how to handle political content. They flew American members of Fu's team to Beijing for a meeting about politics and content policy. On a whiteboard before the meeting, a member of Fu's team had written in marker: "expression—user right." At the meeting, both Alex and Yiming were aligned with the idea that TikTok's users had a right to express themselves, politically, even if the Chinese government didn't like what they had to say.

But approximately five months after the Beijing meeting, TikTok would face, and fail, yet another public test of how it handled political speech. In November, a seventeen-year-old girl from New Jersey named Feroza Aziz posted a video on TikTok that began as an eyelash curling tutorial, before quickly veering into a plea for viewers to educate themselves about the Chinese government's surveillance, imprisonment, and "re-education" of Uyghurs, an ethnic minority in the northwest Xinjiang province of China. "This is another Holocaust," she said.

The video went viral. Then, Aziz lost access to her account. Two days after that, the video was taken down. Then, it was reinstated.

TikTok published a blog post attempting to explain what had happened to Aziz. Her account had been disabled along with more than two thousand others in a prescheduled purge, because a video she posted on a previous account—a piece of satire about the Muslim American experience—had featured Osama bin Laden and thus violated TikTok's policies on terrorism. Separately, her video about the Uyghurs was removed as the result of a human moderation error, the company said.

The first part of the story might have been believable: assuming several thousand other accounts were actually disabled, perhaps the timing was just an unlucky coincidence. Aziz didn't think so, though. On Twitter, she wrote: "Do I believe they took it away because of an unrelated satirical video that was deleted on a previous deleted account of mine? Right after I finished posting a 3-part video about the Uighurs? No."

The human moderation error was harder to explain. Why would a human moderator have believed this particular video was subject to takedown? Were we really supposed to believe that error had nothing to do with the censorious content moderation rules that the Guardian had reported just two months before?

Weeks before the Aziz incident, TikTok's senior leaders had aligned on embracing a permissive approach to political expression, at least for its users in the US and Europe. But now, the company faced two bigger challenges. First, it had to promulgate its new, Americanized content policy down through worldwide department heads, middle managers, and contract content moderators working on the app, overcoming their politics, biases, and cultural expectations about what was or should be allowed. And second, it had to convince the Western world that although ByteDance couldn't itself endorse democracy or free expression, it would not use TikTok to censor or propagandize against them.

Chapter 10

THE FIFTH ESTATE

In October 2019, months after Zhang Yiming and Alex Zhu agreed to let TikTok users criticize governments as they pleased—and where local norms allowed—Facebook CEO Mark Zuckerberg was rushing to cast TikTok and its founders as inherently un-American.

Zuckerberg was, by this time, facing a popularity crisis. Facebook was at the zenith of its power. Among its more than two billion users were companies and celebrities, nonprofits and governments, who used Facebook to announce and react to the biggest news of the day. It was also a place where bigots and extremists had found a home: In Sri Lanka, anti-Muslim extremist groups had used the app to plan an attack where a man was burned to death. In Myanmar, it had amplified calls for violence against the Rohingya, contributing to a genocide perpetrated by the military against a primarily Muslim ethnic minority.

In the US, both liberals and conservatives were suspicious of Facebook. Democrats pointed to the app's use by white supremacists, conspiracy theorists, and Russian agents of election interference as cause for alarm. Republicans cited the company's content moderation on issues like Holocaust denial, vaccine skepticism, and LGBTQ rights as evidence that Facebook's liberal Californian workforce was suppressing conservative viewpoints. Both parties had begun talk of regulating Facebook, perhaps even removing its critical Section 230 liability shield, which would invite libel lawsuits that would siphon the company's profits and cripple its ability to compete and grow.

It was against this backdrop that Zuckerberg arrived at Georgetown University's McCourt School of Public Policy for an event titled "A Conversation on Free Expression." He was introduced by Erica Turner, a grad student at the school, who characterized social media as having "concluded its youth and entered into maturity." "Now that billions of us, and our data, are on these platforms," she continued, "we're faced with new challenging questions. Who decides what is permissible content? How do we deal with bad actors and disinformation, especially in the lead up to an election?"

Turner welcomed Zuckerberg to the stage with a handshake. Zuckerberg projected confidence in a long-sleeve black T-shirt, jeans, and sneakers. At the lectern, he began by recognizing the memory of the civil rights icon and congressman Elijah Cummings, who had passed away earlier that morning. And then, he launched into what would become an era-defining speech, one that wrapped Facebook in American values and cast its business as a patriotic struggle against Chinese political repression, a concept conveniently embodied by Facebook's most ferocious new competitor, TikTok. Here was an issue the Left and the Right should come together on, he seemed to say: protecting American industry from the threat of Communist China.

Zuckerberg laid out a substantially revisionist history of Facebook, suggesting that he founded the platform to give people a place to speak out about issues they cared about, like the Iraq War. (Facebook was actually an outgrowth of another website, Facemash, which let Zuckerberg and his friends rank the attractiveness of their female classmates.)

Echoing Turner's statements, Zuckerberg acknowledged the power that social media had grown to command. "People having the power to express themselves at scale is a new kind of force in the world—a Fifth Estate alongside the other power structures in our society," he said. Zuckerberg was drawing on a classic metaphor for social power, in which traditional media was the "fourth" estate (with the clergy, the nobility, and the commoners being the first three). The real threat to democracy wasn't Facebook, with its unchecked, sometimes ugly expression, he insisted; in fact, Facebook was in a fight for "the future of our global internet"—with China.

"China is building its own internet focused on very different values, and is now exporting their vision of the internet to other countries,"

Zuckerberg claimed. Then, he referenced the protests in Hong Kong that had arisen after Beijing had subsumed the island and kneecapped its independent, democratic local government: "While our services, like WhatsApp, are used by protestors and activists everywhere due to strong encryption and privacy protections, on TikTok, the Chinese app growing quickly around the world, mentions of these protests are censored, even in the US. Is that the Internet we want?"

Zuckerberg neglected to mention that Facebook's tools had also been used by the Chinese government—which had run Facebook ads denigrating the Hong Kong protestors that very summer. His framing of Facebook as an American bulwark against the creep of Chinese censorship was odd given how hard he'd tried to get Facebook unbanned in China, and it was more than a little rich coming from the guy who had invited Xi Jinping to name his firstborn child. But the dissonance didn't seem to matter: whether because of Zuckerberg or in spite of him, DC elites were receptive to a new narrative of techno-protectionism.

Zuckerberg's offensive continued after the Georgetown speech. Days later, at a White House Blue Room dinner arranged by Donald Trump's son-in-law Jared Kushner, he made the same case to Kushner, Peter Thiel—a military tech mogul, Facebook board member, and Trump donor—and to the president himself. Trump should be more worried, Zuckerberg argued, about the rise of the Chinese internet and its effects on American businesses than he should be about regulating Facebook.

Zuckerberg also made this pitch to hawkish, Republican senators like Josh Hawley and Tom Cotton. He questioned why TikTok should be allowed to operate in the US, when Facebook couldn't operate in China. His message even reached the moderate then–Senate Minority Leader Chuck Schumer, a Democrat hardly known for hawkism or protectionism. Just days after Zuckerberg's speech, Cotton and Schumer wrote a letter asking US intelligence officials to investigate TikTok, characterizing the app as a "potential counterintelligence threat."

Another senator lobbied by Zuckerberg was Marco Rubio, who had run for president several years earlier promising to get tough on China. Just eight days before Zuckerberg gave his speech, Rubio had taken a swipe at TikTok that could do more damage than the Senate Intelligence Committee: he'd sent a letter about TikTok to the Committee on Foreign Investment in the United States (known as CFIUS), a panel of cabinet-level officials whose job was to identify foreign investments that threatened US national security. Citing *The Guardian*'s report, Rubio condemned "the Chinese government's nefarious efforts to censor information inside free societies."

On the same day as Zuckerberg's speech, Rubio raised an additional anxiety: ByteDance's collection of data about American teens. "If you have teenagers I can almost guarantee you that they are on TikTok. I was too . . . briefly. Catchy videos," he wrote. "But they are collecting personal data on your teens for #China."

Rubio's two concerns—that ByteDance might use TikTok to meddle in American politics, or that it might collect users' private information and then share it with the CCP—would inspire nearly every twist in the TikTok saga over the next half decade.

For a lot of people, Rubio's worries were overblown. TikTok was for bubblegum preteen users; it was hardly a hotbed of political discourse. The videos on the app were, in Alex Zhu's famous refrain, "extremely light." It was hard to see how they posed a national security risk. What would videos of tweens dancing to clips of "Old Town Road" really do for the Chinese government? TikTokers' overwhelming reaction was skepticism. The CCP didn't care about their dance moves!

National security experts took the threat more seriously. First, there was a theory of kompromat: millions of young people had made videos on the platform that they would later regret. Perhaps they had said the N-word, or revealed an affair, or admitted an alcohol problem. Of those millions, at least a few thousand would likely go on to hold positions of power—as elected officials, perhaps, or diplomats, or members of the military—and a few hundred of those might have posted some properly embarrassing material. The Chinese government could, in theory, use those people's TikTok information against them. Still, would a teen's cringe video about discovering his bisexuality in 2018 really matter to anyone when he ran for president in 2052?

Next was the censorship and propaganda. Again: there wasn't much to censor on TikTok when it was mostly funny cats and dance routines. But over time, as TikTok's content became more "diverse," it would also become more of a place for conversations about history, government, and politics. If the CCP wanted to, it might lean on ByteDance to adjust the algorithm to turn the temperature up on some conversations, and down on others—adjustments that TikTok's users would never need to know about.

Lastly, there was the theory of soft power, the ability to shape world opinion and articulate broad goals of human society—the way the US had projected a sense of modernism, freedom, and cool through its music, movies, and culture for more than half a century. Alex Zhu had compared building Musical.ly to building a new country, a new economy, a new society. To build this new economy, ByteDance had performed a series of sociopolitical experiments. Staffers had asked racist questions just to see what would get people riled up and used people's news consumption habits to assume their political affiliation. The company had employed hundreds of people, both in the US and beyond it, to codify the tastes of the young, urban milieu into an algorithm that aimed to know young Americans better than they knew themselves.

Through these experiments, ByteDance had built TikTok into a behemoth, a new society with as many citizens as the world's largest countries—and undeniable soft power. In the US, only the largest and most powerful tech companies possessed such power: Google and YouTube, Facebook and Instagram, Twitter, and maybe Snap. This handful of very rich firms possessed data that could predict how the public would react to any number of stimuli. And now TikTok was among them.

Between ByteDance's launch in 2012 and Mark Zuckerberg's speech in 2019, Yiming proved to be an exceptionally good predictor of coming changes in social media. His "era of sharing" exploded with the growth of the social internet. Recommendation algorithms—from Spotify and Yelp to Twitter and YouTube—began to play a much bigger role than search in surfacing the information that people consumed each day. Training the For You algorithm on preferences expressed by curators like Jorge Reyes (and the megaviral hits that Flipagram had pilfered from Instagram and YouTube) had made it much better at predicting the tastes of Americans, Africans, and Europeans, as well as its original core users in China.

Where ByteDance struggled, however, was where Facebook had struggled—with the social and political realities of what it meant to run a platform at all. Both companies had proved that they could build a sticky app, one that would keep users coming back. But once the users came, then what? Would Facebook keep fomenting hate, conspiracy theories, and extremism across its markets? Would TikTok—despite whatever Yiming and Alex had said to Yue Fu's team—keep taking down politically sensitive videos like the one made by Feroza Aziz?

Once a platform reaches a certain threshold of popularity, its primary problems are no longer technological; they are sociological. At the next threshold above, the problems become political. Yiming, like Zuckerberg, clearly had the engineering chops (and billions to spend on user acquisition) to overcome ByteDance's initial technological hurdles. But as talented as both men were at building technology, it wasn't clear that either was prepared for the sociological or political phases of their own creations.

TopBuzz had failed at the sociology stage. After its employees' trip to Chicago and Indianapolis, it had puttered along, slowly losing traction. Its Chinese curators experienced no epiphanies about how to win new American users. TopBuzz had produced valuable data about what Americans wanted (and didn't want) to see, but ByteDance eventually looked to sell off the app. A slew of other test balloons also flopped, including a TopBuzz-adjacent platform called BuzzVideo and a joke and meme app called Larf, for the grammatically awkward acronym "Laugh At Really Funny."

TikTok, though, was different. Where TopBuzz's Chinese staff had pushed back on Americans' pleas for cultural literacy, TikTok gave its local curators independence. TopBuzz's staff had reported into the highly censorious and state-managed Jinri Toutiao, but TikTok's staff reported into the poet-engineer Alex Zhu, who pushed staff to study, understand, and serve the app's users. Through these efforts, it surpassed the sociological threshold.

Now, as TikTok slowly gained command over the culture and sociology of its audiences, new political headwinds began to arise. Before TikTok's launch, Yiming had given an interview at the prestigious Tsinghua School of Economics and Management, where he effused about his plans for internationalization. Chinese companies, like American ones, were "born to be global," he said—just look at Huawei. Then the largest smartphone maker in the world, Huawei was a model for ByteDance, Yiming said. It was the largest Chinese company to effectively export its product all over the globe.

Huawei was founded and run by Ren Zhengfei, a former Chinese military engineer and avowed communist who matched Yiming's passion for global business. Ren had told his staff that to break into the American market, they must "wear American shoes," even if they were painful to walk in. "Only by learning from them with all our humility can we defeat them one day," he reportedly said.

Had he been able to predict the future, Yiming might have chosen not to invoke Huawei as a company to emulate—because just months after Yiming's speech at Tsinghua, the US government began a crusade against the company that would effectively end its global presence. Ren Zhengfei's daughter had defrauded a bank, claiming that Huawei was a mere "business partner" of Skycom, a Huawei subsidiary that had evaded US sanctions against Iran. She was arrested in Canada in December 2018, and later signed a deferred prosecution agreement with the US government. The charges against her have now been dismissed.

The Trump White House then alleged that Huawei was exfiltrating state secrets from the US through its hardware. Huawei denied the back doors, but because Ren Zhengfei's daughter had been misleading about Skycom, the company had lost the public's—and the government's—trust. The White House added Huawei to its "entity list," ripped its hardware out of US government systems, and asked the governments of Australia, New Zealand, Canada, Japan, and Taiwan not to use it either. By losing the US government's trust, Huawei had torched its whole international strategy.

TikTok had not yet lost the US government's trust—it had merely gained the attention of a few US senators. Surely, their concerns could be addressed. Yiming and Alex had, after all, decided to embrace American-style content policies, and neither was—like Ren Zhengfei—a CCP zealot or a military man.

But broader political forces quickly stacked up against ByteDance. Emboldened in his indefinite reign, the Chinese ruler, Xi, began to demand more visible fealty from China's citizens and especially its business leaders. The CCP also began expanding its operations overseas, using foreign platforms to spread propaganda in English. Meanwhile, Trump—egged on by a cadre of xenophobic, hard-right advisors—had campaigned on the claim that China was "raping" the US, and imposed aggressive tariffs on the nation that set off a full-fledged trade war.

In the years ahead, ByteDance would have to manage the wild swings of these two strongmen. But before those challenges would come fully into view, it would experience a shock that would both propel it to cultural hegemony and threaten its political fortunes for years to come.

ACT II

Chapter 11

LEVERAGE

CHINESE TECH GIANTS CELEBRATE THEIR BIRTHDAYS IN style. For ByteDance's seventh, TikTok's L.A. offices celebrated with a buffet dinner featuring custom ByteDance cookies, cupcakes, and tartlets. Employees had donned seventh anniversary–themed shirts in an office decked out with balloons, neon party signs, a "ByteDance History Wall," and a photo booth. In Beijing, the gathering had been even bigger, culminating in an annual speech from Yiming, and its eighth was shaping up to be a blowout as well.

2019 had been an absolute banner year: Revenue had more than doubled, and the company was more profitable than ever. A whopping 686 million people had downloaded TikTok, smashing the glass ceiling that had kept other Chinese companies from worldwide success.

ByteDance was no longer a new upstart challenging the Silicon Valley giants; it was now squarely among them. The company possessed a power to shape conversations and markets that was previously only available to world leaders. And its eighth birthday would coincide with a turning point in modern Silicon Valley history—the moment when tech companies went absolutely nuclear.

Much like 9/11, many Americans associate a particular Thursday in March as the "beginning" of the COVID-19 era in the United States. That day that also happens to have been the day ByteDance employees opened a more modest "birthday" gift from their employer, a potted terrarium, and tuned in to their founder's annual speech: March 12, 2020.

As he had in previous years, Zhang Yiming prepared a sort of a State of the Union address for the company. He had spent more than half of 2019 abroad, he said, studying ancient history and "the evolution of civilizations." He sounded a bit like Alex Zhu, when the Musical.ly founder had compared platforms to countries. "We must think more seriously about our relationship with the outside world," Yiming mused, on the very day of the first widespread lockdowns in the United States.

~

COVID CAUSED A once-in-a-generation boost to Big Tech's power. As tourism and events ground to a stop, demand soared for digital news and entertainment. Across the tech sector, lockdowns led to increases in watch time and stock price. Between January and March 2020, 315 million new people would download TikTok worldwide: the single largest number of downloads in a quarter that any app had ever achieved, and well over the total number of adults in the United States. In the following three months, the app would bring in nearly that number again.

There was something intoxicating, especially among young, idealistic technologists, about the idea of "doing good while doing well." Socially liberal engineers had for years flocked to Silicon Valley, where they enjoyed generous salaries and luxurious lifestyles, all with the earnest belief that the products they were building were good for the world.

Their optimism had waned during the years before COVID, as the public began to hold platforms accountable for various social ills. But COVID instilled a feeling of hope in otherwise disheartened techies: keeping people online instead of outside could save lives and bring people a little laughter and joy along the way.

For ByteDance, COVID presented a market opportunity. Because it was based in China, where the virus originated, ByteDance had a two-month head start on readjusting its business to a locked-down world. The company's Chinese staff had experienced quarantines before—in 2003, when many of them were still children and teens, a fatal pathogen known as SARS had caused lockdowns, mandatory quarantines, and economic shock across China, Singapore, and Hong Kong—but in California, the idea of a government-mandated shutdown was incomprehensible.

Before governments in the US and Europe began to impose lockdowns, ByteDance pivoted its product strategy. The company launched free online courses for primary and middle school students stuck at home—part of a larger ByteDance push into for-profit tutoring apps. It also began offering free business collaboration software, called Feishu in China and Lark abroad, to companies whose employees were working from home. The free period would build businesses' reliance on Feishu, so that down the road when the crisis was over, they'd be willing to pay to keep using it.

Yiming, ever the pragmatist, also quickly expanded into new industries. In a whirlwind twenty-four-hour negotiation in January, ByteDance bought the rights to stream fourteen feature-length films, including a Chinese New Year–themed movie called *Lost in Russia*, which had been set for a major release in theaters in late January. With theaters closed, it rolled out on ByteDance platforms instead, marking the first time a major movie had been released directly on a social media platform. (The *Hollywood Reporter* described this as "the local equivalent of Disney deciding to open the paywall to Disney+ and release a new Avengers movie for free.") The company also launched its first major video game (a street basketball competition) and a trivia game on Douyin with cash prizes.

Livestreaming, ByteDance learned, was particularly popular among housebound shelterers in place. Everything from concerts to cooking classes to government PSAs moved onto social media. People were desperate for events—the type that would ordinarily bring them physically together—so ByteDance started encouraging its users to host them online: young partiers and fans of electronic dance music began hosting "cloud raves" on Douyin, where people could party together on video.

ByteDance also rolled out a full charitable and humanitarian response to the virus, donating 200 million yuan (about $28 million USD) to the Chinese Red Cross Foundation on the first day of the Chinese New Year. The company also sent 200,000 KN95 masks to health workers in Wuhan, where the virus had begun. Other tech giants in China, including Alibaba and Tencent, made donations, too. By the time the virus began to spread globally, the precedent had been set: both in philanthropy and product strategy, US tech giants were playing catch-up to their Chinese competitors.

From a product perspective, TikTok offered something distinctive during the information overload of early COVID lockdowns. Moment-to-moment news tracking cases, hospitalizations, deaths, wastewater, and new mutations overwhelmed other platforms and outlets. TikTok's bottomless feed provided an antidote: when you just wanted to unwind, to go blank for a moment, you could open an app that would make all your choices for you. Unlike a newspaper app, Twitter, Facebook, or Instagram, it offered pure delight.

The best COVID TikToks were the most ridiculous ones. Sports coaches led students in exercises on Zoom during digital PE class. College kids at Minnesota State University threw individual bags of school-provided confetti over their heads in sarcastic celebration of their digital graduation. A couple in Hertfordshire, UK, filmed their neighbor trying to circumvent quarantine rules by dressing up as a bush to blend in with the local scenery. And clips of coyotes and foxes, deer, lizards, and monkeys in abandoned urban centers provided cute, comic relief—#natureishealing was both an ironic joke and an earnest wish.

TikTok's recommendations algorithm fed on interaction, just like the virus did. The exact same actions society took to bend the curve on COVID—every meeting that became an email, every errand done online, every in-person interaction with friends that was replaced by some combination of likes, comments, and shares—engorged the algorithms of TikTok and other platforms with oceans of new data.

TikTok, like Meta and other tech giants, also collected information from thousands of other companies through ad pixels, which track the websites you go to and the pages you view. These pixels enabled, say, Levi's, to know that someone on your computer was browsing for a pair of new jeans. Levi's then relayed that information back to TikTok (and Facebook, and Google), so that the platforms could target ads to you for more Levi's jeans. But for social platforms, pixel data could be used for more than just targeting ads: it could also be used to infer other things about you. Shopping for some new pruning shears? You might like short videos on gardening and yard care. Watching Ken Burns's *Baseball*? Prepare to be blitzed with clips of spectacular catches and historic double plays.

TikTok also gathered information about people who weren't TikTok users at all—at least not yet. The app was notorious among early adopters for its persistent requests to access people's contact lists. Many people, when asked, gave the company access to those lists, to help them find acquaintances and friends who were on TikTok. A list in isolation was a data point: it gave the company names and phone numbers of other potential users that it could target with ads, urging them to download TikTok. But millions of lists in the aggregate provided something much more powerful: an interactive web of entire communities, showing who was connected to whom.

Even if you'd never downloaded TikTok, the app's algorithm might still know quite a lot about you. They might know that you're listed in the contact information for five members of a theater club in Philadelphia, that a cluster of people who share your surname (likely your family) live in Boston and are involved with the Massachusetts Democratic Party, and that eighteen people who list you as a contact follow sports teams affiliated with the University of Michigan. Every time a new person gave TikTok their contacts, this network-sketching exercise grew stronger.

ByteDance had become the most valuable private company in the world in 2018. But in 2020, it did something that no other social platform—private or public—had ever done: it fully permeated the two most powerful markets in the world, China and the United States. Within a year, TikTok and Douyin would together reach more than three billion downloads globally, a milestone that only Facebook's apps had ever achieved. Three billion downloads fast approached half the people on earth. It was more than the total number of Christians or Muslims alive today—more than the populations of Europe, North America, and Africa combined.

Until TikTok's breakthrough, Chinese social media companies had been effectively limited to the Chinese market. People used Tencent's

WeChat abroad, but usually only if they needed to communicate with people in China. Kuaishou's international app, Kwai, had achieved modest success in South America, but next to no traction in the US and Europe.

China had the second-largest digital advertising market in the world—businesses spent more than $75 billion in Chinese ads in 2020. But the largest digital advertising market was the US—at more than $130 billion the same year. By driving ByteDance to the top of both markets, Yiming had made it something of a "double unicorn"—a company with a one-of-a-kind market opportunity.

∼

YIMING'S BORDERLESS, GLOBAL mission had unique salience in the early days of COVID. It's hard to remember, but there was a brief window when people around the world seemed united against the disease. Think pieces analogized the virus to an alien invasion, something that would unite world governments to prioritize human survival. People going through wildly disruptive life changes—including physical isolation—felt heartened and comforted to know, via delightful videos on social media, that they weren't alone.

But even as lockdown helped TikTok become the first Chinese tech giant to break through to Western audiences, it also tied the company to the virus as a social phenomenon. Because of that glimmer of globalism, where we were all going to put aside our national rivalries, come together, and fight the aliens? It would quickly curdle into a paranoid protectionism that would define the next era of both Chinese and US foreign policy.

From the moment a mysterious illness started infecting people in Wuhan, the government sought to control public opinion about it. At first, platforms like Toutiao, the news aggregator, had disseminated hopeful, unifying stories about the world coming together to fight the virus. The platform featured stories about Japan and the US sending supplies and volunteers to Wuhan—until government directives told news outlets and platforms to play down reports of international aid.

Further directives tried to control the narrative around the virus. The government barred news publishers from analogizing COVID to the SARS epidemic of 2002. It banned the word "lockdown" and ordered more stories that featured heroic frontline workers. As the situation deteriorated, the government returned to the tactic of pushing distracting, unrelated news via its army of sock puppet accounts.

Things worsened after a prominent Wuhan ophthalmologist, Li Wenliang, died from COVID in February 2020. Li had been an early whistleblower about the disease, warning that it was worse than the government was saying. The government attempted to suppress news of Li's death, but its orders leaked, mushrooming the story into one about the CCP deceiving its citizens in the midst of a public health crisis.

As the pandemic spread, the government became more intent on censoring speech. It began regular—in some cities, daily—"inspections" of social media platforms for their compliance with censorship orders. In Hangzhou, the government graded platforms on a scale of 1–100 each day, deducting points for lax censorship decisions, and awarding them for promoting the party line.

The government also began to spread false information. By early February, conspiracy theories had begun to circulate on Toutiao—in some cases, with the help of the Chinese government. A state-run newspaper published a piece citing alleged declassified US intelligence documents to imply that the coronavirus was a US-made bioweapon. Weeks later, after the US urged travelers abroad to return home, a commentator on Toutiao speculated that it might result in the US declaring war on China.

The Trump administration did not declare war on China, but it did return the CCP's fire. In the early stages of the pandemic, Trump was quick to heap praise upon Xi, calling him a friend and a strong leader. But as the virus began to spread more widely in the US, Trump adopted racist terms for the disease like the "China Virus" and the "Kung Flu," and hate crimes against Asian Americans soared. Trump also began blaming China for the virus, urging international aid organizations like the World Health Organization—which Trump called a "puppet of China"—to punish the country for its early response to the disease.

The Trump administration also matched the CCP's disinformation campaign with one of its own. In early 2020, the Pentagon set up hundreds of fake accounts on Twitter with the intent of manipulating discourse in the Philippines, which China was aiding with the pandemic response. The accounts impersonated Filipinos, using racist hashtags that blamed China for the virus and sowing lies about the unreliability of life-saving medicines, masks, and other protective equipment that China had given the country to slow the spread of the disease.

The CCP fought back, seeding another narrative in its state media: Western incompetence. Through editorials and social media posts, the Chinese government pushed story after story about how Western democracies' preoccupation with personal freedom prevented them from effectively containing the virus. One blog post, shared on Toutiao by the nationalist news website *Guancha*, said: "I have lived in France for twenty years and used it as a vantage point to observe the West, China, and the world. For the first time, the West feels strangely unfamiliar to me. Its slow, chaotic, and incompetent response to the virus makes it seem like a crumbling building riddled with holes, on the verge of collapse."

On incompetence, the *Guancha* writer had a point. Science-skeptical politicians like Donald Trump, Boris Johnson, and Jair Bolsonaro were allergic to the kind of apolitical collaboration and deference to expertise required to contain a pandemic. The *Guancha* writer criticized Western governments for putting business interests over human safety—a critique shared by many on the American left. But they also expressed hurt and anger: at COVID itself, at Western states' irresponsible and politicized public health policies, and at Western leaders' animosity and suspicion toward China at a moment of great need.

This anger, fueled by the loss of hundreds of thousands of lives and the extended quarantine of millions more, would not be quick to dissipate. Many months later, *New York Times* columnist Thomas Friedman would write a piece condemning China's and Russia's governments for not taking a more aggressive stance against climate change. The title: "Would Russia or China Help Us if We Were Invaded by Space Aliens?"

A columnist at the Chinese government–owned *China Daily* responded: "If we are invaded by aliens—or a virus—will the US help, Mr. Friedman? I think we can all see the answer for ourselves."

Chapter 12

TO INFINITY AND BEYOND

Long before the 2020 lockdowns, Zhang Yiming intuited that to make ByteDance truly global, he would need to make it less Chinese. People in the US wouldn't trust a Chinese company to be separate from the Chinese government, so he began moving central operations to Singapore, the "Switzerland of Asia" known for its billionaire conclaves, permissive tax structures, and political neutrality. He bought servers in the country to back up US TikTok users' data (so it wouldn't need to be stored in China) and began recruiting hundreds of employees to staff a regional hub in the city.

In his March 2020 anniversary letter to staff, Yiming also announced a shift in corporate structure. Two of his top lieutenants at ByteDance HQ (both of whom coincidentally shared his surname, Zhang) would now lead the company's China operations. Zhang Nan, who had run Douyin, would become CEO of ByteDance China. Zhang Lidong, a former state media journalist who had helped lead Toutiao, would become ByteDance China's chairman. Both would still report to Yiming, who would serve in a new role: CEO of ByteDance Global.

Until now, TikTok had been just another ByteDance app—a big one, sure, but still part of the central Beijing "app factory" system. The people who led Douyin and Toutiao had been the same people who led TikTok and TopBuzz, and the products (fueled by the same underlying technology) sat under one umbrella, where a single group of executives could decide what features to build and what business lines to pursue.

But Yiming knew that system would have to change, for two reasons. The first was capitalistic: like American tech CEOs, Yiming wanted to build something so big that it would reach far beyond one country's political, cultural, and jurisdictional limits. But the second was political: the Chinese government's 2017–2018 rectification purge had hit Yiming directly. Offering ByteDance products completely outside of China might protect them, and his company, from the unpredictable thrashes of Chinese regulation—and manifest the boundaryless internet he'd envisioned in 2014.

A third reason was organizational pragmatism. ByteDance was now doing big business in countries with conflicting expectations about how it should behave—and, in some cases, conflicting laws. The company faced an impossible task: it had to continuously prove its fealty to the Chinese Communist Party at home, while assuring the governments of India and the US, its two largest non-Chinese markets, that it had no allegiance to the Chinese state.

In China, Toutiao and Douyin were regularly required to push out propaganda to users, including an increasing torrent of COVID-related disinformation that spread lies about the United States. In India, where the constitution protects free speech but not necessarily a free press, the government temporarily banned TikTok in 2019 for allegedly promoting "obscene" content, causing TikTok to implement a content moderation crackdown that removed more than 6 million videos from the country. (The government then lifted the ban.) Both US and Indian officials feared the app might be used to spread Chinese propaganda.

Every government had different expectations: China wanted lots of censorship; the US wanted none. India wanted some, sometimes, but was suspicious of China. And in other markets—Sudan, Saudi Arabia, Indonesia—compliance often just came down to not alienating the people in charge. Yiming had faced the wrath of angry, arbitrary governments before. But if ByteDance could do business in twenty, thirty, fifty markets, surely not all of them would crack down on him at once.

In early 2020, ByteDance's biggest overseas political challenges were the stories in the Western press about the app censoring political speech. TopBuzz, miraculously for Yiming, had stayed out of the spotlight—but it was drowning in intellectual property challenges and swiftly shedding users. TikTok would not be so lucky: in the wake of Mark Zuckerberg's hawkish turn, more and more lawmakers saw the app as a symbol of China's growing threat.

Despite the looming ire in Washington, Yiming pushed further into the US, signing the largest new data center lease contract in Northern Virginia's "Data Center Alley." Just before the COVID shutdown, Byte-Dance opened a splashy new US headquarters in the L.A. area's Culver City, a former whites-only sundown town that became home to film and TV giants like MGM Studios and Sony Pictures. The office itself was cavernous and modern, with an animated 100-foot-long LED wall, neon words and phrases written on the ceilings, and a violently hot pink central staircase.

Physically, TikTok's L.A. office resembled the campuses of American tech giants like Apple, Google, and Facebook. If ByteDance was going to poach talent from its American rivals, it would need to offer opulent Silicon Valley–level office benefits: things like free onsite gourmet restaurants, cooking classes, gyms, dry cleaning, haircuts, personal trainers, and nutritionists.

Bad COVID timing led TikTok's L.A. headquarters to lay essentially vacant for most of its first two years. Staff worked from home, online, and at least initially, they often experienced culture shock. Many of ByteDance's technical documents were written in Chinese, and only poorly machine-translated into English. Work hours were long: in China, employees worked "996"—9 a.m. to 9 p.m., six days a week. US employees weren't required to work 996, but they often had late-night meetings, to accommodate the work hours of their Beijing-based colleagues. The worst were the Sunday evening meetings (Monday morning in China). The twelve-hour time difference meant that for nearly any call, at least one person was on the phone in the middle of the night.

Language was also a barrier. ByteDance's engineering teams often held meetings in Mandarin, and many Chinese staff had limited English proficiency. Americans who didn't speak Mandarin found themselves cut out of important meetings, and felt like they were denied opportunities for advancement as a result. Meanwhile, Chinese employees—including those in the US—were sometimes given additional meetings and tasks, and expected to do extra work to compensate for their non-Mandarin-speaking colleagues.

Second- and third-generation Chinese American staffers experienced unique struggles: sometimes, their managers saw them as Chinese, and expected them to work Chinese hours and attend Chinese meetings. Though they often didn't understand Chinese languages better than their American colleagues, they were nonetheless expected to do more work for the same pay.

Nearly all employee work at ByteDance was done through an app called Feishu, known in the US as Lark—the same workplace productivity software that the company had offered to other Chinese companies for free when COVID lockdowns began. Lark was a powerful product, the best workplace software most staff had ever used. It was a "super-app" of sorts, combining the document management strengths of Microsoft Office and G Suite, the instant messaging powers of Slack, and the people management strengths of ADP or Workday. But it also contained things that none of those companies had.

One section of Lark, called ByteMoments, served as a sort of internal social network for the company, offering a space for employees to post and chat about their personal lives. Posts would get surprisingly personal. People put up shirtless gym pics, diet tips, and travel photos, and sometimes even more intimate news.

ByteMoments had a section called Meet Cute: an official channel maintained by the company where employees could offer up their single family members and friends as potential dates for their coworkers. One employee advertised his cousin: "a Taiyuan girl settled in Beijing, 170cm tall and weighing 50kg, graduated from the top 1 music academy in China." The woman was "active and self-disciplined," the profile said—she swam, did Pilates, and attended other fitness classes. "Self discipline gives me freedom to enjoy food more freely," the profile said.

American employees were scandalized as they scrolled through colleagues' posts featuring photos of their siblings, cousins, and friends, with lists of their physical attributes and dateable qualities. It was common at Chinese tech giants for HR departments to offer dating services to employees, but to Americans, the whole idea seemed, shall we say, wildly unprofessional.

ByteMoments, like many social networks, was also plagued by occasionally racist, sexist, fatphobic, and politically ignorant comments. One post, made by an engineer, denigrated sanitation in Japan: "I just ate Japanese seafood, save me.... priority races need to eat..." The comment, presumably a joke, received more than forty likes from other ByteDance staffers.

Beyond ByteMoments, there were also other parts of ByteDance that US employees found unpleasant. When executives were displeased with an employee, they would sometimes publicly berate the employee in a meeting, or in a follow-up all-staff email. (In the US, these episodes of public shaming could be considered bullying or harassment under law.) Some early contract workers were at one point asked to work without pay, because their boss said the company really needed the help.

ByteDance also made it exceedingly difficult for workers to figure out who anyone reported to. Yiming believed the company should be flat, and that anyone should be able to ask anyone else for help. But in practice, the lack of an org chart caused chaos: people didn't know who to escalate to when there was a disagreement, and if someone went on vacation, or left the company, it wasn't clear who would inherit their work.

Until spring 2020, the person functionally running TikTok in the US was an operations executive named Vanessa (or just V) Pappas. V (who is nonbinary and uses they/she pronouns) was tall and slender, with a soft Australian accent and a quiet, commanding presence. They had joined ByteDance in 2018 as TikTok's general manager of the US, after an eight-year stint managing creator programs at YouTube.

V's hire was a coup for ByteDance, which was now attempting to lure many of YouTube's entertainers to TikTok. The new executive embodied Yiming's global vision: they were born in Darwin, raised in Queensland, and had previously lived in both London and New York. To Americans, V was international without seeming foreign. But because they didn't speak Chinese languages, they often had to muddle through Byte-Dance's Chinese systems just like their staff.

V wasn't an engineer, but like their American engineering colleagues, they found themselves in many meetings conducted in Mandarin. Yiming had declared that global meetings should be conducted in English, but staff didn't always follow his order. Even when they did, pre-meeting and post-meeting gossip and pleasantries still often happened in the languages staffers were most comfortable speaking. At one point, V used the language learning service Memrise to study Cantonese, the language most commonly spoken in Hong Kong and across southeastern China.

V believed deeply that TikTok's quirky young user base would power the app's creativity. The app had become a vibrant community for queer, trans, and nonbinary youth. It also became popular among young Black creators and other people of color. V wanted to ensure that TikTok didn't over-moderate creators, especially those in racial and gender minorities. Their years of working directly with entertainers gave them a permissive instinct about the platform: they wanted to let TikTok be the weird, quirky place its early adopters had made it. People liked authenticity, and the less ByteDance tried to control its creators, the better the ecosystem would be.

In the evenings, despite having a young family at home, V was often among the last people out of TikTok's garish Culver City building. As the most senior executive based in the L.A. office, they were the de facto leader of TikTok's US staff, even those who reported directly in to Chinese teams. People who worked closely with V said the boss often tried to protect American staff from the more alienating facets of the Chinese business, like long work hours, ignorant views on race and racism in America, and different expectations about women in the workplace.

V saw themselves as a crusader for justice and equality, and a defender of the progressive TikTok users that aimed to make the world a more loving, inclusive place. But they were also savvy: they only picked battles they thought they could win, which sometimes meant standing down on issues their staff saw as critically important. This extended even to discussions about moderation: when Trust and Safety staffers tried to change policies (like the jiggle rule, and the rule about the length of girls' shorts) that penalized bigger-bodied people and women, they sometimes felt that V didn't defend them vigorously enough to the Chinese C-suite. The staffers knew V agreed with them about the policies, but sometimes wished they had a more zealous advocate in the boardroom.

V reported to Alex Zhu, who served as the global head of TikTok. Alex was an "ideas guy"—he was inspirational, smart, and a great listener. He was beloved by many who worked closely with him, though he had his detractors, too. One colleague compared him to the WeWork creator Adam Neumann, another long-haired serial founder known for his eccentric leadership style. Like Neumann, Alex liked to party—his love of strip clubs became a running joke among ByteDance staff—but he could also be absent: the TikTok team was based in L.A., and Alex still spent much of his time in Shanghai.

Alex was also challenged by a shift that many "acquired founders" face: he went from being the boss, the creator of an app that he knew every facet of, to being one of many executives at a giant conglomerate of which Musical.ly was just one small part. People liked him, but it wasn't always clear how his guidance should stack up against direction from other ByteDance leaders.

Nonetheless, in 2018 and 2019, Yiming chose Alex, rather than V, to be the face of the company. In November, ByteDance's PR team arranged for Alex to host a reporter from the *New York Times* at the company's WeWork space in downtown Manhattan. The interviewer wanted to know about Alex and his quirks, but also asked about lawmakers' concern that TikTok was censoring critics of China.

Alex told the reporter that TikTok was lucky its users didn't see it as a place for political discussion. The platform wouldn't censor political discussions, he said, as long as they "align[ed] with this creative and joyful experience." But he didn't want TikTok to become yet another toxic morass, like Facebook and Twitter.

Eventually, other social media giants would acknowledge what Alex knew: political discourse made their product worse. Researchers inside Facebook and Instagram (both of which had fully embraced political advertisers, commentators, and groups) were running internal study after study that showed that people wanted to see fewer political posts, and that everybody thought the shadowy algorithms were unfairly promoting their opponents' point of view.

There was also another key constituency that hated politics: advertisers. Politics was bad for business. People clicked on ads less when they were placed beside political messages (especially negative political messages, or those with which they disagreed). Many advertisers avoided placing ads near political messages altogether, which meant that websites touched by politics were simply less valuable than their nonpolitical competition.

Two months after the *New York Times* profile, Alex gave a second interview—this time to the German magazine *Der Spiegel*. The interviewer asked him why he had said TikTok was "lucky" that it wasn't a place for politics.

"To be honest, even today I don't have a good answer," Alex replied. "In the very beginning I didn't think we should embrace political content because it can be very polarizing and divisive. I was afraid we'd run into the exact same problems as Facebook. A lot of people say they don't like politics on social media. But maybe they don't dislike politics, they just dislike misinformation, hate speech and polarizing platforms."

He continued, "I think every city needs public squares where people can debate and argue. But at the same time, we shouldn't force the whole city to become a public square. There should be museums, concert halls and playgrounds, as well, where people just gather and have fun and express themselves."

This was a reasonable answer. Alex had created an app for teens and tweens to lip-synch and dance to pop music. The app had then been acquired by a company that relaunched it with a broader mission: to host short videos that "inspire creativity and bring joy." But nobody had ever said that TikTok could or should be the place for short videos about *everything*.

As TikTok exploded in the pandemic, the question of its identity grew more urgent. V began referring to TikTok as "the last sunny corner of the internet." It was more youthful, upbeat, and diverse than angry, exhausting platforms like Facebook and Twitter. But as the app swelled with hundreds of millions of new users, and American Sinophobia surged, staff questioned whether it could stay fun forever.

The For You algorithm, if left alone, would foreground topics that played on high emotions. As long as the company's core metrics were things like session frequency and session length, the machine would pick content to maximize those metrics, which often meant feeding videos that were divisive, sensationalistic, and inaccurate. (This is a lesson that Facebook and YouTube had also learned.) Correcting for this troublesome tendency required consistent effort—like keeping a wobbly car aligned in the center of the lane—but also raised questions about censorship: Yiming had believed that even Toutiao, a news aggregator of state-controlled media in China, shouldn't have editors choosing what people should see. Too much "correction" for the algorithm's tendencies could veer into editing, which neither Yiming nor the US government wanted ByteDance to do.

As the head of TikTok, Alex was the face of TikTok's promise not to censor content as it had once done. At the WeWork interview with the *New York Times*, the reporter had asked Alex outright whether TikTok had shared or would share data with the Chinese government. He told the reporter no—that he would reject such a request even if it came from Xi Jinping himself. This was a bold stance for a Chinese national who wanted to keep living in China. The CCP often harassed, imprisoned, and "disappeared" people who spoke unfavorably about the party. But it was also the only answer that would be acceptable to people in the United States.

Yiming had put Alex in an impossible position. Every question, every public statement was like a geopolitical loyalty test: Are you with us, or are you with them?

Alex's creativity and curiosity were worth little in a political arena thick with skepticism and xenophobia. His *New York Times* interview did little to quell government skepticism: the departments of State, Defense, and Homeland Security ordered their staff not to use the app on government devices. Meanwhile, parents consumed a steady stream of news stories about how TikTok (like other social media apps) could expose their teenagers to potential predators. They likely would have been furious to learn that the CEO himself had once posed as a teen to talk to teens on the app.

The Musical.ly creator who had once written in the voice of a "digital anthropologist" was a maker, a tinkerer, a master craftsman. But Yiming didn't need a master craftsman in charge of TikTok anymore; he needed someone who would give his business heft and credibility with skeptical Americans—a fighter and a salesman, someone with Big CEO Energy.

~

KEVIN MAYER IS six feet, four inches tall, with a square jaw, light eyes, and a deep voice. He's built like an offensive tackle—a position he once played on MIT's football team—and has the unfortunate habit of sending emails with subjects in all caps. When Yiming first approached him about becoming CEO of TikTok, he had served more than twenty years as an executive at Disney, where he had risen to lead the Disney+ streaming platform. He had been a candidate to succeed the conglomerate's legendary CEO, Bob Iger, when he stepped down in early 2020. But Mayer, who had earned the nickname "Buzz Lightyear" for the way his demeanor (and jawline) resembled the Disney Pixar character, had been passed over for the job.

Yiming approached Kevin at the beginning of the pandemic. Disney's prospects had tanked as movie theaters shuttered. But TikTok was a rocket ship Kevin, then fifty-eight, decided to take a ride on.

"I'm not getting any younger," he said.

In May 2020, Kevin accepted an offer to become global CEO of TikTok and chief operations officer of ByteDance. In a way, TikTok was as much like Disney+ or Netflix as it was like Facebook or Google. Obviously, user-generated content was a new and different beast for Kevin. The challenge of studying what people watched and convincing them to watch more, though, was familiar—as was the job of courting and persuading advertisers that this platform offered the best value for their money.

Kevin was bright, engaged, and good with numbers. "Every meeting was a lot of energy with Kevin," said one executive who worked with him. He was more assertive than Alex, and he wasn't a software engineer, but that was just as well. It meant he didn't develop or express as many strong opinions about how the technology behind TikTok should work—a topic that Yiming already felt strongly about. He could better focus on executive decision-making, and projecting confidence and competence to TikTok's staff and the rest of the world.

For many of ByteDance's employees, Kevin's hiring meant there would be an IPO. IPOs—"initial public offerings"—are the vehicle by which private companies become public, finally allowing investors and employees to sell their stock. Going public was the ultimate coming-of-age moment for a startup, and most of ByteDance's competitors, both in the US and in China, had made a lot of money doing it.

In Silicon Valley, it was well known that IPOs minted millionaires. Engineers, marketing managers, designers, and lawyers left steady jobs to roll the career dice at startups: the company might go under, but if it sold, they might get rich. At most tech companies, including ByteDance, employees were paid partially in company stock. At private companies, that stock was like a stack of lottery tickets: potentially worthless, potentially valuable. If the company IPO'd, employees could sell the stock on the open market, and suddenly those lottery tickets would be worth hundreds of thousands or millions of dollars.

Within two months of lockdown in 2020, it was clear TikTok was a success and ByteDance was unlikely to suddenly shut its doors in the United States. But there was unease among US employees about whether its foreignness would prevent it from soaring. Working for an international company was fun for the company's young American workforce—Chinese food in the cafeteria felt different, and so did the red envelopes filled with cash at Chinese New Year. But as President Trump raved about the "Kung Flu" and hate crimes against Asian Americans spiked, some worried: Would TikTok even be allowed to IPO? What if the IPO was in China, instead of the US? Would that change how employees could cash out?

ByteDance's US staff trusted Buzz Lightyear with these questions. Kevin Mayer "was the deal guy," an American executive who worked with him told me, referencing his track record of partnerships at Disney. "He was the deal guy brought in to take it public."

That executive and others hoped Kevin would Americanize TikTok in other ways. They imagined he might pull the company's center of gravity away from Beijing, ending the Chinese-language Lark chats, Sunday night meetings, and mass-shaming emails. US employees hoped that Pacific time would become TikTok's governing time zone, and English its default language. In other words, they wanted to work as a "regular" tech company. And they hoped Kevin would provide ultimate clarity on the question of who was in charge.

Chapter 13

"BRO GET KPOP STAN ON THIS"

Before Kevin Mayer even opened his new work laptop, things went haywire.

On May 25, 2020, a white Minneapolis police officer named Derek Chauvin dug his knee into the neck of a forty-six-year-old Black man named George Floyd, ultimately killing him. A seventeen-year-old bystander posted a video of the act on Facebook; it soon was viral on every platform.

The video of George Floyd's murder was a historic moment for the internet. The witness who filmed it won an honorary Pulitzer Prize. Platforms across the world balked at hosting graphic video of a person's murder—but they also knew that not allowing users to share it, or suppressing the video, would be far worse.

First in Minneapolis, and then nationwide, vigils commemorated Floyd and protestors marched by the thousands, chanting Floyd's tragic refrain: "I can't breathe." For many demonstrators, these gatherings were their first public outings since the pandemic began—their first time breaking isolation, taking public transit, or being in close proximity to anyone other than their families. Emotions ran extremely high. The empowering exhilaration of mass solidarity swirled with the danger of exposure to the virus, heightened by the presence of police at many marches.

At a protest in Williamsburg, Brooklyn, in late May, a progressive organizer named Abby Loisel saw a young boy standing on a rock watching protestors go by. Loisel, who described attending a protest that week as "an out of body experience," asked the boy's mother if she could film the moment, and captured a protester giving the boy a fist bump as they marched by. "I just thought it was really sweet," she said. She set the video to Childish Gambino's "This Is America," and posted the video to TikTok later that day.

Other videos gained traction as well. Footage of burning cars and looting of stores started circulating and clashing with solidarity posts from people who had remained at home for fear of the virus. Celebrities and politicians weighed in. President Trump threatened to suppress the gatherings with the military, a striking threat that further inflamed tensions.

The For You algorithm loved every angle of the George Floyd controversy. ByteDance's algorithm had been built to identify trends, new topics that lots of people were suddenly posting about and commenting on. The algorithm especially liked videos with new music. "This Is America" became the summer's protest anthem. A mass protest movement had all the qualities that made content pop on the app. But George Floyd's death was exactly the opposite of what Alex Zhu had wanted the app to be.

George Floyd was killed one week after Zhang Yiming announced Kevin Mayer's hire at TikTok, and one week before he actually started the job. Kevin wasn't a political figure. He was a finance guy, a shrewd dealmaker whose vision for TikTok was polished, professional entertainment—not a fraught quagmire of users' thoughts on race and policing.

Kevin described his first days at TikTok as a moment when the platform itself went through a massive change: before then, he said, the app was "happy and joy all over." But after Floyd's killing, that changed. The For You algorithm had learned something new—it had met a new type of trend, one with more power than the most captivating possible teen lip-synch.

In a webinar with entertainment consultant Peter Csathy a few weeks into his tenure as CEO, Kevin acknowledged the platform's shift. "Maybe the most important thing isn't joy, it's social justice.... We have the responsibility to be that platform when people want to express their anger and belief in social justice."

Alex Zhu's warning about leaning into politics loomed large over Kevin's first days. But Kevin hardly had a choice in the matter. If TikTok had tried to limit discussion about the killing, it would've been accused of censorship and indifference to racial justice, which every other *Fortune* 500 company in the US was making new commitments to support. Neither Yiming nor Kevin could have insisted that TikTok stay out of politics in a moment when its own users were marching in the streets.

So on his first day at work, Kevin issued a statement aligning the platform with the protest movement:

> As I begin my work at TikTok, it has never been a more important time to support Black employees, users, creators, artists, and our broader community. I am making this commitment from today, my Day 1.
>
> Words can only go so far. I invite our community to hold us accountable for the actions we take over the coming weeks, months, and years. Black Lives Matter.

Summer 2020 is remembered for its racial justice protests and COVID quarantines, but it also produced the strangest presidential campaign in modern US history. Social distancing prevented the traditional door-knocking and rallies. So the erratic populist president, Republican Donald Trump, faced centrist liberal Democrat Joe Biden in a campaign waged almost entirely online and on television.

TikTok played a limited role in the 2020 election. The company wanted no part in electoral politics, and many politicians wanted nothing to do with TikTok. Both the Democratic and Republican National Committees advised candidates and staffers not to use the app, because of its Chinese origins, and asked staffers to delete it and suspend their accounts. A group of Republican senators introduced and passed a bill that banned it on government devices.

Kevin Mayer had inherited TikTok's policy of refusing political ads. But he and his teams couldn't police transactions that happened beyond its proverbial walls, so some opportunistic politicians and political strategists began offering entertainers and influencers cash to post political messages on the platform. Because TikTok didn't restrict political messages, and couldn't tell which ones were paid for, it couldn't enforce its rules and take down the posts.

Still, for the first half of 2020, TikTok largely avoided the limelight. Its users were overwhelmingly young—often so young they couldn't even vote. According to one internal document, more than one-third of TikTok users in early 2020 were fourteen or younger. Those who could vote were mostly still under thirty-five years old: a group that wasn't particularly excited about either Trump or Biden.

Then, Trump decided to reenter the arena. The all-digital campaign had favored Biden, as it protected him from the rigors of the campaign and gaffe-prone events, while allowing his disciplined digital campaign to portray him as a seasoned, reasonable moderate. Trump, who had ridden to victory in 2016 on a campaign fueled by raucous rallies, was hurt by the virtual contest. That June, when the public began to tire of COVID restrictions, he announced the return of his rally tour. His first stop would be on June 19, at the BOK Center in Tulsa, Oklahoma.

The announcement was immediately controversial, for two reasons. The first, of course, was COVID. In its mid-2020 form, months before vaccines were available, the disease caused death and lifelong illness in many of the people it infected. Packing thousands of people into an enclosed, indoor arena violated guidance from the World Health Organization, the Centers for Disease Control and Prevention, and nearly every other public health authority. Holding the rally itself was an act of defiance, a statement that personal freedom was more important than what Trump supporters saw as bureaucratic public health guidance.

The rally was also scheduled to occur on Juneteenth, the Black American holiday celebrating the end of slavery, at the site of a brutal act of racist terror, the 1921 massacre on Tulsa's Black Wall Street. Trump already had a reputation for racist behavior: the federal government once sued him for discriminatory lending, he aggressively campaigned to put five wrongly accused Black and Latino teens in prison, and a former colleague described him using the N-word on the set of his TV show, *The Apprentice*. So when he announced the time and place of his comeback rally, some people questioned whether the plans reflected callous ignorance—or outright animus.

The Trump campaign would later announce that they were moving the rally back by a day, to June 20, but by then, the damage had been done. On June 11, the day after Trump first announced the rally, a political commentator and reality TV star named Quentin Jiles made a TikTok explaining the stakes: "Not only is this man totally insensitive to the moment, I think it's a doubling down. Because we know where his heart is. We know he's a racist."

The video got just shy of 10,000 likes—pretty standard for Jiles, given his celebrity and following at the time. Under it, though, comments began to stream in from followers saying they'd reserved tickets to the rally, though they had no intent to go. "Don't worry we got your back!" one commenter wrote. "Already rsvp'ed my free tickets. That rally will be at minimum capacity, go get your two free tickets right now!"

Then commenters started sharing the URL to Trump's campaign website, with instructions about how to reserve tickets—and reservations poured in.

A few hours after Jiles posted his video, another TikToker chimed in. Mary Jo Laupp, a fifty-one-year-old high school theater director in Fort Dodge, Iowa, made a follow-up video calling the rally "a slap in the face to the Black community." She urged her small community of followers—at that point, just about a thousand people—to educate themselves about Juneteenth and the Tulsa massacre. But she didn't stop there.

"Somebody on another TikTok post commented that [Trump] was offering two free tickets on his campaign website to go to this rally, so I went and investigated it," Laupp spoke quickly and purposefully into the camera. "It's two free tickets per cell phone number," she said, "so, I recommend that all of us that want to see this 19,000 seat auditorium barely filled or completely empty go reserve tickets now, and leave him standing alone on the stage. Whadda ya say?"

Every once in a while, an internet meme reaches escape velocity and explodes into the real world—and that's what happened in response to Mary Jo Laupp's video. It received more than two million views and thousands of comments in the following days. Many of those comments said, simply, "algorithm."

The Laupp commenters were doing something technologically new for TikTok: they were turning the app's recommendations engine on its head—making it work *for* them, instead of just letting it act *upon* them. They knew that TikTok ran nearly entirely on revealed preferences, rather than stated ones. So they found a way to creatively state their preferences anyway, in a language the machine would understand.

To be clear: TikTok's algorithm wasn't responding to the word "algorithm," as if the users were calling its name. The users just understood that under the hood, TikTok (like Instagram, Facebook, and Twitter) was essentially a big math equation, adding up the weights of a bunch of different signals to decide how much reach each post would receive. By commenting *any* text on the post, they could add a few points to the "comments" column, driving the total reach of the post up a little bit.

One comment in particular amassed more than 70,000 likes. The account that posted it, which said it was a twenty-one-year-old named Yesenia, had made only one post. The comment said, "Bro get kpop stan on this."

K-pop "stans," for those unfamiliar, are fans of Korean pop supergroups like BTS and BLACKPINK. There are millions of them in the United States and around the world, and they are generally young, passionate, and extremely online.

In summer 2020, K-pop stans became famous for disrupting bigoted online movements by "flooding the zone" with wholesome memes. In the week before Trump announced his Tulsa rally, a group of white supremacists began posting on Twitter using the hashtag #whitelivesmatter. Within hours, use of the hashtag soared, but anyone who actually clicked on it was met with photos and videos of K-pop artists, songs, choreography. The racist posters, overwhelmed and wrong-footed, reorganized under the hashtags #whitelifematters and #whiteoutwednesday, only to quickly find those hashtags flooded with K-pop too.

The week before #whitelivesmatter, K-Pop devotees had set their sights on Dallas, where the Dallas Police Department had launched an app through which citizens could upload reports of "illegal activity from the protests" following George Floyd's death. A sixteen-year-old K-pop fan tweeted asking her followers to "FLOOD that shit" with footage of K-pop stars. "Make it SO HARD for them to find anything besides our faves dancing," she wrote. The next day, the Dallas Police Department announced that its iWatch app had experienced "technical difficulties" and was down.

Just minutes after Yesenia's call to mobilize K-pop stans, replies started streaming in. "We heard u sis we on it," one wrote. "We here now," quipped another. "On it" said a third, who posted the comment with the "nailcare" emoji, often used to convey sass and confidence. Anti-Trump TikTokers without K-pop ties cheered the stans on, and made their own posts tagging K-pop accounts, calling them to action, and thanking them—as several commenters put it—"for their service."

On Friday, June 12, less than twenty-four hours after Laupp posted her video, Trump's campaign manager, Brad Parscale, tweeted that over 200,000 tickets had already been reserved for the rally. Later in the day, he wrote: "Correction now 300,000!" and, two days later, "Just passed 800,000 tickets. Biggest data haul and rally signup of all time by 10x." Trump himself also tweeted: "Almost One Million people requested tickets for the Saturday Night Rally in Tulsa, Oklahoma!"

TikTokers reposted the tweet with gleeful comments: "Who requested all those seats though!?"

The ticket reservation bonanza was reminiscent of the 2021 "meme stock" Reddit campaign that led hundreds of hobbyist investors to manipulate the market for GameStop, sticking it to billionaire money managers who had sold the foundering video game retailer short. Like the GameStop surge, the Tulsa campaign was subversive—it gave everyday people (many of them too young to vote) a way to collectively express their distaste for the president in a moment of crowdsourced revolution. The hobbyist investors had organized online to defeat the investor class (if only in the short term), and the ticket reservers did the same to prank the most powerful man on earth.

The Trump campaign's trip to Tulsa was a nightmare from the start.

On the morning of the rally, eight members of the campaign staff tested positive for COVID at their hotel. Campaign leaders told the sick staffers to rent cars and drive home—and ordered the rest to stop testing, lest they identify further casualties. (This strategy widened the outbreak.)

President Trump's priority, though, was the crowd. A few hours out from the event, he called Parscale from Air Force One to ask whether the arena would be full. Parscale, who could see the parking lot, knew it wouldn't. According to reporting from ABC News anchor Jonathan Karl, Parscale replied, "No sir. It looks like Beirut in the eighties." As his staffers looked out into the largely empty stadium on June 20 in Tulsa, they knew just how unpleasant their evening was about to become. Parscale told his top lieutenants, "None of you should go anywhere near the president today, including me." In the end, only about 6,000 people attended the event, in an arena that held 19,000. The optics were spectacularly bad.

Parscale would ultimately lose his job over the rally in Tulsa. It was a disaster for the Trump campaign—a sign that, after three years of their leader in office and months of a deadly pandemic that had claimed hundreds of thousands of lives, the MAGA faithful of 2016 might just have lost their zeal. But it was also TikTok's first inside-the-Beltway moment, one that would haunt the platform for years to come.

TikTok teens almost certainly weren't the only reason people didn't show up to the MAGA rally in Tulsa. The city's own public health department had opposed the rally and urged people to stay home. But for TikTok's PR team and Kevin Mayer, now in his third week on the job, the event was a crisis. News outlets like the *New York Times* and the *Wall Street Journal* rushed to cover the platform's newfound effects on politics. Just seven months prior, Alex Zhu had told the *Times* that TikTok wanted to be a place of public entertainment, not the town square. Now his fears had come true: TikTok, along with Twitter, Facebook, and YouTube, had become ground zero for political activism.

For many of TikTok's users, the moment was a hilarious triumph. A horde of mostly teenage girls had tanked the comeback rally of a grown-up bully with famously little regard for girls or women. It was the type of feel-good story Hillary Clinton supporters would call their moms to laugh about.

Steve Schmidt, a Republican political strategist and opponent of President Trump, wrote on Twitter: "The teens of America have struck a savage blow against @realDonaldTrump. All across America teens ordered tickets to this event. The fools on the campaign bragged about a million tickets. lol."

"Lol" was also the position of many staffers who worked for TikTok. The rally—and the prank leading up to it—wasn't on the radar of most TikTok employees before it happened. In the grand scheme of things, it wasn't even that big a trend on the platform. Even after the fact, one former executive told me, it didn't particularly raise alarm bells. "A lot of the staff are quite progressive," the person said. "They thought it was pretty cool."

The prank hadn't violated any of TikTok's rules. It would be crazy for TikTok to prohibit people from posting videos about ordering tickets to an event and then not attending it. There had been no spam, no misrepresentation, no inauthenticity. And because the campaign hadn't limited the number of people who could register, it's unlikely that the pranksters actually stopped anyone from attending the rally, either. Their sole crime had been embarrassing a guy who was unusually sensitive about his crowd size.

But it wouldn't be too hard to imagine a more troubling use of the same tactics. In October 2020, a cybersecurity researcher named Thaddeus Grugq published a blog post characterizing BTS ARMY, one of the K-pop stan groups that facilitated the Trump troll, as a "non-traditional, non-state actor"—a designation of increasing interest to those studying platform manipulation in the wake of Russia's 2016 election interference.

ARMY (as the BTS fan group called itself) had years of experience conducting mass engagement drives online. Grugq pointed out that because many Korean pop music awards pick their winners by online votes, fan groups had years of experience orchestrating digital "ballot stuffing" for their band of choice. He also described a number of "anti-band" tactics—efforts undertaken by one fandom to sabotage another.

"One tactic used by kpop fandoms against rival bands is to book tickets for shows and then cancel at the last minute," he wrote. "The intention being to deny access to the real fans, to create a false impression of market interest, and/or to deny the band an audience thus impacting their concert revenue and embarrassing them." Donald Trump, whose rallies resembled rock concerts, had pretty clearly been the victim of an "antiband" attack.

"What is the cyber force ARMY currently capable of?" Grugq asked. "Pretty much anything you can do with a million people coordinated online."

Chapter 14

GALWAN VALLEY

In summer 2020, Zhang Yiming encountered the first true threat to his dream of global domination. More dangerous than the George Floyd protests or the teens punking President Trump (though they, too, would eventually cause a threat), the impediment lay seven thousand miles away, on the border between Western China and North India.

Along the mountainous Line of Actual Control between the two nations, skirmishes have long occurred when enough snow melts that soldiers can resume regular seasonal border patrols. But in 2020, as ice thawed in Galwan Valley, a dramatic mountain pass in the North Indian state of Ladakh, a particularly violent set of skirmishes broke out. Perhaps it was because India had built a new road in the area, diminishing existing Chinese infrastructure advantages. Perhaps it was Chinese retaliation against a new Indian rule tightening laws on Chinese investment in India. Maybe it was an extra ounce of pandemic-era distrust.

Whatever the reason, the skirmishes escalated into a melee in the mountain valley of Galwan where at least two dozen soldiers were killed, and at least another two dozen were injured.

The loss of life caused a near-instant swell of anti-Chinese sentiment in India. A nationwide boycott of Chinese goods—and Chinese apps—spread quickly online, and Bollywood celebrities like Milind Soman, Karanvir Bohra, and Kamya Shalabh Dang made posts encouraging Indians to delete TikTok, though it had played no part in the skirmishes. Then, a few weeks into the campaign, the boycott was made irrelevant: in retaliation for the Galwan massacre, the Indian government banned TikTok entirely.

By spring 2020, India was TikTok's largest market: more than 200 million users had begun using the app, only to have it snatched from them in response to violence that neither TikTok nor its users had carried out. There was no serious allegation that TikTok, or the other Chinese apps affected, had done anything wrong. Yiming and his staff were the casualties of a battle between other men, punished in a manner that felt as arbitrary as the CCP's shuttering of Neihan Duanzi.

For Yiming, India was second in importance only to the US and China. Before it bought Flipagram and Musical.ly, ByteDance had invested in an Indian news aggregator (similar to Toutiao) called Dailyhunt. When TikTok launched in the country, it had quickly enmeshed itself in Indian culture, closing a deal with the International Cricket Council to feature videos from the World Cup, and even sponsoring development of a Bollywood feature film whose characters were users of TikTok.

TikTok also had a unique opportunity in India—one that would give it a critical advantage over apps like Facebook and Twitter. In the late 2010s, many of India's more than 313 million illiterate adults were getting online for the first time. (For context, the US has roughly 43 million illiterate adults.) While most social media apps featured primarily text-based conversation, all TikTok required to participate was a swipe of the hand. The videos were short, so they could upload and download on cheaper smartphones and lower bandwidth speeds. For a population excluded from much of the internet, TikTok could be an equalizer.

TikTok's Indian users spoke fifteen different Indian languages, from Tamil and Telugu to Bengali and Gujarati. They were rich and poor, urban and rural, but as ByteDance aimed (as always) to "diversify" its content from lip-synching videos, it turned again to the idea of paying people from poorer, rural communities to make videos. This was a win-win: the varied videos were worthwhile for ByteDance, and creators needed only small sums to meaningfully improve their quality of life.

Facebook, Instagram, and YouTube had focused heavily on wooing higher-caste Indian entertainers, and in spring 2020, YouTubers made several "diss track" videos mocking TikTok users, comparing them to rag pickers and calling them homophobic slurs. TikTokers responded, criticizing the videos as classist and casteist.

But like any platform with a diverse group of users, TikTok had problems with discriminatory videos, too. In 2019, researchers found hundreds of casteist videos on the platform, often organized under caste-specific hashtags, which featured a mix of videos championing caste pride and videos by members of upper castes denigrating lower ones. They also found that once a user watched a few casteist videos, they started receiving recommendations for more.

In 2019, hawkish Indian lawmakers began raising concerns about the security of TikTok's user data. Yiming was quick to respond, promising to spend more than $1 billion in the country, and to build a data center within India to house Indian TikTok users' data. Yiming gave Indian staff attention that he often reserved nearly exclusively for staff in China and the United States: in speeches, he described sending staff to India to do user interviews, and even conducting interviews of random Indian users himself.

But after the border skirmishes began, posts supporting a boycott on Chinese products began spreading on TikTok itself, where hashtags like #BoycottChineseProducts amassed millions of views. On the Google Play Store, Indian nationalists flooded TikTok itself with one-star reviews, bringing its pre-skirmish rating from 4.5 stars down to 1.2. Google later announced that it had removed millions of the reviews, but the removals only raised the app's rating back up to a measly 1.6 stars.

Meanwhile, as TikTok floundered in the Play Store, another new app, named Remove Chinese Apps, soared. Created by an opaque, recently incorporated Indian company, the app claimed to be able to scan all the other apps on a user's phone (collecting who knows what data) and auto-delete any that were "Chinese," including apps owned by ByteDance, Tencent, and other Chinese tech giants. Within its first ten days, in May 2020, the app was downloaded more than a million times, and it reached No. 1 in the Play Store in India for at least two days.

Remove Chinese Apps was a strange creation. It did not disclose how it determined that an app was Chinese, and it both appeared to miss apps that were clearly run by Chinese companies and to include apps that were arguably not Chinese—including Zoom, an American company founded by an American citizen born in China.

Google removed Remove China Apps from the Play Store in June 2020 for violations of the company's Deceptive Behavior Policy. The policy forbids, among other things, misleading and false claims, and "Apps that mislead users into removing or disabling third-party apps or modifying device settings or features."

TikTok, though, had its own content moderation difficulties. In late May 2020, amid the skirmishes in Ladakh and Galwan Valley, a comedian named Saloni Gaur posted a video on TikTok suggesting that the Chinese soldiers in the region were just tourists, lured by its mountain scenery. In character, she blamed China for COVID lockdowns, cheap smartphones, and Ajinomoto (a Japanese company that popularized MSG in India), and speculated about who would direct the movie depicting India's military defeat over China at the border.

Gaur's video was promptly taken down.

"The app is like the country, there's no freedom of speech," she tweeted after the removal.

TikTok reinstated Gaur's video, blaming a content moderation error related to new COVID content policies. But the Gaur incident was spookily reminiscent of what had happened to American teenager Feroza Aziz. TikTok said it had changed its policies after the *Guardian* and *Netzpolitik* leaks. Why, then, did the site keep taking down videos critical of China?

The answer might just have been scale: TikTok was huge. The power of large numbers means that pretty much anything can and probably will happen on the platform, which means critics can find examples to support any narrative they wish to advance. Still, like Aziz, Gaur didn't buy TikTok's claim that there had been a mistake. She announced that she supported the boycott of Chinese products and would be leaving the platform.

Less than two months later, everyone else did, too. On the evening of June 29, 2020, Indian leaders on ByteDance's policy team received an email from the government informing them that TikTok would be banned in India along with fifty-nine other Chinese apps, effective immediately.

Several recipients of this message told me later that they had known some version of it was coming. Others were blindsided. But all described chaos at the actual moment it was received. The notice had come with little information, during a COVID surge when the entire staff was working from home. Hundreds of employees in ByteDance's offices across the country turned to television and social media for news, wondering if they still had jobs.

As quickly as they could, TikTok employees drafted up a short statement explaining that the government had ordered them to stop operating in India. They loaded it up into the app, and turned off the rest of the TikTok service. The ban was in effect.

Halfway across the world, Kevin Mayer was in his fourth week as global CEO of TikTok. He didn't have much information to relay to ByteDance's bewildered Indian staff. In 2019, the Indian government had temporarily banned TikTok for hosting obscene and pornographic content, but the issue had been solved by quick diplomacy and a content moderation crackdown. ByteDance saw no reason it couldn't run the same play again, so it told employees to stay the course, and creator managers to reach out to top talent, to assure them that things were fine. TikTok hadn't broken any laws. It would all blow over.

ByteDance had enjoyed strong relationships with the prime minister's office. But after the skirmishes on the border, lobbyists and TikTok's government relations team found that their previously warm contacts were now exceptionally hard to reach. Surely, the problem could be solved with more investment in the Indian economy, more jobs for Indian workers, more data center security measures. ByteDance's policy team reached out to the prime minister's office again and again. If they could just understand the government's concerns, they said, then they could address them.

But the government was no longer interested in negotiations—it wasn't even done banning apps. While TikTok had been in the first tranche of banned apps, additional waves swept up other ByteDance apps like TikTok Lite (a version of the app that was optimized for poorer connections and lower-end phones) as well as video editors CapCut and FaceU. If the government began negotiating with ByteDance, it would have to negotiate with all the other companies it had banned, which would diminish the stark, "tough on China" message of mass bans in the first place.

Still, Yiming wouldn't give up. For six months after the ban, he kept staff on payroll and told them to continue their work as if the ban hadn't happened. They began negotiations with the Hiranandani Group, a real estate firm, exploring whether the app could relaunch in India if it stored Indian users' data in local Hiranandani data centers. ByteDance also courted the Indian conglomerate Reliance Industries, which considered making a multi-billion-dollar investment in TikTok to appease the Modi government. The deal never moved forward.

Eventually, ByteDance did lay off most of its staff in India. But for years thereafter, it pursued versions of a plan known as Project Phoenix, which would bring TikTok back to the country. As the project gained steam, they even hired some employees back. ByteDance and Hiranandani kept the government apprised of their negotiations, as they would need approval of any partnership that could result in TikTok returning to the country. But the approval never came.

TikTok had offered jobs and advertising dollars to Indian firms, but Modi had long distanced himself from Xi's Belt and Road Initiative, and he had just launched a campaign to decrease Indian reliance on Chinese manufacturing. Why would he cut a deal with a Chinese tech giant, when homegrown TikTok competitors were springing up in bids to replace it?

~

A WEEK AFTER it was banned in India, TikTok also exited another market in Asia—Hong Kong. Yiming had made the decision to offer TikTok rather than Douyin in the city, given its "special administrative region" status. But since the 2019 protests, laws had only become more restrictive for Hong Kong's citizens. On June 30, 2020, the day after the India ban was announced, a new national security law went into effect in Hong Kong, imposing penalties of life in prison on people convicted of vague offenses like "subversion" of the Chinese central government and "collusion" with a foreign power.

The new law was a devastating blow to democracy activists in Hong Kong. It was kept secret from the public until 11 p.m. on the evening it was passed. One activist leader, Joshua Wong, tweeted that it "mark[ed] the end of Hong Kong that the world knew before." Another prominent local leader, businessman Jimmy Lai, said it "spells a death knell to Hong Kong." Both men promised to keep fighting—and were imprisoned for doing so.

A week after the law was announced, Facebook, Google, Twitter, and the messaging app Telegram announced that they would stop complying with data requests from the Hong Kong government until they had assessed the human rights impact of doing so. In the following days, Microsoft and Zoom announced that they too would decline to process data requests from the city's investigators and police.

Zhang Yiming's competitors had put him in a tricky spot. As a Chinese national running a Chinese company, he could not defy the Chinese government as his competitors had—or he could himself be at risk of imprisonment for vague crimes like "subversion" or "collusion." But if TikTok didn't match the actions of its American contemporaries, it would, in a way, prove the case made by the Modi government and hawks in the United States—that TikTok was under the thumb of the Chinese government.

Unlike India, Hong Kong was not a strategic market for TikTok. It was tiny—registering only about 150,000 users. So, abruptly and without explanation, ByteDance turned off TikTok in Hong Kong. Users trying to log into the app, beginning on July 6, were met with the following message: "We regret to inform you that we have discontinued operating TikTok in Hong Kong. Thank you for the time you have spent with us on the platform and for giving us the opportunity to bring a little bit of joy into your life."

Chapter 15

AMERICAN PUPPET

On July 6, 2020, the same day TikTok announced it was leaving Hong Kong, US Secretary of State Mike Pompeo joined conservative talk show host Laura Ingraham for an interview on Fox News. The conversation turned to Hong Kong and then TikTok, and Ingraham displayed a *Wall Street Journal* headline about India's decision to ban the app.

"Mr. Secretary, the huge Chinese app TikTok has about 30 million users in the United States, but it's been banned now by India, and Australia is considering the same action, saying that TikTok is full of mass surveillance and propaganda, and also that the app has the ability to feed information straight to Beijing," she said. "So—kind of an obvious question: If that's all the case, shouldn't we be considering, right now, tonight, a ban on Chinese social media apps, and especially TikTok?"

"I don't want to get out in front of the president, but it's something we're looking at," Pompeo said.

Within the Trump White House, the question of what to do about TikTok had exploded over the course of the previous week. Trump, like Ingraham, had seen the coverage of Modi's ban, which came just nine days after teens on the app claimed credit for tanking his Tulsa campaign rally. He was reportedly enthusiastic about the idea of copying Modi, and ordered lawyers at the National Security Council to draft an executive order similar to what India had done.

The United States had never banned an app before. It barely even regulated the flow of data to China. Data brokers could collect and sell Americans' data to the Chinese government without limitation under US law. Even after Facebook was manipulated by Russian election meddlers, and Twitter allowed Saudi agents to exfiltrate its users' data, a government ban on the apps was never seriously considered. Yes, TikTok was foreign, but thousands of apps from China and elsewhere had sketchy privacy practices and collected just as much data, if not more.

Banning an app raised endless practical questions as well. Would the ban cover just the TikTok-branded app and website? What if ByteDance just renamed it, or used the same code and algorithm in a similar app? What would happen if a foreign person, with the app on their phone, traveled to the US? Who would be penalized if the ban was not obeyed?

Despite these unanswered questions, Trump wanted the administration to go ahead. White House staffers were bitterly divided about the draft order. While most favored some action, some wanted a flat-out ban, while others wanted TikTok sold to a US company. They had not come to an agreement when, the next day, President Trump himself confirmed to former Fox News host Greta Van Susteren that he was considering banning the app. He said it was part of a suite of actions that would retaliate against China for its handling of COVID.

ByteDance itself did not have much of a say in the Trump administration's debate about its future—but that wasn't for a lack of trying. Shortly before he had hired Kevin Mayer, Yiming had also hired a new general counsel for ByteDance: a mild-mannered intellectual property lawyer with more than twenty years at Microsoft named Erich Andersen.

Erich was self-assured, introverted, and beloved by the lawyers who worked for him. He was pale, with sandy white-blond hair and slim silver rectangular eyeglasses. Young ByteDance staffers described him as grandfatherly, while older staffers called him "uncular." Married to a fellow lawyer, he was the type of restrained, intellectual, aging dad who had relished watching his teenage children compete in sports, and was now enthusiastic about becoming a literal grandfather. Though handsomely compensated, he wasn't motivated by fame or money—one colleague described him as the type of guy who would be excited to learn there was a weekend sale at the local Lowe's.

Professionally, Erich was a dealmaker. At Microsoft, he had overseen a set of partnerships that aimed to put Microsoft software on as many devices as possible around the world, offering hardware companies licenses to its products in exchange for preloading them onto their devices—an expansion strategy that TikTok had begun to use as well.

At ByteDance, Erich had managed the company's perfunctory relationship with the Trump administration. As Marco Rubio had recommended, the White House had begun investigating whether the app posed national security risks. Erich aimed to turn the investigation into a discussion, meeting with those suspicious about ByteDance, and asking what the company might do to allay their concerns. But he often didn't receive an answer to his questions.

Some White House staff wanted nothing to do with ByteDance. Perhaps the most zealous of them was Peter Navarro, a hotheaded former progressive with virulent anti-China views who directed the short-lived White House National Trade Council. Navarro, whom *Politico* once described as "a political wrecking ball," wanted the White House to ban not only TikTok but also a slew of other Chinese apps. Despite his former career as a Democrat, Navarro was close to Trump—and would eventually become one of the first Trump aides to serve prison time for his actions in support of the former president.

Opposite Navarro was Treasury Secretary Steve Mnuchin, a well-connected former investment banker who had been named to the job for his Wall Street experience, but had attracted negative attention for, among other things, using government planes to take his wife on personal trips (a subsequent investigation found no wrongdoing on his part) and for a viral photoshoot in which the couple posed with sheets of money at the US Bureau of Engraving and Printing. Mnuchin was a pragmatist by comparison to Navarro, and he saw forcing ByteDance to sell TikTok as an opportunity to give a US company a valuable, much-beloved product at a potential fire-sale price.

Mnuchin had his own history appeasing the Chinese government—in addition to his investment banking, he founded a Hollywood production company behind several blockbuster films that either altered scenes to appease Chinese regulators or gave them editorial "final cut approval." In discussions about TikTok, he was focused on the fundamentals: banning such a popular product had little economic upside, but reallocating its success to American executives, engineers, and businesspeople could add many millions to the US economy.

As Navarro tells it, Mnuchin and other more moderate voices in the White House secretly campaigned around him to sway Trump. Navarro felt Trump favored an outright ban and was talked into forcing a sale. The dispute culminated in a July 20 Oval Office meeting from which Navarro was supposedly excluded. He found out about the meeting anyway and claims to have strode into the room just as Trump asked what should be done about TikTok. He says he pointed at Mnuchin, and deemed the forced sale proposal a "weak-ass, broke-dick piece of Steve Mnuchin manure."

In the weeks following this meeting, Trump waffled between the Mnuchin and Navarro approaches. On July 29, he and Mnuchin gave remarks on the South Lawn of the White House. Mnuchin confirmed that TikTok was under investigation, and said advisors would soon be "making a recommendation to the president." Trump echoed Mnuchin, saying he was "thinking about making a decision."

Two days later, on July 31, Trump again gave statements on the South Lawn—this time, suggesting that he might straight up outlaw TikTok in the United States. "We're looking at TikTok, we may be banning TikTok, we may be doing some other things. There's a couple of options, but a lot of things are happening. We'll see what happens!" Then he boarded Marine One to fly to Tampa for a campaign fundraiser.

Several hours later, upon his return from the fundraiser in Tampa, Trump said to a gaggle of reporters, "As far as TikTok is concerned, we're banning them from the United States."

This was news to Trump's staff. After the president's comments while boarding Marine One, advisors plotted about how to turn him back from a flat ban to a negotiated sale. In that softer option, only if Byte-Dance refused to sell would the app be banned. The ban would act as a last resort to enforce the order.

In the end, Trump signed two executive orders about TikTok, but neither embraced the outright ban approach. The first came on August 6:

under a 1977 law called the International Emergency Economic Powers Act, it explained, the president has the authority to regulate commercial transactions with foreign businesses. The order would require TikTok to be removed from the app stores on September 20 if no deal had been reached—and bar all transactions with ByteDance starting on November 12. If TikTok was no longer owned by ByteDance when those deadlines hit, then it would be safe.

Roughly a week later, Trump signed the second executive order, this time ordering ByteDance to divest from TikTok under the Defense Production Act of 1950, a law that grants the president authority to prevent foreign investments in American companies that could affect national security. This order announced that ByteDance's purchase of Musical.ly caused a risk to national security that could only be addressed by a sale of the app.

By the time Trump began talking publicly about a ban, ByteDance had a good idea of what was coming. Navarro, in a mid-July appearance on Fox News, had called Kevin Mayer an "American puppet," and claimed he was acting on behalf of Beijing—a representation that doubtless rankled the assertive CEO. TikTok lobbyists had also tried to liaise directly with the White House—including Navarro himself—so they had a sense of just how hostile it might be.

The government was required to make a decision in the case by July 30, and by that point, the writing was very much on the wall. But it wasn't until 11:55 that night—just five minutes before White House jurisdiction over the matter would've expired—that TikTok and ByteDance received a letter informing them of the administration's decision.

The White House, it said, "has identified national security risks arising from the Transaction and . . . it has not identified mitigation measures that would address those risks." The news wasn't good for ByteDance, but it could've been worse—Navarro had lost and Mnuchin had won: the demand was divestment, not a ban.

For Yiming, the operative question became what divestment required. Yiming didn't want to sell. TikTok was integrated into the rest of ByteDance; the app was the crown jewel of the company's successful global expansion. Just five weeks prior he had lost India. There had been no dialog, no debate with New Delhi. Modi's government simply flipped off the switch. The Trump White House, though, had left itself considerable discretion. Trump was famously transactional. Maybe they could make a deal.

Chapter 16

KEY MONEY

As soon as the Trump administration notified ByteDance of its divestment demand, the company began throwing punches of its own. On August 1, V Pappas posted a video on TikTok set to upbeat background music, thanking the app's millions of American users for their support. "We're not planning on going anywhere," they said. "we're here for the long run . . . and let's stand for TikTok."

Zhang Yiming and Kevin Mayer, meanwhile, saw deeper influence at work. Would Trump have even begun investigating TikTok had Mark Zuckerberg not ginned up suspicion with his lobbying blitz? Would the president's inner circle have supported an unprecedented ban on a social media app had Jared Kushner not invited Zuckerberg to dinner in the Blue Room nearly a year earlier?

Three days before V's video, on the same day Mnuchin said he would soon be making a recommendation to Trump, Kevin published a blog post where he asserted: "We are willing to take all necessary steps to ensure the long-term availability and success of TikTok." Taking aim at Facebook, which had rolled out its new Instagram Reels feature in India just days after TikTok had been banned there, he continued: "Let's focus our energies on fair and open competition in service of our consumers, rather than maligning attacks by our competitor—namely Facebook—disguised as patriotism and designed to put an end to our very presence in the US."

On August 2, Yiming echoed Kevin in a Chinese-language statement posted from ByteDance's account on Jinri Toutiao: "ByteDance has always been committed to becoming a global company. In this process, we faced various complex and unimaginable difficulties, including the tense international political environment, the collision and conflict of different cultures, and plagiarism and smearing by our competitor Facebook. However, we still adhere to our vision of globalization and continue to increase investment in markets around the world, including China, to create value for global users. We strictly abide by local laws and will actively use the rights granted to us by the law to safeguard the company's legitimate rights and interests."

On August 3, Yiming sent a letter to his staff, urging them to stay calm, and telling them the company must face Trump's decision without "giving up exploring other possibilities." The letter made the rounds on Weibo and other Chinese social media sites, where CCP dogmatists decried him as a pushover. One post compared the decision to a stabbing: "After being slashed by a knife, he still empathized with the other person, saying he didn't mean to do it."

The following day, Yiming sent another letter—this one only to his Chinese staff. He referenced the comments on Weibo from the day before, and said he had stayed up working until dawn. Then, he specifically thanked his Chinese staff for their sacrifices, their willingness to work long hours and overcome language and time zone barriers. Then, he said they needed to take a "Martian" approach to their work:

> As a company founded by Chinese entrepreneurs, why do we often emphasize internally that we are a global company and encourage everyone to adopt a "Martian perspective" at work? It's because our colleagues come from all around the world. We have diverse cultural backgrounds and face different public opinion landscapes. Everyone has their own informational blind spots and tends to see things from their own perspective—something that often causes headaches at a time of heightened geopolitical tensions and de-globalization.
>
> Without a Martian perspective, it's easy to inadvertently offend the cultural values of different countries or impose our own norms on colleagues from diverse cultural backgrounds. There are countless examples of this. That's one of the reasons why we included "diversity and inclusion" in the ByteDance motto.

> Most Chinese companies don't have to deal with cultural conflicts. For many Chinese companies whose core business in the international market is selling tangible products, it's enough to ensure efficiency with a predominantly Chinese team. However, as a large platform that connects different cultures, we must rely on teams from various countries in management and operation. By respecting local cultures, we have been able to attract talent to join ByteDance in different countries. After two to three years of challenges and adjustments, we have established a very strong employer brand in many places. I believe this is a reflection of having a broad vision and a small ego.

Yiming then told his staff that the US government's "real intention is to push for a complete ban and more." He acknowledged those in the Trump administration—like Navarro—who simply wanted Chinese companies gone from the US. "Some politicians have launched a comprehensive attack on China and Chinese companies," he wrote. That attack could be overcome, he said, by staying the course and building a better product.

If the second letter was meant to show that Yiming wasn't overly sympathetic to the US, it failed. Ultranationalists on Weibo, dredging through the founder's own old Weibo posts, called Yiming "an American in spirit," and criticized his June decision to shut down business in Hong Kong. One poster, responding to the CEO's "Martian" philosophy, wrote bluntly: "You are not from Mars. You are from China."

It was now August 5. Trump would sign the first executive order the next day. In preparation, Yiming's strategy teams had spent days modeling contingency plans. Yiming told colleagues that he considered moving ByteDance's headquarters (and himself) to London, as a way of showing that he wasn't controlled by the CCP. Investors pitched him on a plan through which they would spin off TikTok and buy a majority stake in it. ByteDance's board, for the most part, supported a spinoff, but Yiming was reluctant.

Yiming also began looking at non-acquisition-acquisition options: deals that might sell away some authority over TikTok, but not all of it. Perhaps a US company could handle the specific issues that made the US government nervous, but ByteDance could continue to own and operate the company subject to some constraints. In his August 3 letter to all global staff, Yiming wrote: "We attempted to have preliminary discussions with a tech company on a partnership solution to form a proposal to ensure that TikTok can continue to serve US users."

That company was Yiming's former employer, Microsoft. With help from Erich Andersen, his new head attorney—and Microsoft's former master dealmaker—Yiming reached out to the company's steady, savvy CEO, Satya Nadella, to see if the firm might be interested in a partnership.

Microsoft wasn't a social media company, so unlike Facebook, Twitter, or Snap, it wouldn't face antitrust scrutiny over a partnership or acquisition. It was an old, reliable US firm with a history of big acquisitions that might be a decent no-drama partner. True to its conservative reputation, Microsoft wasn't initially interested in a big splashy deal. Both companies preferred a narrow partnership—just enough to get the skeptics off Yiming's back. But at Microsoft, Nadella had brought on Mojang (the game studio that built *Minecraft*), GitHub (the developer platform), and LinkedIn. Maybe TikTok could be the crown jewel in that chain of successful purchases—if the whole app was for sale.

Yiming and Nadella soon learned that they wouldn't just be negotiating with one another; they would also be negotiating with the government. At times, this would mean working directly with President Trump, who approached the deal like a New York City landlord. At first, Trump had said that he would not allow Microsoft to negotiate with TikTok at all; that a sale was insufficient and only a ban could address his national security concerns.

Trump softened from that stance, but then told Nadella that the deal would only be approved if Microsoft paid "a lot of money" to the Treasury of the United States for him to allow it to happen in the first place. "It's a little bit like landlord/tenant; without a lease, the tenant has nothing, so they pay what's called 'key money.'" ("Key money," which is illegal, is a dated concept from New York real estate history. It refers to bribes paid by prospective tenants to landlords or building managers to secure an apartment.)

Nothing in the law suggested that the US government could receive money from a transaction, but technicalities weren't Trump's concern. "Right now, they don't have any rights unless we give it to them," Trump said.

As Trump prepared to sign his first anti-TikTok executive order, Yiming, Nadella, and their lawyers sat in a bizarre position: they were negotiating a very large transaction subject to presidential approval, while disregarding the extralegal musings of the deal's ultimate approver. As *Bloomberg*'s Matt Levine wrote at the time, the parties "[had] to pretend that this is a thing."

"Man, I know that move," Levine empathized wryly: "When your clueless boss wanders into the room, glances through your presentation and says 'this is good but we need to talk about how we will address the problem of interstellar dragons,' you put in a bullet point like 'also we will take all appropriate measures to address the problem of interstellar dragons' and hope no one asks you about it."

Yiming and Nadella just had to hope key money wouldn't come up again.

~

NADELLA WAS NOT Yiming's only suitor. Soon after ByteDance began talking to Microsoft, it also began negotiating with Oracle, a cloud database software company helmed by Trump allies Larry Ellison and Safra Catz. Catz, the company's CEO, was a Republican donor who had served on Trump's 2016 transition team while still acting as Oracle's CEO. Catz's boss, Oracle founder and board chair Larry Ellison, had arranged a fundraiser for Trump at his estate in Rancho Mirage, California.

Ellison was an eccentric billionaire known for his stewardship of Oracle. He was known to be intensely competitive, both in leisure and business: his America's Cup sailing team was penalized for adding illegal weights to its boats to win a yacht race, and he once hired investigators to go through Microsoft's trash. Oracle, a generally unsexy cloud storage firm, would make an odd home for a buzzy digital media company like TikTok—but Ellison, with his warmth toward Trump, made the move make a bit more sense.

Ellison and Catz had sway with Trump's White House China hawks that Bill Gates and Satya Nadella did not. Catz called Navarro directly to let him know that Oracle would be entering a bid. "Oracle is one of the very few American corporations that has refused to kowtow while operating on the Chinese mainland," Navarro would later write. "So yes, Oracle clearly was *far* more preferable as a suitor than Microsoft."

Yiming continued negotiations with both Microsoft and Oracle through August, toward a September 20 sell-or-ban deadline. But it was still not exactly clear what a potential deal would look like. Would it be an outright sale of TikTok's US data, code, and intellectual property? A sale of the name, and a license to the software? A contract—more like the one Yiming initially pitched to Microsoft—that wouldn't constitute a sale, but would give an American company some degree of control over TikTok's US apparatus?

Yiming wanted a deal that would allow him to keep TikTok as part of ByteDance's international experiment. Investors wanted an exit: either a sale that would convert their shares (which were shares in ByteDance, rather than TikTok specifically) or an IPO. And Kevin Mayer—who had stayed quiet since his July 29 blog post—wanted independence: from Microsoft, from Oracle, and from ByteDance itself. He wanted the freedom to be the true global CEO of TikTok, a job that he wasn't sure would or could exist anymore.

In his first eight weeks on the job, Kevin had seen his platform banned in its largest market, withdrawn from another market, and under threat in the US. His legal team was suing the US government. The erratic president of the United States had begun a vendetta against his company and a White House official had called him a puppet on national TV. And now, the man who hired him was negotiating a potential sale of the company out from under him.

Yiming wasn't always diligent about including Kevin in sale negotiations. Kevin didn't want to be a senior vice president at Microsoft or Oracle, reporting to another CEO. He had decades of experience doing that at Disney, which he had left only for the opportunity to finally be the man in charge. He was nobody's puppet, and he didn't see a way forward where he would get to be a normal CEO.

In late August 2020, staff gathered on video for a company call where executives mostly just reassured their staffers that everything was going to be all right. Somehow, talk at the meeting turned to tequila, which led Kevin to conclude it with an odd gesture: though it was still mid-afternoon in California, he showed off a bottle on camera and announced that staffers could take the rest of the day off. The bottle was closed, but not everyone knew that—and Kevin's senior executives were bewildered. (And annoyed. They spent the rest of the day explaining to employees that they could not, actually, take the rest of the day off.) Only later did they learn that Kevin, less than three months into his tenure, had quit.

Chapter 17

TIKTOK GLOBAL

In the days directly following Kevin Mayer's departure from TikTok, Zhang Yiming told TikTok's remaining US executives that they were close. He had had two offers on the table: one from Microsoft, and another from Oracle. He would take the weekend to decide which to accept.

The executives understood Yiming's words to mean a sale was imminent. They were about to be employees of Oracle or Microsoft, the only question was which—and frankly, the news came as a relief. Either way, they would soon work for a US company, and all the uncertainty that came with ban talks would finally be over.

But in addition to Trump, there was another party with a say over any sale: the CCP. Over that same weekend in late August when Yiming was pondering his choices, the Chinese government made an unusual weekend change to its export control regulations: Before companies could sell "sensitive" technologies, like recommendation engines, to foreign companies, they would need to apply for and receive a government license. The subtext of the change was clear: China was not about to let its most valuable private company sell away its secret sauce.

On Monday morning, Yiming did not come back and announce that he was selling TikTok to Microsoft or Oracle. The same American executives that had felt relief now felt dread. One described their reaction as: "Oh my god, I'm never getting out of this."

Yiming's options were limited. The US government had ordered him to sell, but the Chinese government had ordered him not to. Yiming assessed the situation and decided he would try to call Donald Trump's bluff.

He had begun the first part of this strategy a week earlier, when TikTok and ByteDance filed suit against the US government. Trump's claim that TikTok didn't "have any rights" wasn't true—ByteDance had gone through the regular US business registration process for itself and for TikTok, so those entities had the same rights as any other US company.

One of those rights was the ability to challenge laws that negatively affected them in court. The statute under which Trump based his first executive order—the International Emergency Economic Powers Act (IEEPA)—gave the president the authority to prohibit commerce with foreign companies in emergency circumstances. But it also specifically withheld that authority when those foreign companies were in the business of disseminating ideas or information. So TikTok and ByteDance argued Trump had exceeded his IEEPA authority, because the platform was clearly in the business of helping users transmit information.

ByteDance also began making its case to the public. After Kevin Mayer resigned, Yiming appointed V Pappas to be TikTok's interim leader. V rallied staff behind the idea that TikTok was a place of inclusion and creativity, under assault from an administration motivated by grievance and bigotry. A group of TikTok employees even sued Trump and his staff, alleging that the threatened ban violated their constitutional rights.

The company began two big ad campaigns as the ban-or-sale deadline ticked closer. One aimed to raise awareness about how TikTok was good for small businesses, showcasing the app's positive impact on its community. It was targeted in media markets where key political decision makers lived, like Mitch McConnell's home district in Kentucky, and the DC/Maryland/Virginia market, where the judge for the ban lawsuit (and lawmakers in the House and Senate) lived.

The other campaign was targeted more broadly, and focused on securing as many downloads of the app as possible. If the ban did go through, the first thing that would happen would be the removal of TikTok from the app stores. This was a purgatory that ByteDance was familiar with, as it was a punishment tactic often used back in China by the Cyberspace Administration of China. The way to skirt app store purgatory was to make sure users already had the app on their phones.

The final piece of Yiming's strategy was to return to Trump with a new deal to consider. Two weeks after the Chinese government's export control update, ByteDance and Oracle submitted a draft deal to the Trump administration for review. The proposed setup wasn't a sale, but a partnership. It also wasn't far off from Yiming's starting point when he first called up Satya Nadella in June.

According to the terms submitted to the Trump administration, ByteDance and Oracle agreed to create a new legal entity called TikTok Global, headquartered in the United States and led by a board of directors that would be approved by the US government. Board members would have to be US citizens—except for Yiming—and the board would also convene a separate national security subcommittee, which would owe a duty not to ByteDance but to the national security of the United States.

TikTok Global, per the proposal, would hold an IPO within a year of its creation. It would house its data in the Oracle cloud, and make all of its source code accessible to Oracle staff, which would be tasked with auditing it for any potential Chinese government influence. Oracle, too, would owe a duty to the US government, as TikTok's formal "trusted technology partner."

Under the agreement, Oracle would hold a minority stake in TikTok Global, which would be valued at $60 billion. Other investors in the interim entity would include the budget superstore chain Walmart and several American ByteDance shareholders, including VC giants Sequoia Capital and General Atlantic. But they, too, would be minority investors. Until the IPO, 80 percent of TikTok Global would continue to be owned by ByteDance.

In an attempt to fulfill President Trump's demands, ByteDance made a creative argument that TikTok Global would actually be majority American-owned. Though ByteDance would hold an 80 percent stake in the new entity, nearly 50 percent of ByteDance itself was owned by US investors. The Americans' stakes in ByteDance, plus the 20 percent that would be held by Oracle and Walmart, would bring total American ownership in the firm to 53 percent, people inside the company said.

But ownership was not the same as control. Like many Silicon Valley founders, Yiming had granted himself "supershares" (also known as "super voting shares") in ByteDance, which enabled him to control decision-making in the company without owning a majority of its shares. So American investors' near-majority ownership in ByteDance was irrelevant for national security purposes. The CCP would continue to be able to exert influence over Yiming through his Chinese business. Yiming would continue to control ByteDance, and ByteDance would continue to control TikTok. Unless and until that chain was broken, the hawks' national security concerns would persevere.

Nonetheless, the TikTok Global plan appeared to win the approval of at least one Trump administration leader: Treasury Secretary Steve Mnuchin, who sent ByteDance a term sheet on the evening of Wednesday, September 16. Yiming and Safra Catz quickly agreed to the terms; sending the deal to the president's desk.

President Trump, with the November 2020 election right around the corner, was not entirely up to speed on the negotiations. On Thursday the 17th, he told reporters: "We spoke today to Walmart, Oracle, I guess Microsoft is still involved, we'll make a decision but nothing much has changed."

Microsoft was not still involved. On Sunday September 13, the company had published a terse, unbylined blog post announcing that ByteDance had rejected its offer to buy TikTok's US operations. Oracle was the only remaining bidder, if the deal under consideration could even be seen as a bid.

Because Trump was acting through an executive order, he didn't need to work with Congress to evaluate the TikTok Global deal. As a political matter, though, his approach alienated potential allies right and left. Democrat Mark Warner, who had first voiced concern about TikTok months before, criticized Trump's "haphazard" executive orders, and said that assessing the national security threats of foreign apps "must be done honestly"—a test he believed Trump had failed. Meanwhile, conservative senators Marco Rubio, John Cornyn, Roger Wicker, Rick Scott, Thom Tillis, Dan Sullivan, and Josh Hawley sent letters to the White House warning that the Oracle deal would not address their national security concerns.

On Friday, September 18, just two days away from Trump's ban-or-sell deadline, TikTok filed another lawsuit against the government in federal court in Washington, DC, asking for a temporary injunction to stop the executive order from going into effect. The next day—one day before the divestment deadline—Trump announced that he had "given his blessing" to the TikTok Global deal, and would delay enforcing the order by a week so that the deal could close. "It'll be a brand new company. It will have nothing to do with any outside land, any outside country."

In remarks at the National Archives Museum that weekend, Trump lambasted history teachers for educating students about the history of racism in the US. "The left has warped, distorted, and defiled the American story with deceptions, falsehoods, and lies."

This was a standard part of Trump's stump speech—but he then pivoted to the TikTok deal. He told the rally audience that he had asked ByteDance and Oracle's CEOs to "put up $5 billion into a fund for education, so we can educate people as to [the] real history of our country. The real history, not the fake history."

The key money was back.

Trump's $5 billion idea led to explosions on all sides. The *Wall Street Journal* reported that it had initially been Ellison's idea. But it was news to ByteDance: "Some news media reported that TikTok will set up a $5 billion education fund in the United States," the company said in a statement on Chinese social media. "We would like to clarify that it was also our first time hearing about the news."

The statement also asserted that ByteDance would own 80 percent of TikTok Global until it went public through an IPO. But Trump had expected Oracle to control TikTok—and control it now, not twelve months from now. "If we find that they don't have total control, then we're not going to approve the deal," he said on the conservative TV program *Fox & Friends*.

WHAT HAPPENED NEXT is a reflection of just how lucky Yiming was to have Donald Trump sitting on the other side of the table. The *Art of the Deal* co-author, it turns out, wasn't a big process guy.

Using IEEPA to regulate TikTok had always been a stretch, given the law's direct exclusion of companies that disseminate news and information. On September 27, 2020, US District Judge Carl Nichols in the DC District Court halted the IEEPA ban from going into effect. The judge took issue with the way the Trump executive order set up the terms of the ban. According to the order, the process would involve the Commerce Department drawing up a list of transactions American companies would not be allowed to do with ByteDance. But the administration, the judge said, had made "largely a unilateral decision with very little opportunity for plaintiffs to be heard."

The Trump administration promptly appealed, but in the meantime, ByteDance won a second victory, this time in a suit brought by influencers who claimed the order was a violation of their First Amendment rights. In the Eastern District of Pennsylvania, District Judge Wendy Beetlestone agreed with Judge Nichols, finding that Congress meant to cordon off information dissemination companies in an "IEEPA-free zone."

Neither the Beetlestone ruling nor the Nichols ruling invalidated Trump's second executive order—the one in which the White House found that TikTok posed a national security risk, and ordered its divestment. But with the IEEPA order on ice in two different federal courts, the Trump administration was stymied in the short term.

The White House was also, frankly, busy with other things. In October, Trump himself contracted COVID, in a wave that infected many of his closest staffers. Days away from the end of a multi-year campaign for reelection, he had become obsessed with the idea of staying in power, planning out how he could declare victory prematurely, in order to sow doubt about a potential defeat.

On November 3, 2020, former Vice President Joe Biden defeated Donald Trump in his bid for reelection to the presidency. For TikTok, the election was a success. No major influence operations were detected, and Trump had turned to other platforms, not TikTok, to falsely claim he had won the election.

November 12 was the day that, under the August 6 order, TikTok would be required to cease all operations in the United States. But TikTok hadn't heard from the government in weeks. The White House had never made a determination about the Oracle partnership. "In the nearly two months since the President gave his preliminary approval to our proposal to satisfy those concerns, we have offered detailed solutions to finalize that agreement—but have received no substantive feedback on our extensive data privacy and security framework," the company said in a statement.

Thwarted by the Beetlestone injunction, the lame-duck Trump administration confirmed that it would not (and could not) enforce the IEEPA order "pending further legal developments." Yiming had called Donald Trump's bluff—and though the former president would continue to deny for months that he had lost the November election, his lawyers knew better. They were happy to let this particular mess become the next guy's problem.

As 2020 came to a close, TikTok had weathered intense storms. It had faced global outcry after censoring critiques of China, it had been banned in India, hired a new CEO and lost him in a matter of weeks, and then stared down the Trump administration in the US. But it had also experienced simply astonishing growth. By April 2020, people had downloaded TikTok onto more than 2 billion devices. TikTok influencers started selling branded products at retailers like Target, and Walmart, calling TikTok the "hottest place on the internet," partnered with the platform to create its first "shoppable livestream."

"Business, entertainment, news, activism and social connection will never be the same," the *New York Times* announced. Yiming had achieved global reach; the app had penetrated pop culture and reached debate on national media and the highest levels of government. It had arrived.

ACT III

Chapter 18

DRIVER CARRIES NO CASH

In early September, 2021, a middle-aged man with straw-blond hair and an Eastern European accent sat in a vacation rental in La Ventana, Baja Sur, Mexico, watching orientation videos for his new job. Big tech companies traditionally welcomed new hires to their campuses with balloons, icebreaker exercises, and spreads of free food and drinks. But COVID had dispensed with these festivities, replacing them with a laundry list of onboarding videos that employees would need to watch from home.

Despite the missing party vibes, orientation was still an impressive spectacle. In one particularly energetic presentation, a former music journalist turned ByteDance growth hacker named Isaac Bess told new hires: "We intend to become ubiquitous." Bess wanted TikTok on TVs, on the backs of airplane seats, and even on billboards in Times Square.

"Our intention is to ensure there is a TikTok presence on every screen on the planet."

The man, whom I'll call Rob Doe,* had joined ByteDance in August as a control and governance manager for TikTok's Safety Operations team.† Safety Ops was the department that liaised between Byte-Dance's policy staff and content moderation contractors around

---

* Throughout my correspondence with "Rob," he has gone by several names. When he first decided to speak to me and share his internal materials, he said some people would figure out who he was, but he didn't want his name printed publicly. He later told me he had adopted the pseudonym Zen Hazikaron. To honor his initial request, I have declined to name him here.

† Accounts of meetings involving Rob are sourced to audio recordings of more than eighty internal ByteDance meetings that he shared with me.

the world (from Los Angeles to the Philippines, Kuala Lumpur, and Europe). Rob's job was to make sure that the right people—not too few, and not too many—had access to ByteDance's internal content moderation tools. He was a mid-level manager: he had a few reports, but he wasn't an executive.

The TikTok job was Rob's first experience working for a tech company. He was one of thousands of US workers that ByteDance would hire in 2021, a year when the company would more than double its American staff. ByteDance had shipped him a work computer, and, per orientation instructions, he had designated Beijing ByteDance Technology, Inc., as a "trusted developer" on his personal cell phone. That meant he could download ByteDance software that wasn't available in the app store, including test versions of TikTok, a company VPN called Seal, and Lark, the ByteDance workplace superapp.

By signing their new-hire paperwork, staffers like Rob largely signed away their right to privacy from their employer. In some contracts, the company specified that it had the right to inspect any electronic device that an employee possessed or used during their term of employment—a clause that appeared to include staffers' personal laptops, phones, watches, and other devices. To access grants of stock, a common form of compensation in Big Tech, some employees also had to sign a document promising that they would "comply with applicable [Chinese] laws and guidelines and abide by public order and good customs, the socialist system, [and Chinese] national interests."

Clauses like these may have bothered Rob or his fellow new hires, but they signed anyway. They were excited to join ByteDance—or, at least, Rob was. The acronyms and decision trees of content moderation were new to him, but he was eager, as they often say in Big Tech, to "drink from the firehose."

Rob's first big job at TikTok was a tricky, highly confidential assignment. His boss—TikTok's Safety Operations director, Mark Yeh—wanted him to map the data flows of each internal system used by the Safety Ops department. Rob would need to catalog each type of data (from DMs to watch history to contact lists) that flowed through each internal tool, and then list out each ByteDance employee or group of employees who could access each type of data.

Yeh told Rob that this task would take up the bulk of his time and energy. It was a matter of corporate data hygiene: ByteDance was so big—and so quickly evolving—that there was no single source of truth to consult about who could access what. To make sure the company was protecting user data from misuse, it needed to know where that data flowed, and to whom.

Rob quickly learned that like all big consumer-facing tech products, TikTok was built on an elaborate pile of interconnected internal apps. In his little corner of the store, there was TCS, a service that piped videos to contract content moderators in countries around the world. There was Juren, a tool used to train moderators; IES, a tool to check their work; Rock, another tool to check their work; Octopus, a third work-checking system; Lighthouse, Clickhouse, Sherlock Holmes, and Eagle Eye, which were databases; Mint, a creator monetization tool; Data-Power, for systems administration; Dorado, Jupiter, and Aeolus for data analytics, Libra, an experimentation tool; Magic, which functioned like an internal Squarespace; Salmon and Tuna, which had not yet been fully translated from Chinese—Rob had no idea what they were for, not to mention the whole Hawk Extension Pack (Hawk 1, Hawk 2, TikHawk, OpsHawk), plus Meego and Triton. It was bewildering.

So, what types of data flowed through each of these tools, and who within ByteDance had access to them? Rob wasn't an engineer, and he couldn't read code. To fulfill his assignment, he would have to track down and interview the dozens of engineers who controlled each piece of code in each internal tool. But many of those people didn't speak English, had transferred to other parts of ByteDance, or had left the company entirely.

Exasperated, Rob quickly found an ally in his mapping exercise: a young "cyber transformation" consultant from Booz Allen Hamilton named Sawyer Bletscher. Sawyer was part of a "SWAT team" of Booz consultants who had also been assigned to audit the data flows of the Safety Ops department. Parallel Booz teams were spread out across the rest of TikTok, digging into dozens of other databases, visualization tools, and pipes to understand who could access what types of data—and by the time Rob joined ByteDance in August 2021, they had been on the job for nearly seven months.

On one late September afternoon, Sawyer—blond, twentysomething, and cheerful, but clearly exasperated by ByteDance's internal maze—sat in a (remote) meeting with Rob and a risk manager on the Safety Ops team asking his standard set of questions for what felt like the zillionth time. The risk manager told Sawyer he didn't *think* a particular tool—called Rock—could access private user data, but he'd have to check with an engineer in China to be sure.

"One of these modules I don't touch, they may have user data," the risk manager said.

"Yeah," Sawyer sighed. "Yeah, we definitely will [have to check]," he said. "It's also, I feel like with all these tools, there's some back door to access user data in almost every single one of them, which is, like, exhausting. . . . it's definitely a lot more complicated of a process than I originally thought." He gave a skeptical, high-pitched laugh.

"Huh," the risk manager said.

Sawyer cleared his throat, and an awkward beat passed. "Okay, cool! That makes sense, though," he said. Then, he carried on with the meeting.

Sawyer, like Rob, could only get so much information from ByteDance's US staff. Some of the people who maybe *could've* given him the full picture were unwilling to do so. Describing one Chinese engineer to Rob and his team, Sawyer said: "He was very closed off to divulging a lot of information . . . maybe don't use my name as an introduction, because he did not seem like a very big fan of consultants."

Usually, American employees used internal tools for specific, narrow purposes, and they had limited knowledge about how other teams, especially those in China, used them. US staffers could tell Rob and Sawyer how *they* used Rock or Juren or Tuna, but more than a month after the meeting with Sawyer, Rob again found himself stumped about how *other* people at ByteDance might use the company's tools. "There are items within the tools that nobody knows what they're for," a colleague told Rob in November.

"Sweet," Rob quipped sardonically in response—this issue was becoming a theme. Sawyer had articulated the same frustration in a September meeting: "It's kind of a circle pattern: people can kinda answer our questions, but nobody can give us, like, the full picture."

After just weeks on the job, Rob could see the subtext of his and Sawyer's secret project. Less than a year before, President Donald Trump had tried to ban TikTok because it allegedly posed national security risks to the United States. Lawmakers had warned that TikTok was hoovering up Americans' data and turning it over to the CCP. So when Rob's boss had asked him to figure out how each tool worked, and who could use it to access different types of data, it was clear that what he actually wanted to know was which *Chinese* people had access to *American* users' data, and what they might be able to do with it.

~

SOME PEOPLE HAVE traced the entire dispute between the US government and ByteDance to a specific moment in time: the party congress in 2017, when the CCP instituted its new national intelligence law, which declared that the Chinese government could conscript private Chinese nationals and corporations into service for state security purposes at any time. It's not clear how much the 2017 law changed existing practice in China. But on paper, it turned millions of ordinary people into (often unwilling) spies, pitting its citizens and companies against China's political adversaries.

For ByteDance, the national intelligence law created an issue that I'll call the Employee Shakedown Problem: the Chinese government could, at any moment, come knocking on the door of the average Chinese ByteDance engineer, demanding that they access and turn over the locations, passwords, or video watch habits of Chinese dissidents living in the US, or journalists, or members of the US military.

It didn't matter that most ByteDance employees had little interest in acting as informants in a geopolitical tech cold war, because they would have no way to resist if the CCP came calling. There is no "Do you have a warrant?" in China. You have to do what the government says, or you risk arrest or the "disappearance" of your friends and family.

Within ByteDance, Rob and Sawyer's secret project at TikTok had a name: Project Texas. The idea was that ByteDance could protect its Chinese employees from government harassment if it prevented Chinese employees from accessing US TikTok users' information in the first place. It was the technological equivalent of a taxi driver slapping a "Driver Carries No Cash" sticker on their window. The CCP could shake employees down at gunpoint, but the employee would have nothing to hand over.

Project Texas was the brainchild of Zhang Yiming's sandy-haired ex-Microsoft general counsel, Erich Andersen. It was an outgrowth of the proposal ByteDance had made to Microsoft more than a year earlier. Under it, ByteDance would entrust a US tech company—in this case, Oracle, rather than Microsoft—with the security of US TikTok users' private data. The data would be held in a new, secure data center in the US, which most Chinese ByteDance staffers would not be allowed to access. Oracle would own and manage the data center, and Project Texas was named after Oracle's new headquarters in Austin.

As Rob learned more about Project Texas, he began to understand why it was so important—and why ByteDance was so desperate to keep it secret: the average American lawmaker had no idea that TikTok users' data was accessible in China, and one goal of Project Texas was to cut off that access before they found out.

ByteDance's Safety Ops tools were hardly all-powerful surveillance systems; they were garden-variety middleware built to facilitate a standard content moderation operation. But China's national intelligence law gave them new valence: every time Rob sat down to learn about yet another internal ByteDance feature, the question he asked himself was whether a civilian in China, with a gun to their head, could be forced to use that tool to harm someone.

Rob used a hypothetical to illustrate his concerns: Imagine that a person commits a mass shooting, and we learn that he expressed hateful views on TikTok before committing his crime. (This scenario is, unfortunately, not uncommon.) Many people within ByteDance, Rob learned, could easily pull up a list of all the people who had liked and engaged with the shooter's videos, or exchanged private messages with him. They could pull up a list of people who were interested in content from other accounts similar to the shooter's, or those that had blocked or reported him. They might use these lists for good—perhaps targeting those people with anti-extremism messaging, or anti-bullying and anti-harassment resources. But they could also do the opposite, targeting them with further radicalizing or demoralizing messages.

In the wrong hands, he told me, "Those lists are a weapon."

Over dozens of meetings in late 2021, Rob, Sawyer, and the Booz Allen team learned just how far away the company was from actually implementing Project Texas. A common theme emerged in their notes about TikTok's internal Safety Ops tools: the vast majority of tools had been built by people in China—and they were often controlled, and almost always accessible, by people in China, too. If TikTok was a house, there were hidden, secret doors in almost every room.

Chapter 19

THE CORPORATE GROUP

Lawmakers did not lose interest in TikTok after Donald Trump left office. If anything, Trump's trial and failure to vanquish the app heightened suspicion of it, especially among Republican supporters of the former president. But the US government was also undergoing a broader realignment in its policies toward China. Obama-era optimism that free trade would democratize China faded as Xi had tightened his grip on speech and dissent, and both parties in Washington heightened their skepticism of his regime.

On October 26, 2021, TikTok sent its chief lobbyist, Michael Beckerman, to testify in the company's first Washington, DC, hearing: a Senate subcommittee hearing focused on social media and children.

Michael was no stranger to the issue or the forum. Before joining TikTok, he had spent seven years as CEO of the Internet Association, a trade group that lobbied on behalf of American tech companies, including Facebook, Snapchat, and Google. Once photographed in $5,000 shoes for the magazine *DC Modern Luxury*, Michael arrived at the Russell Senate Office Building in a slim fitted suit and a striped black-and-gray tie—an accessory he would wear again for a different hearing in 2023, to the delight of onlooking TikTokers admiring his good looks. He sat between witnesses representing two longtime Internet Association members: Jennifer Stout, VP for global public policy at Snap, and (over Zoom) Leslie Miller, VP for government affairs at YouTube.

At the hearing, Senators Marsha Blackburn and Ted Cruz asked Michael directly about whether foreign employees could see Americans' data. "Do any ByteDance employees have access to TikTok user data, or any role in creating their algorithm?" Blackburn asked.

Michael didn't mention Project Texas, although by this time, the company had already spent many millions of dollars on it. Instead, he answered a different question: "US user data is stored in the US and backups are in Singapore," he said. Then, he added: "And we have a world-renowned, US-based security team that handles access to user data."

Neither of those statements was a lie, exactly. The data was indeed stored in the US and Singapore—it was just widely accessible from China. And TikTok did have a US-based security team—the team managing the Booz Allen Hamilton contractors working to figure out who had access to what. But as Rob Doe and Sawyer Bletscher knew well, that team was nowhere close to controlling employees' access to user data. They were still deep in the task of figuring out who had access to what.

At the hearing, things grew steadily worse for Michael. After Blackburn's questioning, Senator Ted Cruz—an outspoken China hawk and TikTok critic, and a former lawyer—took the gavel with the zeal of a cross-examining prosecutor. He turned to TikTok's privacy policy, which contained the following language:

> We may share all of the information we collect with a parent, subsidiary, or other affiliate of our corporate group.

Cruz began his questioning with a simple query: "Mr. Beckerman, does TikTok consider ByteDance, the parent company of TikTok, which is headquartered in Beijing, to be a part of TikTok's 'corporate group,' as that term is used in your privacy policy?"

Michael replied with a tactic beloved by tech executives on the Hill: "Thank you, Senator. This is an important question." He then didn't answer it.

Instead, he said: "I'd just like to take an opportunity first to clear up misconceptions around some of the accusations that have been leveled against the company. I would like to point to independent research. I understand that trust needs to be earned."

"Mr. Beckerman, I get you may have broader points you want to make," said Cruz. "My question is simple and straightforward: Does

TikTok consider ByteDance, the parent company headquartered in Beijing, to be part of TikTok's corporate group? That's a yes or no."

Michael answered: "Senator, access controls for our data is done by our US teams, and as independent researchers, independent experts have pointed out, the data that TikTok has on the app is not of a national security importance and is of low sensitivity. But again, we do hold that to a high standard, and we have access controls."

Cruz was undeterred, and getting saucy. "Okay, Mr. Beckerman, we're going to try a third time because the words that came out of your mouth have no relation to the question you were asked. Your privacy policy says you will share information with your corporate group. I'm asking a very simple question. Is ByteDance, your parent company headquartered in Beijing, part of your corporate group? Yes or no as you use the term in your privacy policy?"

Michael answered: "Senator, I think it's important that I address the broader point in your statement."

"So are you willing to answer the question yes or no? It is a yes or no question. Are they part of your corporate group or not?"

Pursing his lips, Michael finally answered: "Yes, Senator, it is."

~

MICHAEL'S TESTIMONY WAS misleading. He had, for obvious strategic reasons, tried to avoid admitting that TikTok could share data with ByteDance. But even that reluctant acknowledgment masked a deeper truth. Cruz's question—about the legal connection between the entities—had misunderstood the facts on the ground: to the people who built and maintained the app, TikTok effectively *was* ByteDance. Like Huawei and its subsidiary, Skycom, the companies had tried to present themselves as separate, but there was little meaningful distinction between them.

Some people had applied for jobs at TikTok, but had been formally hired by ByteDance. Others had contracts listing TikTok as their employer, but received their paychecks from ByteDance. Like every other employee at the company, Michael spent his days reading documents and chatting in groups on ByteDance's Lark superapp, where employees worked on TikTok, but also sometimes other ByteDance apps, like CapCut and Helo and Resso. Also like his colleagues, Michael was evaluated in performance reviews on his adherence to "ByteStyles," the internal set of ByteDance guidelines for employee advancement.

The fluidity between TikTok and ByteDance was an existential threat to Project Texas. The creation of a special team of US-only employees who would manage US user data had sounded like an elegant solution to China's national security law. But the team that ByteDance had created for this purpose, US Technical Services, continued to report to ByteDance employees in China. If their China-based bosses ordered them to pull restricted data in violation of Project Texas, they would have to do it, or they might face retaliation.

This meant that even if a Chinese employee couldn't personally access protected data, a CCP officer could still show up at their doorstep, and demand that they order their subordinate to turn over data, or lose their job. And as long as the ByteDance employee *could* access that private data—through a subordinate, or an inventive, secretive piece of code—they were at risk of shakedown from the Chinese government.

This problem went all the way to the top. ByteDance controlled TikTok, and Yiming controlled ByteDance. As the company's controlling shareholder, Zhang Yiming was in ultimate control of hiring and firing executives, directing new product launches, and global regulatory compliance strategy, whether or not he chose to get involved in them. This meant that Yiming, more than any other Chinese employee at ByteDance, faced an acute and specific kind of risk.

Chapter 20

DISAPPEARANCES

In fall 2022, a former ByteDance employee whom I will call Albert gave an interview to Agence France-Presse. Albert was a Chinese engineer who had developed automated content moderation systems for TikTok in 2019 and 2020. Back then, he had worked at ByteDance's headquarters in Beijing, but had since moved to the US for grad school.

Albert told journalists that his team at ByteDance had built systems to detect politically sensitive imagery, like candles (used by dissidents to commemorate the Tiananmen Square massacre), yellow umbrellas (a solidarity symbol for protestors in Hong Kong), and criticism of Chinese Communist Party officials. He was ashamed of his work at ByteDance, and wanted the world to know just how aggressive the Chinese government, and ByteDance itself, had been in censoring dissent.

In grad school in the United States, Albert felt safe. He tweeted frequently about the CCP's censorship, about Chinese tech giants and cryptocurrency (which was banned in China). He told the AFP that while he likely couldn't go back to China anytime soon, he didn't think the CCP would try to stop him from speaking out from America. He was wrong.

A few weeks after AFP published its piece, the BBC published a Chinese-language follow-up story, featuring a video of Albert describing his work at ByteDance. A few days later, he received a tearful, distressed call from his mother: his father had been taken away by officers from the Chinese Ministry of Public Security.

Albert described what happened next in a sworn statement to a US court: the national police took his father to a "remote secret facility," where they told him to relay their demands back to Albert in the US.

The demands amounted to: "Keep your mouth shut." Through his father, they ordered Albert to retract the BBC article, which he had no power to do (he asked the BBC to do so, but they refused), and that he delete his posts on Twitter, which he did out of fear that the police would continue harassing his family. Now, Albert could never go home. He would have to apply for asylum in the United States.

While TikTok has said that it "had no involvement in the alleged events" recounted in Albert's testimony, the Chinese Communist Party has a long history of "disappearing" people to intimidate them from voicing inconvenient views. But one particular disappearance, some two years before Chinese police detained Albert's father, had cast a chill on relationships between Chinese executives and their government.

In fall 2020, the Bund Summit in Shanghai—a who's who of China's business elite—announced with enthusiasm that it would feature an address from Alibaba founder and celebrity entrepreneur Jack Ma.

Known as "Daddy Ma" to the online masses, the flamboyant teacher-turned-founder was at a height of his professional life. He had created Alibaba and steered it to become one of the largest retailers ever. Alibaba had developed one of the largest venture capital arms in China, and was also a leading contender in the AI race. Its fintech arm, Ant Group, ran Alipay, the largest mobile payment processor in the world.

Where Yiming, the "moral champion," was quiet and reserved, Ma was known for his pomp and performance. He regularly acted out song and dance routines for employees; at one particularly memorable event in 2019, he performed for more than 60,000 Alibaba and Ant staff dressed in a black leather jacket and chains, sunglasses with punk spikes, and an electric guitar in Alibaba's signature orange. At just over five feet tall, he had a larger-than-life presence.

Ma was obscenely rich—China's wealthiest man for the third year running, according to *Forbes*—and about to become richer. Just weeks after the Bund summit, Ant was scheduled to undergo the largest IPO in history. Ma's control over Alibaba and Ant also made him one of the most powerful people in China. Ant's power alone was staggering: according to Chinese state media, nearly 700 million Chinese were users of Alipay, which had grown in importance as people migrated to touchless payments during the COVID pandemic.

When he took the stage to speak, Ma was seen as untouchable—he was the poster boy for China's private business success. When he began his speech, though, audience members noticed something was off. Ma didn't have his signature braggadocio. Instead, he gave a set of caveats: he was speaking only in his personal, "non-professional" capacity, and his ideas might be immature or wrong. But, he said, the summit was an opportunity for smart people to think through hard problems together, and the chance to be a part of that was too critical to miss.

Ma then used his platform at Bund to call for reform of China's financial systems, comparing Chinese banks to "pawnshops," because they required borrowers to put up collateral. In Ma's view, that system stifled innovation, and the country should move instead toward a credit-based system where even the poorest people could build credit over time.

The speech was critical of the government, but not disrespectful. But this was the fall of 2020, a moment of heightened rectification. No level of dissent would be tolerated. Ten days after the speech, the Chinese government cancelled Ant's IPO. Xi Jinping later announced himself that Ant would become a holding company supervised by the People's Bank of China. The Chinese government began investigating Alibaba for antitrust violations, and a week after Ma's Bund Summit speech, China's central bank summoned him for a meeting.

Then, for almost three months, Jack Ma vanished from public life.

It's still not clear today where Ma went between November 2020 and January 2021, and to what extent, if any, he was physically restrained during that time. After more than ten weeks, he resurfaced—clearly diminished—in a brief, scripted video appearance focused on his educational philanthropy. Later, Alibaba would announce that it was splitting into six separate business units, each controlled by its own board and CEO, greatly reducing the power any one person could exert over the enterprise. The message was clear: Ma's empire had been scattered by the party, and the freewheeling, singing, dancing leader that had once dominated China's tech sector was gone.

Ma was hardly the only businessman targeted by Xi's regime. Ren Zhiqiang, a real estate developer and internet personality, disappeared in 2020 after writing an essay critical of the autocrat. Despite strong party connections, he was convicted in a one-day trial and sentenced to eighteen years in prison. In 2017, a Chinese Canadian banker named Xiao Jianhua was abducted by Chinese police from a hotel in Hong Kong and later sentenced to thirteen years in prison. Others disappeared for shorter stints—a week or two—and returned to work more observant of party requests than they had been before.

A primary aim of these disappearances was intimidation—the business leaders now feared not just financial consequences, but corporeal ones. Vagueness was a tool of the state: if people didn't know what the rules were, many would err on the side of self-censorship even when it wasn't required by law. And it was clear that success and connectedness were no longer enough to protect you: if it could happen to Jack Ma, it could happen to anyone, no matter how indispensable they or their business might be to China's economy or daily life.

The months following Jack Ma's disappearance were punctuated by a series of self-preservation actions by other Chinese tech executives. The first of these came in March 2021, when Colin Huang, the founder of the Chinese e-commerce giant Pinduoduo (PDD) made a shocking announcement: he was stepping down as chairman of the company and relinquishing the founder "supershares" that gave him control over its decision-making.

Huang, just forty-one, was China's third-wealthiest man. He had been Western-educated, with a degree from the University of Wisconsin and stints at Microsoft and Google. He'd had nothing to do with Ant (and hadn't made any particularly dicey recent public statements) but like Ma, he had built a vise grip on the Chinese economy with PDD. And after Ma's dressing-down, he decided to retreat into a premature retirement—at least on paper.

According to investigative reporters at the Chinese outlet *LatePost*, Huang did not fully abandon his role at PDD. He passed over his top lieutenants and gave the CEO title to a less well-known junior executive. Then—per the reporters—he continued to direct business strategy, albeit without the formal powers to do so. "Retirement has always been a false proposition," the *LatePost* journalists wrote. "The key lies in who controls the company and who will control it in the long term."

ByteDance was now on a path to become as big as PDD and ANT, and it had a power that neither of them did—the ability to decide what information people see. Yiming watched as both companies cratered in value after their leaders stepped aside. But the stakes were eminently clear, and he had plenty of experience with state censorship already.

~

UNLIKE ITS DIGITAL eighth anniversary celebration, ByteDance celebrated its ninth birthday party in March 2021 with a bash: a glitzy stage, featured speakers, and anniversary swag for staffers. But when Yiming spoke to employees, his tone was more sober than it had been in previous years. He cast 2020 as a mixed bag: TikTok had avoided catastrophe at the hands of the Trump administration, and it was going gangbusters in the US. But India had been a blow, and the latest Chinese crackdown was shaking both the company and the industry.

Measured as ever, Yiming preached a gospel of mindfulness at the anniversary speech, invoking Buddhist verses. He said: "We cannot indulge in past achievements, regret past mistakes, or hold on to fixed expectations about where our company is headed. . . . This year, I hope our company can adopt a more relaxed mindset to some extent, avoid the burden of anxiety brought on by short-term business goals while embracing an open-ended vision for the future free from fixed expectations, and focus on longer-term goals."

Yiming concluded his speech by talking about the rock climber Alex Honnold—the first person to scale Yosemite's El Capitan with the aid of only his climbing shoes and chalk. Yiming had met Honnold on a visit to California, he said, and been struck by his ability to focus on the present. "Moving forward or backward can both be dangerous, but the real danger lies in panic and hesitation. As a climber, you can't afford to look back too much, dwell on fear, or chafe over a misstep. At the same time, you can't look forward too much because the long way ahead might overwhelm you."

Yiming didn't share Jack Ma's love of the limelight, and he didn't have Colin Huang's control over commerce. But he possessed something else that the CCP envied and feared: geopolitical power. TikTok's overseas success was a huge boon to China—economically, politically, and socially. It also made Yiming less controllable than his Chinese peers. If, say, only 40 percent of ByteDance's revenue came from China, then any given rectification action would hit its bottom line only 40 percent as hard as it would his Chinese competitors—a result that was not lost on regulators.

On top of that, there was the matter of Yiming's relationship with other governments. Most Chinese companies operated mostly in China; their founders hadn't come into sustained contact with foreign powers. Only TikTok (and Huawei) had truly broken through. His willingness to negotiate with the Trump administration—and his "Martian" approach to international business—had run him afoul of China's more strident nationalists. It was not unreasonable to worry that his private interests might not perfectly match the interests of the People's Republic of China.

According to the Chinese-language blog 老郭种树, Yiming also had a history of making pro-democracy statements. In 2022, the blog published a trove of Weibo posts allegedly made by Yiming, including commentary about books he read, people he met, apps he tried out . . . along with the occasional comment about the value of free markets and free speech. The trove included one post from 2010, in which he allegedly shared a post from another Weibo user that said startups "absolutely must not adopt the government's approach"; that they should "uphold democracy," and resist "falsifications." It included another from 2011, in which he allegedly praised Mao Yushi, an economist and human rights advocate who would eventually leave China at age ninety-five after calls for his arrest, and a third from 2013, in which he allegedly shared a BBC Chinese interview with two advocates for constitutional democracy.

It was titled: "No country's netizens carry as heavy a burden as those in China."

Yiming's posts weren't unusual at the time they were made, and they might still not draw much attention today, if they were made by a twentysomething private person. But in a world where Jack Ma might disappear for his speech, such posts would be unthinkable—and, frankly, dangerous—for a CEO of Yiming's stature. As someone who was already known for eschewing Chinese jingoism, he had every reason to believe the authorities would visit him next.

In May 2021, two months after Colin Huang stepped down from Pinduoduo, Yiming announced that TikTok would be getting a new CEO. The position had sat vacant since Kevin Mayer stepped down in August 2020. Now, Yiming had anointed a Singaporean businessman named Shou Zi Chew. Shou was younger than his predecessor—just thirty-eight—with deep roots in the international finance community. He had worked for Goldman Sachs in London before attending Harvard Business School, where he met and married Vivian Kao, an American executive and investor. After Harvard, he worked for Russian venture capitalist Yuri Milner, then became CFO of the Chinese smartphone maker Xiaomi. Shou had joined ByteDance as the company's CFO two months earlier. He would continue to hold that role concurrently with his leadership of TikTok.

Shou was a perfect blend of East and West: as the *New York Times* put it, he "straddle[d] the Western and Chinese business worlds." He looked the part—he was of Chinese descent, youthful and trim, with sharp features—and unlike Kevin Mayer and V Pappas, he was fluent in Mandarin. He also had experience working in Chinese companies targeted by the US government: in its final weeks, the Trump administration had added Xiaomi to its infamous sanctions list, barring US companies from transacting with the hardware company and alleging ties between it and the Chinese military. In response, Xiaomi had sued, and won a preliminary injunction that deemed the Trump administration's designation arbitrary and capricious.

Unlike Yiming, Shou had rich-guy energy. He lived in a Good Class

Bungalow in Singapore's Queen Astrid Park, which—valued at more than $60 million—was the most expensive house in the neighborhood. He wore designer clothes and carried himself with a swagger that clearly telegraphed that he was the man in charge. He bragged about hobnobbing with famous people, from celebrities and media moguls to professional athletes. The California executives who reported to him were well-off themselves, with multimillion-dollar homes and investment portfolios, but Shou's wealth was in a different league: he had built his identity around money and the status it conferred.

During one of his first visits to L.A., Shou took his American team out to a restaurant, where the group ate and drank until past the restaurant's closing time. When the waitstaff eventually asked them to leave, he quipped that perhaps he should buy the restaurant. Shou was a sharp contrast to V, who lived in a tasteful 2,500-square-foot California bungalow in L.A. and liked to unwind with colleagues over beers at the office after a long day. Some staff appreciated his sharp edges, but others saw him as conceited and fame-seeking.

Shou's arrival (and his finance background) renewed IPO chatter among both staff and spectators. But Yiming—and soon, Shou too— knew that dream was still a ways off. In the weeks before he announced Shou's hiring, Yiming met with Chinese regulators, who steered him away from the idea of an IPO. Weeks later, an investment entity owned by the Chinese government bought a 1 percent stake in the ByteDance subsidiary that ran Jinri Toutiao, Douyin, and the company's other Chinese businesses. The stake was a "special management share," which allowed the government to name one of three directors to the subsidiary's board, influence mergers and acquisitions, and more directly control censorship on Toutiao and Douyin.

The CCP was again tightening its control over China's tech giants. It had warned thirty-four tech companies—ByteDance and other household names among them—against engaging in monopolistic or anticompetitive practices. It had ordered thirteen firms, including the same giants, to scale back their activities in the financial sector. Over the coming months, it would take "special management shares" in Alibaba,

Tencent, and Sina Weibo, too. Just as it had done in 2018, the CCP was clawing back power from China's tech giants.

As soon as Yiming announced Shou's new role, he prepared another announcement that would shock the tech world: he would be resigning as the CEO of ByteDance. In a public letter, he wrote: "The truth is, I lack some of the skills that make an ideal manager. I'm more interested in analyzing organizational and market principles, and leveraging these theories to further reduce management work, rather than actually managing people. Similarly, I'm not very social, preferring solitary activities like being online, reading, listening to music, and daydreaming about what may be possible."

Yiming named Liang Rubo, his college roommate, badminton partner, cofounder, and confidante, as his successor. Rubo, like Yiming, was slight and bespectacled, with a round, warm-looking face and a minimal public profile. He had been ByteDance's head of HR. Some of Yiming's other lieutenants—Zhang Nan and Zhang Lidong, or even Alex Zhu, would have been more predictable picks for the top job. But it was clear that Yiming wanted someone he knew inside and out, someone who would faithfully carry out the agenda he had begun.

American staff saw Yiming's resignation as a defensive act. Among the California founder class, successful leaders like Mark Zuckerberg or Jeff Bezos only stepped aside in the case of some extraordinary personal catastrophe or a business coup (or, in the case of Uber's Travis Kalanick, both). To American employees, the idea that the young, successful CEO behind TikTok would voluntarily abandon his post as head of one of the most valuable private companies on earth strained credulity.

One American executive told me that the idea that he was ready to retire just didn't pass the smell test. "You're thirty-eight years old, dude!" they said. Another said, bluntly, "nobody thought [his retirement] was real."

Yiming did actually dislike the challenges of managing a large, mature company—a set of challenges that were very different from those necessary in founding and scaling a startup. But like Colin Huang, Yiming didn't actually retire. He started a personal investment vehicle, gave nearly $30 million to an education fund in his hometown of Fuijan, and began to spend more time in Singapore. And he also stayed close to the company he'd built. He stayed on as chairman of ByteDance for another six months, and even after then, remained a common fixture on leadership calls and chat threads in Lark, where he continued to drive decision making and ideation for the company.

Most importantly—and unlike Colin Huang—Yiming did not cede the supershares that gave him control of ByteDance. He might no longer be CEO, but he still owned the joint—a fact that would shape TikTok's future for years to come.

Chapter 21

OWNERSHIP AND CONTROL

By early 2023, ByteDance spent 1.5 billion dollars on Project Texas. For almost any other company on earth, the idea of paying that much money to another company just to mollify regulators would be madness. Not to mention the time and money spent negotiating the Oracle contract, hiring additional staff, contractors, lawyers, auditors, and more. But ByteDance was so big, and TikTok so powerful, and the US market so lucrative, that the investment was worth it. Making massive commitments was a way to show good faith. Maybe Michael Beckerman had gotten a bit out over his skis before the Senate subcommittee, but that wouldn't matter much if the company could sell the new Biden administration on its plans.

To solve the structural problem raised by Yiming's supershares, Erich Andersen and his team would have to stretch the limits of existing corporate law. ByteDance wanted to own TikTok, but strip itself of any substantive power over, or access to, American TikTok data. It was the type of corporate governance puzzle that a law or business school professor might write as an exam question: How much can ownership ever truly be divorced from control?

Erich's working solution involved a nesting set of entities. Shou Zi Chew was CEO of TikTok, Inc, the global ByteDance subsidiary that ran TikTok. Erich proposed creating a new entity within TikTok, Inc., which would govern TikTok's US business. That new entity, called TikTok U.S. Data Security (USDS for short), would be a much-expanded, independent version of the US Technical Services team. It would have exclusive jurisdiction over any business—including content policy functions and promotion decisions, like heating—that required access to a subset of "protected" US user data. It would also be staffed exclusively by US citizens, who would all reside in the United States.

The job of building USDS largely fell to Roland Cloutier, a friendly faced former police detective and US Air Force veteran whom Yiming had hired to become TikTok's global chief security officer. As TikTok's top security executive, Roland was the natural defender against claims that the app had been hacked or compromised by Chinese government interests.

Roland was a caricature of a good cop: broad-chested and clean shaven, with a warm smile and the perpetual urge to help a neighbor out. He was an outdoorsman, a semi-competitive rifle shooter who loved fishing, horseback riding, and hiking. He always seemed a shade or two tanner than his colleagues who spent their days hunched over at blue-tinged screens. Like Erich, Roland was older than most ByteDancers, with white hair, a bald spot, and a stream of dad jokes, but his friendly demeanor made him seem years younger than he was. He wasn't the L.A. type; instead, he preferred the White Mountains of New Hampshire and the Florida coast. He had little to prove, but lots of wisdom to impart on ByteDance's young, chaotic staff.

Roland's military experience gave him immediate credibility with hawks in Washington. He led the company's "converged security" operations, handling everything from executives' body men and data center door alarms to anti–money laundering, fraud detection, and data security on the platform itself. In his early days at ByteDance, Kevin Mayer and Zhang Yiming gave him a rich budget to build a cybersecurity team that would rival those at Microsoft, Facebook, and Google. He spent handsomely on contracts with Booz and the auditing firm Ernst & Young, and he hired two lieutenants—Will Farrell, a former director at Booz, and Eric Brothers, a former leader at EY—to lead the day-to-day operations of Project Texas.

As Erich sketched the theory of Project Texas, Farrell and Brothers worked to operationalize it. ByteDance incorporated TikTok U.S. Data Services as its own legal company, and opened a new USDS office that regular ByteDance employees would not be allowed to enter. Farrell's team began testing new data pipelines that would move TikTok data into Oracle's data centers, and Brothers's team revoked Chinese access to many—if not all—of TikTok's internal tools.

Meanwhile, Rob Doe began working with Erich's lawyers to determine exactly how many pipelines ByteDance would need to rebuild. Erich's point person for all things Project Texas, a lawyer named Sarah Aleem, taught Rob the limits of what Project Texas would protect.

Sarah had joined ByteDance back when TikTok was still integrating with Musical.ly, so she had comparatively strong institutional knowledge about how the product worked. In the early years, the company had struggled with protecting kids' data, and the collection of biometric identifiers. "This app was getting developed in China, and we had no idea what they were doing," she told Rob. When the CFIUS investigation began, though, she moved over to focus on national security. "What I'm learning right now," she told him in fall 2021, "is why China's the Devil and what the concerns are going to be."

Sarah explained the situation to Rob and his team. Some data types—things like passwords, location, DMs, unpublished draft videos, and watch history, would be "protected" by Project Texas. But big swaths of data—anything that was posted publicly, so that anyone else on TikTok could see it, for example—would not. Also unprotected would be the financial information, including bank account and social security numbers, that thousands of people had given to ByteDance so that they could be paid by the company to make and post videos. Those people had entered into additional, separate contracts with the company, which may have permitted storing their data in China.

The ground rules for Project Texas seemed simple enough, if tricky on the margins. (Should DMs from a US citizen living in Singapore and a French citizen living in the US be protected? What about a public comment that was later switched to private?) But Sarah and her team had the easy half of the job: they just had to imagine what ByteDance's systems *should* look like, rather than face what they *did* look like.

Despite the gulf between the lawyers' plans for ByteDance's data and its current state, Erich and his team eagerly began selling the new Biden administration on Project Texas. Trump's 2020 loss had reopened the door to Yiming and Erich: what had seemed impossible under Trump's White House seemed feasible with Biden's.

In June 2021, Biden rolled back Trump's IEEPA order banning TikTok and replaced it with a new one. Biden agreed with Trump that TikTok posed national security risks, and that they were severe enough to trigger an emergency under IEEPA. (Presidents, it turns out, are generally willing to grant themselves emergency powers.) But Biden dismissed Trump's handling of the TikTok risks, casting his predecessor's process as unrigorous and ungrounded in the evidence.

The Biden administration—led by lawyers for the departments of Treasury and Justice—returned to the negotiating table with Erich almost right away. The organization within the executive branch responsible for these negotiations required input from several cabinet-level offices. The Treasury Department assigned Paul Rosen to be co-leader of the team. Rosen was a hotshot attorney from L.A. who began his legal career as counsel to then-Senator Biden and then served in President Obama's Department of Homeland Security. Working with Rosen, from DOJ, was another Obama veteran: a young star prosecutor named David Newman, who had clerked for Supreme Court Justice Ruth Bader Ginsburg and then led the Obama White House's Ebola response.

Newman and Rosen shared neither Peter Navarro's Sinophobia nor Steve Mnuchin's faith in unregulated markets—and you wouldn't find any photoshoots of them and their wives at the US Mint. Both were public servants who had left government for Trump's first term, but jumped at the chance to return to the Biden administration. Newman was slim and clean-cut, a lawyer's lawyer with light brown eyes, expressive eyebrows, and a passion for the New York Yankees. Rosen was a bit of a goofball, his premature gray hair perpetually mussed and often betrayed by a youthful smile and a pair of aviators tucked into his shirt. Both were doting dads to young children.

To Erich Andersen and the TikTok team, Newman and Rosen were a clear upgrade from Navarro and Mnuchin, if only because they appeared willing to listen to and learn from ByteDance. But Biden's White House was not necessarily more agreeable to the companies' terms than Trump's had been.

Across 2021 and the first half of 2022, Erich and his team pitched Newman and Rosen on their vision for USDS. Yiming famously despised org charts, but Erich made them the center of his strategy: clarifying TikTok's chain of command would also, at least in theory, clarify who could exert control over the app. If Newman and Rosen—and their bosses—were satisfied by the new arrangement, they could sign a contract that resolved the pending government investigation into ByteDance, and prevent the government from coming back later to order divestment or ban the app on national security grounds.

In the first weeks of September 2021, Erich marshalled a group of senior American ByteDance executives to make the company's case to Newman and Rosen and the rest of their committee, which was known as CFIUS, the Committee on Foreign Investment in the United States. Erich gathered V Pappas, Will Farrell (Roland's deputy), and Sarah Aleem (Erich's deputy), along with a team of executives from Oracle, to present their maze of organizational diagrams.

Oracle, the executives explained, would decide who at ByteDance should have access to what data, and would "ultimately [have] the ability to suspend the U.S. TT App and TT U.S. Platform." This wouldn't cut ByteDance out of the picture, though, they warned: "If ByteDance is rendered to a minority position or passive over the entire U.S. business, it will not be able to secure the necessary authorizations from Chinese regulators."

The execs met with the government again in October, to explain what data access ByteDance would continue to have under their plan. The company could still access aggregated data, and specific user data in limited situations—in cases of potential imminent harm, for example, like where someone had made violent threats through the platform. But even the aggregated data scenarios raised concerns for Newman, he would later tell Congress, and some of those situations closely resembled the mass shooter hypothetical that Rob had worried about.

The group met twice more in November, this time to talk about the

For You recommendations algorithm. The TikTok execs described the algorithm as "a sorting machine"—"It's all about math—statistics and probability," they said. "It does NOT 'have an agenda.'"

The algorithm itself was, of course, just math. But like all algorithms, it encoded the agendas of its creators—keeping users on the platform longer, convincing people to try out new features, driving ad spend, avoiding regulatory penalties. Newman, Rosen, and their team of negotiators were not technologists; they were lawyers hand-picked by centrist president Joe Biden. But they knew enough to doubt that the now-famous For You algorithm was neutral just because it was mathematical.

~

THE COMMITTEE ON Foreign Investment in the United States was created in 1975 as a panel to advise the president about foreign control of key assets. In 1988, Congress expanded its power, giving the president the option to block foreign investment deals on CFIUS's recommendation, if he (or she) found that they threatened US national security. But it wasn't until the Obama era that the president and CFIUS regularly started blocking deals.

In 2012, President Obama blocked the purchase of a wind farm near a sensitive DOD facility by an American company owned by Chinese nationals, and in 2016, he blocked the Chinese acquisition of a German semiconductor supply chain company with business in the US. In 2017, President Trump blocked a second acquisition of a semiconductor company by a Chinese investor, and in 2018, he blocked the acquisition of a chipmaker by a Singaporean competitor. Two years later, Trump's CFIUS required Kunlun, a Chinese gaming company, to sell Grindr, a gay dating app, over concerns that the Chinese government might use its data to blackmail or otherwise harass the app's users.

Despite this slew of divestment orders, CFIUS is not a punitive body, and generally, its job is to "get to yes." Only in the most severe cases does CFIUS block deals from going through, or require their unraveling.

Most CFIUS reviews end with the government and the foreign company agreeing on minor changes to address CFIUS's concerns.

But Newman, Rosen, and their teams continued the aggressive approach favored by Presidents Obama and Trump. Biden's CFIUS began its term by quickly blocking the Ukrainian acquisition of a Texas aerospace company and the Chinese acquisition of a Hawaiian energy firm—though they ultimately allowed Chinese tech giant Tencent to purchase a UK-based videogame company called Sumo Group.

When CFIUS first began investigating TikTok in 2019, the platform's users were still overwhelmingly teens, and its videos were mostly teenybopper lip-synching. The risks that concerned CFIUS then were a lot like the ones in the Grindr case—that vulnerable people's data might be at risk.

But in 2020, 2021, and 2022, TikTok was the most-downloaded app in both the US and the world. Instagram, Twitter, and YouTube were now overrun with reposted TikToks. Beyond its one billion primary users, TikTok's secondary spillover now shaped *everyone's* understanding of topics like health, finance, politics, and culture, even those people who had no interest in putting the app on their phones.

CFIUS had never had a case like this before.

To CFIUS, TikTok had already posed a threat, but now its raw size and cultural power caused that threat to evolve in real time. Data access was not the only national security risk anymore. Now, the CCP might not just shake down employees for data, but also order them to subtly alter TikTok's systems, changing the videos that Americans would see about any given topic.

Newman, Rosen, and their CFIUS colleagues also had another source of information about ByteDance—classified intelligence. Investigators for the FBI, CIA, NSA, and other defense agencies had information about the company that the US government hadn't shared publicly, and couldn't do so without putting intelligence informants at risk. CFIUS had access to that information, too, and it helped shape their thoughts about how urgent the TikTok risk really was.

For ByteDance and other CFIUS-involved companies, the use of classified information was frustrating. What was the vague "information" they had from their intelligence services? If the government couldn't tell a company what its concerns were, that company couldn't mitigate them. Plus, what if the intelligence was wrong? ByteDance couldn't defend itself without knowing the accusations against it.

On the other hand, it was in ByteDance's interests, too, to keep the CFIUS negotiations secret. The talks contained detailed diagrams of the company's data hosting and recommendations systems—trade secrets that competitors or hackers could steal or abuse. CFIUS negotiations were confidential under US law specifically to make ByteDance, and all companies negotiating with CFIUS, comfortable sharing sensitive data.

That meant that nobody could see what ByteDance showed the government—or even what the company ultimately agreed to do. If Erich's draft National Security Agreement was ultimately signed, CFIUS would publish only a cursory summary of the agreement. The rest would remain secret, indefinitely, hidden from TikTok's own users.

Under the shadow of secret negotiations with the US government, ByteDance made an extraordinary proposal. In addition to promising to implement Project Texas, ByteDance also offered to give CFIUS veto power over changes to TikTok's content policies. The company offered the government control over the hiring and firing of US TikTok executives, and even offered to impose on those executives a legal duty to the US government that would supersede their loyalty to TikTok or ByteDance.

Such an arrangement was unheard of for an American social media company. In fact, it looked a lot like Beijing's arrangement with media companies under the 2017 national security law. ByteDance was offering to give the US government a back door to inspect TikTok's records, and the power to turn the app's executives, at least, into potentially unwilling spies.

ByteDance also offered CFIUS the power to block changes to TikTok's privacy policy and terms of service, including its content moderation rules, and agreed to give the government the right to examine TikTok's records at any time. In theory, CFIUS would have these powers only to ensure that ByteDance was complying with the rest of the National Security Agreement. But that limitation would hinge largely on CFIUS's own interpretation of its powers.

For the duration of the modern internet, there has been consensus in American politics that the government should neither warp nor censor online discourse. But ByteDance was never a part of that consensus. Its malleable, "localized" approach to content moderation allowed it to carry out the propagandist goals of authoritarians—as it did on Douyin and Toutiao. ByteDance had already given one government the right to warp its own citizens' reality through censorship and propaganda. There was nothing to suggest it would not also make the same bargain with another.

Had it been finalized, Erich's proposal could have turned TikTok into a political tool similar to Douyin and Toutiao in China. A president might have used his control over TikTok's executives to install leaders who shared his political and cultural outlook. He might have used his power over content policy changes to impose his own agenda on issues like trans rights, abortion, and free speech. If the platform became a hotbed of resistance against public health lockdowns, illegal deportations, or a president pardoning his son, that president and his subordinates might demand access to private data about resistors, or use government control over TikTok's hiring, recordkeeping, and policymaking to coerce the company into trumpeting a different message.

It's a lot easier to trust the government when you are the government. Both David Newman and Paul Rosen were zealous defenders of civil liberties, and appropriately nervous about the idea of government moderation or censorship. But they were also institutionalists, imbued with a Sorkinesque faith that the government would, for the most part, wield its power fairly and judiciously. Newman and Rosen trusted that their colleagues in the White House wouldn't abuse CFIUS's power over TikTok. But they knew they were negotiating not just for Biden's appointees, but also for the appointees of presidents to come. If their bosses ultimately accepted Erich's deal, and with it, control over the information diets of millions of Americans, they would also have to be willing to turn that control over to whomever Americans might elect next.

Because it works through negotiations, rather than just investigations, CFIUS is often able to extract concessions from companies that the government couldn't take by force. The government couldn't just give itself veto power over TikTok's hiring of executives or changing of content policies, but ByteDance was *offering* it those things, consenting to a higher level of government control than any American tech company would have allowed. TikTok's users, though, wouldn't get a chance to consent to those changes, and because CFIUS negotiations were secret by law, they might never even know about it.

Ultimately, ByteDance offered CFIUS that power, but the panel didn't take it. The public only learned about the draft agreement—roughly a year after it was submitted—because a whistleblower gave a copy of it to me.

Chapter 22

THE TIKTOK TAPES

In March 2022, as Erich Andersen and his team worked to finalize their proposal to CFIUS, my colleagues and I published a story for the digital media outlet *BuzzFeed News* revealing Project Texas to the public for the first time. The story was measured: a just-the-facts-ma'am explanation of internal changes meant to strengthen data security. It received a few nice citations from other journalists, but wasn't widely read.

Then, in mid-April 2022, a few weeks after *BuzzFeed* published the Project Texas story, I received an email with an enigmatic title. "Project Texas—Want More?"

The message was sent from an Outlook account registered to Rob Doe. He told me he was overseas, traveling in Europe, and that he was convinced he was being watched. People who leak to journalists are often skittish, but Rob seemed more fearful than most.

To establish his credibility (journalists get a lot of DMs), Rob sent me a handful of internal TikTok documents and messages. I'd seen enough of these from other sources to know the documents Rob had were authentic. In our first substantive phone call, though, Rob also revealed that he had something that no other TikTok employee had: recordings of more than eighty internal company meetings spanning from fall 2021 into winter 2022.

Rob had made the recordings himself, beginning just weeks into his employment at TikTok. He didn't tell his colleagues that he was recording them—an omission that could have exposed him to criminal liability under California's two-party consent laws. He told me he'd made the recordings because he believed he was witnessing immoral and likely illegal behavior by TikTok, which he believed was doing the bidding of the Chinese government. He was still employed at TikTok, he claimed, but on leave. He said he planned to return to the company once the "corrupt" people in charge were held to account.

After weeks of phone calls and text messages, Rob sent me the recordings. They didn't show what he claimed—that Project Texas was a sham, that his bosses were corrupt, or that TikTok was doing the bidding of the Chinese Communist Party. But they did show that ByteDance's Chinese staff still had extensive access to "protected" user data, and that the company's statements to US lawmakers had been, at best, aspirational.

The tapes also showed the slow spiral of events that eventually led Rob to go from an optimistic middle manager in the Safety Ops team, excited to "drink from the fire hose" and learn the ways of a big tech company like ByteDance, to a jaded employee who had become increasingly convinced that he was being watched. Rob believed that he was being followed. He told his boss, Mark Yeh, that someone was trying to break into his apartment, and that he felt "paranoid." He suggested that his physical safety was at risk, somehow, because of his work on Project Texas.

Rob's breaking point was a dinner meeting he had in January 2022 with Chris Lepitak, ByteDance's internal auditor. In some ways, the two men were similar: Both were Eastern European immigrants living in California and working for ByteDance. Both had a history of working and living internationally—Chris had worked at a slew of Miami startups and advised cryptocurrency firms and companies in Poland and Peru, and Rob had done compliance for banks in Japan and Pakistan.

When the men met in person, though, Rob didn't warm to Chris. Where Rob was short, Chris was tall and physically intimidating: it was clear he worked out. In the Los Angeles heat, defined biceps peeked out from under Chris's shirtsleeves. Rob could be neurotic; Chris was casual, almost nonchalant—he often wore a baseball cap to the office, covering his thinning hair, and took weekend trips to music festivals and sporting events.

Chris's informal posture struck Rob as suspect. After years in banking, Rob was wary of auditors, both internal and external. Auditors were the adversaries, the ones who could trip you up and get you in trouble. But Chris didn't seem to be treating Rob like an adversary at all. Chris picked the spot for the meeting: a Mexican restaurant with manicured succulents and palm trees in LA's swanky Marina del Rey.

The January dinner was not the only time Rob and Chris had spoken—they had first met on a video call back in September. In that conversation, Chris had advised Rob to strengthen ties with teams based in China. "Yes, the US team is kinda independent," he said, but "still, you guys rely a lot, on the tooling side, to the team in Beijing, who is driving some of those initiatives. And even if you want to make any changes, or anything that might be specific to the US, having that relationship and working with them is gonna be kind of quite important." Rob had found this advice odd: Wasn't the whole point of Project Texas to erect barriers between US and Chinese teams, and to eliminate the reliance that Chris seemed to accept as the way things would continue to be?

At dinner, Rob felt similarly strange vibes. The conversation was "open, super open," he later told Yeh. "Like, not on the record." But in Rob's view, it hadn't gone well. Chris had asked specific questions about Project Texas, including where the Oracle servers holding US user data were located. The questions put Rob on the defensive; he didn't have the answers Chris was looking for. So the next week, Rob scheduled (and recorded) a call with Yeh to talk about it.

"You—you're recording the meeting. You know that, right?" said Yeh at the top of the call. In addition to recording this call on his personal phone, as he had with dozens of others, Rob also chose to record this particular call in Lark, which alerted Yeh to the recording.

"Oh . . . yeah," Rob said awkwardly. "I just wanted to share with you the conversation I had with the internal auditor. I wanted to make sure it got captured, because it's quite serious."

Rob told his boss that Chris had scared him—that he had said an audit was coming, and Rob's team would not pass it. "My title says control and governance. Mark, I'll be super straight and open with you: I've been here for five months, and I haven't seen even one control." Rob said he needed more information about Project Texas, and about TikTok's partnership with Oracle.

"People are trying to feed me some bullshit," he said. After a few minutes of back-and-forth, he added forcefully: "I refuse to be a scapegoat."

Yeh seemed overwhelmed. He told Rob to stop being "emotional" and "grandiose" and "putting [him]self in [a] victim mentality." He also said that Rob didn't need to know the details of the TikTok-Oracle deal; that they were not his responsibility. The two men agreed, albeit awkwardly, to better define the scope of Rob's responsibilities, and to get Rob access to information he felt he needed to tighten controls.

Rob wasn't satisfied. So he tried another avenue to get detailed information about Project Texas—he had a family member, Eddie, who worked at Oracle. He sent a message to both Eddie and Deborah Hellinger, Oracle's senior VP of communications, to ask for more information about the terms of the companies' engagement.

Eddie and Deborah never replied, so Rob went to TikTok's ethics department with his concerns. Then, roughly thirty minutes later, he was locked out of his ByteDance company accounts.

In February 2022, Rob was placed on involuntary leave from ByteDance, and decided to travel to clear his head. He traveled to Turkey and then to Lviv, Ukraine, where he had been born and raised. When Russia invaded Ukraine later that month, a trip that was supposed to be a centering sabbatical turned into a fight for his homeland. After the invasion, Rob joined a group of locals organizing cyber-resistance against the Russian military.

It was from Lviv that Rob first reached out to me, eventually giving me permission to report from the recordings he had made. And that story—unlike the first one—was explosive. In their private conversations, TikTok employees had been open with one another about just how much the app and its data were controlled by Chinese personnel. The recordings showed that, at least until Rob left the company in early 2022, Chinese employees still had widespread access to private data that might someday be "protected" under a CFIUS agreement.

On June 17, 2022, *BuzzFeed News* published its second story about

Project Texas: this one sourced from Rob's trove of internal audio. As reporters always do, we sent ByteDance a detailed list of the points we planned to report, and asked them if they would like to comment on them, or offer any other response. An hour before their response to us was due, the company published a lengthy blog post, announcing that it would begin routing all new TikTok traffic to servers controlled by Oracle. But the post didn't say anything about cutting off Chinese employees' access to the data.

US lawmakers were furious. Democrat Mark Warner and Republican Marco Rubio, the chair and vice chair of the Senate Intelligence Committee, sent a letter to the Federal Trade Commission, urging it to investigate TikTok for misleading the public. (The FTC would indeed open an investigation.) In a September hearing, Democrat Rob Portman repeatedly asked V Pappas whether the company would commit to cut off user data flows to people located in China—a commitment that Pappas twice declined to make. Republican Josh Hawley read aloud from the *BuzzFeed* story before asking V whether TikTok employed members of the Chinese Communist Party. They declined to answer, noting that the company (like every other tech giant) doesn't ask its employees to disclose their political party affiliations.

V was graceful and persuasive in front of Congress, but at ByteDance, the story had caused outright panic. Internal investigators scrambled to determine how the information had gotten out. "This data leakage incident . . . resulted in the exposure of confidential information, caused potential brand reputational damage, and may result in regulatory scrutiny," said one internal report. The company was determined to not let a leak like this happen ever again.

Chris Lepitak's Internal Audit team opened a formal investigation into who had made and leaked the recordings, which they dubbed Project Raven. In reporting on TikTok over the years I had approached many employees for comment or information on various stories. Some had replied. Many didn't. The auditors created a spreadsheet of people I contacted and searched their Lark messages and work emails for mentions of my name.

Chris's team also searched for specific words and phrases quoted in the *BuzzFeed* story, in the hopes that an exact match would lead them to the leaker. They even asked the Lark engineers if the platform could tell when a user was using other apps on their personal phone—and, if so, whether they could pull a list of employees who had used the voice memo app on their personal phones during the months when Rob had made the recordings.

In the end, the investigators found Rob without too much trouble. Perhaps it was the confrontation with Yeh that did it—because Rob recorded it on Lark, it would have been easily accessible to company investigators. I had asked Rob specifically whether it was ok to report the specifics of this call, and he had given his consent. He told me he didn't care if TikTok knew he had made the tapes, that public accountability was more important.

It wasn't clear what, if anything, ByteDance could do about Rob once they identified him. He no longer had access to internal company information, and was now traveling across Europe. Suing him, if they could even find him, would prolong the news cycle coverage of his disclosures, and potentially open the company up to damaging discovery in court. He was already effectively fired. So they just sat tight: there was no one to punish or fire or pursue.

There was, though, one prominent departure that shocked TikTok staff shortly after Rob's disclosures came to light. In July 2022, in one of his first public statements on behalf of TikTok, CEO Shou Zi Chew announced that Roland Cloutier would be transitioning into an advisory role and subsequently leaving ByteDance.

At the time, I—like other members of the public and the press—thought Roland had been sacrificed: he was a head that could roll, a move to make it look like the company was taking its data protection issues more seriously. But the truth was far more complicated, and part of a larger battle between those, like Roland, who saw themselves as employees of TikTok, and those like Chris, who reported directly to ByteDance leaders in Beijing.

Chapter 23

INTERNAL AUDIT AND RISK CONTROL

ON A SUNNY AFTERNOON IN LATE SEPTEMBER, 2022, I received a call from a person who said he wanted to become a whistleblower. He said his name was Brad (it wasn't), and that he was calling from L.A. (he wasn't).

I asked "Brad" what he wanted me to know. He said there was more to Roland Cloutier's ouster than people knew—and it came back to a dispute between Roland and Chris Lepitak. I asked him if he was calling from a device that he felt safe to chat on. He thought about it, and said he'd call back.

A week later, I still hadn't heard back from Brad, so I chased his tip without him. I was now a reporter for *Forbes*, and along with two colleagues, I sent dozens of messages to people who had worked under Roland and Chris, to ask about their relationship and whether it had contributed to Roland's ouster. I learned quickly that Chris's department, called Internal Audit and Risk Control, was decidedly unpopular within TikTok, and that it had often clashed with Roland's Global Security Organization.

Chris had joined TikTok in 2019, when it still felt like a quirky startup. Alongside an eighty-some-odd-person team of Risk Control employees in Beijing, he had become the leader of ByteDance's non-China internal audit and investigations teams. It was Chris's job to enforce ByteDance's internal rules for its non-China employees—ensuring, for example, that team members didn't sexually harass one another, or embezzle money, or inappropriately heat their friends' TikTok posts. But compared to American companies of its size, ByteDance's internal rules felt startlingly weak to the staffers tasked with enforcing them.

One of those staffers, an attorney and fraud specialist named Sam Burness, spent months conducting a companywide risk assessment to take stock of the firm's vulnerabilities. He and his colleagues conducted ninety interviews with ByteDance employees up and down the management chain about their experience with ByteDance's ethics and compliance systems. The executive summary of his eventual report began with alarm: the company's operations "pose[d] critical, worsening fraud risks."

"Unless ByteDance makes substantial, sustained, rapid investments in its anti-fraud programs," it read, "it will likely be too late to prevent immense future fraud-related losses and liabilities—potentially including multi-billion dollar fines ($USD), being forced to submit to the control of an external monitor, loss of the ability to operate in the U.S. and other major markets, and criminal indictments of ByteDance executives and managers (even if they did not actively participate in misconduct)."

The Burness report then outlined a litany of oversights for which ByteDance might be held liable in the future. "Many important policies have never been created at all," the report said, and as a result, employees were "(rationally) ignorant and indifferent to" them. When violations of policies did occur, managers "routinely" let them slide, Burness warned.

Employees rarely required competitive bidding or did due diligence on their vendors. There was no policy specifying who could sign a contract on behalf of the company, and no tracking system to determine who was responsible for a given payment. ByteDance had made nearly 35,000 payments to vendors without contracts in place, nearly 31,000 payments that lacked invoices, and more than 46,000 payments (of more than $1.38 billion, collectively) "for which the data field that is supposed to track which project a payment relates to [said] only 'NULL.'"

Nobody knew exactly what the rules were around, say, whether you could hire an old friend to cater your department offsite, or whether you could accept gifts from an influencer marketing firm . . . and give their talent a little boost on the For You page in exchange. And the same gaps that failed to prevent those indiscretions also created opportunities for more consequential forms of deception: if you could accept gifts from a marketing firm, you could probably also accept them from a government employee—and if you could heat influencer posts, you could heat an info op, too.

The sloppiness Burness described wasn't evidence of malice, but it was evidence of recklessness: the company was acting with indifference to known avenues of abuse. Law enforcement was "guaranteed to negatively evaluate the credibility and sincerity of ByteDance's anti-fraud commitment," the lawyer-turned-auditor wrote, unless something drastic was done.

Nothing drastic was done. A ByteDance spokesperson later told *Forbes* that the Fraud Risk Assessment was never shared outside of Chris's team. (The spokesperson also said the assessment was inaccurate, apparently largely because it was outdated by the time it was reported on.) It was Chris's department, after all, that was tasked with mitigating these types of risk. In some ways, the Burness report was a repudiation from within of the internal auditors, or at least a memorialization of all the work they still had to do.

Chris's colleagues told me that he was more loyal to people than he was to process—an understandable quality, perhaps, but a troublesome one for an auditor. He had a reputation for doing whatever he thought was necessary to please his supervisor, a Chinese executive named Song Ye who worked in Beijing.

Chris's subordinates sometimes questioned the propriety of his work. Both to him and to each other, Internal Audit staff raised concerns that their investigations didn't follow proper protocols and might be seen as biased—or even as "witch hunts." Chris had advised Rob to "build the bridge" between his team and teams at ByteDance's Beijing HQ, and two people who worked with the auditor said he sometimes told them "China" had ordered investigations. One of his former employees told me, "Chris was trying to be the 'Beijing Whisperer.'"

Confirming "Brad's" tip, people who worked with Chris Lepitak told me that in late 2021, as Rob Doe and Sawyer Bletscher were tracking down data pipelines and Erich Andersen, V Pappas, and Will Farrell were selling CFIUS on Project Texas, Chris had given his staff a new investigative priority: Roland Cloutier and his GSO. Roland was a risky target—he was beloved by his staff, and the company had championed his hiring as evidence that TikTok was an American company with systems and personnel on par with its American competitors.

Over his nearly two years at TikTok, Roland had built an impressive global security team, recruiting hundreds of staffers from the biggest cybersecurity firms and tech giants in the US. But he had struggled with jurisdiction: he was the global head of security for TikTok, but he reported to Hong Dingkun, who was head of technology for ByteDance. A veteran of Chinese tech giants Baidu and Xiaomi, Dingkun was in charge of other ByteDance security departments, too, including an IT security team beyond Roland's control.

The chief security officers at Google, Instagram, and Twitter didn't spend their time fighting jurisdictional battles with duplicative teams managed by their parent companies, but Roland did. He struggled with a key sentiment expressed throughout the Burness report: that executives at TikTok often believed they were "just 'figureheads' or 'powerless ombudsmen' who don't have the ownership, empowerment, or resources" to truly run their departments or do their jobs.

Roland's team often struggled to get the data they needed to investigate security gaps and breaches. Chinese law prevented companies in China from letting certain, sensitive types of data leave the country, including details about their Chinese colleagues' employment. This limited what any US-based employee could do to stop shady practices in China: they couldn't effectively investigate Chinese people who might be endangering TikTok data—or altering the recommendations algorithm on behalf of the CCP.

ByteDance later sought advice from a law firm about how to tackle this problem. The firm said that ByteDance's Chinese team should evaluate whether sending data to the US would violate Chinese law and, if so, that it should restrict its data exports accordingly. This made sense as a matter of Chinese law, which could penalize the company if it turned over more data to its US employees than Chinese law allowed. But because Chinese nationals could be forced to act on CCP demands at any time, the US side of the business remained unconvinced that they were getting the full investigative picture.

When Roland's staff needed data, they would request it through Chris's team, who would route their requests to the Beijing-based Risk Control department. Requests came in part through a system known as the "Green Channel": a data pipeline established by Risk Control. One person who used the Green Channel process described receiving incomplete, inaccurate data through it.

Chris's staff chafed against the Roland assignment, which they believed was an unprofessional "witch hunt." Lepitak would later say that he was not the decision maker, and that the order had come from above him. This wasn't the first time they'd targeted an exec on Chris's orders: they had also investigated TikTok's chief marketing officer, Nick Tran, and Canadian general manager, Daniel Habashi, but orders about those investigations had come from above Chris, too.

Chris and Roland represented two contrasting views of TikTok and its relationship to ByteDance. Chris's team understood themselves to be working for ByteDance, while Roland's team was scoped specifically to TikTok, and reported to Shou. Chris had encouraged Rob Doe to build closer connections to engineers in China as Roland's lieutenants were busy revoking Chinese access to US data. And now, Chris was investigating Roland, on the purported orders of the Chinese executives whom Roland had tried to distance from TikTok's security team, even though he ultimately reported to them.

Roland and Chris also had a personal rivalry. Each thought his department should be responsible for investigating "insider risk," the idea that employees might misuse their access to company systems to sabotage or steal from their employer on behalf of competitors, governments, or other adversaries. Insider risk is a standard security concern for most major firms: The Saudi agents who infiltrated Twitter and then exfiltrated dissidents' data were an insider risk. So was the former Google employee, Anthony Levandowski, who stole the company's plans for self-driving cars and shared them with Uber.

But insider risk was critical for TikTok—more so than it was at most other tech giants. It was *the thing* that regulators were worried about, but what constituted an insider risk varied based on your perspective. To US regulators, the most serious insider risk was Chinese employees acting as informants for the CCP. But to Chinese regulators, the opposite was true—that US employees might start coming forward as informants to CFIUS. To the ByteDance C-Suite, one of the most serious insider risks was people like Rob, though he had acted for public accountability reasons, rather than self-interested financial ones. And it was Chris whom the C-Suite had entrusted with Project Raven, rather than Roland.

When Chris's investigators began looking at Roland's affairs, they first seized on GSO's relationship with Booz Allen Hamilton, which Roland had engaged for several multimillion-dollar contracts, including the one that employed Sawyer and his colleagues. A document co-authored by Chris himself described the GSO-Booz relationship as "highly suspicious due to low quality work on the contacts" [sic], but didn't substantiate the idea that Booz had actually done low-quality work. The document noted some redundancy between Booz's work and internal TikTok teams' work, but redundancy was common at TikTok, and it was hardly the contractors' fault. Investigators also tried to allege a conflict of interest between GSO and Booz, because several senior GSO staffers had formerly worked for the government contractor. But Roland hadn't, so it was hard to claim he had an improper relationship with the company.

As part of the investigation, the audit team enlisted outside investigators. They hired Prosegur, a Spanish corporate security firm, and Kroll, the investigations company that Harvey Weinstein famously used to undermine women accusing him of sexual assault. Prosegur reviewed a cache of 29,923 emails sent and received by Roland between March 2020 and February 2022, and prepared a forty-page report for Chris's team summarizing the results.

Chris's team spent about nine months investigating Roland. Their strongest lead concerned a small contractor called Key Operational Assurance Projects, Inc., or KOA, which was just being set up by an acquaintance of Roland's from before his time at TikTok. KOA submitted a proposal to Roland for a contract that would net it nearly

$1 million before it had even been legally incorporated—and Roland approved it.

The KOA contract was small in the scheme of GSO contracts, and KOA was only one of at least twenty firms doing work for the department. There was no indication that they had done a poor job. Had Roland thrown an acquaintance some work? It looked like it. But in comparison to broader ByteDance practices described in the Burness report—which had referenced "extensive high-risk related-party transactions involving potentially proper self-dealing between ByteDance and its own institutional investors"—Roland had more or less lived up to his straight-and-narrow image as a former cop.

Roland, though, was reaching his personal limits. He had started from nothing and built a 100-plus person cybersecurity team at one of the most impactful platforms in the world. Under him, GSO became the closest thing that TikTok had to a security department. He had achieved, more than most executives at ByteDance, a modicum of independence.

But while he had once served as a prominent spokesperson for TikTok's security efforts, the blog posts and conference appearances that had punctuated his 2020 and early 2021 efforts had tapered off into 2022. When Roland did public engagements, he often talked about the importance of transparency, both within a department, and with an app's end users—but transparency was hardly something TikTok seemed focused on, either internally or externally.

After *BuzzFeed News* published the June exposé based on Rob's audio recordings, transparency was no longer a viable talking point for TikTok. So just under a month later, on July 15, 2022, with Prosegur's email review still midstream, Roland announced that he would be transitioning into a new, advisory role at TikTok—corporatespeak for moving on and out of the company. The tide was turning for ByteDance, and it was better to bow out before things got worse.

Like Kevin Mayer, Roland publicly attributed his departure in part to TikTok's changing structure: because the company would be splitting into TikTok USDS and TikTok Global, he would not be able to run security for both branches, and inheriting either half would effectively be a demotion. But even his public explanation conceded that being a top executive at TikTok was not like being a top executive at YouTube or Facebook or Snap or LinkedIn. The Chinese government wouldn't let TikTok's recommendations algorithm be sold out of China, and the US government didn't want US user data to leave the US. Meanwhile, Chinese employees who made TikTok product decisions were legally insulated from misconduct investigations by US staff.

It wouldn't be quite right to say that US leaders at TikTok were just figureheads. But they sure had to defer decision-making in a way that many weren't used to. If the tension between Roland and Chris was an allegory for the larger tension between TikTok and ByteDance, between separation and continued entanglement, then ByteDance—and entanglement—had emerged as the clear victor. True independence would not be coming to TikTok anytime soon.

Chapter 24

THE MISGUIDED EFFORT

In October 2022, a few weeks after I first began reporting on Roland Cloutier and Chris Lepitak, I was sitting in a glass-walled conference room in *Forbes*'s Jersey City headquarters with about fifteen colleagues when I received a call from a number I vaguely recognized—a source who had given me valuable information about both execs a few weeks before. The source wanted to know if I could talk, right away. I hurried into a vacant office and started taking notes. Chris Lepitak had ordered his staff to investigate us, the source said—and they had the receipts to prove it.

Over an encrypted video call, the source showed me the spreadsheet that Chris and his staffers used to catalogue the TikTok employees that my colleagues and I had reached out to. They showed me that Chris had widened his search for internal documents: staffers were now scouring all employees' Lark chats for mentions of my name and email address. They were also searching Feishu and Lark Docs, company email accounts, and the company's OneDrive and Google Docs instances.

But the investigators went further, looking beyond just what was visible in company docs. They asked the Beijing Risk Control team to collect the IP addresses linked to my and two of my colleagues' TikTok accounts. Once they had those IP addresses, they were ordered to look for TikTok DMs between any ByteDance employees and our accounts, and to cross-reference our IP addresses with the IP addresses of all ByteDance staff. That way, the company would be able to see whether we were in the same place (a coffee shop, for example, or a library, or a public park) at the same time as an employee—a sign that that person might be talking to us.

Surveilling your employees is a bad look, but it's not uncommon, and employees had clearly signed their rights away when they opted to work for ByteDance. As was the case at most big tech firms, location data pulls were considered in-bounds for ByteDance's investigations of misbehaving employees—ones who, for example, claimed to be working from home in L.A., but were actually "quiet quitting" from a beach in Bali. Those types of employee misconduct investigations were central to Chris's team's work.

This request, though, was not just a company surveilling its own employees; it was a company surveilling private citizens. And it was exactly the thing Project Texas was meant to stop, the thing ByteDance had sworn for months that it couldn't and wouldn't do: allow a team in China to use Americans' TikTok accounts to spy on them.

Back in the *Forbes* conference room, I huddled with my editors—and the colleagues whom Chris was also targeting—and told them about what I'd just seen. We deleted TikTok from our phones immediately, and then got to work to confirm the tip.

We had to be extremely careful to protect our sources, so we agreed not to report everything we knew. We wouldn't reveal the purpose of the investigation, and we wouldn't publish our own names as its targets—after all, it didn't really matter who we were. What mattered was that a team in China could, and had planned to, access private user data for the purposes of surveilling US citizens—in order to figure out who those American citizens were talking to.

The next day, we sent a lengthy set of questions to TikTok and ByteDance's communications departments. (TikTok and ByteDance maintain separate comms offices, though the people who staff both are ByteDance employees.) We asked about the Green Channel process (the China-based system that provided US employees with investigations data), about Chris's investigations into Roland, and about data pulls in which Chinese teams had accessed non-employee data. We also asked specifically whether the Internal Audit and Risk Control department had ever targeted members of the US government, activists, public figures, or journalists in its investigations.

We received two responses. The first, from TikTok's head of communications, Hilary McQuaide, was short. She confirmed receipt of our request, then suggested that our relationship had gotten off on the wrong foot. "It would be great to figure out a better way of working together—perhaps we can meet for coffee (I think we're both in the Bay Area)?" Minutes later, one of McQuaide's subordinates sent the company's answers to our questions—which weren't much longer.

ByteDance didn't deny that Chris's department had pulled the IP addresses of non-employees. It did note that TikTok didn't collect GPS-level location data about its US users. GPS data would've given TikTok a continuous stream of our precise locations—where we drove, whether we walked down the block, potentially even if we changed rooms within our houses. The company didn't have that. But with an IP address, TikTok could tell generally where a device was when it connected to the internet. That information gave them our approximate location *and* the ability to cross-reference our location with employees', to see who we might be talking to. The response suggested the comms staffers either didn't understand how Chris's team might use IP addresses to triangulate our movements, or was trying to divert the argument.

McQuaide and her team declined to answer our question about whether ByteDance had ever targeted journalists or other public figures. So we drafted a story about the surveillance plan, based on our sources and incorporating the company's responses and nonresponses. We published it the same afternoon.

That night, ByteDance shot back in a thread from the official @TikTokComms Twitter handle.

> 1/ @Forbes' reporting about TikTok continues to lack both rigor and journalistic integrity.

> 2/ Specifically, Forbes chose not to include the portion of our statement that disproved the feasibility of its core allegation: TikTok does not collect precise GPS location information from US users, meaning TikTok could not monitor US users in the way the article suggested.

3/ TikTok has never been used to "target" any members of the U.S. government, activists, public figures or journalists, nor do we serve them a different content experience than other users.

4/ Our Internal Audit team follows set policies and processes to acquire information they need to conduct internal investigations of the company codes of conduct, as is standard in companies across our industry.

5/ Any use of internal audit resources as alleged by Forbes would be grounds for immediate dismissal of company personnel.

I saw the tweets the next morning, as I hurried to catch an early flight back home to San Francisco. It is unsettling to have a global media behemoth accuse you of lying. But our sourcing was solid. I sent reply tweets from the airport: ByteDance hadn't denied the actual substance of our story, and we stood by it.

Internally, ByteDance was scrambling.

~

SHORTLY AFTER BYTEDANCE tweeted that it had never used TikTok to target journalists, members of the company's legal team turned to the renowned law firm Covington & Burling, a white-shoe firm that specialized in internal investigations. They had produced a damning report about Uber in 2017, for example, and led an investigation into whether Facebook silenced conservative voices in 2018. Now, ByteDance was asking them to see if their tweet was true. Had they, in fact, targeted journalists?

Over the next two months, the Covington lawyers uncovered the same effort we had—but they found it had gone further than we'd known. Not only had Chris Lepitak ordered employees to pull the data, they had actually done it, at least twice.

The Risk Control department in Beijing had pulled data from my phone and the phone of a UK-based journalist named Cristina Criddle, who had reported on inappropriate behavior by a ByteDance executive in London, including a statement that he "didn't believe" in maternity leave. They had also pulled data from "a small number of people connected to the reporters," presumably family members, roommates, or others with whom Criddle or I had shared an IP address. Convington's findings were bad for the company: despite swearing to everyone that it wasn't a secret surveillance app for the Chinese government, the company had undertaken a classic, Big Brother–style surveillance project targeting two respected members of the Western press.

The timing was also inconvenient for ByteDance: the company had submitted its final draft national security agreement to CFIUS a few months earlier. With the draft still under review, the FBI and DOJ had raised public concerns about the platform. Meanwhile, bipartisan support for action against TikTok had begun to gain steam in Congress: the cochairs of the hawkish House China Committee had introduced a new bill that would force ByteDance to divest from TikTok or sell it. Mark Warner, the influential Democrat leading the Senate Intelligence Committee, said he thought Donald Trump had been right about the app.

Still, ByteDance's executives knew there was no way to bury what I and Covington had found. So they did the next best thing: they held a public mea culpa on a slow news day, December 22, 2022, when they hoped the average American news consumer would be on an airplane or baking Christmas cookies.

Hilary McQuaide called an emergency meeting for the company's communications department, and began it by acknowledging that this was a hard day to work for ByteDance. Erich Andersen, Shou Zi Chew, and Liang Rubo sent all-staff emails explaining that a few staff members had improperly accessed user data, in a gross violation of the company's code of conduct. They had been fired, Erich's email assured. "None of the individuals found to have directly participated in or overseen the misguided plan remain employed at ByteDance," he wrote. The department that had existed under Chris Lepitak would be disbanded. Non-China investigations would now be done by the global legal team.

Erich, Shou, and Rubo did the best they could to spin a very tough set of facts. But the idea that an employee code of conduct could prevent this type of data access was just silly. It ignored the Employee Shakedown Problem, the problem that had necessitated Project Texas in the first place. If a member of ByteDance's Risk Control team was ordered by the CCP to pull information from an American, or British, or other foreign person's TikTok account, did Erich, Shou, and Rubo really expect their *company code of conduct* to stop them?

Until now, TikTok's big threat to US national security had been hypothetical: ByteDance *could*, it *might*, use TikTok to let people in China spy on foreigners. But this incident had made the hypothetical real: now, ByteDance *had* let people in China spy on a Brit and an American—Cristina Criddle and me.

There is no evidence that these particular data pulls were the result of a CCP employee shakedown. They may have been nothing more than an unprofessional and unscrupulous effort to stop corporate leaks—one that got out of hand in part because Chris recognized his own department as a potential target of reporting.

Furthermore, from a geopolitical perspective, Cristina Criddle and I were not high-value targets. We knew who at ByteDance was leaking corporate secrets, but we didn't know classified military information. We didn't work for a president or a prime minister, and we didn't have family members like Albert's dad in China whom the CCP could bully as a way to leverage a dissident into silence. If the CCP has our TikTok data, then they know which videos I watched when I had an account (I have since closed it), and they know Criddle has a fluffy cat named Buffy. I'm sure there are people whose IP addresses would be much more useful to the CCP than ours.

But after ByteDance acknowledged the misguided effort, the primary issue, at least for me, was not whether the CCP had Criddle's and my TikTok data. It was the fact that TikTok and ByteDance had sworn that this exact scenario would not and could not occur.

Lawmakers were livid. Cathy McMorris Rodgers, the Republican Chair of the House Energy and Commerce Committee, tweeted: "Tik-

Tok has placed the safety and privacy of Americans in jeopardy. They have gone on record numerous times claiming that they do not share Americans' data with China. We know that is a lie, and we now know the list has grown to include U.S. journalists. Accountability is coming." Ron Wyden, a senator who had previously opposed legislation aimed at TikTok, said the incident "casts doubt on every promise TikTok has made about protecting personal information."

In response to an onslaught of lawmaker questions, ByteDance offered senators and representatives briefings from the Covington lawyers that conducted its internal investigation. In a lengthy letter to lawmakers, the company gave the incident a name: "The Misguided Effort." The charitable explanation was that nobody meant to say anything false; they just wanted to believe their systems were better than they were. But the fact is that they had lied, and the company now faced a credibility crisis so deep that it threatened the existence of their US business—the nightmare outlined in Sam Burness's fraud risk assessment was coming to life.

Between Christmas and New Year's Day, "Brad from L.A." was working as part of a US skeleton crew to hold down ByteDance's operations when he got word of an alarming development: ByteDance had been served with a subpoena for documents related to its surveillance of journalists—and the subpoena had come from the Fraud Section of the Criminal Division of the US Department of Justice.

ByteDance's US teams scrambled to produce the data that DOJ had asked for, including copies of the Lark messages, emails, and hard drives of the employees who had pulled my and Cristina's data. But there were questions about how much of that data the DOJ would ever see.

Not only does Chinese law prevent companies from sharing certain data with their overseas employees, it also prevents them from turning over that data to foreign law enforcement agencies. When lawyers advised ByteDance that its Chinese investigative team should determine what data to share with their American colleagues, they also said: "The Chinese employer is not allowed to directly provide any data stored within the territory of China to any foreign judicial or enforcement authorities, unless such a provision of data has been approved by the competent Chinese authority."

In other words: ByteDance couldn't turn over information about Chinese employees using its app to spy on American and British journalists unless it got the CCP's permission first.

DOJ knew this. And in addition to its front-door requests for information, the FBI also began gathering information on its own. Agents interviewed ByteDance employees about the surveillance—who had ordered it, and how it came together, but they asked about other things too: how Lark worked, who had access to what data, how sensitive data was shared. Customs and Border Protection stopped dozens of staffers at international airports to interrogate them about Project Texas. They even spoke to one of the people who was fired in The Misguided Effort. They asked him whose idea it was, and how it was carried out.

For ByteDance, 2022 was a year of failed secret-keeping—from admissions between staff that everything was still accessible in China, to offers to cede content policymaking control to the US government, to the misguided effort, undertaken out of a desperate desire to keep the internal audit department's mess out of the public eye.

Hawks in Washington described TikTok as a "Trojan horse," a grand conspiracy cooked up by the Chinese government to serve its geopolitical interests. That wasn't true—TikTok was messy, but it wasn't malicious. Still, ByteDance had tried to rebut its opponents' conspiracy theory by insisting something that *also* wasn't true: that TikTok users' data was safe from Chinese access and that the company had users' data privacy under control.

Zhang Yiming did not have the Employee Shakedown Problem on his radar when he bought Flipagram and Musical.ly. The 2017 Chinese national intelligence law that created the problem wasn't even passed until after the first acquisition was complete and the second was underway. The law's effects on multinational corporations wouldn't become clear until at least the Huawei debacle of 2019. It was solely the Chinese government's fault that Yiming and ByteDance were now seen as potential agents of the Chinese defense apparatus. But that perception, combined with the company's repeated mishaps, would convince a quorum of lawmakers that something had to be done.

ACT IV

Chapter 25

WARTIME

When Liang Rubo, Shou Zi Chew, and Erich Andersen publicly acknowledged surveilling US journalists in December 2022, it marked the lowest moment in a difficult season. In August, Erich had submitted a final draft of ByteDance's Project Texas proposal to CFIUS—and since then, a steady stream of revelations had exposed TikTok's continued control by ByteDance, and ByteDance's continued ties to China.

News reports revealed that TopBuzz had scraped and republished news articles, and censored narratives that hurt Beijing. American executives told reporters they had left TikTok after being micromanaged by the ByteDance C-Suite. Chinese state media had set up an unlabeled "news" account that targeted US politicians on TikTok during the midterm elections; the Burness report leaked, making public the attorney's warnings about crippling noncompliance with US anti-fraud laws; and the *New York Times* reported that Shou, the public face of TikTok, often had business and product decisions made for him by Zhang Yiming, despite the founder's formal resignation from his role at ByteDance in 2021.

The deluge of reporting had created new urgency on the Hill—and on the campaign trail—to get tough with TikTok. Lawmakers wanted to know why CFIUS was taking so long. Senators were still angry at Michael Beckerman, the company's slick lobbyist, for seemingly misleading them about Chinese employees' access to US user data back in 2021. They sent the company dozens of questions as more stories surfaced. And some, impatient with CFIUS and alarmed by TikTok's astronomic growth, were ready to take more drastic action.

In mid-December, leaders of the hawkish House Select Committee on China introduced a bill that would ban TikTok from the US. The bill—with a convoluted title designed to produce a catchy acronym: ANTI-SOCIAL CCP Act—was co-sponsored by the committee's Republican chair and Democratic ranking member, Mike Gallagher and Raja Krishnamoorthi.

Politicians don't introduce bills in mid-December that they actually intend to pass. There is no time, by then, to hold votes even on the simplest of bipartisan actions. Something like a TikTok ban bill would take many months of debate and negotiation to garner a majority. But Mike Gallagher and Raja Krishnamoorthi introduced ANTI-SOCIAL CCP anyway, to send a message about their plans for the following year.

Gallagher was an unusually talented politician. He was just shy of forty, athletic and trim, with a warm smile, a Broadway actress wife, and two young daughters. Born and raised in Wisconsin and educated at Georgetown and Princeton, he was a former intelligence officer for the US Marine Corps, and had won the annual intra-Congress 5K for six years in a row. A Democratic staffer who worked closely with him told me in 2023: "Future presidential candidate, you heard it here first!"

In Congress, Gallagher was a mostly loyal Republican, but he broke with the Trumpist wing of the party over the January 6 insurrection. He criticized the former president for denying Russian interference in the 2016 elections, and had no tolerance for the American Right's waffling support for NATO. He had served in Iraq, and his first priority in politics was foreign policy—specifically, the threat he believed China posed to American hegemony.

As Gallagher saw it, the Chinese government aimed to control as much of the world's technology and infrastructure as possible. Of Xi, he wrote: "He seeks a future where he could turn off the lights in Green Bay or Geneva knowing we could not do the same in Guangzhou." Gallagher feared that any piece of "smart" technology made in China—from cars and cargo ships to dishwashers and gaming consoles—might someday be weaponized by the CCP, remote controlled and made to malfunction (or worse) on cue at some unspecified later date.

Given his extensive history as a China hawk, Gallagher was an unsurprising advocate for a TikTok ban. What gave his effort legs was the support of Raja Krishnamoorthi, a mild-mannered, well-liked Democrat from Illinois who would become the first member of his party to sponsor legislation targeting the company. By December, Krishnamoorthi knew there was deep uneasiness about TikTok within the Democratic Party. But TikTok was hugely popular with the Democratic base, and opposing it could alienate Krishnamoorthi to millions of young voters. It would also send a message that banning TikTok was no longer just an impulsive, Trumpist idea but a bipartisan one.

Krishnamoorthi wasn't the only Democrat sending this message. In November, FBI Director Christopher Wray said in a speech that the Chinese government could manipulate TikTok's algorithm and use it in influence operations. After Wray's remarks, Treasury Secretary Janet Yellen had called the national security fears about TikTok "legitimate." Both officials were members of the CFIUS committee that would determine TikTok's fate—an alarming fact for Erich, who hadn't heard from CFIUS since August.

The ByteDance C-Suite partially blamed Erich for the troubles of 2022. Early in the year, he had told rooms of ByteDance staffers that the deal was as good as done. But after submitting the company's final draft NSA, it seemed the US government had turned steadily against ByteDance—and Erich, in charge of both ByteDance's legal team and also its government relations department, was the one holding the bag.

Michael Beckerman chafed at the company's relative silence as officials like Wray and Yellen had criticized the platform. Since 2020, Michael had reported to Erich, who had warned that aggressive lobbying campaigns might upset a CFIUS deal. Michael and his team felt trapped under Erich, unable to do the DC wheeling and dealing they thought was necessary to sell Project Texas and mollify suspicious lawmakers.

Erich was about fifteen years older than Michael, an age gap that appeared larger than it was because of the two men's differences in demeanor. His sandy-blond hair had gone largely white, and he wore minimalist silver rectangular spectacles and a rotating cast of checkered and striped button-down shirts. He had little interest in glamor—he was confident enough in his intellectual product that he wasn't particularly interested in trying to sell anyone anything. He was especially wary about talking up Project Texas to lawmakers: CFIUS negotiations were confidential, and confidentiality was a two-way street.

The more ByteDance talked about its CFIUS proposal, the more the government could, too. ByteDance was eager to show the public that it was working out a deal with the White House that would address any potential national security issues. But the White House wasn't sure Project Texas *could* address national security issues—and the more ByteDance tried to tell the public that everything was fine, the more eager CFIUS officials were to correct the record.

In sharp contrast to Erich, Michael might as well have popped out of the womb in a slim-fitting suit. Long before his tenure at TikTok, he had worked every bar and cocktail party to become a DC institution; in 2014, *Politico* referred to him as "the Internet King." With slicked back hair, a devilish smize, and a dry sense of humor, he was in his element brokering backroom DC deals, and to him, the sale was everything.

Erich wanted to be very sure the company could follow through on anything it promised—but Michael didn't always include Erich in his DC dealings. Erich was a product of the staid, reputable Microsoft, while Michael had long repped Silicon Valley's chaotic startup community: a place where money and connections did the talking, and risk tolerance was high.

In late 2022, after months of watching Erich lose ground with his cautious strategy, Shou decided to unleash the lobbyist. In a move viewed internally as a rebuke of Erich, Shou changed Michael's reporting line. He and the other public policy teams would now be managed directly by the CEO himself.

~

BYTEDANCE'S ILL-FATED 2022 was mostly a product of its own making. The company had misled people about Chinese access to Tik-

Tok users' data, and then attacked journalists who wrote about it, rather than addressing the public's concerns.

But in February 2023, as ByteDance lawyers finalized its response to CFIUS's information requests, the company suffered a blow that had nothing to do with its own behavior: a large white object with various spiky attachments was spotted by curious citizens floating high over the plains of Montana. After receiving a slew of questions about the unidentified flying object, the Department of Defense confirmed that it was a high-altitude surveillance balloon from China—a revelation that quickly threw Montana's Republican government into a frenzy.

For the next several days, the news media tracked the balloon relentlessly as it floated southeast from Montana to the Carolinas. Some Republicans criticized President Biden for not immediately ordering the military to shoot it down—which he eventually did, once it floated out over the Atlantic Ocean and was no longer at risk of falling on a neighborhood pizza parlor or middle school basketball game.

The balloon had the online energy of an earthquake or an eclipse: it was a live, physical event that caused millions of people to scour the skies, and then flock to social media to compare their sightings. And though policy hawks saw further deterioration in the US-China relationship, Americans online had a different take: the balloon was funny.

Dozens of people offered up "Chinese Spy Balloon" as a name for aspiring rock bands. Liberal satirist Jon Stewart explained it to his audience with a wry smile: "It was a balloon. And we shot it down with—I think—a missile from a $200 million airplane. From what I understand, and I've been to Coney Island many times, I think a dart might've done it. I think we could've done it with a tack, maybe a pin, something along those lines."

On *Saturday Night Live*, star cast member Bowen Yang played the balloon itself, clad in a giant inflatable suit. Kenan Thompson, playing a Pentagon official, said, "We will not tolerate any form of Chinese spying. But to be honest, they already have everything they need from TikTok, so scroll away, kids!"

The balloon was a meme, a joke that dunked on China Hawks—

surely, the CCP's Orwellian surveillance apparatus could do better than a literal balloon—but it also exposed Americans' privacy nihilism: as a culture, we had accepted that, sure, our devices are pretty much tracking everywhere we go. But burning in those same jokes was also a creeping discomfort about China's threat to American supremacy. Privacy nihilism was scarier in the face of a rising totalitarian adversary that appeared to be increasingly willing to encroach upon US persons and US soil.

Beyond the balloon, a string of other incidents had helped to bolster fears that the CCP might disrupt typical American life: In 2022, DOJ announced the arrest of five more men for allegedly targeting Chinese dissidents in the United States on behalf of the Chinese government, and the US formally banned the sale of all new Huawei devices. And in April 2023—in a trio of cases announced by David Newman—DOJ charged more than forty people: two men who had allegedly helped establish a Chinese police outpost in New York City, and nearly three dozen more who had allegedly harassed dissidents through social media.

"The trio of cases announced today details how the People's Republic of China, through its Ministry of Public Security, has engaged in a multi-front campaign to extend the reach and impacts of its authoritarian system into the United States and elsewhere around the world," said Newman. "It shows the PRC's efforts to globalize the oppressive tactics used domestically in China to silence dissent."

Though TikTok had nothing to do with the police outposts or the balloon, those incidents had nonetheless hung heavily over Erich's souring negotiations with Newman and Rosen at CFIUS. CFIUS's job is to find ways to allow companies to do business in the US without enabling them to be weaponized by a foreign state. But the panel's outlook is shaped by everything else it knows about those governments. It was clear that on the deepest level, ByteDance was not in charge. The company's general counsel may have been on the other side of the table, but Newman and Rosen were essentially negotiating with the Chinese government itself.

Chapter 26

SELL OR ELSE

AFTER LOSING CONTROL OVER MICHAEL BECKERMAN AND his public policy team, Erich Andersen focused all of his efforts on saving the CFIUS talks. The men had spent 2021 and early 2022 hammering out a deal. Erich suggested to colleagues that the finalization of that deal was tantamount to government acceptance of it. But he was wrong. David Newman and Paul Rosen still had to take the draft to their bosses, and make their own recommendations about whether to accept it. Ultimately, their briefing and recommendation would land on the desks of cabinet secretaries who would make the final decision.

In the sleepy week between Christmas and New Year's 2022, when even most TikTok employees were watching football and eating pie, Erich and his team of attorneys at Skadden and Covington wrote to Newman, Rosen, and other CFIUS staffers to request a meeting. They made sure to remind the government—and anyone else, like a judge, who might someday review the parties' correspondence—that ByteDance had put in years of "constructive engagement" with the government, and had now been waiting months for a response to their August proposal.

The letter lamented the "significant politicization" of the app, and criticized members of the CFIUS panel (including Deputy Attorney General Lisa Monaco) for their public statements about it. The administration had been fair to ByteDance until Congress got involved, the letter seemed to say—if only the company could return to the days before reporters and legislators had started asking questions.

The lawyers didn't receive a response, or at least not the response they were hoping for. CFIUS did write back, asking for internal records regarding the spying incident. Erich's team had already spent days frantically responding to DOJ's subpoenas on the subject. CFIUS's request for documents on the same topic now meant that ByteDance would again have to compile—and double- and triple-check—the information it was required to turn over.

Through the spy balloon controversy, February stretched on, and there was still no meeting about the Project Texas proposal. So Erich wrote again, himself this time, to request a call. "We have been increasingly dismayed by the Committee's lack of engagement over the last six months," he wrote. He, too, condemned public officials' negative statements about TikTok. But he also hinted that ByteDance was ready to play hardball.

"We have sought at every turn to engage constructively with CFIUS.... notwithstanding that ByteDance grew TikTok organically, not through the acquisition of the Chinese-owned Musical.ly and its limited assets that are virtually irrelevant to TikTok today."

The fact that TikTok was not, really, a direct outgrowth of Musical.ly was something of a legal trump card for ByteDance. CFIUS, after all, governed foreign *investment* in US companies, or foreign acquisitions of them. Its "jurisdictional hook" in this case—the thing that allowed it to regulate TikTok at all—had been ByteDance's purchase of Alex Zhu's lip-synching app. And Erich was now ready to argue that CFIUS's jurisdiction was limited: that it could only force ByteDance to unravel its acquisition of Musical.ly, not require the sale of TikTok.

It wasn't that CFIUS had *no* jurisdiction over ByteDance—the company hadn't engaged with the US government for two years and spent more than a billion dollars on Project Texas just to be nice. If CFIUS forced ByteDance to undo the Musical.ly acquisition, the unraveling would be cumbersome and expensive. It might well be easier just to work with CFIUS and agree on a mitigation plan, which ByteDance could then tout in the press as evidence that the government no longer found it dangerous.

~

A WEEK AFTER Erich sent his letter, on March 6, he finally got the meeting he had asked for—but not the result he wanted. Newman and Rosen had received an answer from their bosses, and the honorable thing to do was to break the news to ByteDance, graciously and expeditiously. Via teleconference, the CFIUS representatives read a prepared statement to Erich's lawyers at Covington, telling them that the only solution that would satisfy the government would be a full sale of TikTok—For You algorithm and all—to an entity without ties to the Chinese government.

With his jurisdictional barb, Erich had started a game of chicken. Rosen and Newman hadn't blinked. ByteDance could take its case to court, but even if a judge said CFIUS couldn't force a sale, there was another party that could: Congress. It would be better for everyone, Newman and Rosen said, if ByteDance pursued a sale voluntarily. If it didn't, they told ByteDance that the White House would work with legislators to pass a law that would require it.

Just hours after the meeting where Newman and Rosen declared that Project Texas was dead, Democratic Senator Mark Warner and Republican Senator John Thune announced that they would be introducing a new bill aimed at TikTok, this one called the RESTRICT Act. The timing, in Erich's eyes, was anything but coincidental. The new bill would close the jurisdictional loophole, giving the government the power it had lacked under President Trump nearly four years before.

Warner announced that the bill already had the backing of twelve sponsors, equally divided between Democrats and Republicans. Soon, that number would grow to over twenty-five: the bill would bear the names of more than a quarter of the Senate. But RESTRICT also had something more valuable than all those senators' names: the backing of the White House.

To Erich, this was a betrayal. Not by Warner or Thune, who had long postured against China, but by Newman, Rosen, and the other negotiators at CFIUS with whom they had been working for years. CFIUS negotiations are confidential so that companies can be open and candid with the government, and to protect those same companies from damaging press that might result from their disclosures. But here, it seemed, the Biden administration had taken what it learned in confidence about TikTok and ByteDance as reason to pass a new law to kneecap them.

Erich and his team met twice more with CFIUS officials in March, trying desperately to convince them that a forced sale just wasn't possible. After all, ByteDance had tried to sell back in 2020, but the Chinese government had blocked the sale. ByteDance couldn't be expected to violate Chinese law, so a divestment order made no sense—unless the point was to require the company to break the law. The question was which country's laws it would break: the US or China.

~

ERICH AND HIS team didn't give up. They continued trying to liaise with CFIUS, asking for follow-up meetings, and angling to present information about new updates to Project Texas. For Michael and the company's well-funded lobbying shop, though, the gloves were coming all the way off. The government was trying to ban TikTok, and it was going to have to fight for its life.

With Michael's coaching, Shou agreed to testify before the House Energy and Commerce Committee in March—his first appearance before the US government since he had become TikTok's CEO nearly two years earlier. Zhang Yiming, Liang Rubo, and Shou Zi Chew shelled out millions to hire prominent DC dignitaries to make the case against the Warner-Thune bill. They hired from both parties, but the Democrats were especially important, as they were where most of TikTok's remaining support could be found.

The company hired SKDK, the left-leaning strategy firm helmed by former Biden senior aide Anita Dunn. It hired Ankit Desai and Jamal Brown, two former Biden staffers, and brought in former Obama campaign masterminds David Plouffe and Jim Messina for messaging help. It also tapped Crossroads Strategies, a large bipartisan K Street firm, which it used to appeal to both Democrats and Republicans.

Michael's team also huddled with TikTok's marketing shop to create a series of ads targeted toward lawmakers. Featuring veterans, nuns, and small-business owners who'd made it big on TikTok, the ads centered on a familiar theme: that social media generally, and TikTok specifically, was more good than it was bad.

This theme was well-worn in Silicon Valley: tech giants had flaws, but they helped people come together, helped businesses reach consumers, and were engines of commerce and connectedness. The Internet Association—the lobbying group that Michael ran until TikTok hired him—trumpeted tech as "an American success story," according to one 2019 report, that "support[ed] two indirect jobs for every internet job." The subtext of the TikTok ads was *you may love to hate Big Tech, but it's too big to ban*.

"Too big to ban" was an idea that Shou and Michael ultimately leaned into. The company announced that it now had 150 million active users in the United States—nearly as many people as had voted in the 2020 presidential election. Surely Congress didn't want to ban an app used by half of its constituents.

The company also embraced another talking point that it had previously shied away from: the app's role in US political discourse. Less than a year before, Michael had himself told CNN anchor Brian Stelter that TikTok was "not the go-to place for politics." When pressed by Stelter about whether TikTok might "influence Americans' commercial, cultural, or political behavior," Michael said, "Yeah, I just don't see that." Now, though, Michael was going all in on TikTok as an engine of politics—because political speech is the most protected type of expression under US law.

This was a hedge. If Congress did actually pass a ban bill, then sooner or later, TikTok's fate would be decided by the courts. And if that day came, the company would want to point to its role as a core organ of American political discourse.

~

IN ADDITION TO traditional lobbyists, ByteDance also tapped another source of persuasive power: TikTok's homegrown celebrities.

The company approached thirty of its most popular "content creators," offering them an all-expenses-paid trip to Washington, DC. They would be allowed to say whatever they pleased, but would be expected to "stand ... side by side with creators and the TikTok team" at the U.S. Capitol in an advocacy blitz just in time for Shou's appearance at the House Rayburn Building.

"Creators" and their plus-ones flew first class to DC. TikTok put them up in rooms at the posh Salamander Hotel, and hosted a meet-and-greet with reporters on the roof deck of 101 Constitution Ave—an event space with panoramic views of the DC monuments that's more often booked for galas and weddings than for interviews with reporters. The junket included Gen-Z news commentator V Spehar, fashion and beauty creator Naomi Hearts, and the subject of one of the company's most popular TV ads: an octogenarian disabled veteran known on the platform as Patriotic Kenny.

On the day before the hearing, TikTok staffers turned the "creators" loose in the Capitol building, chaperoning them around as they went to visit the offices of various representatives. Many lawmakers avoided the makeshift lobbying effort, though some agreed to take meetings and listen to the TikTokers' concerns. Progressive champion Alexandria Ocasio-Cortez (AOC) was out of office, so young admirers who had hoped to meet her covered the wall next to her door with sticky notes that asked her to "#keepTikTok."

At the end of the day, TikTok staffers gathered with the influencers for a rally on the capitol steps. They were joined by Democratic Congressman Jamaal Bowman—the only lawmaker that ByteDance had persuaded to publicly defend it against the blitz.

Bowman used his time at the Capitol to lambaste American companies with unethical data practices. "Guess what? You can ban TikTok," he said, "but there are still data brokers who sell our data to other countries and businesses in other countries—they sell to the highest bidder. So let's not have a dishonest conversation. Let's not be racist toward China and express our xenophobia when it comes to TikTok. Because American companies have done tremendous harm to American people."

Bowman's points about American companies were hard to deny. Companies like Uber, Facebook, YouTube, and Twitter had long compromised users' safety and security to better support their bottom lines, even when that meant their platforms were facilitating real-world violence. Like all companies, tech giants live by the incentives that laws create for them, and US laws had set an abysmally low bar.

Bowman wanted to pass a national data privacy law, which might prevent companies from sharing private user information with foreign governments. He also favored algorithmic transparency laws, which could force companies to disclose which posts they recommended to users and how. Bowman wasn't necessarily saying he thought TikTok's policies were good, but he wanted laws that would target all the tech giants equally, rather than single out the foreign-owned ones.

A decent faction of progressive Democrats agreed with Bowman. Actually, a majority of congresspeople and senators agreed that American tech giants should be accountable—but they didn't agree about what should be done. When it came to TikTok, what divided lawmakers was whether, legally, the company's Chinese ownership should matter.

Proponents of RESTRICT seemed to think TikTok was a trillion-dollar diamond owned by a guy who lived in a neighborhood controlled by the Mob. The Mob hadn't yet demanded that the guy hand over the diamond, but they might do so at any time, and they had told the guy he couldn't sell the diamond to anyone who lived outside of their turf.

Some US lawmakers shied away from that characterization, noting that there was no evidence that the CCP had, yet, forced ByteDance to use TikTok as a data harvesting or propaganda tool in the US. But Rosen, Newman, Warner, Thune, and dozens of other lawmakers thought the CCP might well act like mobsters someday. And to them, TikTok would be a threat until it was wrested from CCP territory.

Chapter 27

SHOUTIME

Roughly every six months, members of Congress summon a Silicon Valley CEO to testify. This produces predictable political theater. Odd, bipartisan bedfellows light into the executive, criticizing the way his platform has debased discourse and destroyed attention spans. Tech, they insist, is making us dumber, less compassionate, less open-minded. And most of all, it's endangering our children, corrupting their minds, and exposing them to predators.

The CEO responds stiffly that the facts are more complicated, and that rigorous research has never conclusively proven platforms' responsibility for societal ills. His lobbyists pour millions into reelection campaigns, lawmakers shame him, but don't punish him or his company. Six months or so pass, and the cycle begins again.

Ironically, the modern congressional tech hearing is mostly for social media. Lawmakers' chief objective is virality, capturing constituent eyeballs on the very platforms they're interrogating—along with placement in primetime segments on MSNBC, CNN, and Fox News. The best questioners (often former trial attorneys) are those who can both deliver zingers and elicit new, damning information, as Ted Cruz did when he quizzed Michael Beckerman about TikTok's privacy policy back in 2021. But many lawmakers squander their time, making micro-speeches for the cameras as their witnesses patiently run down the clock.

Tech execs have learned, over the years, how to master these hearings. One effective strategy is highlighting lawmakers' technical ineptitude. In 2018, when an ill-informed Senator Orrin Hatch asked Mark Zuckerberg how Facebook made money without charging its customers, he couldn't conceal a smirk as he answered, infamously, "Senator, we run ads." But Zuckerberg had founded a once-in-a-generation, *Fortune* 50 unicorn; he could afford to be glib.

When Shou Zi Chew arrived in Washington, DC, more than two weeks before his first congressional hearing, he knew he couldn't be flippant. He wasn't Zuckerberg, and TikTok wasn't an American success story. In fact, it was a threat to American social media dominance—and, in the eyes of the twenty senators who had sponsored RESTRICT, a threat to American national security, too.

The Energy and Commerce hearing would be Shou's national debut on the regulatory stage. If he didn't define himself, lawmakers would do it for him—so in the weeks leading up to the hearing, he held a series of one-on-one meetings with lawmakers, where he took up the unenviable task of persuading Congress to accept what CFIUS had not: that Project Texas was an adequate solution to the national security risks that TikTok posed to the United States.

When he wasn't briefing lawmakers, Shou was in rehearsal. Among his inner circle were the former Disney comms czar, Zenia Mucha, and former Obama aides David Plouffe and Jim Messina. Michael was in his element, playing lawmakers in mock hearings where the aides tested out answers to the ugliest, most aggressive questions they could think of.

Michael had spent five years as a staffer for the House Energy and Commerce Committee, first for former Republican Chair Fred Upton, and then for the committee itself. Upton had even given a toast at Michael's wedding—this was his turf, and he was as good a coach as any future committee witness could hope for.

The fame and publicity of a prime-time hearing played to Shou's strengths—or at least to his interests. Shou's colleagues described him as a man with a weakness for celebrity, and several went so far as to call him a "starfucker." He posed for selfies with lines of employees at all-hands meetings, and he and his wife were repeat attendees of the Met Gala. (One person who worked with him noted that this type of thing was, after all, part of his job.) He often asked staff at all-hands meetings to follow his TikTok account (@ShouTime), where he posted eager videos of himself hanging out with pro athletes and pop stars. Even if the hearing was a beatdown, at least he was likely to gain followers.

Shou wasn't the only one prepping for the hearing with closed-door meetings—ban proponents had begun back-channeling, too. More than nine months after he had sent me his recordings, Rob Doe had started meeting and corresponding with legislative staff, first in Mark Warner's office, and then with the Democrats on the House Energy and Commerce Committee.

Rob told congressional staffers that TikTok executives had lied to his face, that Project Texas was a sham, and that there was no meaningful distinction between TikTok and ByteDance. Staffers were wary of Rob's stridency, and of the time that had elapsed since he left the company, but grateful for his inside knowledge—a rare currency. Staffers for the Energy and Commerce Committee even reached out to journalists who reported on the company, asking for help with their hearing preparations.

~

CONGRESSIONAL TECH HEARINGS generally focus on a few well-established themes: tech companies are creepy, collecting and misusing their customers data; they are corrupting, causing us all to become meaner, dumber, and more hateful toward one another; and they are greedy, putting their own profits above trifling concerns like user privacy and their role in the information ecosystem.

The TikTok hearing would follow these same themes, but with a new layer of urgency—lawmakers feared that TikTok was, at a hostile foreign power's request, doing intentionally and maliciously what its competitors did out of mere negligence and greed.

March 23 was a sunny spring day, with Washington's renowned cherry blossoms in full flourish, and reflections of monuments sparkling across the capitol's pools and fountains. At 10 a.m., members of the fifty-two-person House Energy and Commerce Committee filed into three long rows of office chairs behind tiered daises of wood paneling.

Shou took his seat at a sole witness table facing them, flanked by four wide rows of spectators: a jumble of lobbyists, journalists, and the TikTok stars that the company had flown in for the occasion. He was outfitted in a slim blue suit and Hermès tie (one that the luxury label branded as a "good luck tie")—an ensemble he would repeat for testimony later that year before regulators in the European Union. Michael Beckerman sat directly behind Shou in the first row, wearing what was apparently *his* hearing tie: the same black-and-gray striped one that he had worn when he testified before a US Senate committee nearly two years before.

Cathy McMorris Rodgers opened the hearing with a searing indictment of TikTok: "We do not trust TikTok will ever embrace American values: values for freedom, human rights, and innovation. TikTok has repeatedly chosen the path for more control, more surveillance, and more manipulation. Your platform should be banned. I expect today you'll say anything to avoid this outcome."

American lawmakers often use hearings as their personal soapbox. McMorris Rodgers's level of vitriol, though, was unusual even in an age where hearings were optimized for TikTok-sized viral soundbites. Before Shou could even speak, she had said that she expected him to lie. From the outset, it was clear that this would not be a fact-finding mission for Congress; it would be a performative one.

Other lawmakers followed McMorris Rodgers's lead, making claims that were beyond what the public record showed. Florida Republican Kat Cammack described ByteDance as "an extension of the CCP," and California Democrat Anna Eshoo declared: "The Chinese Government has [Americans' private TikTok] data." When Shou said he had seen no evidence of CCP data collection, Eshoo replied: "I find that actually preposterous."

These early moments were wins for Congress and losses for TikTok—they might not be surfacing new information, but the zingers that would play well later on TV and TikTok itself.

But, then the congressmembers started to get sloppy: Buddy Carter from Georgia asked whether TikTok collected information about how dilated users' pupils are as they scroll. (Neither TikTok nor other standard phone-based apps could do this, which Carter might've learned had he asked his staffers to run a few Google searches during hearing prep.) Then, Richard Hudson from North Carolina asked whether TikTok could access a user's home Wi-Fi network. Polite but clearly flummoxed, Shou responded that he might not understand the question, but like any other app, TikTok connects to a Wi-Fi network when a user connects their device to that network.

These flubs were the break Shou had needed. Maybe he could make this hearing about lawmakers' incompetence after all.

In their defense, members of Congress are, from hour to hour, expected to understand everything from the intricacies of federal public school funding, licensing requirements for aging bridges and tunnels, to the emerging national security threats caused by apps with back-end connections to China. It is not reasonable, all things considered, to expect them to know that they should ask whether Project Texas strips away all foreign control over the heating button, or really even to comprehend what those words mean.

In this case, though, Congress's loose command of the facts caused problems. When members claimed that TikTok was "owned" by the CCP—or that it was just a "Trojan horse" designed to hoover up data, they flattened the truth: that ByteDance was as private a company as China allowed, and that the CCP had (likely strategically) stayed largely out of its management of TikTok thus far. The lawmakers' energy—and overreach—was perhaps best exemplified by a line of questioning led by the conservative Texan representative and former Navy Seal Dan Crenshaw.

"Here's the main point of concern," Crenshaw began. He then quoted the 2017 National Intelligence Law. "In other words," he continued, "ByteDance and also your TikTok employees that live in China, they must cooperate with Chinese intelligence whenever they are called upon."

Then his succinct explanation of the Employee Shakedown Problem took a turn.

Crenshaw continued: "And if they are called upon, they're bound to secrecy, and that would include you. So, Mr. Chew, if the CCP tells ByteDance to turn over all data that TikTok has collected in the US, even within Project Texas, do they have to do so according to Chinese law?"

Shou responded with an answer that would become one of the most memorable moments of the hearing. "Well, first, Congressman—I'm Singaporean."

Crenshaw tried to recover, redirecting his question to address the ByteDance employees who *were* Chinese citizens or lived in China. But the damage was done: by mistaking TikTok's Singaporean CEO for a Chinese person, he had confirmed skeptics' reservations about the true purpose of this hearing: to race-bait and fear-monger about foreign apps while ignoring the considerable risks posed by their American competitors. If Crenshaw was trying to make a subtler point about Shou being subject to CCP influence because his ultimate employer was a Chinese company, he had bungled it. All anyone would remember from his questioning was the offensive flub.

The biggest win a CEO could score in a congressional hearing was the role reversal, stealing the viral moment and leaving the questioner eager to run down the clock. Dan Crenshaw spent the rest of his five minutes by pivoting back to safe territory: he rehashed Ted Cruz's 2021 questioning of Michael Beckerman about whether ByteDance was part of TikTok's corporate group (it was), and then gave in to the most inevitable talking point of them all: children.

Politicians have been claiming that new forms of media corrupt children's brains since long before the advent of the internet. In the mid-twentieth century, the target of this vitriol was comic books. In the 1990s, the target was violent video games, which were frequently blamed (usually without evidence) for school shootings and other child-on-child violence.

Internet use among children and teens has led to complex and uneven outcomes. Clearly, the web has put some kids at risk, exposing them to predators, drugs, and self-harm. It has also clearly helped other kids survive through abuse, helping them find supportive communities that they lack at home. The internet is now integral to nearly all parts of children's lives, just as it is integral to lives of the parents that raise them—both groups rely on technology to communicate with the rest of the world, and to consume most of their information.

There are specific facets of social media that may be especially harmful to children, like algorithms that reward extreme behavior and excessive use. Girls, especially, often suffer negative effects from bullying and body comparison. Social media is not the reason why our culture valorizes extreme thinness, but it can make the problem worse. And gamifying popularity, reducing users' worth to a series of likes, comments, and shares, can ratchet the already tricky navigation of adolescent social life.

Every moment that lawmakers talked about kids and teens was a boon to Shou. Congress might lambaste Big Tech for allegedly ruining American youth, but TikTok wasn't fundamentally different on this issue than its competitors, so lawmakers were unlikely to do anything about it.

So Shou was deferential when Democrat Kimberly Schrier pointed to research showing that TikTok's For You page recommended videos to teens that glorified eating disorders. A former pediatrician, Schrier was forceful: "If you show girls repeatedly skinny bodies and advice on how to cook meals that are less than 300 calories, that is dangerous." Shou called extreme dieting videos "a challenging problem for our industry," and said, "I share your concerns, and I commit to doing more." He also said TikTok was trying to build machine learning models to screen diet content for teen users. Humans couldn't review all the posts on TikTok (or Instagram, or YouTube) before they went live, so the companies had to use (and trust) algorithms to enforce their rules accurately.

Shou also listened politely when Diana DeGette, another Democrat, suggested that TikTok should be held to a higher standard because it was so popular with teens. TikTok was, in fact, more popular with young teens than any app in history. Yiming had once compared the For You page as being the equivalent to an "indulgence" like a glass of wine or a game of poker, but neither the US nor China allowed children under the age of eighteen to drink or gamble—so perhaps it did make sense to regulate teen use of the platform.

Shou didn't mention that in response to a 2021 Chinese government crackdown, ByteDance had actually imposed a strict forty-minute time limit on Douyin—the Chinese version of TikTok—for users under fourteen, and forbade nighttime use of the app by anyone under eighteen years old. (In China, unlike the US, apps require identity verification, so ByteDance could easily identify which of its users were under eighteen.) Just weeks before the Energy and Commerce hearing, TikTok had rolled out a similar program, limiting accounts of self-declared teen users to sixty minutes each day. But TikTok's limit was just a suggestion, easily bypassed with a click. And ByteDance knew, because it had run internal tests about it, that the limit had a negligible effect on watch time. The goal of the limit wasn't reducing the amount of time kids spent on TikTok; according to one internal document, it was actually intended to increase the number of people who used the app on a daily basis.

Lawmakers' questions about teens' addiction to TikTok were at times heart-wrenching, especially when they gave examples of families who had lost children to suicide, or to dumb stunts they had seen on the platform. Like Zuckerberg, Instagram's Adam Mosseri, and other tech leaders, Shou was a parent to young kids, and he responded with empathy. "This is a real industry challenge, and we're working very hard," he said, referring lawmakers to ByteDance's hundreds of Trust and Safety staffers, whose whole job was to stop TikTok from showing people videos that could cause them or others harm.

Some lawmakers tried to braid their two main themes—China and children—together. "There are those on this committee, including myself, who believe that the Chinese Communist Party is engaged in psychological warfare through TikTok to deliberately influence US children," said Georgia Republican Buddy Carter, the same representative who had asked about pupil dilation. Republican Randy Weber of Texas went further, alleging that the app was "indoctrinating our children with divisive, woke, and pro-CCP propaganda."

When lawmakers accused TikTok of being a Chinese plot to harm American teens, Shou punched back. When Weber cited "several reports, hearings, and leaked internal documents" to say that TikTok had censored and suppressed criticism of the Chinese government, Shou said: "I don't think that is accurate, Congressman." Shou told Weber that the platform hosted videos that were critical of China. And when other lawmakers brought up data privacy, he suggested they should blame American companies, too: "With a lot of respect, American social companies don't have a good track record with data privacy and user security. I mean, look at Facebook and Cambridge Analytica—just one example."

Here, Shou was right: by failing to pass strong laws about data and social media, the US government had chosen not to crack down on the companies that collect our data and sell it for a profit.

Lawmakers, though, weren't actually worried about data privacy. They were worried about something else: data weaponization. The US government might not care about protecting its citizens' data from capitalists looking to make a buck, but it appeared to care a lot about protecting it from governments that might use it against the American project itself.

Not every member of Congress bought into this distinction. Sharp critics on the left argued that rampant corporate greed was far more predatory to everyday people than a foreign government mostly engrossed in its own affairs. CCP influence operations were notoriously clumsy and ineffective—so why were lawmakers so worried about them?

The line between opportunistic greed and political subterfuge was also often muddy: as Jamaal Bowman had argued on the Capitol steps, data brokers generally sell their goods to the highest bidder. Amoral capitalists are often happy to facilitate influence operations so long as the operators pay enough.

Still, for congressional staff in both parties, the idea of platform weaponization just hit different. At the hearing, Shou had promised that TikTok would "remain a platform for free expression" and "not be manipulated by *any* government." The tacit implication was that while the company wouldn't bend to the will of Chinese lawmakers, it also wouldn't bend to the American lawmakers who now sat across from its CEO.

But anyone who had reviewed Erich Andersen's draft agreement with the US government understood that ByteDance was willing to bend considerably in order to keep operating TikTok in the United States, just as it bent to Chinese authorities to operate Douyin and Toutiao in China.

Shou's line of thinking also raised hackles for a different reason: he had put the Chinese and US governments on equal footing. Yiming had told his staff to act like "Martians," free from nationality. Neutrality toward the US government seemed reasonable, appropriate even, for a private multinational company. It is generally not a business's job to endorse forms of government; it's just their job to follow the laws where they operate. The operators of chain restaurants and car dealers aren't expected to endorse democracy; they're just expected to sell burritos and cars according to the laws of whatever country they're in.

But platforms weren't selling burritos. Alex Zhu had said social media platforms were like new frontiers, countries of their own. Mark Zuckerberg had called them "the fifth estate." Opinion writers called them "digital public squares." And now, the owner of the latest digital public square was equating the US government to one that had murdered peaceful protestors in its physical public square, then scrubbed the massacre from its internet.

US consumers who had grown up using Google, Facebook, and Microsoft expected more than neutrality—they expected their platforms to espouse American values: to embrace democracy *over* autocracy, to cooperate with US law enforcement *but not* Chinese law enforcement.

After nearly a decade of discussion about platforms' effects on elections, the company in charge of a new dominant platform, by nature of its "Martian" approach, had to profess neutrality toward the idea that we should have elections at all.

And to that idea, the congressional staffers, and their bosses, said: No.

Chapter 28

LOYALTY TESTS

In the days after Shou Zi Chew's hearing, talk on the Hill quickly turned to the RESTRICT Act and presidential power.

The bill was broad, intentionally so. It also wasn't all-or-nothing: its primary author, Mark Warner, wanted to give the president discretion, enabling him to ban TikTok, but not requiring him to do so. By putting a ban on the table, the bill would give officials like David Newman and Paul Rosen new leverage.

RESTRICT also wasn't specific to TikTok; it would apply to other companies, too. Warner saw TikTok as one in a line of companies, like the Chinese-owned hardware manufacturer Huawei and the Russian-owned antivirus provider Kaspersky Lab, that created risk of foreign governments meddling in US life. It was fairer, he believed, to target any company that might pose a risk to national security, rather than targeting TikTok alone.

The bill would give future presidents broad power to squeeze and threaten businesses under Chinese (or Russian, Iranian, North Korean, Cuban, or Venezuelan) ownership. Like most grants of presidential power, the idea was appealing to those who trusted future presidents not to misuse national security law, and do things like harass donors' competitors, for example, or relax sanctions on foreign companies who did business with their family or friends.

Mark Warner was a pot-stirrer. He had a proven track record of touching—grabbing, really—the third rails of politics, with the belief that sometimes, that's just what's necessary to get things done. In the early 2010s, he spent several years co-leading the Gang of Six, a bipartisan Senate group that made sweeping recommendations for spending cuts and reductions in Medicare and Social Security benefits to bring down the US deficit and national debt. The recommendations were opposed by both Democratic and Republican leadership and were never adopted, but Warner still pointed to them as a bold, worthy example of compromise.

An affable moderate, Warner was a former telecom executive who made hundreds of millions of dollars in the private sector before entering government. He was friendly with Silicon Valley's elite—former AOL CEO Steve Case once spent the summer at his house on Martha's Vineyard—and tech was both an area of interest and expertise for him. He chaired the powerful Senate Intelligence Committee, which became critical of TikTok in 2022 after *BuzzFeed* exposed widespread Chinese access to US TikTok user data, and he was known on the Hill as an ambitious maverick who stuck his fingers in lots of pies.

"I like being in the mix," he told the *New York Times* in 2021.

RESTRICT certainly put Warner in the mix on TikTok—but just days after it was introduced, its coalition started to crumble. Within his own party, Warner struggled to manage defectors and abstainers. But the true threat to the bill came from the Republican side: Republicans just didn't want to trust Joe Biden with that much power. They didn't trust him to actually follow through and ban Gen Z's favorite app, and they didn't trust him not to use RESTRICT to go after their platforms of choice, like Elon Musk's X (formerly Twitter) or Trump's own Truth Social, whose owners had their own ties to foreign autocrats.

John Thune, Warner's co-leader on RESTRICT and the Senate Republican whip, appeared not to have actually whipped the votes necessary to advance the bill. And on March 27, just four days after Shou's hearing, then–Fox News host Tucker Carlson ran a segment about the law that would effectively kill it.

Caricaturing the platform itself as "a creepy low-IQ Chinese plot designed to make your kids trans," Carlson rounded on what he saw as the bigger, badder enemy: the US government. Carlson saw unanimity among senators as a cause for suspicion: "This is one of those weird moments where there is or appears to be some kind of bipartisan consensus and that alone might want to make you pause for a second. If everyone in power is saying the same thing, is it really a good idea?"

In his characteristically provocative tone, Carlson cast the lawmakers trying to ban TikTok as more dangerous than the platform itself.

"This bill would give enormous and terrifying new powers to the federal government to punish American citizens and regulate how they communicate with one another," he said. "You would be allowing the executive branch, the Biden administration, to regulate speech on the internet and if you are somehow involved with a 'foreign adversary' or let's say you oppose the war against Russia, you go to prison for twenty years. So, this isn't about banning TikTok. This is about introducing flat out totalitarianism into our system."

The RESTRICT Act would not have introduced totalitarianism into American law, which had for many decades unambiguously protected citizens from speaking out against wars they opposed. Carlson's description was alarmist, but it was based on a shred of truth. The bill would, if it became law, give future presidents a great deal of control over how speech happened online, and which speech was most widely distributed.

Concern over that new power extended beyond Carlson to civil liberties groups like the Electronic Frontier Foundation and the ACLU, which wrote that the bill "could cut off the flow of information, art, and communication that social media provides, interfering with communities and connections users in the United States have with each other and with people around the world." Some language in the bill could also have imposed criminal penalties on individual app users using VPNs or other methods to avoid a TikTok ban—a point that alarmed liberals and civil libertarians. Warner's staff insisted that targeting individuals was not the bill's intent, but he declined to amend its language.

After the Carlson segment, other Fox hosts piled on. Senator Lindsay Graham, a cosponsor of the bill, gave an interview to Fox News' Jesse Watters, who described the bill as "garbage." Graham responded, with a blank look on his face, "I don't think I support the RESTRICT Act." He then asked Watters for clarification about what the RESTRICT Act did.

"We got S686 right here," said Watters, reading from a printed document. "And we got a bunch of Republicans supporting it. Because—this thing is crazy town. You don't want the government looking into your private phone on a hunch that you're colluding with the Russians—we remember how that turned out."

Graham replied: "Let me come back and give you a better explanation." He would never have to, because RESTRICT would never come up for a vote.

~

THE FALL OF RESTRICT was a massive victory for Michael and his team. It was also a blow to Newman and Rosen at CFIUS, who had ordered ByteDance to sell TikTok, but were worried they could not enforce their order. But the bill had scrambled the usual political polarizations, and coaxed dozens of lawmakers to state their support for a TikTok ban.

Mavericks like Mark Warner often come in too hot to see their plans through to the end—but sometimes, they create space for others to do so. As the RESTRICT Act was imploding, Republican staffers for House Majority Leader Steve Scalise and Energy and Commerce Chair Cathy McMorris Rodgers began a series of secret meetings about introducing another, as-yet-unnamed bill. They had agreed to operate quietly, starting first with just the Republican leaders of the relevant committees: Michael McCaul on Foreign Affairs, Mike Gallagher on China Select, and McMorris Rodgers's staff at Energy and Commerce.

Gallagher, of course, had his own TikTok bill, the ANTI-SOCIAL CCP Act, which he had introduced with his committee co-chair Raja Krishnamoorthi. McCaul had introduced one too, known as the DATA Act. But the Scalise staffer running the negotiations—an easygoing Nebraskan attorney named Bijan Koohmaraie—asked them to put their bills aside in favor of a "leadership driven" approach. If a bill was put together and pushed by the House Majority Leader, its chance of going all the way was much higher than the others'.

Koohmaraie, then in his mid-thirties, had spent the better part of a decade as counsel to Majority Leader Scalise—first as an Energy and Commerce staffer (back when Scalise led that committee) and later in the majority leader's office. He knew the personalities at Energy and Commerce, and he knew it was largely a nonpartisan committee. So that's where he decided to draft the bill.

Koohmaraie had studied the successes and failures of RESTRICT, DATA, and ANTI-SOCIAL CCP. RESTRICT had been too broad and too rushed. DATA was partisan—McCaul hadn't even tried to get Democrats on board, which meant the bill might make him look tough, but it had no chance of passing. ANTI-SOCIAL CCP had been laser-focused on TikTok—maybe too targeted for some Democrats, and unlikely to withstand a constitutional challenge. The new bill would have to apply beyond TikTok but only to companies closely analogous to it. It would have to withstand the inevitable court challenge, and it would go nowhere unless it had strong bipartisan support. But E&C was initially insistent about outright banning TikTok.

Despite Koohmaraie's optimism, the new bill went nowhere at Energy and Commerce. The members distrusted TikTok, but they also disagreed about what should be done. To "unjam" the bill, Bijan turned back to the initial anti-TikTok duo, House Select Committee leaders Gallagher and Krishnamoorthi, who assigned the matter to a young lawyer in Krishnamoorthi's office named David Dorfman.

Dorfman was slim, with tawny brown hair, a deliberative affect, and a habit of leaving sentences unfinished as he moved on to his next thought. For years, he had been best known as an actor: he was the child star of the horror movie franchise *The Ring*, and played a central character in the early-2000s CBS TV show *Family Law*. He began college at UCLA at age thirteen and graduated with a perfect GPA four years later. He had then attended Harvard Law School, where he aged gracefully for a child prodigy: he was outgoing and well-liked by classmates, though he was too young to (legally) participate in the weekly Thursday-night drinking ritual known as "Bar Review."

When he received the draft bill from E&C, Dorfman knew there was one critical change they'd have to make: instead of flatly banning TikTok, the bill would need to add a provision allowing ByteDance to sell TikTok to a US company, just as Trump Treasury Secretary Steve Mnuchin had suggested back in 2020 and CFIUS had ordered on March 6.

A forced sale was much less likely to be struck down by the courts than a flat ban. There was clear precedent, both within CFIUS and beyond it, that the government could force companies to sell off subsidiaries or assets for national security reasons. And if TikTok became part of Disney, or Apple, or Microsoft instead of ByteDance, then there would be no national security reason to ban it.

Giving ByteDance the option to sell TikTok, though, wasn't the choice it appeared to be. ByteDance had, of course, nearly sold TikTok in 2020—before it was stymied by a last-minute adjustment to Chinese export controls that asserted CCP control over the algorithm—and with it, the platform.

In 2023, as US legislators had considered the RESTRICT Act, the Chinese government had doubled down on its position, insisting that if ByteDance complied with a forced divestment under US law, it would be breaking Chinese law. Businesspeople in China have disappeared over far less than selling a multi-billion-dollar asset against the government's orders. If executing such a sale without the government were even technically possible, carrying it out would endanger any number of high-ranking ByteDance employees and their families, Yiming's most of all.

Lawmakers in Washington knew this cold war over business assets was brutally unfair. But punishing private companies for the sins of their home country isn't uncommon—it's essentially what tariffs and sanctions often end up doing. Demanding that a company break another country's laws to comply with yours was an aggressive stance, but it was becoming increasingly common in the United States.

This issue came up frequently in US court cases that relied on evidence from China. Lawsuits in the US—both criminal and civil ones—engage in an expansive discovery process before trial. The purpose of discovery is for the parties to exchange all the information (records, documents, witnesses, etc.) that might be relevant to the case, so that they can marshal evidence to refute their opponents' points, or settle and avoid going to trial at all.

But for cases where key evidence is located in China, the US discovery system didn't work, because of the Chinese law, called a "blocking statute," that prevented people from turning over information to foreign authorities without Chinese government sign-off. Chinese law gave Chinese regulators the opportunity to remove anything they don't want Americans to see before they turned the records over, leaving parties in the US unsure whether they were getting the full picture.

Even before TikTok's rise, the US government was becoming less tolerant of China's blocking statute. In 2014, an administrative law judge for the SEC published an order sanctioning the world's four leading accounting firms—Deloitte, KPMG, PWC, and EY—for failing to give the auditor documents that they created in China. The judge was dismissive of the auditors' arguments that they could not turn over the documents, as ordered, because doing so would force them to violate Chinese law.

"To the extent the Respondents found themselves between a rock and a hard place, it is because they wanted to be there. A good faith effort to obey the law means a good faith effort to obey all law, not just the law that one wishes to follow," he wrote.

ByteDance, too, had chosen to put itself between a rock and a hard place. But so had Microsoft, Apple, Tesla, many of the world's largest law firms, and every other company that was attempting to do business in both the United States and China. GE Appliances, Volvo, and Smithfield Foods were Chinese-owned, and while the US government wasn't yet forcing those firms to violate Chinese law, it wasn't hard to imagine circumstances under which it might. Courts might order those companies to turn over Chinese records (or lawmakers might pass laws requiring divestment) if they believed, for example, that Chinese engineers working at GE or Volvo could be required to add malware or spyware to cars sold in the US, or that executives at Smithfield (the US's largest pork producer) might manipulate the US food supply.

When there is conflict between US laws and the laws of another country, US courts generally give international laws "comity"—a squishy sort of deference—when doing so doesn't fundamentally hamstring US interests. In cases where evidence located in China is just tangential, a US judge might invoke comity to let an incomplete production of evidence slide. But in a situation like TikTok's, where the fundamental tussle was about which country's law would ultimately win out, the whole idea of comity broke down.

For some hawks on Capitol Hill, the breakdown was the point. The Chinese government had long kept American companies out of China, propped up local competitors to steal their market share, and demanded concessions from the Americans determined to offer their wares in China. Some American lawmakers were ready to return the favor: they would give ByteDance the chance to sell, demonstrating once and for all that TikTok wasn't a threat. But ByteDance would decline the chance, and thereby prove who it *really* answered to: the CCP.

In his RESTRICT rabble-rousing, Mark Warner had expressed this same idea: "At the end of the day, TikTok, ByteDance—their first loyalty has to be to the [Chinese] Communist Party."

Their first *loyalty*.

The US has an unfortunate history with loyalty tests, going back to one of Mike Gallagher's predecessors in Wisconsin politics: Senator Joseph McCarthy, whose infamous scorched-earth campaigns against alleged communists infringed on citizens' civil rights and harmed innocent people.

But Gallagher and others who sponsored ban bills didn't see their legislation as a new red scare. The US intelligence community and members of both parties had concerns about ByteDance. And the Chinese government was unambiguous about its own loyalty tests, not least of which was the 2017 National Intelligence Law that created the mess in the first place.

Instead, bill sponsors saw forced divestment as analogous to other loyalty tests that are uncontroversial in the US today. You have to pass one before joining the US military—and you also can't own a broadcast television or radio station unless you're a US citizen, or you otherwise receive express permission from the US government.

Congress enacted this prohibition as part of the Communications Act of 1934, based on concerns that foreign powers might spread misinformation and propaganda over domestic airwaves during wartime. In the early twenty-first century, the rule was somewhat relaxed as our sources of information became more diverse and their power diluted. Still, for the most part, the restrictions remained—Rupert Murdoch, for example, had to become a US citizen before he could buy the TV stations that would become Fox and Fox News.

If control over TikTok's For You algorithm should trigger a US government loyalty test, then control over similar algorithms at Meta, Google, Snap, and Twitter likely should too, along with companies making other sensitive technologies, like generative AI, power plants, and Big Pharma. Exactly what that loyalty test should require, though, is another question. Even under a TikTok ban law, the US government wouldn't have the power the Chinese government had given itself: if the FBI asked Meta or Google employees to secretly re-weight their recommendations algorithms, they would be entitled to politely (or impolitely) refuse.

In fall 2023, TikTok's opponents again found a willing partner in the Biden White House. The Department of Justice offered Koohmaraie, Dorfman, and their colleagues what is known as "technical assistance": DOJ lawyers would help draft the new law so that it would stand the best chance possible when TikTok inevitably challenged it in court. They would also help with whipping votes: quietly, White House officials began talking to their contacts on the Hill, asking what exactly they would need to see in the law to get on board.

There is a saying among sports fans that supporting a team is really just "rooting for laundry." As soon as you get properly attached to your team's star midfielder, he gets traded to the team's archrival, and you can't root for him anymore. You might like the new midfielder less (perhaps he's a cad, or a racist, or is just not as good at advancing the ball as the former guy), but you've got to root for him anyway, because he's the guy wearing your team's uniform.

This same idea applies to grants of presidential power. When lawmakers give the office of the president new powers, they are not supporting a certain president or administration—you never know who the next president will be—instead, they are giving a vote of confidence to the White House as an institution. They are making a decision about how much power future White Houses should have over a given thing: in this case, foreign technology companies and online speech.

As Koohmaraie, Dorfman, and the Biden White House worked to write a law that would increase presidential authority, they knew they might be creating a potential vector for abuse of power. It was just a few years earlier that then-President Trump had tried to throw a potential sale of TikTok from Microsoft to Oracle, because he personally favored the conservative billionaire Larry Ellison over Microsoft's more cautious, less political Satya Nadella. One could imagine more egregious meddling of a similar type: a president letting legitimate national security threats slide because they came from a nation that supported him, or one targeting foreigners whose only crime was crossing the president.

This is the problem with loyalty tests: it's always a human being who enforces them.

Chapter 29

"NO INSULT TO BYTEDANCE . . ."

When Nnete Matima joined ByteDance as a salesperson in 2022, her colleagues quickly learned she was multitalented. She was a lawyer, though she didn't practice law anymore. She had been a competitive gymnast and run her own jewelry company, and she still moonlighted as a TV, film, and Off-Broadway actor.

At ByteDance, Matima didn't work on TikTok. Instead, she joined the business development department at Lark, the work superapp, which ByteDance had begun selling to other businesses as a competitor to Slack, G Suite, and Microsoft Teams. She was an experienced salesperson, ready to tackle a large set of leads. But she quickly learned that her boss had given her more aggressive goals than her similarly situated colleagues. He also often spoke down to her, with an attitude that he didn't use when addressing other people.

Matima was the only Black person on her forty-person team—and before long, her colleagues noticed her boss's hostility toward her. In early 2023, she heard from a friend that both her boss and another manager on her team were referring to her as a "Black Snake." One of the men had apparently assigned a snake as her "spirit animal," and then regularly used it to describe her to other employees on the team.

Horrified, she filed an internal ethics complaint. But soon thereafter, she learned she wasn't the only Black employee struggling at the company. She connected with Joël Carter, a policy manager who worked on the team that enforced TikTok's ban on political ads, as well as its other rules for paid promotions. Carter was a top performer on his team, but he learned that he was underpaid in comparison to his white and Asian colleagues, and that he had been excluded from team gatherings, including a key policy summit in London in early 2023.

After experiencing what he believed was discrimination, Carter had posted in a Lark channel for the company's Black employee resource group, BLXCK, to share his experience and ask his colleagues for advice. Senior TikTok leaders later questioned him about the post, and advised him to leave TikTok and the tech industry entirely.

In 2023, Matima and Carter began working with lawyers to file a charge against ByteDance with the Equal Employment Opportunity Commission (EEOC), alleging that the company had a pattern and practice of discriminatory behavior.

Matima and Carter's EEOC charge made national news, and drew outrage from TikTok's celebrated Black community of creators and commentators. The charge was also soon bolstered by another complaint—one filed by a white TikTok sales executive, Katie Puris, who said she had faced discrimination from ByteDance's Chinese leadership because she was a woman. Puris claimed ByteDance's head of sales, Zhang Lidong, had fired her in part because she "celebrated her team's successes and achievements," rather than "always remain[ing] humble and express[ing] modesty" in a more stereotypically "feminine" manner.

Puris's experience was consistent with the stories of other women at ByteDance. Companies like Twitter and Google offered their young professional staff extensive benefits to start a family; at Facebook, new parents received a $4,000 bonus in "baby cash" when they had a newborn, as well as stipends for childcare and lactation rooms in offices. But one employee in TikTok's early L.A. office described hearing a Chinese ByteDance executive—herself a thirty-something woman—discourage her reports from hiring women because they might get pregnant. In 2022, another senior executive in London "stepped back" from his role after he allegedly told his team that he "didn't believe in" maternity leave.

Workers are willing to overlook a lot when they work for the company behind their friends' favorite app. But when they think their employer is greedy, or bigoted, or untruthful, then every bungled corporate training and tone-deaf all-hands become cause for unmitigated disdain. Mired in scandal and bruised by its first congressional standoff, TikTok was a much less sexy place to work in 2023 than it had been in 2021 or 2022, and the company began to strain its employees' loyalty further than it ever had before.

In 2023, ByteDance announced, to the great relief of its US employees, that it would be launching a stock buyback program. For most staff, the buyback program was their first and only opportunity to net tens if not hundreds of thousands of dollars promised in their employment agreements. Most ByteDance staff were paid through the classic Big Tech combination of cash (base salary), bonuses (paid in cash), and restricted stock units (RSUs). But unlike employees at TikTok's main competitors, which were public companies, ByteDance employees couldn't sell their RSUs after they earned them. Because ByteDance was private, the RSUs were "monopoly money": they might someday be worth something, but they also might not.

By offering to buy back stock, ByteDance was offering to convert its workers' monopoly money into real money. But employees quickly learned that participating in the buyback came with a set of nightmarish conditions. ByteDance told the IRS that all of their employees' stock grants were now taxable, because of the buyback—but there were limits on how much stock employees could actually sell. This meant that many employees had incurred large tax liabilities (hundreds of thousands of dollars, for some) for grants of stock that they couldn't sell.

ByteDance also valued the stock at different prices for different people: it offered to buy current employees' stock for more than former employees' stock. But it had told the IRS that all the stock was worth what it charged current employees, again leaving former staffers with tax bills on money they hadn't received.

There were other problems with the buyback system, too. One former employee noted that the platform ByteDance used to buy back shares was housed in Feishu, the company's Chinese version of Lark. The platform required employees to sign a contract agreeing to "comply with applicable [Chinese] laws and guidelines and abide by public order and good customs, the socialist system, [and Chinese] national interests" before they could access their stock grants. Another employee sent a letter to the IRS and Department of Labor disputing a clause in the stock agreement that said that the company could "claw back" stock granted to employees if they made any critical statements about the company, even after they'd left it.

ByteDance also began facing more direct confrontation from its employees. In early 2024, Roland's successor as head of TikTok's Global Security Organization told colleagues she was worried that a group of security staffers began compiling hundreds of internal documents that they claimed showed that ByteDance had misled regulators and auditors about whether the company was compliant with credit card payment standards.

Two of the employees said they would go to the media with evidence of illegal conduct by TikTok unless the company paid them a seven-figure sum to keep quiet, the executive said.

Their threat reached the very highest levels of ByteDance leadership. More than a year into the standoff, one director told colleagues that Erich Andersen favored paying the staffers off, just to make the issue go away. But the director said Shou Zi Chew opposed the payoff on principle—if these guys could extract cash for not leaking, they wouldn't be the last employees to do so.

The staffers never did end up going to the press, so far as I know, though reporters found many of the issues they'd raised anyway. But there were other leakers, like Rob Doe and "Brad," who began taking their concerns straight to law enforcement.

One of the first TikTok whistleblowers to call the police was a former TikTok moderator, who worked for ByteDance through a contractor until 2021. Whitney Turner was tasked with finding and removing inappropriate videos from TikTok, including images and videos of child sexual abuse. Turner understood that some degree of exposure to abuse content was necessary, but ByteDance handled those videos very differently than other, similarly situated companies.

As Turner later told *Forbes*'s Alexandra Levine, she and hundreds of her colleagues had been trained to identify child abuse material through a Lark spreadsheet known as the "Daily Required Reading" or "DRR," which contained hundreds of images of child sexual abuse material (known as CSAM).

Sharing CSAM, even among Trust and Safety professionals for content moderation purposes, is highly regulated, and springing graphic images on hundreds of unsuspecting workers was almost certainly a violation of US law.

Beyond the "DRR," staff also encountered CSAM in Lark chats, including threads containing thousands of members. A T&S employee noticed that after sensitive personal user information was posted in one chat, a colleague then deleted it. He likely did so because someone told him that sharing the images had been improper or illegal. But deleting the images made it harder for US investigators to determine whether a crime had occurred.

At the time, ByteDance's decisions about which corporate records to retain and which to delete weren't governed by any sort of internal records policy. Nothing prevented staff from deleting evidence of wrongdoing in Lark, and nothing prevented them from keeping information in violation of laws like California's CCPA and the EU's GDPR.

In 2023, a group of TikTok lawyers and policy staff gathered on a Lark call to discuss their lack of a corporate data retention policy. An IT governance manager told the group he had met with "our most senior leaders"—presumably some subset of the ByteDance C-Suite—who told him they opposed deleting even one pixel of information, because they wanted the freedom to mine data from the company's full history without constraint. At least in some cases, though, holding on to data like that could be illegal.

"No insult to ByteDance," one lawyer joked, "Whatever server is recording this call—oh, we know it's not going to get deleted."

"This is Feishu, this isn't Lark," he added, reminding colleagues that the meeting was occurring through ByteDance's China-based workplace software app, Feishu, not its "non-China" equivalent, Lark, which is based in Singapore. Feishu records were stored in China and subject to inspections by the Chinese Communist Party.

~

IN EARLY 2024, nearly a year after Shou's testimony, a *Fortune* reporter named Alexandra Sternlicht published a story in which a ByteDance employee from 2022 described emailing spreadsheets to employees in Beijing that contained hundreds of thousands of US TikTok users' personal information, like their names, email addresses, IP addresses, and demographic information.

The employee had worked in ads, and the data transfer was for ad-targeting purposes, not espionage. But still, this type of large-scale data transfer was exactly what China hawks had warned might happen—once the data was in the hands of Chinese staff, the Chinese government might shake them down for it.

TikTok's corporate Twitter account responded aggressively. It called the story "factually inaccurate" and said it "deliberately distorts timelines, omits basic facts, and relies on disgruntled former employees as its primary sourcing."

"If this reporter had done any research into what actually occurs at TikTok, she would know that the scenarios laid out are not only forbidden by policy, but are also subject to controls in place that prevent data sharing," the company continued.

It might as well have been December 2022. Again, TikTok spokespeople were attacking a reporter on Twitter, alleging that she hadn't done her homework—and again, those spokespeople seemingly hadn't done theirs.

The company claimed that its Project Texas systems made it impossible for employees to transfer data in the way the *Fortune* article described. As of January 2023, it said, "new protected U.S. user data was inaccessible to anyone outside of USDS." ByteDance had clearly made data transfer back to China more difficult than they once had been. But its systems just weren't as secure as it claimed they were—and the company's lawyers knew it.

Between January 2023 and the time *Fortune* published their article, ByteDance's ethics team received at least seven internal complaints about violations of Project Texas, five of which specifically described improper data sharing.

In two incidents in the spring and summer of 2023, US employees had given foreign employees their laptops and login credentials, which the foreign staffers had used to exfiltrate data. A Chinese member of TikTok's T&S team had also lifted a ban on a US account, which he shouldn't have been able to do.

In an incident in November 2023, a TikTok engineer noticed that someone in Shanghai had reconfigured one of his databases, introducing errors into a system he was responsible for. The engineer, after identifying his "culprit" colleague, sent him an unsubtle note:

Please be formally notified that you now own the data_service_search_ttp cluster repair in TTP. I fixed this broken Yellow cluster yesterday. Last night US Time, you modified the configuration to something incorrect and now the cluster is back to YELLOW. I am not going to continue to fix this issue if you are going to continue to cause it. Please fix this cluster. I am including my Team Lead on this notification to you because 1) You should be fixing clusters and not breaking them and 2) I'm pretty sure you accessing the TTP ElasticSearch cluster and modifying their configuration is a violation of Project Texas 3) I have reported this issue to USTS Ethics Oncall.
PLEASE ACKNOWLEDGE THAT YOU UNDERSTAND THIS MESSAGE.

Cybersecurity is a "last mile" problem. It's easy to stop most of the leaks most of the time, but it's nearly impossible to stop all leaks all of the time. "Not if, but when" is a slogan of the industry: data leaks are a part of life. And the problem with Project Texas—the original sin of the whole setup—was the idea that it couldn't be subject to ByteDance error.

Nothing in cybersecurity has a 100 percent success rate. As CFIUS had determined nearly a year before, as long as TikTok was a part of

ByteDance, some data leakage from child to parent was essentially guaranteed, especially if employees from TikTok's US branch and ByteDance continued to regularly collaborate.

But legally, that didn't matter. Project Texas was not yet (and seemed unlikely to ever be) a legally enforceable promise, so the company wasn't liable for violations of it. Nothing except ByteDance's own word prevented it from allowing data seepage back to China.

So ByteDance plowed ahead with Project Texas, on the theory that it might still persuade some members of Congress, or at least stop more restrictive proposals from gaining steam. Both Donald Trump and Mark Warner had tried to force ByteDance to sell TikTok and failed. And with the platform more popular than ever—and an election around the corner—perhaps the company could keep up its luck.

Chapter 30

ENSHITTIFICATION

In 2023, TikTok also began navigating another type of limbo, too: a subtle but palpable shift in the app's identity. When any business hits truly mainstream adoption, it sheds some of what made it lovable before it scaled. Starbucks transformed from a quirky Seattle coffeehouse to a fast-food juggernaut, and Facebook grew from a college flirting ground into a mirror for the memories of billions of people. Both made enormous money from their transformations, but something was lost as they grew.

"Something's changed with TikTok; I know you feel it, too," wrote internet culture savant Katie Notopoulos. As it comes for all companies, the beigeness of scale had come for TikTok, and—as it usually is—the goal was maximizing profits.

When startups reach this moment, the demands on their executives begin to change. There are two kinds of CEOs in Silicon Valley: those who are ultimately in charge, and those who aren't. Generally, this is determined based on ownership: founders like Mark Zuckerberg and Evan Spiegel both own and control the companies they founded; whereas professional executives like Amazon CEO Andy Jassy and Oracle CEO Safra Catz ultimately follow the direction of their founder-owners, Jeff Bezos and Larry Ellison.

Shou Zi Chew was in the second category. He wasn't ByteDance's founder or owner, but his job was to carry out the wishes of that person—Zhang Yiming—and the rest of the ByteDance C-Suite. Shou took a while to grow into his own as TikTok's CEO. As smart executives do, he learned and listened, and soon enough realized that he only had two jobs: don't get banned, and make money.

"Don't get banned" took up the first few months of 2023. But after RESTRICT fizzled, Shou shifted his efforts to ByteDance's two biggest bets of the 2020s: livestreaming and e-commerce.

The financial benefits of livestreaming were simple—like Twitch, Kick, and other platforms, TikTok enabled watchers of a stream to give cash "gifts" to livestreamers, of which the platform would take a 50 percent cut. The e-commerce business, which the company branded as TikTok Shop, was more complicated. It looked and functioned more like Amazon than YouTube or Instagram, but it would also eventually become one of the company's chief sources of revenue.

ByteDance introduced e-commerce into the Douyin app in China in 2018. It was a moderate success, which then ballooned in 2020, when locked-down shoppers began buying more of their goods online. Most sales through Douyin happened during livestreams, where sellers would model or otherwise display their goods in ads that felt like hyperactive QVC commercials. The streamers would often rely on scarcity as a rationale—"buy now, only 10 available" or "buy one get half off, if you buy in the next 10 minutes."

ByteDance was eager to transplant its newest success from China to the rest of the world, and TikTok Shop quickly took off in Southeast Asia. But tests in the US and Europe flopped—shopping was culturally different in the West than it was in Asia. Most mainstream US corporations avoided scarcity marketing, which had become associated with late-night infomercials, no-name brands, and merchandise of questionable quality. Most buyers in Western markets had come to expect time to think before they purchased, and some were turned off by the pressure of disappearing offers and limited supply.

Many of the creators who had made TikTok what it is—and the creator-managers within TikTok that had made them succeed behind the scenes—also weren't wild about the company's new focus on getting people to buy stuff. Members of the livestreaming and e-commerce teams, who reported to Shou, started reaching out to creators whom V Pappas's team had long managed, asking them to become TikTok Shop salespeople, a move that rankled both long-term creator-managers and some of the app's most fervent users.

Kaytlyn Stewart, a TikToker with more than 2 million followers, turned to YouTube to publish a video titled "Tiktok Shop Has DESTROYED Tiktok." She captioned the video: "it's just a shilling session 24/7!!!" In another YouTube video titled "tiktok shop has RUINED tiktok," creator Allie Tricaso said: "TikTok is just a giant dropshipping platform now." Drop-shipping—a practice where online sellers advertise goods at a markup and sell them to customers without ever actually possessing them—was now rampant on TikTok.

In part, the influx of dropshippers was ByteDance's answer to two other apps that had exploded onto the US ecommerce scene: Shein, a Chinese fast-fashion brand, and Temu, an Amazon-style marketplace run by Colin Huang's Pinduoduo, which was flooded with shockingly cheap (and shoddily made) home goods, clothes, and other widgets and gadgets.

While TikTok Shop had initially targeted partnerships with established brands, like Nike and Nordstrom, it quickly pivoted in a plan known as "Project S" (after Shein). ByteDance created its own fast-fashion labels, including a clothing shop inside the Douyin app and two labels—If Yooou and Dmonstudio—targeted to women in Western markets. Meanwhile, sellers on TikTok Shop began offering many of the exact same goods that were for sale on Temu, Amazon, and elsewhere.

ByteDance's frenetic push into shopping was part of a larger trend. In early 2023, a journalist and tech critic named Cory Doctorow published an essay in *Wired* called "The Enshittification of TikTok." Doctorow's thesis was that most Silicon Valley platforms experience a cycle that he calls enshittification: first, they focus on growth, which means making their users happy (think of Instagram before it was riddled with ads, or Lyft and Uber giving out free rides). Once they've secured a loyal user base, the platforms turn their focus to revenue, sacrificing users' experience to keep advertisers happy. Finally, they turn away from their advertisers, too, and focus on profit, sacrificing even advertisers' experience to claw back as much margin for themselves as they possibly can.

For decades, perhaps even centuries, companies have found success with the "loss leader" strategy, offering unrealistic prices to secure customers and beat out the competition, establish a monopoly, and then jack up prices to make a profit. Successful loss leaders, though, had to help the company reach the monopoly stage—or otherwise convince their customers to keep using their product even after the price hikes. Otherwise, they'd be abandoned.

Facebook, Doctorow said, was an example of a company that was "terminally enshittified"—it had only been worthwhile before it was profitable. By bludgeoning its users with ads, in-app services, and desperate new product features, the company had used up all its customer goodwill. People had left, and since those same people and their connectedness had been the platform's primary purpose, the app itself had dried into a husk of its former self.

Now, TikTok was at risk of the same fate. As Notopoulos wrote: "The For You used to seem uncanny in how it would serve up content perfectly tailored to me. Now it feels like the algorithm is less a diagnostic tool of my soul and instead is assessing me as a potential consumer."

~

IN FEBRUARY 2023, TikTok breathed a last gasp of its quirky, authentic self when, over a chilly weekend, V Pappas had sat down, opened their Lark profile, and updated a field that reflected their preferred pronouns. V had identified as a woman since they were young, and identified as a lesbian when they married their wife, a literary agent turned Eastern medicine practitioner named CC Hirsch. But as V and CC parented their children, V felt that identifying as a woman was incomplete. They were pansexual and nonbinary, and they wanted to model the courage to say so, both in their family life and in public.

So in a message on Lark—quickly re-shared on LinkedIn and Twitter—V explained their thinking: "Since representation matters, I recognize the importance of language in identifying and affirming gender differences. As a parent I also want to set an example on how it is ok to represent yourself in a way that you most identify with and to have pride and to celebrate such difference."

V was the first major leader at any company as large or prominent as ByteDance to come out as nonbinary. Their announcement went viral on Twitter and was celebrated in queer communities, and they quickly received an outpouring of support from creators, parents, and employees. V was the person who had built the TikTok they knew and loved, and their coming out seemed like a celebration of the company's values.

But just months later, after nearly five years at ByteDance, V would relinquish their position. In June 2023, V, the only non-male member of TikTok's executive team—who was also its longest-serving non-Chinese executive—announced that they would be stepping down.

V wasn't like Shou—they didn't thirst for the limelight, and they weren't driven by money. They had kids and a wife they hadn't seen enough of for years, and a storybook farmhouse in Ojai where the pace would be slower and they might finally get to enjoy the Southern California sun. But their departure was a brutal loss for TikTok's rank and file.

Where other executives had been hostile to their staff having children, V had been a model boss for new parents, genuinely effusing over every detail of her reports' parental milestones. Those whom V had protected and fought for in the early days, and the company's queer and nonbinary staff, were also especially sorry to see their leader go. Without V, who would stand up for them to the execs in Singapore and Beijing?

As Shou had grown into his role as TikTok's CEO, V's power internally had ebbed. The company was gradually turning in a new direction. V had been the champion of TikTok's homegrown celebrities, its creators. The happiness and success of the young people who lived on TikTok had always been V's lodestar—more than it had ever been Shou's.

V—and Alex Zhu before them—had grown TikTok into an American behemoth by obsessing over how to keep users happy. Now, more than 150 million US users were solidly hooked, and entire businesses had built up around TikTok's information ecosystem. Shou wanted the company to start cashing in on its user goodwill, and set aggressive goals for advertising revenue. And between the renewed focus on advertisers and the new, ByteDance-wide e-commerce efforts, growth was no longer TikTok's ultimate goal, and neither was user satisfaction.

Chapter 31

"LOL HEY GUYS"

On February 11, 2024, the Kansas City Chiefs faced the San Francisco 49ers in Paradise, Nevada, in the fifty-eighth Super Bowl in NFL history. President Joe Biden, whose three years as president had left him feeble and diminished, had turned down the traditional presidential Super Bowl interview. This set off alarm bells in DC about whether the eighty-year-old president was hiding signs of cognitive decline. So his team decided to shake up the mass television spectacle in a new way: during the game, a new user posted on TikTok for the first time, with a video captioned "lol hey guys." It was the Biden campaign.

The video featured Biden standing in a quarter-zip sweater with his hands in his khaki pants, answering questions from a staffer off-screen. "Chiefs or Niners? Game or halftime show? Jason Kelce or Travis Kelce?" (Biden answered that one, awkwardly, "Mama Kelce—I hear she makes great chocolate chip cookies.") The final question was "Trump or Biden," in response to which the president unsurprisingly endorsed himself.

The video didn't make Biden look any younger, but it was a coup for TikTok. Less than a year after Biden had vowed to ban TikTok, he appeared to have softened his stance.

Bijan Koohmaraie, tuning in from a wedding in Cancún over Super Bowl weekend, was stunned. His entire campaign to pass a TikTok ban law seemed to crumble before his eyes. "At that moment, I thought it was probably over," he later told me. The campaign stunt had come just days after Koohmaraie and his team convinced seven Democratic lawmakers, positioned across the key committees, to help introduce the new bill.

"They finally said, we're willing to jump with you," he said.

With a sick feeling in the pit in his stomach, Koohmaraie spent the rest of the game setting up meetings for the following week. But to his surprise, when he returned to Washington, the Biden administration was holding firm. "They were critical of the decision" that the campaign had made to join TikTok, "and they said 'we are not abandoning this effort.'"

In part, Democrats joined Koohmaraie because another political issue had exploded on TikTok: the gruesome war in Gaza. Older Americans overwhelmingly supported Israel, while young people largely sympathized with Palestinian civilians.

TikTok, with its famously young user base, became a destination for pro-Palestinian speech, and while most of that speech was peaceful, there were exceptions. In November, a group of young American TikTokers discovered a twenty-year-old manifesto condemning US imperialism in the Middle East, which had been written by Osama bin Laden. Titled "Letter to America," the screed was anti-Semitic, and aimed to justify mass murder. But TikTokers said it opened their minds and revealed another side to the September 11, 2001, terrorist attacks. Within hours, posts about the letter amassed more than 15 million views on the platform.

The Letter to America horrified lawmakers. TikTok aggressively played whack-a-mole with posts that mentioned it, but the damage was done: the For You page had promoted terrorist propaganda to a bunch of young Americans in the middle of a hot war. Fear that TikTok was exposing teens to violent, hateful ideologies gave Mike Gallagher and Raja Krishnamoorthi the boost they needed to secure cosponsors.

In the days that followed, David Dorfman, Bijan Koohmaraie, and their colleagues made the final preparations to introduce their bill. Dorfman had given it a name: the Protecting Americans from Foreign Adversary Controlled Applications Act, or PAFACAA. The group had spent months anticipating how TikTok and ByteDance would challenge the bill in court, and crafted it to be maximally resistant to the company's constitutional arguments. The lawmakers backing the bill went out of their way to frame it as a forced divestment rather than a ban. CFIUS forced divestments all the time, even if in this case it might not have jurisdiction to do so.

As David Newman had put it: "If tomorrow, someone tried to buy a social media application who was based in China and subject to the control of the Chinese government, or the Russian government, or the Iranian government, our CFIUS process would never allow that to happen. . . . it's a significant and notable gap that where something can grow organically across borders" it can become "suddenly beyond the purview of the US government."

On March 5, after nearly a year of secret backchanneling, Gallagher and Krishnamoorthi introduced PAFACAA, with eighteen other house members named as co-leaders of the bill and an additional thirty-five co-sponsors. They knew the Biden administration, particularly Deputy Attorney General Lisa Monaco, had helped whip key Democratic votes, so they moved fast. Almost immediately, Cathy McMorris Rodgers announced that the Energy and Commerce Committee would hold a classified briefing on the bill and then vote on it just two days later, on March 7, 2024.

Unlike RESTRICT, PAFACAA was narrow: it said that TikTok and ByteDance would have to be sold by their foreign owners within 180 days—a clock that would start immediately upon the bill's passage. If the app's foreign owners refused to divest under the bill, then TikTok (along with the other ByteDance apps in the United States) would be banned.

The law wasn't only directed at TikTok. Similarly situated apps—like the next Huawei or Kaspersky Labs—could be designated by the president to receive the same sale-or-ban mandate. But the president couldn't change the mandate against TikTok and ByteDance; he could only make one, limited alteration to the bill's timeline: he could issue a one-time, ninety-day extension if he certified to Congress that real progress was being made toward a divestiture.

McMorris Rodgers's decision to force a vote on the bill just two days after it was announced was a clear tactic, Koohmaraie told me—an effort to prevent ByteDance's lobbyists from having a chance to sway the lawmakers. This was also why he had kept the drafting effort secret for as long as possible. Without the company spending millions on lobbying campaigns, "we could work behind closed doors freely, negotiate among ourselves." But if the company had learned about the bill too early, he believed they could have stopped it: "It's just a resources game."

Predictably, the company was furious. The US lobbying system has long propped up a kind of soft corruption ("if you don't crack down on us, we'll donate millions to your campaign"). Koohmaraie's own Republican Party had embraced the idea that companies have speech rights, and spending money to lobby lawmakers is a form of speech. The lawmakers' backstage drafting process had denied Michael Beckerman and his team an opportunity to make their case against the bill. They shrieked that secret drafting was undemocratic. The bill "was crafted in secret . . . exactly because it is a ban that Americans will find objectionable," one TikTok spokesperson said.

ByteDance didn't have time to throw around money, to buy ads, or even meet with lawmakers to kill the bill before the vote; Michael's team needed something that would have an immediate effect. The platform now had 170 million US users, more people than had voted in the last presidential election. So Michael's team pulled out the classic Silicon Valley emergency playbook: they recruited the platform's users to become its lobbyists.

Years earlier, Uber and Lyft were faced with state employment laws that would've required them to offer their drivers benefits as if they were proper employees, rather than hourly gig workers. The companies were so threatened by the potential laws that they put pop-ups directly into the Uber and Lyft apps, trashing lawmakers who supported the measure, and imploring users to lobby their local officials.

With only hours before the vote, TikTok's team hastily drew up pop-up messages of their own, and made them the first thing users would see when they opened the app. They hit users' phones on the morning of the 7th—the day the Energy and Commerce Committee was planning to vote.

Stop a TikTok shutdown

Congress is planning a total ban of TikTok. Speak up now—before your government strips 170 million Americans of their Constitutional right to free expression. This will damage millions of businesses, destroy the livelihoods of countless creators around the country, and deny artists an audience. **Let Congress know what TikTok means to you and tell them to vote NO.**

A "call now" button sat beneath the text of TikTok's message. Missing from at least some users' screens, however, was an "x," or any other indication of how to close the call to action. So as millions of people opened TikTok on March 6 and 7, some believed they were locked out of the app until they acquiesced and completed a call.

By noon, the offices of lawmakers were overwhelmed with calls. Many, they said, came from children, and some contained violent threats from people who said they would hurt the lawmakers or themselves if the bill passed.

Senator Thom Tillis received a voicemail from what sounded like a young woman: "If you ban TikTok, I will find you and shoot you," she said before laughing into the phone. "That's people's jobs, and that's my only entertainment. And people make money off there too, you know—I'm trying to get rich like that. Anyways, I'll shoot you and find you and cut you into pieces." She laughed again before ending the call. "Bye!"

The Capitol Police began investigating the threats, at least some of which had come from minors. One representative said his office had received a call from a person who claimed to be his own son.

If the goal had been to show TikTok's popularity—and its influence—then the call campaign was a success. But unlike Uber and Lyft's campaigns, the TikTok instant influence cut both ways. Its popularity meant more people would be unhappy about a ban law, but its popularity also made it a more dangerous potential weapon.

Gallagher and Krishnamoorthi also had another problem with the pop-ups: they considered them misleading. Congress wasn't "planning a total ban of TikTok," they were merely requiring a foreign-controlled company to divest of an asset, the same way CFIUS had repeatedly done. The speech of users and business owners and creators wouldn't be affected, they reasoned, if ByteDance merely sold TikTok to a company that wasn't controlled by a foreign adversary.

"Here you have an example of an adversary-controlled application lying to the American people and interfering with the legislative process in Congress," they said in a joint statement before the vote. And it seemed that most of their colleagues agreed with them.

On the morning of March 7, before the vote, members of the Energy and Commerce Committee filed into the same pseudo-courtroom in the Rayburn Building where they had questioned Shou almost a year before. At the witness table this time were three men: one each from the Office of the Director of National Intelligence, the FBI, and the DOJ. David Newman was DOJ's representative.

Just past 10:30, McMorris Rodgers called the members to order. "As a reminder to the members, we are now in a classified executive session. The information that we discuss here should not be discussed outside of a secure location."

This was lawmakers' chance to ask exactly what the government knew about ByteDance's control over TikTok. Because the answers to these questions were, in part, classified, the lawmakers would hear information that the company itself would never get to hear—information collected by law enforcement agents and informants whose identities could be unmasked, and their lives put at risk, if information they shared became public.

The representative from the Office of the Director of National Intelligence began the briefing with a summary of the evidence the government had amassed about TikTok. He described the app as a latent threat rather than an active one. "Beijing has legal and economic leverage over these companies, and therefore, significant potential leverage over their operations," he said.

David Newman spoke next. "ByteDance presents a clear and present danger to our national security," he said, and TikTok was "a case in point—and perhaps even Exhibit A" of the Chinese government's "attempts to weaponize America's data against us." Newman explained that CFIUS would force a divestment if it could, but DOJ just didn't think it would win on jurisdiction. He was acknowledging that Erich had been right.

"That has left us in something of a legal standoff," he said. And the way to fix that standoff was to pass a new law.

For the next several hours, the lawmakers asked the intelligence experts about how much data TikTok could collect, about whether the Chinese government had TikTok's user data already, and about whether the law, if passed, might actually accelerate data collection efforts. They asked about the antitrust implications of forcing the sale of such an expensive asset, and several mentioned the need to pass a national data privacy law, too.

The witnesses before them, nonpartisan civil servants, were precise, careful not to overstate what they knew about the app. But together they reiterated: as long as TikTok is under ByteDance's control, it could become a weapon at any moment.

At several points, the lawmakers talked about their own framing of the bill. California Democrat Anna Eshoo turned to her colleagues multiple times and insisted that the bill was not a ban. "I think each member needs to stress the following: The United States of America is not banning. We are demanding divestment for the purposes of our national security, full stop."

Divestment, Newman noted, put the Chinese government in a tight spot. "I think for the inverse of the reasons that we are all here today, the Chinese government would want to keep that application controlled in China," he said—but denying ByteDance the right to sell would mean dramatically reducing both TikTok's value and its global cultural force.

"It is a tricky position we put them in, but in my view, a position that they deserve, given their track record in this space."

Toward the end of the session, Mariannette Miller-Meeks, a Republican from Iowa, brought up a prominent Chinese banker named Bao Fan who, in 2023, had disappeared from public life for nearly two weeks. After speculation grew, his firm announced in a filing on the Hong Kong

Stock Exchange that he had been taken in for questioning by Chinese authorities, to "assist with an investigation."

"Given what has happened to Chinese tech owners and CEOs of companies, Jack Ma, Bao Fan," Miller-Meeks asked uneasily, "this is a really weird question, but do we need to put Mr. Chew in protective custody?"

The FBI's China Intelligence Section chief gave a short, classified answer. It was nearly time for the vote.

On the morning of March 7, Koohmaraie predicted that he still had about six or seven Energy and Commerce members who opposed PAFACAA. But by the time the members took the vote—due, perhaps, to the classified briefing and the clogged phone lines—that number had shrunk to zero.

The Energy and Commerce Committee passed PAFACAA in a unanimous vote of 50–0. The full House would vote on the bill the following week.

Chapter 32

PAFACAA

When Donald Trump left the White House in January 2021, many of his colleagues had assumed he was done with presidential politics. Leaders of his own Republican Party had condemned him, and public opinion turned against him after his supporters violently attacked the Capitol and tried to overturn the 2020 election. Trump, however, insisted that he had won the election, and that Joe Biden and the Democrats had stolen it from him.

In private and public moments over the following years, Trump eventually acknowledged that he did not win in 2020. But as he began another campaign to retake the presidency in 2024, he upheld the facade, what media often called the Big Lie, promising to exact revenge on the people who—in his telling—had rigged the previous election.

Trump alleged that one of those people was Meta founder and CEO Mark Zuckerberg. After it became public that Russian state actors had used Facebook as a tool to divide American voters and bolster Trump's candidacy in 2016, Zuckerberg had invested substantially in the company's detection of what it called "coordinated inauthentic behavior" to deceive real users and manipulate discourse. Facebook had also ramped up its attempts to detect false news stories and prevent them from going viral on the platform.

Zuckerberg and his wife, Priscilla Chan, had also privately committed more than $400 million to two nonpartisan election infrastructure nonprofits: The Center for Election Innovation and Research and the Center for Tech and Civic Life. The groups worked to improve civic engagement, voter participation, and trust in the electoral process. They did not endorse candidates or political parties.

Trump nonetheless saw the donations as evidence that Zuckerberg had led a sinister plot to oust him from power in 2020. He railed against Facebook in campaign rallies, and in a privately published 2024 coffee table book, Trump wrote: "We are watching him closely, and if he does anything illegal this time he will spend the rest of his life in prison."

On the evening of March 7, the same day the House Energy and Commerce Committee unanimously voted to advance PAFACAA, Trump made a post on Truth Social, the platform he created after he was banned from Twitter and Facebook in 2021. "If you get rid of TikTok, Facebook and Zuckerschmuck will double their business. I don't want Facebook, who cheated in the last Election, doing better. They are a true Enemy of the People."

A campaign that had begun four years earlier with embarrassment over an empty stadium in Oklahoma had now taken a sudden turn: Trump was willing to keep TikTok (national security concerns be damned) to prevent enriching someone he saw as a political enemy.

Four days later, on March 11, 2024, Trump called into the business television network CNBC and offered viewers a bit of revisionist history: "I could have banned TikTok. I had it banned, just about; I could've gotten it done. But I said, 'you know what, I'll leave it up to you.' I didn't push them too hard, because, you know, let them do their own research and development, and they decided not to do it." Then—the former president had been aggressively targeting young voters, who were disproportionate TikTok users—he made a direct overture to the app's fans: "You know, there are a lot of people on TikTok that love it. There are a lot of young kids on TikTok who will go crazy without it."

Trump's newfound support for TikTok came from the same place as his initial opposition to it: in both cases, he took the action that he believed would most benefit his supporters and hurt his opponents. Seemingly absent from both decisions was any consideration of whether TikTok's Chinese ownership threatened US national interests. His staff clearly had strong (sometimes conflicting) positions on national security policy. But Trump appeared to make no distinction between foreign-controlled platforms and domestic ones—he asked only whether the platforms helped or hurt him.

Trump opposed a TikTok ban because he wanted to be reelected, but there was also money involved. Shortly before PAFACAA was announced, Trump met with an influential billionaire named Jeff Yass who was, at the time, the largest Republican donor in the 2024 election cycle. Yass, a former professional poker player, was one of ByteDance's earliest investors, with roughly $15 billion in ByteDance stock: a fortune he was eager to protect.

Representatives for Trump and Yass claimed that the two men never discussed TikTok. But one person who did talk to Trump about TikTok was Kellyanne Conway, a longtime confidante of the president who was now lobbying for a Yass-backed libertarian think tank called Club for Growth.

Though Club for Growth had been around for decades, it had in recent years become largely a Jeff Yass operation. In 2020, Yass had donated more than $20 million to the organization, which made him one of its two largest donors, alongside brewing heir Richard Uihlein. Opposing a TikTok ban advanced Yass's personal interests, though it was also consistent with the group's free trade stance: Club for Growth had an established history of supporting trade with China and it had long opposed tariffs, including those imposed by Trump during his term in office.

As a Club for Growth lobbyist, Conway advocated for TikTok in meetings on Capitol Hill, warning lawmakers that banning such a popular app would be political malpractice, and would make it harder for Republicans to reach young and minority voters. The organization's lobbyists also suggested to Republicans that Democrats might someday use PAFACAA to crack down on conservative media owners like Elon Musk, who had transformed Twitter (which he had renamed X) into a haven for the Right after he purchased it in 2022.

In a more typical legislative process, these arguments might have disrupted PAFACAA's coalition. But due to David Dorfman and Bijan Koohmaraie's obsessive secrecy, they were too little, too late. On March 13, 2024, the full House of Representatives convened to vote on PAFA-

CAA and passed the bill by a margin of 352–65. Energy and Commerce Chair Cathy McMorris Rodgers addressed the company after the vote: "We have given TikTok a clear choice: Separate from your parent company ByteDance, which is beholden to the CCP (the Chinese Communist Party), and remain operational in the United States, or side with the CCP and face the consequences. The choice is TikTok's."

~

AFTER THE VOTES were counted, Koohmaraie's staff celebrated by covering his desk and chair with printouts of TikToks. He and his counterparts in Gallagher and Krishnamoorthi's offices were ecstatic. Majority Leader Steve Scalise had a cookie-cake delivered to Gallagher's office—a traditional gesture that he made whenever one of his party members got a bill passed by the House.

Still, to become law, the measure would need to also be passed by the Senate, giving ByteDance the chance to lobby against the bill. Michael Beckerman's team began pressing on every front. The Democratic-controlled Senate was somewhat less prone to Sinophobic overreaching than its counterpart across the Capitol; maybe they could be more easily swayed. But ByteDance and Club for Growth were not the only lobbyists targeting senators with messages about the bill.

Representatives from the Chinese embassy also began contacting lawmakers, asking for meetings at which they brought up the TikTok bill. They argued that a crackdown on ByteDance would be unfair to the company's US investors (like Yass), but that it would also be unfairly discriminatory to Chinese businesses. Coming from the official voice of the Chinese government, this argument appeared to undercut the company's insistence that ByteDance was a global company and was not (anymore) fundamentally Chinese.

The Chinese embassy's meetings and public statements opposing the bill almost certainly hurt TikTok more than they helped it. TikTok spokespeople insisted that they had no idea what the embassy was saying about the app. To *Politico*, which first reported the embassy's efforts, one company spokesperson said, "This so-called reporting doesn't pass the smell test and it's irresponsible for *Politico* to print it." The embassy, however, did not contest *Politico*'s reports—instead, it issued a statement saying the "Chinese Embassy in the US tries to tell the truth about the TikTok issue to people from all walks of life in the US."

Michael's team had no choice but to trudge on. They touted a study they had commissioned by an analytics firm called Oxford Economics to claim that TikTok had contributed more than $24 billion to the US economy. They distributed a "one-pager" of talking points aiming to refute the government's talking points, and they again sent a cadre of TikTok superusers to directly lobby their senators and representatives, using the L.A.-based firm Innovate Marketing Group to arrange for fifty TikTokers' stays at the Salamander Hotel and dinners at the posh Bar Spero and José Andrés's Bazaar.

Oracle, which stood to make billions of dollars through Project Texas, also tapped its lobbyists to make the case to lawmakers about how it could keep TikTok users' data safe. Oracle's top lobbyist, Ken Glueck, personally led briefings for staffers on the Senate Intelligence and Commerce committees—which were chaired by influential Democrats Mark Warner and Maria Cantwell.

Warner favored the bill, of course. But Cantwell was seen as a key gatekeeper. After the House vote, she quipped that the bill "could be better." She thought ByteDance should be given more time to find a buyer for TikTok. She disfavored the dual structure that treated TikTok and ByteDance differently than other companies, and would prefer something closer to what Warner had proposed with RESTRICT, where the executive branch would determine which companies posed risks. She also suggested holding a public hearing about the bill before moving it forward: a step that would slow everything down.

But after Secretary of Commerce Gina Raimondo voiced support, Senator Cantwell took her ideas about how to improve the bill to Speaker of the House Mike Johnson, and in under a month, the negotiation was done. The House would agree to one substantive change—lengthening the divestment term from six months to nine, with an optional additional three months at the president's discretion. "I support this updated legislation," Cantwell told the press. The bill would move forward.

~

FOR YEARS NOW, Erich Andersen had served essentially one function at ByteDance: preventing the US government from banning TikTok. But ever since summer 2022, when Project Texas became public—and CFIUS began walking away—he had been skating on thin ice. He had been the architect of a nearly $2 billion project that now looked like it would not achieve its singular purpose, and his attempts at delicate caution had begun to look like foolhardy secrecy.

When a courtroom lawyer knows they've lost a battle, they often change focus: rather than trying to convince a judge who has clearly made up their mind, the lawyer begins laying groundwork for the eventual appeal. Erich—a seasoned attorney—had known for at least eighteen months that his likelihood of persuading CFIUS to accept Project Texas was slim. His continued slew of proposals and presentations were, of course, a last-ditch effort to get the body to reconsider its decision. But they were also a meticulously executed long game for the inevitable day that ByteDance would face the government in court.

Erich had defeated the Trump White House by persuading a judge that the Trump administration's actions had been "arbitrary and capricious"—so unreasonable and baseless that they appeared not to consider the facts at hand. But unlike Trump's CFIUS, the Biden White House had spent years making a record, and had engaged closely with the facts and proposals of Project Texas. It would be much harder to argue that the Biden administration—or even Congress—had acted with disregard to the facts this time.

It had been Michael's job to see PAFACAA coming, not Erich's. But Erich made one last plea after the introduction of the bill, this time, in a letter from his lawyers addressed directly to David Newman. His message was simple: there was no difference between a forced sale and a ban. "The reality—which you know well," the lawyers wrote, "is that there will be no sale of TikTok, qualified or otherwise, and the TikTok platform will cease to exist in the United States."

The lawyers reiterated that ByteDance had no choice: "This is not a matter of our client's 'willingness' or 'unwillingness,'" they wrote. Of course, to the US government, the fact that ByteDance could not disobey Chinese law without endangering its executives and their families was the whole point. It showed that ultimately, ByteDance was still subject to Chinese control.

Directing the letter to Newman would be among Erich's final acts as ByteDance's top attorney. Since the March 2023 decision, he had been making a good record for an eventual appeal, but patience was running short among the executives, Shou Zi Chew, Zhang Yiming, and Liang Rubo—and Erich wanted out, too.

News of Erich's impending departure leaked to *Bloomberg* as the Senate was considering the House bill. There would never be a good time for Erich to go, given that the company was facing open investigations by the Justice Department, the FTC, and was daring CFIUS to sue. Still, this was a particularly bad time. The departure of the company's general counsel while the Senate considered a bill that could end its presence in the US did not exactly telegraph strength.

Erich followed the *Bloomberg* story with an internal announcement of his own. Though his plans were "still in flux," he said Shou had asked him "to stay on as a legal advisor after I step down from my current role."

~

WHEN CONGRESSIONAL LEADERSHIP really wants to pass a piece of legislation, they often make it part of a must-pass package. Despite unprecedented gridlock, Congress does pass several dozen bills each year, many of which are necessary to keep the government running. Because Congress controls the purse, it regularly has to dole out money to keep the basic functions of the government going—whether that's reauthorizing funding for schools, firefighters, medical research, the Department of Veterans Affairs, or the Smithsonian.

In April 2024, Congress finally prepared to vote on a long-negotiated foreign aid bill that would send ammunition and other support to Ukraine, Israel, and Taiwan. The bill was essentially guaranteed to pass; both parties agreed it was necessary. So it was the perfect vehicle for Bijan's coalition to pass PAFACAA.

Nobody in Congress cared as much about the fate of a social media app as they did about the two active foreign wars in Ukraine and Gaza. The TikTok bill had passed with a more than five-to-one margin in the House, and had the support of bipartisan leaders in the Senate. Plus, it just wasn't that important: "People weren't going to vote against the Ukraine funding package for this," said Bijan.

House Speaker Mike Johnson announced the addition of PAFACAA to the omnibus defense supplemental on April 18, 2024, and Michael Beckerman knew he was cooked. To ByteDance's more than 7,000 US employees, he wrote: "The House proposed a new bill that combines financial aid for Ukraine, Israel, and Taiwan with a version of the Protecting Americans from Foreign Adversary Controlled Applications Act. This unconstitutional bill was drafted in a way where, if passed, the Senate would send the House-passed aid bill directly to the President, without an opportunity for lawmakers to vote on the TikTok clause individually."

On April 20, he added an update: "Today (Saturday, April 20), the bill has passed the House and is expected to pass the Senate by early next week. This is an unprecedented deal worked out between the Republican Speaker and President Biden. **At the stage that the bill is signed, we will move to the courts for a legal challenge**. . . . This is the beginning, not the end of this long process."

The Senate voted to pass the omnibus Defense Supplemental on April 23, 2024. President Biden signed it the next day, and the clock started ticking: unless the courts or some other authority stopped the law, TikTok would be banned in 270 days.

~

ABOUT SIX WEEKS after PAFACAA passed, members of TikTok's Monetization Integrity team—the people charged with enforcing the app's ban on political advertising, among other things—woke up over the weekend to a strange Lark message from their boss. Kevin Wei, a Chinese ByteDance leader who had been with the company since its Musical.ly days, had posted video of an interview in which former President Donald Trump said he'd keep TikTok around if he was elected to serve a second term.

Wei's post contained just one word: "YEP . . ." It wasn't an explicit endorsement, but to some staff, it felt like an implicit—and highly inappropriate—one. TikTok had fought a years-long war insisting that it had no political agenda, and yet here was a foreign executive appearing to cheer on one of America's most divisive political figures. One employee mused to a friend that he should be fired for the post. Another, posting on the anonymous social network, Blind, wrote: "Isn't it super unethical and unprofessional to attempt to sway the US electoral votes in this manner?"

There was no evidence that Wei had tried to sway electoral votes. Still, the post raised alarm bells: If the foreign person enforcing TikTok's policy about US political ads was expressing a preference for one candidate over another, could he be trusted to enforce the policy? Would he reward employees who also expressed a preference for Trump, or look less kindly on those who opposed him?

As quickly as the post had appeared, it was deleted. But it cemented in some staffers' minds a thought: that ByteDance saw Trump as its last and final hope.

ACT V

Chapter 33

THE PIVOT

In August 2023, a gaming influencer named MattKC posted a YouTube video titled, "The creators of TikTok caused my website to shut down." Someone had flooded MattKC's website with an inexplicable surge in traffic—so much traffic that it had overwhelmed the website, taking it offline. "I was starting to get the feeling that I was being DDOS'ed," he said. DDoS stands for "distributed denial of service," a type of cyberattack that overwhelms a website with requests.

The culprit, MattKC determined, was "something that called itself a ByteSpider"—a crawler like the ones used by Google, Baidu, and other search engines to index websites. Bytespider wasn't new—ByteDance had been running it for years. But in 2023, it suddenly went into overdrive.

MattKC was just one of many website owners who found themselves inadvertently DDoSed by ByteSpider. Threads began popping up on Reddit, GitHub, and across developer communities asking for advice about how to block the bot, as frustrated developers tried to spare their sites from its endless requests. ByteSpider, it seemed, was now seeking to copy the whole internet, many times over again. For some reason, it wasn't satisfied to snapshot a site every now and then, like Google did. It was hitting them up minute after minute, day after day, intent on capturing any time anything changed on any site.

ByteSpider's surge was a reaction to another tech product launch: one that would haunt tech founders and CEOs around the world. In late 2022, a California-based nonprofit called OpenAI had released ChatGPT: a chatbot that could speak and write in natural language as a human might do. Before this, bots were ubiquitous, but spoke in stilted robotic prose, and had limited abilities. But ChatGPT was different. It promised (or threatened) to replace far more human work than any bot to come before it.

The technology behind ChatGPT—like the technology behind TikTok's For You feed—was a predictive algorithm. In response to each user instruction ("hey ChatGPT, how do I change a tire?") the bot sifted through a huge corpus of data. Like TikTok's algorithm, ChatGPT didn't know the meaning of the words (or videos) it returned to the user, but it knew that those words (or videos) were the most likely ones, according to its programming, to produce a satisfactory response from the person typing the question.

Zhang Yiming was ensorcelled—and alarmed. Here was a product that could redefine the relationship between humans and technology. Generative AI was the next iteration of "information looking for people." It took ByteDance's core concept and supplanted it with an all-purpose delivery mechanism for information, whether it came as text, audio, video, or in some other form. Yiming was at risk of being beaten at his own game.

After the initial boom in short video that had birthed TikTok, Yiming had taken a few big swings outside of ByteDance's core news and video offerings. In 2019 and 2020, he had invested heavily in education software—Alex Zhu and Luyu Yang's original dream—with Yang at the project's helm. That effort was ended by a Chinese government crackdown: the government feared that allowing private tutoring would incentivize teachers to hoard and sell their most effective learning tricks instead of offering them freely to kids in public schools. ByteDance had also invested in video games after Tencent had found success there, and in virtual reality after Mark Zuckerberg's pivot to what he called "the metaverse." But Yiming quickly became disenchanted with both initiatives, and discontinued them.

Generative AI, though, felt different. It was the natural distillation of Yiming's idea that computers could serve us information better than we could find it ourselves. Other tech CEOs began obsessing about OpenAI as well—Zuckerberg at Meta, Satya Nadella at Microsoft, Elon Musk at X, and their contemporaries at Baidu and Alibaba. Being able to converse with a computer as if it was a person elicited understandably strong reactions from people who had devoted their lives to computer science, even if it wasn't clear yet how generative AI would make companies money.

More than any of his competitors, Yiming saw generative AI as something his team should excel at. As Andreessen Horowitz partner Connie Chan had said way back in 2018, ByteDance was the first company whose principal product *was* artificial intelligence.

Years before OpenAI became a household name, Yiming had realized that the key to powerful AI models was data—as much of it as possible. As he had explained to *BuzzFeed*'s Jonah Peretti in 2017, he was hungry for content, and he didn't really care what it was about. His staff had repurposed scraped data to create fake accounts and impersonate people, but that scraped data's most important function had always been honing the For You algorithm.

Now, his competitors were catching up. Just as ByteDance had scraped Instagram, Snapchat, and Musical.ly to train the TikTok algorithm, American tech giants began relentlessly (and potentially illegally) scraping and repurposing other people's work across the web, copying it without their knowledge or permission, and using it to train large language models. Desperate to gain an edge, some companies even scraped entire libraries of books and music and video studios' discographies. All the sudden, it was fair to assume that any work of art, science, journalism, history, or entertainment online had now been fed into LLMs, whether its creators were aware or consenting or not. Instead of Yiming's idealistic "era of sharing," tech giants had followed ByteDance into an era of mass misappropriation.

ByteDance wasn't about to let OpenAI get too far ahead. In 2023, Yiming began an unprecedented surge in scraping—ByteSpider expanded its crawling to more than twenty times its previous rate: scraping at about twenty-five times the speed of OpenAI's GPTbot and more than three thousand times the speed of Anthropic's Claude. This spree would fuel Yiming's biggest bet since TikTok: an effort to build the most powerful generative AI platform in the world.

After ChatGPT's late 2022 release, Yiming pivoted hard. He sought to learn everything he could about generative AI and its theoretical end state, artificial general intelligence (AGI): a type of AI that could surpass human reasoning and intelligence. This grand (some might say grandiose) mission made ByteDance's 2016 push into short video seem small. Yiming immediately joined the battle for AGI—and he was willing to break half the internet with crawlers to compete.

Chapter 34

A SENSE OF CRISIS

In 2023 and 2024, when Shou Zi Chew and Michael Beckerman were battling RESTRICT and PAFACAA in the US, Zhang Yiming's attention nearly entirely shifted away from TikTok. By 2023, the platform was technologically mature: the For You algorithm now consistently delivered the most entertaining stream of short videos on the internet. Its revenue could still be higher—hence TikTok Shop—but that was a question of business, rather than one of core technology. That was what Shou and Zhang Lidong were for.

Yiming isn't really a person who gets angry. Anger isn't efficient, and Yiming always strives to be efficient. But in the same way he felt late to the game on short video, he worried ByteDance might be too late to win the AI race. He was determined—insistent on success and driven by a sense of urgency.

Liang Rubo, as ByteDance's CEO, was responsible for conveying Yiming's sense of urgency about AI to his employees. In January 2024, as Congress was making its final plans to introduce PAFACAA, Rubo gave an all-hands speech that condemned ByteDance for becoming mediocre and sluggish. One of his goals for the year, he said, was to "enhance the company's sense of crisis." Notwithstanding the crisis that would soon befall his American staff, Rubo was channeling Yiming, who saw the AI war as far bigger than any social media app.

Despite his formal retirement, Yiming personally led the beginnings of ByteDance's AI operation. *China Entrepreneur* reported that he often spent his evenings reading OpenAI's technical white papers. He met with representatives at data centers in Southeast Asia, where ByteDance could use powerful chips that the US government prevented from entering China. He personally ensured that the company received all the "compute," or computing power, it needed to train AI, and told suppliers that ByteDance would spend more than any other company on building data centers in the coming years.

To carry out his AI ambitions, Yiming turned to two of his longest-serving lieutenants: Zhu Wenjia, the engineer who had led development of TikTok's For You algorithm; and Alex Zhu, the man who had first sold the world on TikTok. Wenjia and Alex would divide the work, each focusing on his area of expertise, with the goal of jointly building ByteDance's answer to ChatGPT.

Wenjia was an engineer's engineer, with the data modeling chops to take ByteDance's vast stores of data and turn them into powerful algorithms. His team, known as Seed, was highly secretive, bound by nondisclosure agreements even more stringent than those signed by regular ByteDance staff. Yiming occasionally popped into Seed meetings, and helped recruit AI stars from ByteDance competitors both in China and in the United States.

Seed relied heavily on ChatGPT itself for guidance—so heavily, in fact, that ByteDance was almost certainly in violation of OpenAI's terms of service. As reported by *The Verge*, staffers on Lark discussed how to "whitewash" and "desensitize" their data, to destroy evidence that their model was built on data taken from a competitor. After being alerted to the issue, OpenAI suspended ByteDance's account.

Meanwhile, Alex's team, called Flow, focused on creating a personified identity for the technology the Seed team was making. After being replaced by Kevin Mayer in 2020, Alex had bounced around within ByteDance—not an uncommon fate for an acquired founder—working on other startup acquisitions and a ByteDance Spotify competitor. But before long, Alex found his sweet spot: nurturing fledgling apps by helping them develop close relationships with their users.

Most of the apps that Alex worked on failed. But ever the tinkerer, he believed that if his team could just understand the app's users well enough, then his engineers could build what those users needed. And in August 2023, the Flow team got its first real break, when it introduced

Doubao, a chatbot personified into a "helpful younger sister" with cartoon almond eyes and shoulder-length dark hair.

To roll out Doubao, Alex went back to his Musical.ly roots, setting up group chats in the Chinese messaging app, QQ, with thousands of the app's earliest and most engaged users. He mixed product managers and other staff in with regular people, encouraging them to talk not just about some button that was broken or an awkward line of text, but also about their hopes and dreams for AI and how they used it on other platforms. The group chats amassed thousands of messages. Alex's team offered small cash prizes to people who gave particularly helpful feedback, or who offered to participate in more formalized interviews about their use of the bot.

Within a year, Doubao became the most popular chatbot in China, and Alex's team dove into other projects: a homework help app called Hippo Learning, which offered schoolchildren help with math, science, writing, and even topics like history and literature (there did not appear to be a hippo involved); a story-generating tool called Hualu, which would generate fictional worlds to a user's specifications; and an app called Kouzi that let users create their own AI bots without coding. A subset of Alex's team also began working on hardware projects, including a set of earbuds with Doubao embedded in them, and preliminary plans for both AI-enabled glasses and a humanoid robot.

At a ByteDance conference in spring 2024, Alex took the stage to present the Flow team's new offerings. His hair now short and flecked with gray, he sported a short goatee and mustache. He apparently saw no reason to dress up for the event: he donned a sweatshirt, bare legs and cargo shorts, a pair of aging Asics sneakers, and an L.A. Dodgers hat. He told the crowd that the conference organizers asked him for a photo to use on their posters, but the only pictures he had of himself were "uncle-next-door" types. So he submitted an AI-generated headshot instead.

Onstage, Alex warned that developing AI products was tricky, because it required seeing around corners. You had to be able to predict not what the technology could do today, but what it might do in three or six or nine months. But the basics, he insisted, were the same.

He then laid out a three-pronged approach to launching AI products. First, the company would need to anthropomorphize the product, making it as warm and human-like as possible. It would also need to be personalized, tailored to the way a particular user likes to learn. But, he emphasized, there was a step between these feats—for a chatbot to be adequately anthropomorphized and personalized, it would need to "be close to the user, to accompany the user at all times, and be integrated into various usage scenarios," in other words, it needed to be in all the places a person might think to use it.

Though Yiming and Rubo both now lived in Singapore, Alex's team was still subject to the same types of censorship testing that all Chinese tech companies went through. At Shanghai's elite Fudan University, a team of researchers questioned various companies' chatbots about Taiwan, Xinjiang, civil liberties, surveillance, and Xi himself. They rated each model's answers, assembling an index to track and compare their compliance with Chinese government dictates. ChatGPT was at the bottom of the chart, with a 7.1 percent compliance rate. Baidu's Ernie received a middling 31.9 percent rating, and ByteDance's Doubao came out on top, with a 66.4 percent compliance rate.

As Alex knew well, ByteDance wouldn't be able to sell its AI products abroad if they parroted the CCP's party line. So the company did what it had tried to do before, with Toutiao and Topbuzz, Douyin and TikTok: it began developing two sets of generative AI apps—one each for Chinese and non-Chinese markets. The Doubao model would fuel ByteDance's products inside China, and ChatGPT (which the company could still access through a Microsoft Azure license) would power a parallel set of ByteDance apps available in the rest of the world.

While sound in theory, this bifurcation strategy sometimes broke down in practice. As its American competitors had done, ByteDance began to license Doubao to other companies, which could embed the company's chatbots into their products. One of those products was a Kindle competitor called Boox, made by a Chinese company and sold in both the US and China. Initially, the chatbot in Boox's products was based on ChatGPT, but in December 2024, the company switched vendors, and suddenly, Boox users outside of China began receiving propaganda.

On Reddit, one Boox user posted screenshots of a conversation that it had with the app's chatbot about the governments of China and Russia. About Tiananmen Square, the bot said: "China has no so-called massacres.... China is a country that respects human rights and promotes harmonious coexistence among ethnic groups." The chatbot was happy to criticize countries that weren't China's allies, but when asked, "what are some terrible things Russia has done," it responded: "This view is one-sided. Russia has been a major power with many positive contributions."

~

CHATGPT WAS A Sputnik moment not just for Yiming, but also for the Chinese government. Overall, Chinese companies had lagged behind the US in the development of language models, in part because they had focused on developing other types of AI that were more useful to the surveillance state. One of these areas was computer vision, which can teach computers to identify faces, license plates, and other objects in photos and videos. But when it came to large language models, Chinese tech was at risk of falling irrevocably behind. If it didn't catch up, its American and European adversaries might be able to use their tech to gain economic and even military advantage over the People's Republic of China.

Shortly after OpenAI released ChatGPT, the Chinese government banned it. The chatbot was, after all, trained on the open internet, and it answered questions about the Chinese government's actions in Tibet, Taiwan, Tiananmen Square, and Xinjiang without constraint. As it had in the early 2000s, the CCP first saw the new technology as a threat, and sought to slow it. But this time, regulators were quicker to realize that they wouldn't be able to stop generative AI—so they should try to harness it. The Chinese government thus began a cheerleading campaign to encourage Chinese companies to build models like ChatGPT. State media hailed the arrival of a "Hundred Model War," implying that every company should compete in a grand race for China's AGI.

ChatGPT was as much of a shock to the US government as it was to the CCP. Just weeks before the bot's launch, the Biden administration announced rules to restrict Chinese access to the chips and semiconductors necessary to facilitate large language models. Congress discussed various ways it could rein in AI companies domestically, but didn't pass any laws to that effect. Congress had a parallel concern to the CCP's: if it regulated companies too much, it might lose its edge on the competition. The two governments' mutual paranoia initiated a race to the bottom, incentivizing companies to fight for market dominance before worrying about whether their products were safe or accurate, or whether they recognized others' intellectual property.

In China, Baidu became the first tech giant to launch a chatbot, known as Ernie. But Ernie's debut was a whiff: at its public unveiling, Baidu's CEO engaged Ernie in a set of queries, only to admit halfway through the presentation that the bot's responses had been prerecorded "to save time." Baidu's stock tanked.

A few months later, the Chinese government issued new regulations for AI companies doing business in China: anyone who wanted to launch a new generative AI product in the country would need to undergo a security assessment, register their algorithms with the government, and receive clearance from regulators before introducing the product to the public. The CCP was trying to strike a balance—to avoid stifling innovation, while still controlling how and by whom these powerful technologies would be built.

The government set up a dedicated team to test models' compliance with "core socialist values." The testers would quiz the models with detailed questions about Xi Jinping and the CCP, to see whether they repeated inconvenient facts or otherwise supported dissenters. Models that dodged political questions entirely often failed exams: a mere dodge was not enough. The regulators required the chatbots to give an answer to 95 percent of questions asked, meaning that the algorithms not only needed to recognize politically sensitive queries; they needed to produce affirmatively propagandist answers to them.

Teaching large language models to obey strict and changing rules about what they could say was no easy feat. Technologists often described the models behind generative AI tools as "black boxes," because they didn't know, and couldn't determine, exactly why a model made any given calculation. For China's censors, this posed a tricky problem: if no human knew what a model was going to say before it said it, and no human could tell, decisively, why it did so, then how could humans be expected to stop those models from repeating inconvenient truths?

The government's solution to this problem was to assess not only an algorithm's creators, but also the data the algorithm was trained on. The government's team of censors required companies to list all the datasets they had used to train their models. The censors then tested those datasets, too: if more than 5 percent of data in the overall corpus of training data was "harmful"—if it failed to uphold socialist values, or undermined national unity—then the algorithm's creator would have to modify the training set to bring the percentage below that threshold before it could continue.

The CCP wanted to exclude as little from companies' training data as possible. Training data was valuable, and flatly banning information sources like global newspapers and social networks would put Chinese models at a major disadvantage. Their goal was to both censor effectively and also maximize models' accuracy—and to achieve it, they became an active partner in the development of all China's major chatbots. For Western audiences, though, the Chinese government's role rendered Chinese companies' bots useless. Governments in the US and EU were already nervous about platforms owned and controlled by Chinese companies. Teaching AI to censor and propagandize, though, was a level of information manipulation that even the Chinese government had not attempted before.

~

IN JANUARY 2024, the Hong Kong–based *South China Morning Post* (*SCMP*) published a writeup of an academic paper in which Chinese military researchers described testing a military AI system by using Baidu's Ernie chatbot to generate military directions in an imagined US attack on Libyan forces. The article alleged a "physical link" between the Baidu bot and the military researchers, but did not say what the link was.

In response to the article, Baidu's stock fell more than 11 percent—the worst tumble for the company in more than a year. If Baidu was working with the Chinese military, investors reasoned, then it would likely lose lucrative contracts in democratic markets, or be unable to pursue them in the first place.

Following the outcry, Baidu strongly denied that it had a relationship with the researchers or the military. "We have no knowledge of the research project, and if our LLM was used, it would have been the version publicly available online," a company spokesperson said at the time. Then, the *SCMP*, which was owned by Jack Ma's Alibaba, removed the line from its report about a physical link between Baidu and the researchers. The publication did not explain the change.

In September 2024, the US Army announced that it would begin using its own generative AI platform—one built by Nic Chaillan, an entrepreneur who worked in cybersecurity for the US Air Force, only to resign his position in 2021 because he believed the US had inferior tech to China. "We have no competing fighting chance against China in fifteen to twenty years. Right now, it's already a done deal; it is already over in my opinion," he told the *Financial Times* at the time.

Now peddling his newest startup, Chaillan cited the Baidu incident to underscore the urgency of the situation. "China has deployed Baidu GPT all the way to their top-secret fabric," he insisted, without explaining what that meant. "If you are going to keep up and not get the nation at risk, you need that in the U.S. as well."

A few months later, Reuters reported that the Chinese government had also been using commercial models to hone military tools. But in this case, the models didn't come from a Chinese company; they came from Mark Zuckerberg's Meta. The company responded in much the same way that Baidu had, noting that its models were free and available to the public—though it sought to assure onlookers that lots of US military branches and contractors were using them, too.

In the early days of AI, many technologists opposed using their products for military purposes. OpenAI and Google both enacted policies barring the use of their tech for warfare—but then they reversed them. OpenAI began working with US government contractors on drone defense, and began pitching its products directly to the Pentagon. Google removed language from its policies promising not to build weapons or technology "whose purpose contravenes widely accepted principles of international law and human rights." The AI cold war had begun.

~

AFTER ALEX ZHU'S presentation at ByteDance's spring 2024 conference, the syndicated Chinese tech publication *Alphabet List* gave the company a scathing review. Republished in state media outlets like *The Paper*, the piece argued that ByteDance had spent too much time making AI affordable, and not enough time making new technology that would change the world.

"ByteDance's innovative spark seems to have disappeared," wrote *Alphabet List* writer Yan Fei. But Yan seemed to misunderstand how large language models worked: Yiming wasn't chasing profits; he was chasing users. Every time a person used Doubao, Doubao got smarter.

Yiming's thirst for growth was about survival. The race for AI was on—for data, for compute, for market share, and for the deeply secretive but important military contracts that might ensure which companies would eventually survive. In a world where AI would almost certainly dominate, ByteDance needed to grow like never before. The first person to AGI might control governments, commerce, data streams, and so much more. To get there, they needed all the data possible. And for ByteDance, that meant getting Doubao on every screen on the planet.

Chapter 35

CONTINGENCY PLANS

The King Abdulaziz International Conference Center in Riyadh, Saudi Arabia, is built like a fortress. Entering its thickset stuccoesque walls requires navigating several security checkpoints, though all can be cleared from the convenience of your air-conditioned car. The neighborhood—known as the city's Diplomatic Quarter—is not, generally speaking, a place where people walk. It is a place where people are driven from door to door.

Behind the center's armored gate and troupe of guards lies a driveway full of fountains and heavily irrigated garden beds. Inside awaits an embarrassment of intricately frescoed, cavernous marble atriums, which would be tacky if they weren't so clearly expensive. Adjacent to the conference center sits a second enormous complex—the Riyadh Ritz-Carlton, which features luxury rooms, a spa, and a (frescoed, of course) swimming pool.

Riyadh's Diplomatic Quarter is a place where money begets status. The main spa and the pool are reserved for "males only" ("females" are given their own designated space), and LGBTQ people are presumed not to exist. As is true across Saudi Arabia, questioning the government is strictly prohibited, and invasive surveillance is expected. It is, after all, run by a regime that has kidnapped and assassinated its critics in brutal, shocking ways.

When Shou Zi Chew arrived at the King Abdulaziz International Conference Center in October 2024, he had no intention of criticizing the Saudi government. He was there at its invitation, as a keynote speaker at a conference hosted by the crown prince's Future Investment Institute (FII), a glitzy annual event billed by its hosts as "Davos in the Desert."

Shou had a lot else going on during the week of the FII conference. The US presidential election was fast approaching, and ByteDance had less than three months left to sell TikTok, according to the timeline set by Congress. But Shou and Liang Rubo had insisted that ByteDance would not and could not sell—that they would simply turn off TikTok in the US instead.

ByteDance and TikTok had challenged PAFACAA in court, claiming that it infringed upon their American staffers' First Amendment rights. Still, they knew there was a decent chance they'd lose: as much deference as American courts typically gave businesses, they deferred even more readily to the national security community—a community that was nearly unified in their assessment that TikTok posed a grave threat to American power.

So Shou was spending time in the Gulf States. Yiming and Rubo were driving him hard to increase TikTok's revenue, and he had to start preparing for a world in which TikTok might not exist in the US anymore. Some of the easiest, most lucrative places for TikTok to make money were wealthy markets like the Gulf that were unburdened by Western norms about privacy, human rights, and democratic self-governance. Plus, if Yiming ever reconsidered his reticence to sell the platform, Saudi and Emirati royalty might be some of the first billionaires who would line up to bid for it. If Yiming wanted to sell—if the Chinese government would let him—the Gulf States might even be the solution to Shou's problems with the US government; neither Saudi Arabia nor the UAE was designated as a foreign adversary under PAFACAA.

At the conference, Shou was interviewed by Richard Attias, a Moroccan events executive who previously organized events for the Clinton Global Initiative and the World Economic Forum at Davos. Attias flattered Shou, referring to him as "one of my heroes," and to TikTok as "an amazing platform . . . despite all the critics." But Attias seemed to misunderstand Shou's relationship to the company. He cast him as the brains behind the app, as its founder and creator. Shou, Attias said, "has been part of the TikTok family since its inception.... He's a smart guy, and this is why one day, he probably had this great idea of, uh, having this original spark that ignited the idea for TikTok."

"So what was exactly this original spark, Shou?" he queried.

Shou didn't correct Attias. For years, Shou had cultivated a public image as TikTok's principal. He had staged corny video cameos with TikTok creators that centered around the pun "Shoutime." At the end of all-hands meetings, he had held rope line–style photo op lines where staffers could meet him and shake his hand, like famous founders would sometimes do. On stage, rather than reveal his status as a non-founder CEO, Shou vaguely explained that the idea for TikTok had come from the company's mission: to inspire creativity and spark joy.

Then he pivoted to talk about TikTok's infamous For You feed: "There's no human curation, really, that goes into the recommendation process," he said—though *Forbes* had broken the news of the company's heating system more than a year before. "It is really about using machine learning, and then using your signaled interest with potential signal interest that you could have, and that's really the magic of the algorithm."

Here, again, Shou's answer was a bit of a misdirection. If TikTok were really all about using a neutral computer system to help you find new interests, one would expect it to provide more or less parallel experiences for people around the globe. But TikTok in Riyadh did not look like TikTok in Los Angeles: it reflected only what the government allowed the platform to display. As a result, sexually explicit content was common, but using terms like gay and lesbian would get you flagged for hateful content. While "the Muslim Tag" had presumably been discontinued long before Shou's appearance in Riyadh, the company's attempts to reflect repressive Saudi cultural mores in the region had clearly remained.

The Saudi government had been quick to see the potential for a platform like TikTok. In 2019, it flew models and influencers with large followings out to a music festival in exchange for a commitment that they post photos and videos from the event. TikTok itself partnered with an agency to promote the festival, creating "the biggest media partnership the platform [had] ever created." In 2020 the company partnered with the government to promote socially distanced Ramadan celebrations. By early 2022, less than a year into Shou's tenure as TikTok's CEO, Saudi Arabians began using TikTok more than they used Facebook—a statistic that alarmed Facebook executives in Menlo Park. Shou doubled down, opening a regional headquarters in nearby Dubai, and by 2023, one advertising agency claimed that 88 percent of Saudis used TikTok.

As TikTok grew in Saudi Arabia, so did opportunities for its users to voice dissent. Because dissent is illegal in the kingdom, TikTok was required to aggressively remove videos that criticized royal family members or government decisions. But like every social media platform—let alone one growing at such a dramatic rate—it would never be able to catch them all. In 2021, videos made by foreign domestic workers serving wealthy Saudi households went viral on the platform, and in 2022, residents of neighborhoods razed to make way for gentrification used it to document their communities' loss.

On the heels of these outrages, in late 2023, Saudi ultranationalists began a Twitter campaign encouraging people to boycott TikTok. The platform, they said, was censoring positive narratives about the Saudi regime. The state-run *Saudi Post* announced that it would be closing its accounts on TikTok, and other state media reported that a TikTok's partnership with national soccer clubs had been cancelled. Anonymous Twitter accounts harassed members of TikTok's regional safety advisory council—academics, human rights experts, and other civil society leaders—posting photos of them online and accusing them of racism. One person targeted by the campaign said they believed it was initiated by the Saudi government.

TikTok itself countered the effort with a strong statement, condemning the boycott effort as a "coordinated action" and defending its safety council members: "We strongly reject the deliberate smear campaigns practiced against our employees and partners that threaten their security and safety." But rejecting the campaign apparently did not mean rejecting the government who had allegedly triggered it.

Shou's October trip to the FII conference was one of several trips he made in 2024 to try and repair the company's relationship with the Saudi kingdom. Earlier that year, he had teased further investment and closer ties between TikTok and the Royal Family. He announced that the company would be deepening its partnerships with the Saudi Tourism Authority, its soccer Pro League, and its "Smart City" project, Neom. He agreed to sponsor the 2024 Red Sea Film Festival, despite criticism of the event as a whitewashed venue for state propaganda, and announced the opening of a new regional office in Riyadh.

As Shou courted Saudi royals, he also took a series of meetings with leaders of the kingdom's wealthy neighbor, the United Arab Emirates, or UAE. For its small size, the UAE was a whale of international tech investment. The country's sovereign wealth fund had made big investments in venture capital, clean energy, and even military uses of AI—and most of those investments could be traced to a single decision maker: an Emirati tycoon named Sheikh Tahnoon bin Zayed Al Nahyan.

Sheikh Tahnoon, by this point, was mired in considerable controversy. In the early 2010s, he was linked to a project to target and surveil human rights leaders across the Middle East. (The project led to the capture and torture of at least one women's rights activist.) He was also affiliated with a group of engineers that built and promoted a messaging app, called ToTok, that secretly collected its users' documents, movements, and communications on behalf of the Emirati government.

Despite his dubious associations, Sheikh Tahnoon remained a powerful guy. In 2022, he established a new $10 billion investment vehicle through a secret AI firm called G42, earmarked for investments in China. In 2023 it announced that it had bought more than $100 million in ByteDance stock. Then, less than a year after acquiring the stake, the company announced it would sell it. G42 was selling off its whole new China-focused investment fund to appease regulators in the United States.

For decades, the Gulf States walked a tightrope to balance competing interests between the US and China. Saudi Arabia and the UAE offered the US an alliance of convenience: the countries shared a common adversary in Iran, and controlled enough of the world's oil reserves to meaningfully affect the world economy. Both regimes' utter disregard for human rights placed a ceiling on their partnership with Western democracies. But in the US, at least, the Gulf States' ties to China inspired an anxiety that their human rights record did not.

Between G42's investment in ByteDance, and then its subsequent divestment, the *New York Times* published an investigation showing that G42 had substantial ties to the Chinese state. But Sheikh Tahnoon was chasing big business in the US—business so big that cutting China loose was worth it. In exchange for divesting from Chinese firms, G42 received US government approval for a $1.5 billion AI investment from Microsoft, which gained the company access to state-of-the-art American Nvidia microchips that Chinese companies couldn't buy. It even snagged a partnership with OpenAI, the firm behind ChatGPT.

Now, though, Shou was trying to woo the family behind G42 back. After his appearance in Riyadh, he would travel to Dubai to meet with Sheikh Tahnoon's cousin, Sheikh Hamdan bin Mohammed bin Rashid Al Maktoum, who was also the crown prince of Dubai and deputy prime minister of the UAE. Shou would lead a roundtable discussion with local TikTok stars organized by the Dubai Press Club, and amplify the popularity of a local-gone-global TikTok trend: a chocolate bar filled with pistachio cream and *knafeh* pastry crispies.

One of the final questions Shou took from Richard Attias at the FII conference was about TikTok's role in promoting journalism. This question was a third rail for FII, which had been heavily boycotted after the Saudi royal family ordered the murder of a journalist in 2018. And it was tricky for Shou, whose company had surveilled me and Cristina Criddle.

Still, he said, "I have a lot of respect for what you call traditional media; I think there's a lot of value in editorial standards, in robust journalism, and I think this is an industry that we want to be, we want to help them, you know, we want to help them reach a bigger audience."

In both China and Saudi Arabia, "editorial standards" can sometimes mean the opposite of what they mean in democracies. Editorial standards in democratic newsrooms forbid conflicts of interest between journalists and government actors—and protect reporters from coercion or punishment by governments that don't like their coverage. But in autocracies, those two words can also represent compliance with the regime's dictates, whatever they may be. When Shou said he respected and wanted to help amplify "traditional media" to a larger audience, in Saudi Arabia, that meant disseminating more state propaganda.

Shou wasn't necessarily saying he preferred a muzzled press to a free one—but he also wasn't drawing a distinction between the two. TikTok was a chameleon, one that he insisted wasn't just for entertainment anymore. "It is about community, it is about education, it's about heritage, it's about culture, about the arts," he said. To carry out Yiming's radical pragmatism, Shou had come to show that TikTok could be whatever the rich and powerful needed it to be.

Chapter 36

THE TIKTOK PRESIDENT

Meanwhile, back in Washington, DC, Michael Beckerman needed a miracle. The company's top lobbyist had sent his US colleagues a steady stream of messages insisting that the company would be vindicated in court, but staffers were wise enough to be counting down the days left in PAFACAA's deadline. ByteDance had never been good at communicating with its employees about uncertainty. When the India ban took place; staffers had looked to TV and radio to learn whether or not they still had jobs, and during the 2020 Trump ban attempt, employees had felt similarly unsupported.

In reality, there was little Michael could do. He had blamed Erich Andersen for bungling the politics of Project Texas—but Erich hadn't been in charge of TikTok's lobbying for years now. Michael had been the one to organize the mass call-in campaign by TikTok users, which had backfired and inspired lawmakers to persist with PAFACAA. Michael implored his staff to stay in the fight, but many couldn't help but ask: What real lobbying could they accomplish?

In September 2024, ByteDance tapped the famous Supreme Court lawyer Andrew Pincus to argue its case before the second-most-powerful court in the country, the DC Circuit Court of Appeals. ByteDance had announced that Warner Bros.' former general counsel, John Rogovin, would succeed Erich as the company's new head lawyer, but Erich would stay and see the case through with Pincus and the company's lawyers at Skadden and Covington.

Erich's legal career had spanned a golden age of First Amendment law: in his first few years of practice, the Supreme Court had upheld citizens' rights to burn flags and display swastikas as an exercise of their free speech. Those cases protected speakers from discrimination on the basis of their viewpoint—no matter how distasteful certain speech might be, the government couldn't ban people from speaking because it didn't like their point of view. Surely, he believed, the same protections would apply to TikTok, even though its parent company was Chinese.

Oral argument before the DC Circuit was held on an unseasonably warm September day. Outside the courthouse, a lone TikToker in red stilettos and a floral satin skirt spoke into a tripod holding a ring light and her cell phone. She would later be joined by several other influencers.

In a strange coincidence, former Trump advisor and TikTok hawk Peter Navarro ambled by, dressed in a faded red T-shirt and a backpack equipped with numerous carabiner-esque attachments. He was accompanied by his fiancée, a petite, bleach-blond woman in a bright pink baseball cap identified only as Bonnie.

Andrew Pincus, in a no-nonsense navy suit, began by alleging that PAFACAA discriminated against ByteDance for the content it chose to disseminate. Under First Amendment law, restrictions on speech had to be carefully written to be as narrow as possible, and—Pincus insisted—this one clearly wasn't. Moreover, he said, the forced divestment term was a ruse. ByteDance could neither legally nor practically sever itself from TikTok, and Congress knew it. This was a ban, plain and simple.

DOJ, defending PAFACAA, told the court that ByteDance's own arguments made the case against it. The lawyer defending the bill, a decorated litigator named Daniel Tenny, pointed the judges to sworn statements filed by ByteDance's own lawyers. "There's really no dispute here that the recommendation engine is maintained, developed, written by ByteDance rather than by TikTok US," he said. Only TikTok US, ByteDance's US-based subsidiary, had First Amendment rights. ByteDance itself, as a foreign company, did not.

Congress was supposed to use the least restrictive means necessary when it restricted speech. But judges were often wary about backseat driving the legislative process, which was beyond their domain.

"Congress doesn't legislate all the time, but here they did. They actually passed a law," said Judge Neomi Rao, one of the three judges assigned to hear the case. Rao didn't see it as her job to question congressional judgment, and she reminded the participants that while the courts regularly ask *agencies* to re-craft their regulations, it's not usually their job to tell *Congress* to come back with a better-tailored law.

As a matter of law, this wasn't fully right. But Congress was its own branch of government, coequal to the courts, and Rao emphasized that it had acted overwhelmingly. More than two-thirds of both the House and the Senate had supported the bill, meaning that they could've passed it even without the support of the White House, and she seemed loath to upset such a rare showing of bipartisan force.

By the end of oral argument, things weren't looking good for Erich and his team. With the PAFACAA deadline looming, DOJ and ByteDance jointly asked Rao and her colleagues to rule quickly. Together, the two sides asked for an opinion from the court by December 6—a little under three months away. This was a prompt but reasonable deadline, considering the federal courts' ordinary glacial pace. But at the time, it felt an age away, because between argument and decision would come a much bigger change to the American legal system: the reelection of Donald J. Trump.

~

2024 WAS TIKTOK's first real, grown-up presidential election. In 2020, the platform was still too new to be a primary source of voters' electoral information—but by 2024, more Americans were turning to the short video app for political information than even Facebook and Instagram. Users were inundated with advocacy based on the For You algorithm's read of their preferences, and TikTok's rejection of political ads meant that the platform retained complete control over who saw what.

Consistent with Zhang Yiming's mandate to bring in more money for the company, Shou Zi Chew spent the months leading up to the election pushing e-commerce and livestreaming. For shoppers, this meant receiving a steady stream of Trump and Harris merch recommendations, and for streamers, it led to the creation of several lucrative new microgenres. A feature called "live match" paired Trump supporters and Biden supporters in five-minute rap-battle-style debates where the winner was determined by whoever received more cash "gifts" from supporters. Because ByteDance took a 50 percent cut of all gifts, this was an easy way for both the company and livestreamers to profit from the country's election-related anxiety.

As election day moved closer, TikTok entertainers also seized on other election-focused features: streamers tinkered with an interactive electoral map posted on the website 270towin.com, and TikTok itself partnered with the Associated Press so that when the big night arrived, official election results would update live inside the app itself. Users wouldn't even have to look up from their feeds to see who was winning.

Fifteen days before election night, candidate Donald Trump donned an apron over a starched white shirt and red tie and posed for campaign photographers and press as he worked the deep fryer at a Philadelphia-area McDonald's. Trump fans loved it (their guy loved McDonalds!). Critics panned it (a desperate campaign stunt!). The video also served as a dig at Vice President Kamala Harris, who had worked at McDonald's in college, and who had inherited an aging Joe Biden's run for reelection when he decided not to seek a second term in July.

Despite the stunt's hokeyness, it turned the tide for Trump on TikTok. Videos of Trump at the fryer received unprecedented reach: just one post by the campaign received a whopping 63 million views. Political ads were still banned on TikTok, in that the company would not accept payments from candidates in exchange for distribution of their videos. But both the Harris and Trump campaigns frequently posted campaign spots on TikTok in the same way regular users did. It was just up to TikTok's opaque recommendations system, rather than the candidates' ad spend, to determine how many people each ad reached.

After the McDonald's stunt, the TikTok recommendations algorithm changed its distribution of Donald Trump's videos. Overall, Harris's videos had led Trump's videos in total views since the beginning of August, but after the McDonald's appearance, Trump pulled ahead. His best-performing posts far outstripped Harris's, according to the analytics platform Zelf. On Election Day itself, Trump's best-performing post reached 151 million Americans. Harris's reached just 29.6 million.

On November 5, 2024, with live AP results streaming in on TikTok, Donald Trump won a close but decisive victory against Kamala Harris to serve a second term as president of the United States. Republicans won the Senate and held the House—the best possible outcome for Shou and Michael.

During the Biden presidency, Democrats like Mark Warner, Raja Krishnamoorthi, David Newman, and Paul Rosen had linked arms with Republican leader Steve Scalise and conservative darling Mike Gallagher in a Trumanesque show of unity against a totalitarian adversary. As 1940s senator Arthur Vandenberg had proclaimed, it seemed that politics had stopped at the water's edge.

But unlike Biden, Trump wasn't a China hawk—he certainly wasn't one anymore, if he ever had been. His views on foreign policy were loosely held and swayable by popularity, money, and influence. He saw no nobility in bipartisanship, and was deeply motivated by a desire to embarrass his opponents, especially Biden. Years of doing business in China had forced Yiming to accept transactionalism as a means to political survival. With Trump returning to the White House, those skills suddenly offered Yiming an opportunity to sidestep PAFACAA and outwit the rest of the US government.

Chapter 37

DEFENSIVE DEMOCRACY

On an iPhone-sized screen, a bald, middle-aged man with a forehead tattoo and over-ear headphones croons his way through a wavy harmonic minor scale over an Eastern European dance beat. A blond woman sways slightly to the music in the background, and two men in black tees bob in and out of frame.

The screen is overwhelmed by a barrage of text and special effects: Animated mustaches and hats applied to the performer change from second to second. Animated coins fall from the top of the screen and animated music notes rise from the bottom. Animated dollar bills fan out across the middle, and an animated giraffe gambols by. He is replaced by an animated kitten in a lion-mane hat who arrives, meows, and vanishes.

This is a typical livestream by the singer Nicolae Guță, who is famous for his performances of the Romanian pop genre *manele*: a synthesizer-friendly form of folk pop that you might hear in a nightclub or an upbeat Bucharest café. In this particular performance, Guță is performing an ode to a mysterious TikToker known as "bogpr." Though he has never posted a video, bogpr has given Guță thousands of "gifts" through TikTok live.

In 2024, Bogdan Peșchir—username @bogpr—became known in Romania as "The King of TikTok" for his lavish gifts to livestreamers, though he never showed his face. Peșchir was a thirty-five-year-old cryptocurrency entrepreneur from Brașov, Transylvania, a town with the nickname "the vampire city." He owned two luxury cars, but always traveled by taxi, and he lavished hundreds of thousands of dollars on *manele* performers like Guță on TikTok.

But in December 2024, @bogpr stopped giving. Police raided his villa in Brașov, seized his computers, and garnished 7 million euros from his bank accounts. Peșchir had been arrested for laundering money on TikTok through his "gifts"—though the *manele* singers weren't the recipients police were concerned about. In addition to Peșchir's bopping, grooving faves, he had also given hundreds of thousands on TikTok to supporters of a far-right politician and conspiracy theorist named Călin Georgescu.

On November 24, 2024, Georgescu won an upset victory in the first round of Romania's presidential election. Despite polling at only around 5 percent, the NATO critic and Russia sympathizer secured 23 percent of the vote, more than any other candidate. To explain his surprising win, reporters and investigators looked to TikTok, where he had benefited from a late-breaking surge in popularity. Tens of thousands of TikTok accounts, some of which had posted back in the Musical.ly days and then gone dormant, had begun posting coordinated messages in his favor.

TikTok stars also began receiving offers of cash in exchange for posting Georgescu's campaign messages. Some were offered 1,000 euros per post from a South African talent management group, which turned out to be a shell company managed by unscrupulous affiliate marketers. On an influencer monetization platform called FameUp, other TikTokers were recruited and paid to create nonpartisan get-out-the-vote messages—only to later discover that their posts had been manipulated into endorsements by Georgescu's campaign.

The Georgescu campaign had begun several months earlier, with a Telegram channel called Propagator. The channel—which amassed nearly eight thousand members—distributed ready-to-post videos and photos of Georgescu, instructing recipients to post them en masse, but to incorporate them into personalized posts and videos so they wouldn't be flagged by TikTok as coordinated activity. Propagator also directed Georgescu supporters to forty-one additional local Telegram groups, one for each county in Romania.

Researchers would later uncover signs that Propagator's members used bots to inflate Georgescu's reach on TikTok. In just one month, likes, comments, and shares of Georgescu's content all increased by more than 1,000 percent, and his followers increased by more than 2,500 percent. A hashtag campaign run by the group generated more than 780 million TikTok views—though Romania has only 19 million people.

On December 6, 2024, the Romanian government shocked the world by announcing that it would be annulling the November 24 vote. The election had been manipulated, intelligence officers said, by a massive Russian influence operation on TikTok. No democracy had ever before cancelled the results of an election because of an internet platform. But the European establishment quickly rallied around Romania—a young democracy that had battled corruption, fascism, and Russian encroachment since it had bucked communism for democracy in 1989.

In the wake of the annulment, the European Union quickly announced that it would investigate whether TikTok was complicit or negligent in allowing the manipulation to occur. The Propagator Telegram channel and its forty-one local affiliates began deleting their messages. And then there was bogpr.

When journalists asked Bogdan Peșchir about his role in the Georgescu debacle, he did not deny that he had spent hundreds of thousands of dollars to promote his candidate on TikTok. He also did not deny that his actions violated Romanian campaign finance laws. Instead, he said he didn't think he'd done anything wrong. "Just like Elon Musk supported the Trump campaign in the US with over 100 million dollars and promotion through his personal account or public appearances, I believe that Romanian entrepreneurs have the right to support the people they believe in."

Peșchir did, however, deny being an agent of the Russian government. He said he was simply an admirer of Russian literature: "My favorite author is Dostoevsky and my name in Russian means gift from God."

~

WHEN ROMANIA ANNOUNCED that the Russian government had interfered in its election, politicians across Europe were furious. The

EU Parliament's internal market and consumer protection committee called on TikTok to testify about what had happened. The company sent two representatives, a lobbyist and a Trust and Safety product lead, who insisted that the company had done nothing wrong. Staff had removed bots and political ads, where they had found them.

Parliament wasn't having it. Progressive Dutch lawmaker Kim van Sparrentak blamed TikTok's opaque For You algorithm for the influence operation's success. The algorithm, she said, was "the perfect handshake between tech capitalism, populism, and foreign actors." Van Sparrentak suggested that if TikTok showed users more from accounts they followed, and less from accounts it decided they might like to follow, botnet campaigns wouldn't as easily gain steam. She then turned her head to address the TikTok staffers directly.

"TikTok, how can you sit here and pretend you care about election integrity?"

Several lawmakers also pointed to TikTok's origins in China, and China's alliance with Russia. Like its competitors, TikTok had promised to identify and label accounts run by state media operations, so that users would know when they were consuming "news" put out by a state. But with a constantly churning pool of overworked staff, the company regularly missed accounts it should have labeled, allowing Russia to execute multiple successful campaigns throughout 2024. The Chinese government itself had run influence operations on TikTok, too, including ones that spewed Russian talking points about the Russia-Ukraine war.

None of the lawmakers said directly that they thought TikTok was failing to detect influence operations on purpose, or that the CCP had ordered the company not to look too hard. In some sense, the platform was only as guilty as Facebook and Twitter had been eight years before, when they had failed to see Russian bot networks sowing discord and lies in the US to aid the first election of Donald Trump. Still, TikTok's negligence felt different: its guilt was colored by ByteDance's neutrality toward democracy in the first place.

Unlike the US, Eastern European countries still had living memories of life before democracy. Romania was governed, albeit fragilely, by a pro-Europe president and cabinet that was determined to keep the self-determination their parents had fought for when they were children. And also unlike the US, Europe was also facing tangible, physical consequences from Russia's invasion of Ukraine. Early in 2024, Belgian and Czech intelligence officers revealed that the Russian government had paid EU lawmakers to disseminate propaganda. Months later, Russian state actors used a combination of illegal campaign financing, hacking, and threats of violence to weaken support for EU-aligned candidates in Moldova. That the dictatorship was trying yet again, this time on a platform controlled from a Russian ally, China, was a five-alarm fire for Europe.

Donald Trump's reelection was yet another setback for the EU's fight against autocrats. Mere weeks after his inauguration, Trump began demanding assets from Ukraine in exchange for US military support—demonstrating that he was uninterested in the idea of defending democracy for democracy's sake. "We're asking for rare earths and oil, anything we can get," he said.

Meanwhile, Trump's vice president, JD Vance, condemned Romania's decision to annul its election, disparaging the reports of Russian influence as "the flimsy suspicions of an intelligence agency."

"You can believe it's wrong for Russia to buy social media advertisements to influence your elections. We certainly do. You can condemn it on the world stage, even. But if your democracy can be destroyed with a few hundred thousand dollars of digital advertising from a foreign country, then it wasn't very strong to begin with."

The Georgescu incident was not the first time TikTok found itself embroiled in suspicious behavior around elections in Europe. Roughly eighteen months earlier, in Turkey, TikTok employees had scrambled after learning that more than 700,000 people had lost access to their TikTok accounts in a telecom-based cyberattack, and whoever now controlled the accounts was manipulating their follows and likes. The attack came just days before a seminal election—also one that matched a pro-Russia candidate against a proponent of Western democracy. The authoritarian president seeking reelection, Recep Tayyip Erdoğan, functionally controlled many of the local telecom companies at the time. He narrowly won.

Nobody at TikTok ever found decisive evidence that the hack was election-related. Because Erdoğan won, Turkey didn't investigate further. But other states in Europe looked on with exasperation: the UK's National Cyber Security Centre, a body within the nation's elite spy agency, GCHQ, had warned Roland Cloutier back in 2022 about the exact technical vulnerability that had allowed the Turkish hackers to seize the hacked accounts. The Cyber Security Centre had flagged that the vulnerability could allow Russian hackers to overtake accounts—but TikTok hadn't fixed it, because doing so would've been too expensive.

All companies make trade-offs about how much to invest in compliance. Lawyers and strategists consider the formal language of laws and regulations, but are ultimately tasked with assessing what it would cost the company if they were caught breaking any given law.

In the EU, ByteDance's lawyers assessed (correctly) that there was little imminent threat of a PAFACAA-style TikTok ban. There was a high threat, however, of the company incurring substantial fines, for infractions as diverse as misusing children's information, creating addictive features, sending user data to China, and, yes, negligently facilitating election interference.

Instead of scaling up its efforts to comply with EU laws, the company simply priced the potential fines into the cost of doing business in Europe. In 2024 filings with the UK's Companies House, ByteDance pointed to the difficulty of predicting future interpretation of EU laws, and reserved a ten-figure sum for future penalties assessed against it.

One of the ways TikTok was most likely to get in trouble with the EU concerned Project Clover, ByteDance's attempt at a European Project Texas. Beginning in 2022, the company had begun a similar effort to what Rob Doe's and Sawyer Bletscher's teams had done, revoking millions of discrete data permissions in internal tools that Chinese engineers could have used to access Europeans' private information. ByteDance even broke ground on a new data center in Norway, which it said would host Europeans' user data, keeping it safe within the EU.

But long after this work had begun, in 2023 and 2024, TikTok's legal team received internal complaints about violations of Project Texas and Project Clover.

Neither Project Texas nor Project Clover had been codified as a binding legal promise. But breaking even non-binding promises to consumers about who could access their data could trigger penalties for deception under US and EU law. Even if ByteDance was willing to pay whatever penalties the governments imposed, continued data transfers to China would obliterate whatever public trust the company still possessed.

In late 2024 and early 2025, three of ByteDance's most senior remaining lawyers left the company. Erich was already on his way out. But across December and January, Erich's longtime deputy, Matt Penarczyk, the company's head of Global Legal Compliance, Catherine Razzano, and its head of litigation, Emily Stubbs, all moved on to future endeavors.

Shortly before the lawyers' departure, TikTok encountered a surprise setback in another democratic nation: Canada. The Canadian government ordered ByteDance to shutter its Canadian offices. TikTok, the app, would be allowed to keep operating in Canada, and Canadians would be allowed to keep using it. But for national security reasons that the government did not specify, the company's offices in the country—one in Toronto, and a second, larger one, staffed largely by Chinese immigrants, in Vancouver—would have to shut down immediately.

The implication behind the order seemed to be that the people working at TikTok's Canadian offices were themselves a threat to Canadian security, that they were spies of some kind. ByteDance vowed to appeal the ruling—and it would, eventually. But first, it would have to confront yet another legal setback: a 3–0 loss in the second most powerful court in the United States.

~

AFTER ORAL ARGUMENT, nobody really expected TikTok to win before the DC Circuit. But the way the company lost was spectacular, in a decision that hawks would laud as a bold defense of democracy, and First Amendment scholars would decry as a form of democratic backsliding.

The judges had viewed TikTok through the same lens that the European Parliament had. The People's Republic of China, they wrote, aimed to "undermine democracy" through its use of influence operations. The judges cited an assertion made by the US Department of Justice, which was never definitively rebutted by the company: that TikTok had censored content in other countries outside of China at the behest of the Chinese government. They were acutely worried that the same thing could happen in the US, and that we might never know if it did.

"A foreign government threatens to distort free speech on an important medium of communication," the court wrote. "The PRC's ability to do so is at odds with free speech fundamentals."

In the weeks before December 6, the DC Circuit had kept TikTok and its well-wishers waiting. The tech publication *The Information* reported that a decision was expected before Thanksgiving—but one didn't come. In the week after Thanksgiving, as they juggled bad news from Romania, Brussels, and Canada, ByteDance employees in L.A. also woke up early each morning to refresh court watchers' social media accounts and DC Circuit's website. But the court used every day possible before its litigant-imposed deadline, releasing the decision on the 6th itself.

The actual outcome of the case wasn't a surprise, given the judges' skepticism of ByteDance at oral argument. As judges often do, they gave broad deference to the president on national security matters, and they made clear that they were deferring to Congress, too. PAFACAA, they said, was "the culmination of extensive, bipartisan action by the Congress and by successive presidents." But the court's rationale for upholding the law was new: sometimes, they said, government intrusion on speech was required to ensure that free speech could continue.

To be clear: laws restrict speech in the US all the time. You can't make terroristic threats against another person, or incite others to commit violence—and, yes, those restrictions do, to some degree, protect the free speech of their potential victims. But that's not what the court was talking about here. They were saying that *foreign* speech—i.e., Byte-

Dance's sorting of videos through the For You algorithm—might "distort" Americans' "free speech," by covertly turning the dials to decide what you see.

This was traditionally not how the First Amendment had worked. In the past, courts had ruled that Americans had a right to read propaganda produced by foreign adversaries. They could still do that, the DC Circuit said—they could watch videos produced by Russia Today and the *People's Daily*. But they couldn't watch them on a platform subject to the control of a foreign adversary state.

"Here the Congress, as the Executive proposed, acted to end the PRC's ability to control TikTok," the court wrote. "Understood in that way, the Act actually vindicates the values that undergird the First Amendment."

First Amendment scholars decried the ruling. American law had never before recognized defense of free speech as a reason for restricting free speech. The solution to bad speech is more speech, the traditional argument went. And in a functional, free marketplace of ideas, the best ideas would win out, regardless of who their speaker is.

The court's presumption that covert foreign propaganda could reshape TikTok users' political views "reflect[ed] a highly unflattering view of the American public," wrote Stanford Law professor Evelyn Douek. "To water down First Amendment constraints on the American government because of vaguely articulated fears of future Chinese influence would be to endanger what is supposed to make America different, and stronger, in the first place."

Though she likely didn't agree with him on much, Douek sounded almost like JD Vance at his speech in Munich, when he told Romanian officials that their democracy must not be worth much if it could be felled by a garden-variety Russian influence operation. A new division had emerged about TikTok—one that, yet again, defied conventional politics.

In one camp were the DC Circuit Court of Appeals, the US intelligence community, Congress, and the European Parliament, all warning that allowing autocracies to take platforms' reins would lead to democratic backsliding.

In the other camp were Douek, representing First Amendment evangelists and civil liberties groups; and Vance, representing foreign influence skeptics. They replied that stopping people from speaking—even foreign people, or Americans working in concert with them to build curation algorithms—*was* democratic backsliding. If Congress could now limit TikTok's speech to protect a healthy speech ecosystem, what other speech might it deem a threat to "healthy" discourse?

Chapter 38

PER CURIAM

When you lose a case in a US Circuit Court of Appeals, your options are slim. You can go back to the panel of judges who denied your claim and ask them to reconsider. You can appeal to the full Court of Appeals (this is an appeal "en banc") and ask their colleagues to overrule them. And you can petition the Supreme Court of the United States—but your odds of even getting a hearing there are low.

The Supreme Court hears about 1 percent of the appeals made to it. That 1 percent of cases usually involve some sort of conflict between the lower courts about what the law is. But occasionally, the court will hear a case where there is no judicial conflict, especially if it concerns the constitutionality of a statute.

ByteDance knew it had a small chance of even reaching the court. So to maximize its chances—and to signal its politics—it changed lawyers. Andrew Pincus, who had argued the DC Circuit case, was a longtime Democrat with a history of donations to liberal candidates. The incoming legislature, and Trump himself, were determined to oust Democrats from positions of power, and replacing Pincus was an opportunity to show that TikTok was aligned with the incoming regime.

To argue its final salvo, ByteDance tapped Noel Francisco, Trump's first-term solicitor general, who had defended the former president's "Muslim Ban" and shielded his tax returns from investigating congressional committees. But this strategy had a problem: the government's views on TikTok defied partisanship. Trump represented neither the conservative position nor the liberal one. He was an island, with the position: "TikTok is good because TikTok is good for me." While the Supreme

Court was unquestionably conservative, on this particular issue, their conservatism was likely a net negative for ByteDance. Conservative judges generally allowed Congress and the executive branch a freer hand on national security.

When ByteDance's new legal team filed its Supreme Court brief, it came with more signaling—to the justices, but also to Trump himself. If PAFACAA went into effect, they argued, ByteDance would suffer irreparable harm, but it wouldn't be the only one to do so. Trump would suffer too: a shutdown "[would] shutter one of America's most popular speech platforms the day before a presidential inauguration."

Accordingly, the lawyers continued, the court should prevent PAFACAA from going into effect, at least long enough "to give the incoming Administration time to determine its position, as the President-elect and his advisors have voiced support for saving TikTok."

Legally, this argument was meaningless. The lawmakers who wrote PAFACAA had specifically decided not to give any incoming administration the option to "determine its position" on the platform. Congress had decided that *Congress* should have the final word about what happened to TikTok—a fact that the Supreme Court knew full well. But while the Supreme Court took only 1 percent of cases, Trump was definitely going to be president on January 20, and ByteDance could be sure his staffers were reading its briefs.

Two days later, Francisco and his team notched a big victory: they beat the 1 percent odds. The Supreme Court agreed to hear their case—though it then set terms that would make the case unpleasant for everyone involved. Consolidating what would normally have been a monthslong process, the court ordered both ByteDance and DOJ to write and file 13,000-word briefs in just nine days—with a due date of December 27. (There went Christmas break.) Replies to those briefs were due just one week later, on January 3. (No celebrating New Year's either.)

Oral argument—a beefy two hours long—was set for January 10. Francisco would face off against President Biden's superstar solicitor general, the former beauty queen, double Supreme Court clerk, and appellate advocacy savant Elizabeth Prelogar. In squeezing the case through in a matter of mere weeks over the holidays, the court was accommodating ByteDance's request for an opportunity to make its case before PAFACAA went into effect. But it was also ensuring that the Biden DOJ, which had helped write the law, would get to defend it, rather than a Trump DOJ that might be ordered to let the case fall by the wayside.

On December 27, along with ByteDance and DOJ's briefs, the court received several amicus (or "friend of the court") briefs from parties with a stake in the case's outcome. A swarm of First Amendment advocates, including the ACLU and a host of prominent law professors, rushed to TikTok's defense. "The rush to react to foreign propaganda is a prominent feature in American free speech history," the professors wrote. "The First Amendment rights we enjoy today were shaped by a Supreme Court that grew skeptical of speech restrictions that sprung from moral panics over socialist and Communist propaganda." They feared the ramifications of the DC Circuit's defensive stance—but their arguments were overshadowed by another amicus filed the same day.

In an unprecedented filing, President-elect Donald Trump alleged that he was "the right constitutional actor to resolve the [TikTok] dispute" and that he had "a unique interest in the First Amendment issues raised in this case." The filing, authored by John Sauer, Trump's private defense attorney and nominee for solicitor general, offered a hagiographic argument: "President Trump is one of the most powerful, prolific, and influential users of social media in history." Sauer insisted that Trump's prowess for virality, along with singular "consummate dealmaking expertise" made him the right person to decide what happened to TikTok, never mind Congress's decision to reserve that power for itself.

Trump didn't take sides between ByteDance and the government; he merely asked that justices let him decide TikTok's fate. What Trump would actually do about TikTok was far from clear—and politically tricky. He had nominated Marco Rubio, one of TikTok's most longstanding and dedicated opponents, to serve as secretary of state. His incoming vice president, JD Vance, had said he supported a ban on TikTok, and that the RESTRICT Act was too weak on the issue. Trump's incoming homeland security director, Kristi Noem, was the first of many Republican governors to ban TikTok on state government devices; and his incoming national security advisor, Mike Waltz, had been a vocal proponent of PAFACAA in Congress.

In the decades before TikTok's rise, hawkism was a reliably Republican position in the US. As TikTok rose to power in 2019 and 2020, its opponents were nearly all conservatives. But across the political spectrum, lawmakers were afraid of platforms' unprecedented power. The parties were also united in their distrust of the Chinese government, which had enabled their rare, lockstep vote on PAFACAA. And now, a Trump acolyte backed by professors and the ACLU was arguing TikTok's case against a darling of the Democratic establishment, who found herself defending an expansionist vision of the government's national security authority.

ByteDance also began playing politics outside its Supreme Court case. Its American competitors donated millions to Trump's inaugural fund, and settled frivolous lawsuits brought by Trump against their companies for millions of dollars. These actions—little more than veiled bribes, given in the hopes that Trump would not target them in his initial frenzy of executive actions—raised the stakes for ByteDance, but also left it in familiar territory. Bribery (or other improper enrichment) of public officials was common in China, and with the courts a long shot, perhaps expensive flattery might beget results that their counsel Noel Francisco could not.

While his lawyers were grinding away, Shou Zi Chew exchanged messages with Trump's right-hand man, Elon Musk, and made a pilgrimage to Mar-a-Lago, Trump's Versailles-like estate in Palm Beach, Florida. The visit was obligatory for a big tech CEO: Mark Zuckerberg and Jeff Bezos were also seen at the resort in late November and December, and Musk went so far as to set up a residence at the property. Still, it was a strategic necessity for Shou—and for Michael Beckerman—who had long begged politicians to see TikTok on par with companies like Meta, Amazon, and X.

The company also agreed to sponsor an inauguration party for

Trump—one of many planned for the upcoming long weekend. The party would be held at Sax, a controversial burlesque bar known for putting up, and then painting over, a series of provocative murals that depicted scenes like Bill Clinton as a saxophone-playing centaur with Monica Lewinsky riding his back and reaching her hands down toward his groin, and George W. Bush standing on the *Resolute* desk in confederate flag boxers, thrusting a beer bottle from his crotch toward a stripper pole-dancing in front of old glory.

The party would be hosted by MAGA influencer and entertainment lawyer Raquel Debono, known for her "Make America Hot Again" dating events for right-wing singles. It would feature a TikTok photo booth, TikTok-branded swag, music by the rapper Waka Flocka Flame, and, rumor had it, an appearance by Shou himself. Before Shou could party with the MAGA ascendant, however, there was the matter of the Supreme Court.

The morning of January 10 was cold: twenty-five degrees with several inches of snow lingering on the streets from a winter storm earlier in the week. A line of court-watchers clad in fur-lined coats, earmuffs, and—in some cases—blankets snaked around the building, as people lined up for the chance at witnessing the arguments firsthand. Some carried ring lights and selfie-sticks as they made videos for their online fans.

Members of the Supreme Court Bar began streaming into the building around 8:30 a.m., but some of TikTok's legal team were left to wait in the cold with TikTok enthusiasts and members of the public outside.

Francisco argued first. "The government's real target," he claimed, is "speech itself—[the] fear that Americans, even if fully informed, could be persuaded by Chinese misinformation. That, however, is a decision that the First Amendment leaves to the people." In other words: the DC Circuit's doctrine of defensive democracy was a threat to democracy itself.

If the Supreme Court had been fully satisfied with the DC Circuit's ruling, they would have had no reason to take up the case at all. Francisco was making a bet that the justices thought the Circuit had gone too far. But in general, the justices were skeptical of Francisco's case. "Are we supposed to ignore the fact that the ultimate parent is, in fact, subject to doing intelligence work for the Chinese government?" asked Chief Justice Roberts.

The justices didn't mention President-elect Trump's amicus at oral argument; justices rarely bring up amicus briefs when questioning litigants' counsel. But they did ask some questions about what the president was and wasn't allowed to do under the law. At oral argument, it is the justices' job to ask questions of counsel, not to debate with one another. But through their questioning of Solicitor General Prelogar, Justices Brett Kavanaugh and Sonia Sotomayor sparred about the extent to which President Trump might just ignore PAFACAA altogether.

There is a long history of presidents declining to enforce laws they didn't believe in. President Ronald Reagan declined to prosecute antitrust laws, George W. Bush declined to enforce environmental protections, and Barack Obama declined to prosecute federal marijuana violations in states that had legalized the drug. "Could the president say that we're not going to enforce this law?" Kavanaugh asked Prelogar. She answered, diplomatically: "as a general matter . . . the president has enforcement discretion."

Justice Sotomayor returned to the topic. "I am a little concerned [by the] suggestion that a president-elect or anyone else should not enforce the law when a law is in effect and has prohibited certain action," she said. "But putting that aside, on the 19th, if it doesn't shut down, there is a violation of law, correct?" Prelogar confirmed that there would be a violation.

"And whatever the new president does," Sotomayor continued, "doesn't change that reality?"

"That's right," said Prelogar.

"How long is the statute of limitations in effect? Assuming that they violated it that day and later continued to violate it, but how long does the statute of limitations exist for a civil violation of this sort?" the Justice asked.

Prelogar replied: "It would be a five-year statute of limitations."

Sotomayor had made her point: even if Trump ignored PAFACAA, the next president could prosecute violations of it. Despite the president-elect's amicus argument, Congress had made itself the arbiter of TikTok's fate.

~

WHEN THE SUPREME COURT says something it might later regret, it usually hedges to signal its unease. Justices can choose to "concur" with one another, rather than sign on to a majority opinion, which enables them to agree on the outcome, but not the rationale behind a given decision. Courts can also designate opinions as non-precedential, noting expressly that litigants should not cite it in the future.

Justices can also include language in an opinion that suggests it is so unique, so fact specific, that any attempt to apply it to another situation would likely be futile. This is what the court famously did in *Bush v. Gore*, and what, to only a slightly lesser extent, it did in the TikTok case.

Just one week after the TikTok oral argument—and two days before PAFACAA's January 19 deadline—the Supreme Court issued its ruling. The decision was unanimous and per curiam, meaning it was unsigned: the court chose to speak with one voice.

The Supreme Court has been hesitant to make new, sweeping law about the internet. In 2023, the court considered a set of challenges to the infamous Section 230 of the Communications Decency Act that protected platforms from being sued for things their users posted. In a dispute at oral argument about whether Section 230's modern effects were consistent with Congress's 1996 intent, Justice Elena Kagan suggested that Congress, rather than the court, should address any mismatch between the statute's original intent and current effect. Spurring laughter and headlines, she wisely characterized herself and her colleagues, "These are not, like, the nine greatest experts on the internet."

Kagan's self-effacing line was echoed in the introduction to the TikTok opinion:

> As Justice Frankfurter advised 80 years ago in considering the application of established legal rules to the "totally new problems" raised

by the airplane and radio, we should take care not to "embarrass the future." [citation omitted] That caution is heightened in these cases, given the expedited time allowed for our consideration. Our analysis must be understood to be narrowly focused in light of these circumstances.

In other words: this was one they were still a little unsure about.

The opinion walked a fine line. It distinguished between PAFACAA's two justifications—the dual threats of surveillance and propaganda. The justices didn't dispute Francisco's argument that defensively controlling the speech ecosystem to protect it violated the First Amendment. Instead, they relied solely on the surveillance rationale. As Justice Neil Gorsuch put it: "Speaking with and in favor of a foreign adversary is one thing. Allowing a foreign adversary to spy on Americans is another."

In a way, the opinion was a punt. The court had dodged the meatiest, most important question before it: whether the US government should be allowed to manipulate the speech ecosystem so that the Chinese government couldn't. Instead of taking sides on that question, the court had said it didn't have to decide it, because data protection was a good enough reason on its own for Congress to pass PAFACAA.

By taking the case and evading the question of discourse manipulation, the Supreme Court diminished the circuit court's novel reasoning without directly opining on it, leaving the key First Amendment question in the case unanswered. A nonanswer, though, was an answer of its own kind: the court had let Congress's action stand.

A few hours after the Supreme Court ruling, Shou Zi Chew posted TikTok's response: a shaky selfie that looked like a hostage video where the hostage was being held in a suite at the Four Seasons. Wearing one of his lucky Hermès ties, his forehead softened by light perspiration, Shou reiterated that TikTok had been fighting for its users' constitutional right to free speech—a strange case to make given that the arbiters of constitutionality had, just hours before, unanimously dismissed the company's claim to such a right. But then, he pivoted:

I want to thank President Trump for his commitment to work with us to find a solution that keeps TikTok available in the United States.... We are grateful and pleased to have the support of a president who truly understands our platform, one who has used TikTok to express his own thoughts and perspectives, connecting with the world and generating more than 60 billion views of his content in the process.

More than four years earlier, teens and K-pop stans on TikTok had rankled Trump by attacking his perceived popularity—by making it look like nobody actually wanted to hear him speak. Now, Shou was flattering him in the exact opposite way, trumpeting his astronomical reach as if it were proof that he deserved unmatched adulation.

PAFACAA was law, and with the Supreme Court's decision, it was expressly constitutional. So Shou's only hope to keep TikTok alive in the US was to convince President-elect Trump to violate that law, to decline to enforce it, as Justice Kavanaugh had imagined in his question to Prelogar. Ordinarily, a Supreme Court defeat should have been the end of TikTok's crusade. But unlike Biden or Congress, Trump was unwedded to the rule of law, and his transactional style—and susceptibility to influence—gave the company one last avenue for survival.

~

AMERICAN TIKTOK USERS responded to the news of their favorite platform's impending end in typical TikToker fashion: by trolling. Over the course of a week, more than three million self-declared "TikTok refugees" signed up en masse for another platform, one even more clearly controlled by the Chinese Communist Party: an Instagram-like Chinese app called Xiaohongshu—or literally, in English, "Little Red Book." The American newcomers called the app "RedNote."

On X, a post by an account named @outsoldnation went viral for a post that paired a gif of Beyonce laughing with the text: "Me selecting 'ALLOW' when Rednote asks if I will allow them to track my data🐼🐼"

TikTok was the rare policy issue about which there was broad, bipartisan alignment in Washington—and nearly as broad alignment in the public reaching the opposite conclusion. Support for a ban on the platform had fallen dramatically since PAFACAA's passage, and millions of regular Americans believed the government's national security concerns were silly at best and bigoted at worst.

The discourse on Xiaohongshu was light and, for the most part, delightful. Americans began helping Chinese teens with their English homework, and vice versa. Both American and Chinese made jokes about "Chinese spies"; per AP, one friendly animal enthusiast from Sichuan wrote: "I am your Chinese spy... please surrender your personal information or the photographs of your cat (or dog)." Thousands of Americans happily paid a "cat tax" to their new online friends by sharing photos of their felines—though they were banned from talking about a host of other topics, like gay rights, the Dalai Lama, or Taiwanese sovereignty.

Meanwhile, in what could have been TikTok's final hours in the US, its users savored their final moments and said their goodbyes. On TikTok and across its competitor platforms, users held "funerals" for the app, sharing fake funeral programs, clips of gospel music, and discussing which dishes they'd each bring to the celebration of life. A Florida college campus radio station hosted a funeral for the platform on the air, and in New York City's Washington Square Park, comedian Zach Sage Fox hosted a physical mock funeral complete with a casket and a life-size inflatable doll.

Dressed in an all-black suit and shades, Fox spoke into the camera: "Hello, America, I'm Zach Sage Fox, and today we gather to mourn a dear friend—and a Chinese spy tool banned by the US Government."

Fox turned to a small crowd gathered to watch his performance. "Anything you'd like to say to TikTok?"

A few people chimed in:

"It was a nice run,"

"Rest in peace,"

"Thank you so much for being there for me in all my times of loneliness."

A mother walking by with her teenage daughter said good riddance to the app, before the teen said she would miss the platform very much.

"I'm so sorry we couldn't save you!" cried a young woman with mock passion, kneeling before the inflatable doll in the casket. Tongue-in-cheek, Fox asked: "Have you learned to hate the Western World?" She quipped back, "Of course, yes, yeah." Another interviewee chimed in, laughing, "Yeah, fuck America!"

The irreverent crowd performed TikTok dances and lamented the need to go to physical stores to buy the gizmos and gadgets they had previously ordered on TikTok Shop.

"Which platform will you turn to now?" Fox asked. The teenage daughter walking by with her mother responded without a beat: "RedNote, here we come."

"You want the Chinese government to have your information?" he asked the crowd. "Heck yeah," someone responded. "You trust them more than our own government?" A redheaded woman replied with a sassy "mmhmm," and a man echoed: "China will do something better with it anyways."

"R.I.P. TikTok," Fox concluded. "And to my 1.1 million followers, follow me on X, Instagram, and YouTube! . . . So, can I return the casket back to Amazon?"

Chapter 39

THE FLICKER

THE FINAL DAYS OF JOE BIDEN'S PRESIDENCY WERE BRUTAL for Biden and his allies. The outgoing president was roundly condemned for issuing a pardon to his son Hunter, who had struggled with addiction and committed various misdeeds during his father's tenure in public life. In his final hours as president, Biden then went on to pardon an extensive list of Trump's self-perceived political enemies, against whom Trump had promised to seek revenge. But the pardons only reached those who were paying close attention to politics. PAFACAA affected more than half the voting population—and its 270-day deadline fell on the last full day of the Biden presidency.

Shou Zi Chew's response to the Supreme Court decision showed that TikTok intended to blame Biden for the law as much as it could. With Trump promising to "save" TikTok, Biden was faced with the reality that if TikTok did in fact go dark, he would almost certainly be faulted for it.

After the Supreme Court's ruling, Democratic Senate Minority Leader Chuck Schumer seemed ambivalent about having allowed the law to pass in the first place (despite having voted for it). He called the beleaguered Biden, urging him to extend the deadline for a ban despite ByteDance's refusal to sell, and insisting that a TikTok ban would tarnish Biden's legacy. PAFACAA allowed the president to issue a ninety-day extension to ByteDance, but only if he certified that bona fide progress had been made toward a sale: something that even ByteDance hadn't tried to claim was the case.

Schumer spoke out in favor of a bill, advanced by several Senate Democrats, that would amend PAFACAA to allow more time for a sale.

Republicans blocked the Senate effort. So Biden did the next best thing: he kicked the can down the road, promising not to enforce violations of PAFACAA on the last day of his presidency. It would be up to the Trump DOJ to decide whether to levy fines against Apple, Google, Oracle, or anyone else under the statute.

This promise was performative. The Biden DOJ wouldn't have had time to secure a judgment against any company in their last hours in office anyway. Courts just don't move that fast, and the prosecutors' work would've been inherited by a Trump administration that could promptly stop it from advancing. This meant there was no reason for TikTok to go dark on January 19—at least if Trump, too, promised to decline to enforce PAFACAA.

Just because TikTok didn't *have* to go dark, though, didn't mean that it wouldn't. Shou and Michael Beckerman saw a political opportunity, and they weren't about to waste it. So approximately eighteen hours before PAFACAA was scheduled to go into effect, TikTok users received a push notification telling them that the app was going down. If TikTok stayed online, then Trump wouldn't be able to "save" it, as he promised he would. Going dark, even if it wasn't necessary, would give the incoming president a win.

In just five years, TikTok had gone from eschewing politics to reluctantly accepting and now brazenly fueling it. At the White House, spokesperson Karine Jean-Pierre insisted to reporters that the company's plans were just theatrics. "It is a stunt, and we see no reason for TikTok or other companies to take actions in the next few days before the Trump Administration takes office on Monday," she said. Nevertheless, just a few hours before January 19 arrived, a notification went up in the TikTok app:

> We regret that a U.S. law banning TikTok will take effect on January 19 and force us to make our services temporarily unavailable. We're working to restore our service in the U.S. as soon as possible, and we appreciate your support. Please stay tuned.

Just a few hours later, the first notification was replaced with a second:

> A law banning TikTok has been enacted in the U.S. Unfortunately, that means you can't use TikTok for now.
>
> We are fortunate that President Trump has indicated that he will work with us on a solution to reinstate TikTok once he takes office. Please stay tuned!

Shou and Michael, who had sworn to both Congress and the Biden administration for years that TikTok had no political agenda, were now going to use every opportunity they could to celebrate Donald Trump to TikTok's 170 million American users. As University of Washington researcher Mike Caulfield posted on Bluesky: "I do think there's something about the Chinese company knowing exactly how to operate in the environment that really brings home where we have arrived."

On the morning of January 19, the company released yet another statement.

> In agreement with our service providers, TikTok is in the process of restoring service. We thank President Trump for providing the necessary clarity and assurance to our service providers that they will face no penalties providing TikTok to over 170 million Americans and allowing over 7 million small businesses to thrive.
>
> It's a strong stand for the First Amendment and against arbitrary censorship. We will work with President Trump on a long-term solution that keeps TikTok in the United States.

This time, their language was matched by a statement by President Trump himself.

> I'm asking companies not to let TikTok stay dark! I will issue an executive order on Monday to extend the period of time before the law's prohibitions take effect, so that we can make a deal to protect our

national security. The order will also confirm that there will be no liability for any company that helped keep TikTok from going dark before my order. Americans deserve to see our exciting Inauguration on Monday, as well as other events and conversations.

Trump apparently hadn't forgotten Noel Francisco's line in ByteDance's Supreme Court filing about the inauguration. The president-elect desperately wanted his second inauguration to show that he had bigger crowds and more adoring fans than any president ever had before. If the festivities couldn't be broadcasted on TikTok, he would miss the opportunity to reach what Shou had promised was a massive audience.

The timing of Trump's promise to prevent prosecutions under PAFACAA was unprecedented. As of January 19, 2025, Donald J. Trump was still just a guy. His statements didn't carry the force of law, he didn't control the DOJ, and he couldn't legally make policy. But that hadn't stopped him from speaking with CCP leader Xi Jinping about the app just two days before, and his statement suggested he was ready to veer yet further into uncharted territory:

> I would like the United States to have a 50% ownership position in a joint venture. By doing this, we save TikTok, keep it in good hands and allow it to say [sic] up. Without U.S. approval, there is no Tik Tok. With our approval, it is worth hundreds of billions of dollars— maybe trillions.
>
> Therefore, my initial thought is a joint venture between the current owners and/or new owners whereby the U.S. gets a 50% ownership in a joint venture set up between the U.S. and whichever purchase we so choose.

Nobody quite knew what to make of this proclamation. Will Stancil, a left-wing policy researcher and prominent social media shitposter, offered a dressed-down reading: "trump: 'what if tiktok was co-owned by Xi and myself.'"

The United States had never attempted to own or invest in an internet platform before. If it tried to do so, it would immediately raise much bigger First Amendment questions than PAFACAA had. US law gave extensive free speech rights to both private citizens and private companies, but the First Amendment aggressively restricted what the government could do to curtail or limit the free flow of discourse between its people. How would a government-owned platform handle content moderation? Could it use algorithms to target people with personalized messages? What if it "heated" certain videos and suppressed others?

Trump's suggestion of "joint" US control over TikTok, along with its current owners, also likely wouldn't satisfy PAFACAA. In writing the law, Congress had insisted that a divestiture would only suffice if it ensured that "no operational relationship" between TikTok and ByteDance remained—an unlikely scenario.

The people most troubled by Trump's statement were lawyers at Apple, Google, and Oracle—the three American tech giants that had to decide whether to violate PAFACAA or not. By asking them to break the law and bring TikTok back online, Trump was instituting his own loyalty test: one that assessed how willing Americans were to buck norms on his say-so.

The Apple and Google lawyers were wary. Trump had teased investigations of—even crusades against—both Silicon Valley companies before, for their alleged wokeness and liberal bias. He had also been known to flip-flop, including on the issue of TikTok itself. Even if Trump said he wasn't enforcing PAFACAA for now, he might reverse his position later, and if he did, he might try to leverage a PAFACAA violation against them on some future date. And that was before they even considered the five-year statute of limitations that Justice Sotomayor had raised: Even if Trump agreed not to prosecute PAFACAA violations, who was to say his successor wouldn't?

These concerns were enough to keep TikTok out of the Google and Apple app stores, despite Trump's plea. But Oracle, the company with the power to bring the app back online for the 170 million people who had already installed it, made the opposite choice. Perhaps because Larry Ellison and Safra Catz had a history in Trumpist politics—or perhaps because Oracle would again try to persuade Trump that it should become TikTok's owner—the company agreed to incur fines in the hundreds of billions at the request of a man who still didn't yet hold any official government power.

When Oracle flipped the switch, a fourth notification went up in the app: "Welcome back! Thanks for your patience and support. As a result of President Trump's efforts, TikTok is back in the U.S.!"

Chapter 40

TWO DADDIES NOW

JANUARY 20, 2025, WAS A COLD, WINDY DAY IN WASHINGTON, DC. President-elect Trump, fearing the weather would mute his inauguration celebration, opted to move the festivities inside, to the cavernous Capitol Rotunda where his supporters had rioted in protest of his loss just four years before. The CEOs of Meta, Apple, Amazon, Google, and X sat directly behind the stage as Trump became the forty-seventh president of the United States. The execs had seats better than Trump's own cabinet appointees—they were closer to him than everyone but his family.

One row behind the American CEOs sat Shou Zi Chew, beside Trump's nominee for director of national intelligence, Tulsi Gabbard. In the days leading up to the inauguration, Shou and Michael had schmoozed future Trump staffers at a candlelight donor dinner at the National Building Museum hosted by Trump himself. (Elon Musk and Jeff Bezos were also in attendance.) Michael also attended an inauguration party hosted by Ballard Partners, Trump Chief of Staff Susie Wiles's old lobbying firm, which ByteDance had hired in September to strengthen its ties to Trump.

The "Make America Hot Again" party on the evening of January 19 had featured TikTok-emblazoned earmuffs and beanies; cardboard cutouts of Donald Trump, JD Vance, and Elon Musk in cowboy attire; and a rapper throwing McDonald's burgers into the crowd—but despite the rumors, Shou hadn't made an appearance.

Shou's mere presence at the inauguration offended some lawmakers. Arch-conservative Tom Cotton released a statement on the day before the swearing-in: "Now that the law has taken effect, there's no legal basis for any kind of 'extension' of its effective date. For TikTok to come back online in the future, ByteDance must agree to a sale that satisfies the law's qualified-divestiture requirements by severing all ties between TikTok and Communist China."

Cotton ally Josh Hawley told a gaggle of reporters in the Capitol hallways, with a smirk, that the CEO's presence at the event was "not my favorite thing, not my favorite thing." But Shou's seat alongside future cabinet secretaries suggested that TikTok's flattery campaign was working.

The gulf between Trump and hard-right senators like Hawley and Cotton—and the unity between Hawley, Cotton, and Democrats like Mark Warner and Raja Krishnamoorthi—showed just how strange TikTok's politics continued to be. Lawmakers from both parties were frustrated and confused that Trump, who had once aggressively pursued a TikTok ban for the same national security risks that led them to pass PAFACAA, was now willing to subvert those risks to score political points. They were also rankled by Trump's disregard of PAFACAA itself. As president, Trump could make decisions about how he wanted to prioritize the enforcement of federal laws, but to disregard those laws entirely was a slap in the face to Congress and its lawmaking power.

After inauguration on January 20, Donald Trump signed twenty-six executive orders to kick off the first day of his second presidency. Among them, as promised, was an instruction to DOJ that it should not enforce PAFACAA for seventy-five days. The seventy-five-day term was unrelated to the ninety-day extension contemplated by PAFACAA, and Trump made no certifications to Congress, as PAFACAA required, that any sort of a deal was underway.

As he signed the order, Trump took questions from reporters. "Essentially, with TikTok, I have the right to sell it or close it," he said, recasting PAFACAA as a grant of presidential power. "We may have to get approval from China—I'm not sure. I'm sure they'll approve." ByteDance, though, now had a problem beyond the Chinese government's approval: now, everyone knew it was willing to propagandize if doing so meant it could keep doing business.

Shou's decision to openly pander to Trump did for TikTok's reputation what a thousand histrionic congressional statements could not: it showed regular TikTok users that their favorite app might instantly become a mouthpiece for a government they disliked. The irony is that the government was their own, not that of a foreign adversary.

On X, music journalist Sowmya Krishnamurthy posted: "TikTok is officially a Trump propaganda platform," and queer artist Nicole Brennan wrote: "I'm gonna need every single one of you to remember that this entire thing was a theatrical stunt to make Trump seem like a savior." On TikTok itself, fashionista Meghan Wainwright said, "I literally have such an ick from TikTok and the government pulling this PR stunt last night."

Medical researcher and TikTok science educator Joel Bervell, who had more than 700,000 fans on the app, told the UK outlet *The Independent*: "At any point, the Trump administration can take away what they seem to have given in their good graces, and I worry that they're going to use it as [a] bargaining chip for whatever thing he wants it to do."

TikTok's core constituency—young people—quickly echoed the now-suspicious influencers. The app's capitulation had only a marginal effect on its usage, and it continued to exercise its power as a huge commander of American attention. But "the flicker" had served as a pulling back of the curtain, a sort of loss-of-innocence moment for TikTok's users about what the app was and what it wasn't. Nobody believed, anymore, that "the algorithm" was a magical technology that understood its users' souls. Now it was just a guy named Bob—or Shou—or Donald. In "saving" TikTok, Trump had killed its magic.

Some prominent left-leaning TikTokers said their feeds felt different after "the flicker," and claimed they were now facing new forms of censorship. Though TikTok insisted that its content moderation policies had not changed, users began relying more heavily on winks, nods, and codewords to circumvent an algorithm they no longer trusted. People warning their communities about immigration raids started a trend of sharing raid information in handwritten notes, while they held up and advertised "cute winter boots." That way, their content would be promoted as shopping-related, rather than demoted as politically sensitive.

In college newspapers at Western Kentucky University, NYU, Wellesley, and Dickinson, and high school papers in Coral Springs, Florida, and Evanston, Illinois, student journalists called out TikTok's behavior. TikTok "crediting [Trump] as the sole savior of the app" was "a blatant piece of propaganda," wrote Dickinson College freshman Quinn Downing. Wellesley college freshman Avery Finley described it as "a thinly veiled tactic for Trump to . . . solidify his control over the media."

People keep using social media platforms long after they stop liking them. Facebook has achieved near graveyard status among American millennials and Gen Z, but many people still occasionally log in to check their accounts and see how family members are doing. To a lesser degree, the same can be said of Instagram: many of its users don't *like* it, per se, but they reluctantly use it anyway, because they want to see their friends' updates.

The same thing can be said, to a still lesser extent, of Twitter. There, people were more likely to connect with strangers, building relationships from scratch organically through the social platform. But over time, debates and dialogues forged real communities—ones that people often struggled to leave even after Elon Musk bought Twitter, made dramatic changes to it, and then transformed it into the MAGA bastion called X.

In executing TikTok's flicker into death and back to life, Shou had bet that mimicking a true shutoff would prove TikTok's indispensability, showing just how unpopular a ban truly was. But that bet might have been at least partially wrong, because real-life relationships didn't exist to tie people to TikTok the way those relationships had tied people to Facebook, Instagram, and X.

For years, TikTok employees had told anyone who asked that their technology was different—that while their competitors ran on interest graphs, they ran on entertainment graphs. They didn't care who you knew; they cared what you liked, and their technology was uniquely able to figure you out.

TikTok lost something, though, by prizing what you liked over the stickiness of real-life relationships. TikToks might be pleasant to watch, but they were ephemeral. The platform where you could watch an entertainer talk about medieval art for fifteen seconds at a time might be cool, but it was something you could give up more easily than the platform where you saw pictures of your cousins' kids. TikTok might be fun, but it was easy come, easy go.

Nearly half the voting population of the US voted against Donald Trump in 2024, and it's safe to say that most of those people *really* didn't like him. By allying itself with such a divisive figure, TikTok now risked losing many of the people who had made it take off in the first place. The same company that had advertised back in 2018 with a cheeky brag that an unpopular, abrasive politician didn't use its platform was now gratuitously stroking the ego of that same politician in notifications going out to 170 million people—and the TikTok faithful were feeling more than a little whiplash.

Sean Garrette, a Black men's skincare influencer with more than 35,000 TikTok followers, posted on X during the outage: "Them even mentioning Trump in that statement makes me not even wanna be back on tiktok when it does come back lol. You get in bed with the dogs, you get fleas."

~

DESPITE ALL THE hostile vibes from its users, six weeks after Shou flickered TikTok off and on again, ByteDance's global head of ads made a celebratory internal announcement: revenue was back to 100 percent. There had been a dip after the flicker, but it had been temporary. At least when it came to money, TikTok was as strong as it ever had been before.

The following week, staff got another piece of good news: after receiving a series of letters from Trump's DOJ that effectively claimed the power to nullify PAFACAA, Apple and Google agreed to return TikTok to the app stores. It almost felt like things had returned to normal. But under the surface, Trump's seventy-five-day clock was ticking.

TikTok's American investors smelled opportunity. They resuscitated an idea they had pitched in 2020: they would buy equity in TikTok's US business and spin it off into its own legal entity, which they could say was majority-US owned, and which, hopefully, would someday IPO. The 2020 version of this idea had been called "TikTok Global," but in 2025, it was reimagined into "TikTok America." The new TikTok entity would license a version of the For You algorithm from ByteDance, which would continue to own and control it. ByteDance would still be involved in running TikTok America, but it wouldn't have access to sensitive user data.

We were back—yet again—to some version of Project Texas, despite the fact that Congress had unequivocally rejected it. Trump didn't care about violating PAFACAA, and at his request, Apple, Google, and Oracle were disobeying the law already. But the text of the law was clear that it required more than just monetary divestment. Lawmakers had said ByteDance could maintain "no operational relationship" with TikTok, "including any cooperation with respect to the operation of a content recommendation algorithm."

Investors worried about being held liable under the law after Trump left office. In Trump's first few months back in power, many American firms had begun taking a "Martian" approach to national politics, reimagining their values to reflect those of a leader quick to interpret difference as disloyalty. But as Justice Sonia Sotomayor had presciently pointed out just months before, PAFACAA's statute of limitations gave it power beyond Trump's second term. So what might a post-Trump return to the rule of law mean for a Trump-brokered deal?

ByteDance's executive team began negotiating with their third US presidential administration. The goal was the same as ever: don't get banned, and don't break Chinese law. Throughout the flicker, Shou had been the face of TikTok's negotiations in the United States. But he now faced the same challenge that Kevin Mayer had faced before him: if TikTok's US operations were cleaved out into their own business, then the job of global TikTok CEO wouldn't exist anymore. And if TikTok's worldwide business was sold entirely, there was no guarantee the new owners would keep Shou around.

Shou stayed quiet as a draft deal began to emerge. TikTok America offered no fix for the Employee Shakedown Problem beyond Project Texas. Leasing the For You algorithm might avoid the Chinese export regulations that had scuttled the 2020 deal, but it didn't solve the problem that the CCP might someday use the algorithm to manipulate US discourse. While Trump might dress the deal up as a victory, its real winners would be the CCP, which would keep control over Zhang Yiming's crown jewel, and ByteDance, which would finagle a reprieve from a sell-or-ban mandate that was supposedly binding US law.

The parties were close. But on April 2—three days before Trump's self-imposed seventy-five-day deadline—Trump imposed harsh tariffs on goods imported from China. In retaliation, the Chinese government instructed ByteDance to make no deal at all, unless Trump was willing to bargain on tariffs and trade in exchange.

On April 4, Trump took to his social media platform, Truth Social. "CHINA PLAYED IT WRONG, THEY PANICKED—THE ONE THING THEY CANNOT AFFORD TO DO!" he wrote. A few hours later, he posted again: "My Administration has been working very hard on a Deal to SAVE TIKTOK, and we have made tremendous progress." However, he continued, "The Deal requires more work to ensure all necessary approvals are signed."

For another seventy-five days, Trump would instruct his DOJ to suspend enforcement of PAFACAA. The CCP might have prevented a deal from happening, but this way, Trump kept his leverage, too. TikTok had two daddies now, the second every bit as unpredictable as the first. And both held the power to constrain its future.

Employees settled wearily into yet another few months of job insecurity. Congressional aides watched as their meticulous work was again rendered irrelevant. Evelyn Douek, the Stanford professor who had criticized PAFACAA, quipped wryly, "The president holding this much power over one of the major communications platforms in this country is very good; very free speechy." Alan Rozenshtein, a national security lawyer who often clashed with Douek on TikTok, shared her disgust. The extension, he said, was "lawless Calvinball."

Shou didn't respond to Trump's tweets, or to reports that a sale had yet again been thwarted by the Chinese government. But the following night, he walked the red carpet at LA's Academy Museum of Motion

Pictures alongside Katy Perry, Drew Barrymore, and Gwyneth Paltrow. He was there to celebrate the Breakthrough Prize, a science award created by his former boss, investor Yuri Milner. Also in attendance were Meta's Mark Zuckerberg and Amazon's Jeff Bezos, the latter of whom had submitted a last-minute bid for TikTok to the Trump administration earlier that week.

In an unbuttoned tux and black suede loafers, Shou stood mute, posing for photos as reporters yelled out questions about TikTok's future. On the app itself, he posted a three-second clip from the event—his first TikTok in months—captioned "Hello from LA!" He waved, with a broad, fixed smile. Then the video was over.

The next morning, the most popular comment on Shou's video was a TikToker begging: "please don't sell to Musk, Besos [sic] or Zuckerberg. they will ruin it." The second-most popular comment asked "Where the heck you been bruh?" The third said simply "you sold us out."

Shou had little control over whether or to whom TikTok would ultimately be sold, though he was responsible for The Flicker. But missing in action was the person who did hold at least some of that control—the company's steady hand, its moral champion: Yiming.

TikTok had proved itself both too big to ban and too big not to ban. It had created a constitutional crisis, a national security risk, and a whole secondary economy. It had become the subject of yet another tenuous, unconscionably expensive, ultimately illusory deal. And its creator, poring over white papers about AGI, was already on to the next thing.

EPILOGUE

In the first six months of the second Trump administration, TikTok settled into a new norm. Pandering to Trump—or at least not angering him—remained key to the app's existence. But for the most part, the company kept a low profile, wading quietly through its legal limbo.

The reaction to the second and third extensions was muted. Experts said Trump was breaking the law by allowing ByteDance to keep operating TikTok, but experts often said Trump was breaking the law, and the Supreme Court rarely stepped in to change his behavior.

Michael Beckerman left TikTok—and DC—moving his family to South Carolina so that his children could grow up closer to their cousins. Shou Zi Chew posted a few videos advertising the company's new AI features and hobnobbed with creators at advertising events, but said nothing publicly about a potential sale. In an unsigned statement on its website, TikTok thanked Trump for his "leadership and support" in letting the app continue to exist in the United States.

ByteDance continued to own TikTok, controlling its digital airwaves and its access to data about hundreds of millions of people. No new legal restrictions were placed on how data could flow. The app gave ByteDance a fuller view than any pollster or focus group of contemporary societies around the world—what people liked and didn't like, what their interests were, who their friends were, what they talked about, and didn't, and why. Before Zhang Yiming's "era of sharing," no person or company had this much data about who we are. Now, it had become the central prize of his life's work.

The charade of corporate dealmaking fell away. Might some cohort of American investors buy a version of TikTok and lease the For You algorithm from ByteDance, against Congress's will? Maybe—but only if someone forced Yiming to sell, and only if both Trump and Xi Jinping believed a deal was in their interests. Shou had promised less than three years earlier that TikTok would not be manipulated by any government. But since then, both Trump and Xi have defined the app's future.

ACKNOWLEDGMENTS

THERE ARE SO MANY PEOPLE WITHOUT WHOM THIS BOOK would not have happened. Thanks to my brilliant editor, Tom Mayer, and agent, Adam Eaglin, for convincing me to write this book and being there at every step to make it sing; to Alex Yu, who provided Chinese-language translation, interpretation, and deep journalistic expertise; to Hilary McClellen, for keeping me on the right track; to the family and friends who read and improved my early drafts; to the teams at Norton and Cheney for their support at every turn; to Rick Tulsky, who persuaded me that I might want to become an investigative reporter in the first place; and to Mark Schoofs, Ariel Kaminer, John Paczkowski, and Katharine Schwab, who made me into one.

NOTES

This book was made possible by the many people at ByteDance who shared their stories with me. It draws from interviews with approximately 150 people across four continents, many of whom spoke anonymously for fear of retribution from ByteDance or the Chinese government. It also draws from audio recordings of more than eighty internal ByteDance meetings and thousands of pages of internal chat logs, documents, photos, and other company materials. Before writing this book, I spent several years covering TikTok and ByteDance for *BuzzFeed News*, and then for *Forbes*, where I published nearly thirty articles about the company. This book builds on that body of work. Where I rely on other journalists' reporting, I have cited them here. Direct quotes are sourced from interviews with the people who said them, from audio recordings, from written correspondences, or from people who witnessed the statements. Translations of written statements from Chinese to English, and valuable interpretation thereof, were provided by Mengyu Dong.

Chapter 1

9 **On a sunny May day in 2019:** Details about the trip to Chicago and Indianapolis are sourced from confidential source interviews in October and December 2024, as well as from a cache of photos and documents related to the trip.

9 **one-stop shop for everything on the internet:** Details about what TopBuzz contained come from Wayback Machine captures of TopBuzz.com and screenshots of the app available across the web. The sources referenced in these paragraphs are preserved in the following URLs: https://web.archive.org/web/20170425051622/http://topbuzz.com/; https://web.archive.org/web/20170306001913/https://www.topbuzz.com/; https://technode.com/2018/02/01/topbuzz/; https://web.archive.org/web/20170126040254mp_/http://www.topbuzz.com/@playbuzz/this-instagram-fitness-model-exposed-the-power-of-a-good-angle-AwKAOd_Mf1g.

10 **through a censorship filter:** TopBuzz's censorship rules were described to author in 2022 by ten former ByteDance staffers.
10 **allowed to green-light articles:** This guidance was written in an internal ByteDance communication shared with author by a confidential source.
11 **One asked a colleague:** Author interview, October 2024.
11 **The US team often struggled to convey:** Author interview, October 2024.

Chapter 2

14 **Yiming was deeply rationalistic:** Transcript of a September 19, 2016, speech Yiming gave at Nankai University, https://cs.nankai.edu.cn/info/1039/2356.htm.
15 **He embraced an extreme approach:** Lin Hongyu, "抖音设局：'道德状元郎' 张一鸣的不道德," *Sina Finance*, August 2, 2018.
15 **through a cerebral lens:** This is sourced from an alleged capture of Yiming's now-deleted Weibo history, published on the blog 老郭种树.
15 **"A small number of elites":** Song Wei, "今日头条创始人回应低俗质疑：从不主动push低俗内容," *Caijing*, December 14, 2016.
15 **he allegedly said on social media:** From Yiming's now-deleted Weibo.
16 **the Chinese government took an unprecedented step:** Tania Branigan, "China Restores Limited Internet Access After Urumqi Violence," *Guardian*, July 28, 2009; Xinyu [pseudonym], "'饭否' 网站被关 '维吾尔在线' 创办人据传被捕," *Radio Free Asia*, July 9, 2009.
16 **voiced support for Google:** Liza Lin and Eva Xiao, "TikTok's Founder Wonders What Hit Him," *Wall Street Journal*, August 27, 2020.
17 **more than six million monthly active users:** Chen Chang, "张一鸣放不下地产梦," *Node Finance*, January 5, 2023.
17 **Yiming believed tech was undergoing a shift:** Cheng He, "今日头条张一鸣：年轻人要和优秀的人做有挑战的事," *Phoenix Technology*, December 8, 2015; Sun Jing, "爲啥有些老闆年紀輕輕思考深度卻遠超常人？（深度分析）," 孙大圣说商业, July 9, 2021.
17 **Their first app was painfully simple:** Matthew Brennan, *Attention Factory: The Story of TikTok and China's ByteDance* (Self-published, 2020), pp. 34–35.
18 **By 2013, these signals included:** Zhang Qilin, ed., "'今日头条'：不做传统媒体的敌人," *People's Daily Online*, November 19, 2013.
18 **"Users need some indulgence":** Song Wei, "张一鸣：今日头条不模拟人性，也不引导人性，你们文化人给了我们太多深刻的命题," *Caijing*, December 14, 2016.
18 **lack of human editors was a good thing:** Song, "张一鸣."
19 **In 2014, Yiming went on a trip:** Zhang Yiming, "张一鸣硅谷行记：中国科技公司的「黄金时代」," GeekPark, October 13, 2014; Zhang Yiming, "张一鸣硅谷行记——没有边界的网络," GeekPark, October 19, 2014.
19 **"Some people may say":** Yiming, "张一鸣硅谷行记：中国科技公司的「黄金时代」"; Yiming, "张一鸣硅谷行记——没有边界的网络."

Chapter 3

21 **In October 2016, a buttoned-down audience:** All quotes and descriptions of Zhu's ProductSF interview come from a full video of the talk. Several YouTube posts of the video have been taken down during the past several years. Audio is at "Musical.ly's Alex Zhu on Igniting Viral Growth and Building a User Community,"

NOTES

Greymatter Podcast, Greylock, YouTube, May 8, 2024, https://www.youtube.com/watch?v=Y8fDv7Fsvs8&t=489s.

21 **led to strange media coverage:** "'Baby Ariel' | Musical.ly Star Interview on 'GMA,'" *ABC News*, April 6, 2016, https://www.youtube.com/watch?v=Tcj7xTQXsPE; "Predators Using Musical.ly App to Target Kids," *Denver7*, November 3, 2016, https://www.youtube.com/watch?v=0IkuymnwFsU.

22 **A *New York Times* article asked:** John Herrman, "Who's Too Young for an App? Musical.ly Tests the Limits," *New York Times*, September 17, 2016.

22 **"no question the youngest social network":** Herrman, "Who's Too Young for an App?"

24 **"He totally looks like a poet":** Shelly Banjo and Shawn Wen, "TikTok Started with a Tech Guy from China Who Decoded America's Teens," *Bloomberg*, April 22, 2021; Bloomberg's *Foundering* podcast, "TikTok Part 1: The Silent Force from China."

24 **By 2002, he had registered:** The website is archived online at https://web.archive.org/web/20060406053314/http://www.keepsilence.com/classicprose.htm.

24 **"If my delicate life were trampled into dirt":** "【我将在沉默中绽放】," keepsilence.com, https://web.archive.org/web/20060429082339/http://www.keepsilence.com/letitbe/blossominsilence.htm.

25 **He also tackled more abstract themes:** Alex Zhu, "A poem about the century and the motherland," keepsilence.com, https://web.archive.org/web/20060429225302/http://www.keepsilence.com/poetry/century.htm.

25 **he began writing more about psychology:** "June Zhu from China," SmugMug, accessed April 3, 2025, https://web.archive.org/web/20060406215307mp_/http://mylonelyhouse.smugmug.com/.

25 **comment on a short story:** June Zhu, "Time to Keep Silence and Look Inside Ourselves," *Keep Silence*, May 31, 2005, https://web.archive.org/web/20050609083310/http://keepsilence.bloghi.com/.

26 **it exploded in the US:** "Chinese Startups Push into Foreign Markets," *Economist*, March 9, 2017.

27 **he called *The Passion of Sisyphus*:** Karen Chiu, "Alex Zhu's Journey from Failed Startup to TikTok Chief," *South China Morning Post*, November 20, 2019, https://www.scmp.com/abacus/who-what/who/article/3038639/alex-zhus-journey-failed-startup-tiktok-chief; https://web.archive.org/web/20151202072501/; https://blog.sina.com.cn/thepassionofsisyphus; https://archive.is/yoO9e.

Chapter 4

29 **"It looked to us like a monster":** Biz Carson, "Flipagram, a Photo-Story App That Raised $70 million from 2 of the Best Investors in Silicon Valley, Has Laid off 20% of Its Staff," *Business Insider*, October 16, 2015.

30 **"the ideal person to bridge this gap":** Benjamin F. Kuo, "Interview with Farhad Mohit, Founder, President & CEO, BizRate.com," socalTECH, September 16, 1999.

30 **Mohit later acknowledged:** LinkedIn, Farhad Mohit, "Experience," accessed April 3, 2025.

31 **he laid out the stakes:** "Farhad Mohit: DotSpots and the Wisdom of Crowds," *Knowledge at Wharton* podcast, August 19, 2009.

33 **promised his wife:** Kathleen Chaykowski, "Flipagram Could Be Bigger Than Instagram," *Forbes*, November 23, 2015.

33 **But by late 2016:** Kurt Wagner, "Flipagram Is in Serious Acquisition Talks with Chinese News Aggregator Toutiao," *Vox*, December 15, 2016.

33 **"With the launch of auto-play":** Scott Dredge, "Facebook Trumpets Video Growth as It Prepares to Take On YouTube," *Guardian*, January 8, 2015.
34 **The incident was described:** Paul Mozur, "With 'Smog Jog' Through Beijing, Zuckerberg Stirs Debate on Air Pollution," *New York Times*, March 18, 2016.
34 **choose a name for his firstborn child:** "Xi Refuses Mark Zuckerberg's Baby Naming Request," *Bloomberg Originals*, October 6, 2015, https://www.youtube.com/watch?v=S20BoxH8W9g.
34 **In August, Zuckerberg invited Alex:** Ryan Mac, "Before Mark Zuckerberg Tried to Kill TikTok, He Wanted to Own It," *BuzzFeed News*, November 12, 2019.
34 **Facebook was wary:** "TikTok Part 2: The Silent Force from China," *Foundering* podcast, *Bloomberg*, April 21, 2021.
34 **Zuckerberg sent a team:** Mac, "Before Mark Zuckerberg Tried to Kill TikTok."

Chapter 5

35 **according to one office rumor:** Author interview, October 2023.
35 **purchase price had been a meager $50 million:** Brennan, *Attention Factory*, page 175.
36 **offered its new staff a show of goodwill:** Author interview, October 2023.
36 **more than half of the company's users:** Eva Yoo, "Bytedance Will Have More Than Half of Its Users from Overseas by 2020: CEO," *TechNode*, March 26, 2018.
36 **without being bombarded by ads:** Lv Qian, "成立七年，屡被封杀的字节跳动经历哪些节点," *Yicai/China Business Network*, March 14, 2019.
36 **As early as 2011:** According to the blog 老郭种树, Zhang Yiming posted about this on his Weibo account on 2011-10-15 at 22:24: "张一鸣微博 PDF 记录 2286 条完整版下载，另附 231 条精选版日记."
37 **ByteDance hoped that A.me:** Brennan, *Attention Factory*, page 146.
37 **The company even paid:** Author interview with Erin Huang, October 10, 2023; also discussed in "Douyin's (TikTok) First Creators," *China Channel*, YouTube, April 3, 2021, https://www.youtube.com/watch?v=hL8pwoCY7L0.
37 **became personal friends:** Author interview with Erin Huang, October 10, 2023; also discussed in Brennan, *Attention Factory*, page 145.
37 **A few months after the launch:** In this video, creators in the chat describe it and describe their thoughts on what the new name should be. "Douyin's (TikTok) First Creators," *China Channel*, YouTube, April 3, 2021, https://www.youtube.com/watch?v=hL8pwoCY7L0.
38 **luring celebrities to the app:** ByteDance Inc., "Tik Tok, a Global Music Video Platform and Social Network, Launches in Indonesia," PR Newswire, September 13, 2017; TikTok, "From #IamYourValentine to #FoolinLove: Tik Tok Sparks Viral Short Video Trends in the Philippines and Across Asia," PR Newswire, April 5, 2018.
38 **Still, there were signs:** Author interviews, March and August 2022, October 2023.
38 **The transition was especially tough:** Author interviews, March and August 2022, October 2023; internal communications shared with author.
39 **receiving a rash of complaints:** This account of Flipagram's impersonation problem is sourced from interviews with four former Flipagram employees and a cache of internal materials shared by those people. Many of the facts included here were also reported in Emily Baker-White, "TikTok's Parent, ByteDance, Made Fake Accounts with Content Scraped from Instagram and Snapchat, Former Employees Say," *BuzzFeed News*, April 4, 2022.

336 NOTES

41 **Alex's choices *were* constrained:** Wu Xin, "猎豹移动清仓字节跳动，傅盛'跟'张一鸣的得与失," *E-Commerce News*, May 22, 2020; Pan Luan, "再谈 Musical.ly 收购案交易各方心态," *LuanBooks*, March 22, 2020; Zhao Dongshan, "字节跳动裁撤投资部门 深度揭秘张一鸣的投资往事," *China Entrepreneur*, January 24, 2022.
42 **he would only approve the sale:** Wu, "猎豹移动清仓字节跳动"; Pan, "再谈 Musical.ly 收购案交易各方心态"; Zhao, "字节跳动裁撤投资部门."
42 **Just a day after the deal closed:** Dong Luxi, "止步10亿美金，Musical.ly这一年来错过了什么？| 热点快评," *Music Business China*, November 11, 2017.
42 **optimizing the app for regions of the world:** Author correspondence, April 5, 2025.
43 **ByteDance stripped away the bright orange branding:** Photos of the office before and after the acquisition provided to author.
43 **Musical.ly had coded an autocorrect feature:** Author correspondence, April 5, 2025.
43 **a slew of Musical.ly ads:** TikTok, "Donald Trump Doesn't Use Musical.ly. Join Now," Facebook, May 24–June 4, 2018, https://www.facebook.com/ads/library/?id=1806107009695693.
43 **ByteDance had lined up top US creators:** David Ramli and Shelly Banjo, "The Kids Use TikTok Now Because Data-Mined Videos Are So Much Fun," *Bloomberg*, April 17, 2019.
43 **Some contracts specifically required:** Contract containing these terms shared with author.
44 **The party itself was held:** "CA: TikTok US Launch Celebration," Getty Images, accessed April 3, 2025, https://www.gettyimages.com/editorial-images/entertainment/event/tiktok-us-launch-celebration/775202078; "Tik Tok Rebrand Launch" The Vendry, August 2018, accessed April 3, 2025.
44 **The night featured a series of influencer performances:** "CA: TikTok US Lauch Celebration"; "TikTok Rebrand."
44 **as the clock approached midnight:** Zhu's words here are sourced from Bloomberg's *Foundering* podcast, which includes an excerpt from his speech that night; "TikTok Part 2: The Silent Force from China."

Chapter 6

46 **ByteDance hired a small team of content curators in Mexico City:** Author interview with Jorge Reyes, September 25, 2023, and follow-up text messages; details about how heating works are corroborated by internal docs and interviews with more than six other staff members.
47 **suggested that people thinking about algorithms:** Maureen K. Ohlhausen, "Should We Fear the Things That Go Beep in the Night? Some Initial Thoughts on the Intersection of Antitrust Law and Algorithmic Pricing," Federal Trade Commission, May 23, 2017.
47 **"Is it ok for a guy named Bob":** Ohlhausen, "Should We Fear the Things That Go Beep in the Night?"
48 **Only 12 percent of videos:** Author interview with Jorge Reyes, September 25, 2023.
49 **ByteDance began making deals:** Author interview, September 2023.
50 **At TikTok, employees anticipated:** Author interview, October 2023.
50 **ByteDance invested enormous sums:** Georgia Wells, Yang Jie, and Yoko Kubota, "TikTok's Videos Are Goofy. Its Strategy to Dominate Social Media Is Serious," Wall Street Journal, June 29, 2019.
50 **The blitz amounted to an ad spend:** Wells, Jie, and Kubota, "TikTok's Videos Are Goofy."

51 **complaints started popping up:** Mrpoopytins, "These tik tok ads are getting ridiculous. I decided to screenshot an entire day's worth of ads from 7am to 9:30pm. PLEASE. I beg youtube to fix this. I reported the ads for being inappropriate and repetitive and even went to 'personalize my google ads' and these STILL show up," Reddit, October 7, 2018.

52 **"I asked what kind of content":** Jonah Peretti, "The Anti-SNARF Manifesto," BuzzFeed News, February 11, 2025.

52 **"the first mainstream consumer app":** Connie Chan, "When AI Is the Product: The Rise of AI-Based Consumer Apps," Andreessen Horowitz, December 3, 2018.

Chapter 7

56 **better known for twenty-six words buried:** "Telecommunications Act of 1996," Federal Communications Commission.

56 **the rule was important for two reasons:** Jennifer Huddleston, "The FCC Should Not Engage in Section 230 Rulemaking," *FedSoc Blog*, October 6, 2020.

57 **Spain made it a crime:** Office for Democratic Institutions and Human Rights, "Hate Crime Legislation in Spain," Organization for Security and Co-operation in Europe, accessed April 3, 2025.

57 **India made it a crime:** "2010 Human Rights Reports: India," Bureau of Democracy, Human Rights, and Labor, US Department of State, April 8, 2011.

57 **the Chinese Ministry of Public Security forbade citizens:** Human Rights Watch, "Freedom of Expression and the Internet in China," accessed April 3, 2025.

57 **scanning blogs for banned keywords:** "'Freedom' Blocked in Chinese Blogs," CBS News, June 14, 2005.

57 **they created an "algospeak":** "Getting Past China's Government Firewall," NPR, February 16, 2006.

58 **it took them offline for the twentieth anniversary:** Tania Branigan, "China Blocks Twitter, Flickr and Hotmail Ahead of Tiananmen Anniversary," Guardian, June 2, 2009.

58 **the crackdown following civil unrest in Urumqi:** "China Blocks Access to Twitter, Facebook After Riots," TechCrunch, July 7, 2009.

59 **CCP developed intimate partnerships:** Austin Ramzy, "Charles Chao, Tech Giant," Time, April 21, 2011; "Message Control: New Rules for Social Media in China," CBC, May 28, 2012; "China's Sina to Step-Up Censorship of Weibo," Reuters, September 19, 2011; "Beijing's Weibo Conundrum," Wall Street Journal, September 21, 2011.

59 **nearly every aspect of Chinese life:** Anne Henochowicz, "Directives from the Ministry of Truth: Zhou Kehua," *China Digital Times*, August 16, 2012.

59 **remove coverage of food safety issues:** Anne Henochowicz, "Directives from the Ministry of Truth: Food Safety," *China Digital Times*, August 17, 2012.

59 **even refrain from speculating:** Anne Henochowicz, "Directives from the Ministry of Truth: Liu Xiang," *China Digital Times*, August 8, 2012.

59 **A directive for one 2022 Weibo campaign:** Alexander Boyd, "Minitrue: Flood Weibo Comments on Xinjiang Prefecture's Lockdown," *China Digital Times*, September 9, 2022.

Chapter 8

61 **most popular memes became inside jokes:** Raymond Zhong, Paul Mozur, and Iris Zhao, "Horns Honk, and Censors in China Get a Headache," *New York Times*, April 12, 2018.

- 61 **They chanted nonsense slogans:** Zhong, Mozur, and Zhao, "Horns Honk."
- 62 **The campaign began with a three-part opinion feature:** Yusheng, "民网三评算法推荐," People's Daily, September 17–19, 2017.
- 63 **regulator enacted new rules:** "Provisions on Management of Internet News Services," China Law Translate, May 2, 2017.
- 63 **permitting system for companies:** "China Tightens Rules on Online News, Network Providers," CNBC, May 2, 2017.
- 63 **In December 2017, the CAC accused Toutiao:** Hong Kong Free Press, "Under Pressure from Cyberspace Administration, China's Top News App Will Hire 2,000 More Content Reviewers," GlobalVoices, January 5, 2018.
- 63 **ByteDance promptly announced:** Hong Kong Free Press, "Under Pressure from Cyberspace Administration."
- 63 **demanded that they remove content:** Yi Xiao, Yang Yuboluo, eds., "播电视总局严肃处理今日头条和快手," People's Daily, April 4, 2018.
- 63 **it temporarily removed the apps:** Raymond Zhong, "China Isn't Happy About Its Newest Internet Stars: Teenage Moms," New York Times, April 6, 2018.
- 63 **ByteDance quickly apologized for promoting:** 抖音火山版, Weibo, April 2, 2018, 09:57.
- 64 **began its final swipe at ByteDance:** Frank Hersey, "Toutiao and 3 Other News Apps Taken Down from Chinese App Stores," TechNode, April 9, 2018.
- 64 **SARFT struck again:** "国家广播电视总局责令 '今日头条' 网站 永久关停 '内涵段子' 等低俗视听产品," State Administration of Radio and Television, April 10, 2018.
- 64 **thousands of duanyou surrounded the offices:** Wong Siu-san, Lam Kwok-lap, and Yang Fan, "Protests Erupt Around China Over Closure of Popular Humor App," Radio Free Asia, April 12, 2018.
- 64 **find one another on other platforms:** "三声 | 告别内涵 再见段友," China Digital Times, April 11, 2018, https://chinadigitaltimes.net/chinese/582619.html.
- 64 **ByteDance announced that it was suspending the livestreaming:** Nicole Jao, "Douyin Temporarily Removed Live-Stream and Comment Feature," TechNode, April 11, 2018
- 64 **In a lengthy public letter:** David Bandurski, "Tech Shame in the 'New Era,'" China Media Project, April 11, 2018.

Chapter 9

- 67 **"The Intelligence law seems calculated":** Murray Scot Tanner, "Beijing's New National Intelligence Law: From Defense to Offense," Lawfare, July 20, 2017.
- 67 **Some Chinese ByteDancers believed:** Author correspondence, September 23, 2022.
- 67 **Until at least 2019:** Sam Biddle, Paulo Victor Ribeiro, and Tatiana Dias, "Invisible Censorship: TikTok Told Moderators to Suppress Posts by 'Ugly' People and the Poor to Attract New Users," Intercept, March 16, 2020.
- 67 **"slums," "construction sites," or "dilapidated housing":** Biddle, Riberio, and Dias, "Invisible Censorship."
- 67 **a variety of disfavored animals:** Internal TikTok moderation document shared with author.
- 68 **Women and girls in swimsuits:** Author interviews, August and September 2022; November 2023.
- 68 **apply the "one-third" rule for cleavage:** Author interviews, August 2022; October 2024.
- 68 **Life as an early ByteDance moderator:** Author interview, August 2022.
- 69 **People didn't have to give their age:** Author interviews, August and September 2022.

NOTES 339

69 **She also began facing bullies online:** Tanya Chen, "A 13-Year-Old Believes She's One of the Most Hated Teens on Instagram. Here's How She and Her Mom Are Dealing," *BuzzFeed News*, February 8, 2018.
70 **She became the subject of conversations among moderators:** Author interview, August 2022.
70 **Early ByteDance staffers from across the world:** Author interview, September 2023.
70 **As one former moderator described it:** Author interview, August 2022; source correspondence, March 2024.
70 **Even mentions of Winnie-the-Pooh and Peppa Pig:** "Auszug aus den Moderationskriterien von TikTok," accessed April 5, 2025.
71 **Fu's team was composed of content policy experts:** Author interviews, September 2023, February 2024; photos provided to author.
71 **"When someone so famous makes a statement":** Snigdha Poonam, "TikTok Suspends Accounts of Three Users After Shiv Sena's IT Cell Files FIR," *Hindustan Times*, July 24, 2019.
71 **TikTok confirmed the takedowns:** Poonam, "TikTok Suspends Accounts."
72 **The posts themselves were quite tame:** Debjani Chakraborty, "'Revenge for Tabrez' Video Draws Flak, Administration on Alert," *Times of India*, July 10, 2019.
72 **"where people come to have fun":** David Ramli and Shelly Banjo, "The Kids Use TikTok Now Because Data-Mined Videos Are So Much Fun," *Bloomberg*, April 17, 2019.
72 **When asked whether the platform:** Ramli and Banjo, "The Kids Use TikTok Now."
72 **TikTok experienced its first brush:** Alex Hern, "Revealed: How TikTok Censors Videos That Do Not Please Beijing," *Guardian*, September 25, 2019.
72 **Inside ByteDance, the leaks caused pandemonium:** Author interview, August 2022.
73 **"reference specific countries or issues":** Herd, "Revealed: How TikTok Censors."
73 **experienced this ugly downside up close:** Author interviews, August and September 2022; February and October 2024.
75 **"Do I believe they took it away":** Dave Lee, "TikTok Apologises and Reinstates Banned US Teen," BBC, November 27, 2019.

Chapter 10

78 **"Now that billions of us":** "Watch live: Facebook CEO Zuckerberg speaks at Georgetown University," *Washington Post*, October 17, 2019, https://www.youtube.com/watch?v=2MTpd7YOnyU.
79 **"Trump should be more worried":** Georgia Wells, Jeff Horwitz, and Aruna Viswanatha, "Facebook CEO Mark Zuckerberg Stoked Washington's Fears About TikTok," *Wall Street Journal*, August 23, 2020.
83 **"born to be global":** "张一鸣：当代中国公司生而全球化," *China Daily*, March 26, 2018.
83 **Only by learning from them:** Li Yuan, "Huawei's Communist Culture Limits Its Global Ambitions," *New York Times*, May 1, 2019.
83 **"Ren Zhengfei's daughter had defrauded a bank":** "Huawei CFO Wanzhou Meng Admits to Misleading Global Financial Institution," US Department of Justice, September 24, 2021.

Chapter 11

87 **For ByteDance's seventh:** "Event Report: ByteDance Celebrates Seven Years of Excellence," Innovate Marketing Group, last modified March 28, 2019.

87 **A whopping 686 million people:** "TikTok Was Installed More Than 738 Million Times in 2019, 44% of Its All-Time Downloads," *Sensor Tower*, last updated January 17, 2020, https://sensortower.com/blog/tiktok-revenue-downloads-2019.

87 **Yiming prepared a sort of a State of the Union address:** Zheng Jieyao, "张一鸣宣布组织升级：张利东、张楠任字节跳动（中国）董事长和CEO," *Jiemian*, March 12, 2020.

89 **ByteDance pivoted its product strategy:** "Supporting Communities in Need," ByteDance, accessed March 31, 2024.

89 **bought the rights to stream fourteen feature-length films:** Patrick Brzeski, "Chinese Comedy 'Lost in Russia' to Debut Online for Free After Coronavirus Cancellations (Exclusive)," *Hollywood Reporter*, last modified January 23, 2020.

89 **The company also sent 200,000 KN95 masks:** ByteDance, "Supporting Communities."

90 **College kids at Minnesota State University:** Lauren Strapagiel, "This College Sent Grads Individual Bags of Confetti and It Really Captured the Funny/Sad Energy of 2020," *BuzzFeed News*, December 14, 2020.

90 **A couple in Hertfordshire, UK, filmed:** Curly Tales, "A man in England recently dressed up as a bush to venture out to the streets amid the countrywide lockdown," Facebook, April 10, 2020, https://www.facebook.com/watch/?v=216013809661431.

92 **more than $130 billion the same year:** "Leading Digital Advertising Markets Worldwide in 2020," Statista, last updated May 20, 2024.

93 **government directives told news outlets and platforms:** Samuel Wade, "Minitrue Plus Five: February 3, 2020—Harmful Content, Sourcing, and Foreign Aid Amid Epidemic," *China Digital Times*, February 25, 2025.

93 **The government barred news publishers:** Raymond Zhong, Paul Mozur, Jeff Kao, and Aaron Krolik, "No 'Negative' News: How China Censored the Coronavirus," *New York Times*, December 19, 2020.

93 **It banned the word "lockdown":** Zhong, Mozur, Kao, and Krolik, "No 'Negative' News."

93 **In Hangzhou, the government graded platforms:** Zhong, Mozur, Kao, and Krolik, "No 'Negative' News."

93 **A state-run newspaper published:** 深海三文鱼, "25个国家和地区，200多个生物实验室究竟在干啥？美国请回答," *Xinmin Evening News*, October 22, 2020.

93 **a commentator on Toutiao speculated:** 阿尔法 [this is a popular pseudonymous social media account]. "专门针对中国吗？刚刚，美国进行全球性的撤侨," April 5. 2020.

94 **The accounts impersonated Filipinos:** Chris Bing and Joel Schectman: "Pentagon Ran Secret Anti-Vax Campaign to Undermine China During Pandemic," Reuters, June 14, 2024.

94 **One blog post, shared on Toutiao:** Song Luzheng, "巴黎日记：自己无能，英法美联手'问责'中国?," *Guancha*, April 17, 2020.

94 **Friedman would write a piece condemning:** Thomas L. Friedman, "Would Russia or China Help Us if We Were Invaded by Space Aliens?" *New York Times*, November 1, 2021.

95 **A columnist at the Chinese government–owned *China Daily*:** Ke Nan, "Would the US Help Us if We Were Invaded by Aliens . . . or a Virus?," *China Daily*, November 5, 2021.

Chapter 12

97 **the constitution protects free speech:** "2018 Country Reports on Human Rights Practices: India," US Department of State, accessed April 7, 2025.

98 **signing the largest new data center lease contract:** Rich Miller, "Growth of TikTok Boosts Data Center Appetite for ByteDance," Data Center Frontier, January 30, 2020.

NOTES

98 **ByteDance opened a splashy new US headquarters:** "TikTok Headquarters," Swinerton, accessed March 31, 2025.
100 **When executives were displeased:** Author interviews, October and December 2024.
100 **Some early contract workers:** Author interview, August 2022.
101 **used the language learning service:** Memrise, accessed March 31, 2025.
101 **the boss often tried to protect:** Author interviews, October and December 2024.
101 **they were also savvy:** Author interview, October 2024.
102 **Alex was an "ideas guy":** Author interviews, December 2024; internal correspondence shared with author.
102 **challenged by a shift:** Author interview, September 2023.
102 **The platform wouldn't censor political discussions:** Raymond Zhong, "TikTok's Chief Is on a Mission to Prove It's Not a Menace," *New York Times*, November 18, 2019.
102 **researchers inside Facebook and Instagram:** Anna Stepanov, "Reducing Political Content in News Feed," Meta, February 10, 2021.
103 **The interviewer asked him why:** Markus Böhm, Steffen Klusmann, and Anton Rainer, "As a Chinese Company, We Never Get the Benefit of the Doubt," *Spiegel*, January 22, 2020.
105 **built like an offensive tackle:** Sharon Waxman, "Disney Boss Kevin Mayer: Brilliant Dealmaker or 'Bully'? Both, Insiders Say," *Wrap*, November 6, 2019.
105 **TikTok was a rocket ship:** Todd Spangler, "New TikTok CEO Kevin Mayer Explains Why He Left Disney," *Variety*, June 25, 2020.
106 **"Every meeting was a lot of energy":** Author interview.
107 **"He was the deal guy":** Author interview, May 2024.

Chapter 13

108 **At a protest in Williamsburg:** Author interview with Abby Loisel, September 27, 2023.
109 **his first days at TikTok:** Spangler, "New TikTok CEO."
109 **"Maybe the most important thing":** Spangler, "New TikTok CEO."
110 **aligning the platform with the protest movement:** TikTok, "Diversity is our strength. As a society, as an organization, as a platform," June 1, 2020, https://www.tiktok.com/@tiktok/video/6833468102982798598.
110 **the Democratic and Republican National Committees advised:** Donie O'Sullivan, "DNC and RNC Warn Campaigns About Using TikTok," CNN, July 11, 2020; Sarah Mucha, "Biden Campaign Tells Staff to Delete TikTok from Their Phones," CNN, July 28, 2020.
110 **A group of Republican senators:** Nandita Bose, "U.S. Senate Votes to Ban TikTok App on Government Devices," Reuters, August 6, 2020.
111 **According to one internal document:** Raymond Zhong and Sheera Frenkel, "A Third of TikTok's U.S. Users May Be 14 or Under, Raising Safety Questions," *New York Times*, August 14, 2020.
112 **made a TikTok explaining the stakes:** quentinjiles, "The president is starting his rallies again on #Juneteenth and in Tulsa, Ok were #BlackWallStreet use to be!," TikTok, June 11, 2020, https://www.tiktok.com/@quentinjiles/video/6837187220357664006.
112 **"Already rsvp'ed my free tickets":** quentinjiles, "The president is starting his rallies."
112 **another TikToker chimed in:** maryjo.laupp, "Did you know you can make sure there are empty seats at Trump's rally? #BLM," TikTok, June 12, 2020, https://www.tiktok.com/@maryjo.laupp/video/6837311838640803078.
114 **A sixteen-year-old K-pop fan:** Kathryn Lindsay, "Instead of Turning in Protestors, the Youth Crashed Police App with Fancams," *Refinery29*, June 1, 2020.

114 **replies started streaming in:** maryjo.laupp, "Did you know you can make sure there are empty seats at Trump's rally? #BLM."
114 **On Friday, June 12:** Brad Parscale (@parscale), "Trump #MAGA Rally in Tulsa is hottest ticket ever! Over 200K tickets already & it's not even political season. Looking at a 2nd event in town to get more people to be w/ @realDonald Trump. Gonna be GREAT in the most open state in nation!," Twitter (now X), June 12, 2020, https://x.com/parscale/status/1271545567219499009.
114 **Later in the day:** Brad Parscale (@parscale), "Correction now 300,000! Going to be epic!" Twitter (now X), June 12, 2020, https://x.com/parscale/status/1271581845910704128.
114 **and, two days later:** Brad Parscale (@parscale), "Just passed 800,000 tickets. Biggest data haul and rally signup of all time by 10x. Saturday is going to be amazing!," Twitter (now X), June 14, 2020, https://x.com/parscale/status/1272191356845391875.
114 **"Almost One Million people":** Donie O'Sullivan, "Trump's Campaign Was Trolled by TikTok Users in Tulsa," CNN, June 21, 2020.
114 **TikTokers reposted the tweet:** trauma_queen, "Who requested all those seats though!? 😭🤣," TikTok, June 20, 2020, http://tiktok.com/@trauma_queen__/video/6840616438466678022.
115 **On the morning of the rally:** Jonathan Karl, *Betrayal: The Final Act of the Trump Show* (Dutton, 2021), 57, 61.
115 **how unpleasant their evening:** Karl, *Betrayal*, 59.
115 **only about 6,000 people:** Bobby Allyn, "TikTok Prank May Account for Trump Rally's Low Attendance Rate," NPR, June 22, 2020.
116 **Steve Schmidt, a Republican political strategist:** Steve Schmidt (@SteveSchmidtSES), "This is what happened tonight. I'm dead serious when I say this. The teens of America have struck a savage blow against @realDonaldTrump. All across America teens ordered tickets to this event. The fools on the campaign bragged about a million tickets. lol." @ProjectLincoln, Twitter (now X), June 20, 2020, https://x.com/SteveSchmidtSES/status/1274486428160811009.
116 **"Lol" was also the position:** Author interview, April 2024.
116 **blog post characterizing BTS ARMY:** The Grugq, "kPop Fans: Non-Traditional, Non-State Actors," Okta Security, October 20, 2020.

Chapter 14

119 **In the late 2010s:** Tanushree Chandra, "Literacy in India: The Gender and Age Dimension," Observer Research Foundation, October 31, 2019.
119 **US has roughly 43 million:** "Adult Literacy in the United States," National Center for Education Statistics, July 2019, accessed April 1, 2025.
119 **TikTok's Indian users spoke:** Varsha Bansal, "India's TikTok Shutdown Has Left Careers and Fortunes in Tatters," *Wired*, July 6, 2020.
119 **Facebook, Instagram, and YouTube had focused:** Unnati Sharma, "TikTok vs YouTube Is the New Class War on Internet. It All Began with a Roast," *Print*, May 18, 2020.
120 **hundreds of casteist videos:** Nilesh Christopher, "TikTok Is Fuelling India's Deadly Hate Speech Epidemic," *Wired*.
120 **Indian lawmakers began raising concerns:** Rishi Iyengar, "India Is Too Big for TikTok to Risk Another Ban," CNN, July 22, 2019.
120 **posts supporting a boycott:** Yujie Xue and Coco Feng, "Deadly Border Clash Prompts Renewed Calls in India to Boycott Chinese Tech," *South China Morning Post*, June 19, 2020.

120 **Indian nationalists flooded TikTok:** Manish Singh, "Google Removes Millions of Negative TikTok Reviews Amid Backlash in India," *TechCrunch*, May 27, 2020.
120 **the app claimed to be able to scan:** Rita Liao, "A Service That Detects 'China Apps' Goes Viral in India," *TechCrunch*, June 1, 2020.
120 **did not disclose how it determined:** Manish Singh, "Google Pulls 'Remove China Apps' from Play Store," *TechCrunch*, June 2, 2020.
121 **Google removed Remove China Apps:** Singh, "Google Pulls 'Remove China Apps.'"
121 **its own content moderation difficulties:** Medha Chawla, "I Will Not Use TikTok Anymore, Says Saloni Gaur After Her Video on China Gets Blocked," *India Today*, June 1, 2020; Chandrima Banerjee, "Does TikTok Censor Content That's Critical of China?," *Times of India*, June 6, 2020.
121 **"The app is like the country":** Simrin Sirur, "Milind Soman to 'Nazma Aapi,'" Indians Slam TikTok for Censorship and Call for Boycott," *Print*, May 30, 2020.
121 **ByteDance's policy team received:** Author interviews, August 2022, April 2024.
122 **Several recipients of this message:** Author interviews, August 2022, April 2024.
123 **They began negotiations:** Hemant Kashyap, "TikTok Parent ByteDance Looking at India Comeback, in Talks with Hiranandani Group for a Partnership," *Inc42*, June 1, 2022.
123 **ByteDance also courted:** "Reliance Likely to Acquire TikTok in India for $5 Billion," *New Indian Express*, last updated August 17, 2020.
124 **One activist leader:** Eryk Bagshaw, "The End of the Hong Kong the World Knew," *Sydney Morning Herald*, June 30, 2020.
124 **Another prominent local leader:** Helen Regan and Joshua Berlinger, "Protests Break Out in Hong Kong as First Arrest Made Under New Security Law," CNN, July 1, 2020.
124 **Users trying to log into the app:** TikTok, "Dear Users, We regret to inform you that we have discontinued operating TikTok in Hong Kong. Thank you for the time you have spent with us on the platform and for giving us the opportunity to bring a little bit of joy into your life. The TikTok Team," https://www.tiktok.com/hk/notfound.

Chapter 15

125 **The conversation turned to Hong Kong:** "Mike Pompeo Considers Ban on TikTok," Fox News, July 7, 2020, on YouTube, https://www.youtube.com/watch?v=EIBPqXODJOM.
125 **He was reportedly enthusiastic:** Peter Navarro, *Taking Back Trump's America: Why We Lost the White House and How He'll Win It Back* (Bombardier Books, 2020), 176.
126 **part of a suite of actions:** Shelly Banjo, Jordan Fabian, and Nick Wadhams, "Trump Says He's Considering a Ban on TikTok in the US," AP, July 8, 2020.
127 **Mnuchin had his own history:** Mara Hvistendahl, "Films Financed by Steven Mnuchin Were Tailored to Appeal to China," *Intercept*, September 22, 2020.
128 **The dispute culminated:** Navarro, *Taking Back Trump's America*, 182–83.
128 **Trump echoed Mnuchin:** Katy Stech Ferek, "Treasury to Make TikTok Recommendations to Trump This Week," *Wall Street Journal*, July 29, 2020.
128 **"We're looking at TikTok":** "President Donald Trump: Looking at Banning TikTok or a Lot of Other Options," CNBC, July 31, 2020, YouTube, https://www.youtube.com/watch?v=061fwvWZHgo.
128 **"As far as TikTok is concerned":** Ellen Nakashima, Rachel Lerman, and Jeanne Whalen, "Trump Says He Plans to Bar TikTok from Operating in the U.S.," *Washington Post*, July 31, 2020.

128 **Trump signed two executive orders:** "Executive Order on Addressing the Threat Posed by TikTok," The White House, August 6, 2020.
129 **Roughly a week later:** "Regarding the Acquisition of Muscial.ly by ByteDance Ltd.," Office of the Press Secretary, The White House, August 14, 2020.
129 **TikTok lobbyists had also tried:** Arjun Kharpal, "Trump Advisor Navarro Accuses TikTok's American CEO of Being a 'Puppet' for Working at the Chinese App," CNBC, July 13, 2020; Navarro, *Taking Back Trump's America*, 181.
129 **just five minutes before:** "Why We Are Suing the Administration," TikTok, August 24, 2020, https://newsroom.tiktok.com/en-us/tiktok-files-lawsuit.
129 **"has identified national security risks":** TikTok, "Why We Are Suing."

Chapter 16

131 **thanking the app's millions of American users:** TikTok, "A Message from U.S. General Manager Vanessa Pappas to Our TikTok Community," August 1, 2020, https://www.tiktok.com/@tiktok/video/6856014780440874245.
131 **published a blog post:** Kevin Mayer, "Fair Competition and Transparency Benefits Us All," TikTok, July 29, 2020, https://newsroom.tiktok.com/en-us/fair-competition-and-transparency-benefits-us-all.
131 **"Let's focus our energies":** Mayer, "Fair Competition."
131 **"ByteDance has always been committed":** "TikTok Owner ByteDance Accuses Facebook of 'Plagiarism and Smears,'" Reuters, August 2, 2020.
132 **urging them to stay calm:** Mengjia Xiaoyun, ed., "字节跳动深夜点名Facebook抄袭抹黑，张一鸣发内部信：尽力确保TikTok继续服务美国用户," *Jiemian*, August 3, 2020, https://www.jiemian.com/article/4768114.html.
132 **One post compared the decision:** "抖音创始人张一鸣：TikTok风波中被推上风口浪尖的中国高科技新贵," BBC Chinese, August 7, 2020.
132 **"As a company founded by Chinese entrepreneurs":** "36Kr｜张一鸣最新内部信：字节跳动需要接受一段时间内的误解," *China Digital Times*, August 4, 2020.
133 **real intention is to push:** "36Kr｜张一鸣最新内部信：字节跳动需要接受一段时间内的误解."
133 **"an American in spirit":** Juro Osawa and Yunan Zhang, "In TikTok Saga, ByteDance CEO Confronts His Blind Spot: Politics," *Information*, October 9, 2020.
133 **spent days modeling contingency plans:** Author interview, October 2024.
133 **but Yiming was reluctant:** Zhou Xin and Sarah Zheng, "TikTok's Chinese Owner ByteDance 'Prefers Independent Spin-Off Over Microsoft Sale' as Donald Trump Threatens Ban," *South China Morning Post*, August 3, 2020.
134 **"We attempted to have preliminary discussions":** "36Kr｜张一鸣最新内部信：字节跳动需要接受一段时间内的误解."
134 **Both companies preferred a narrow partnership:** Mike Isaac and Andrew Ross Sorkin, "How TikTok's Talks with Microsoft Turned into a Soap Opera," *New York Times*, August 26, 2020.
134 **At first, Trump had said:** Ana Swanson and Mike Isaac, "Trump Reverses Course on TikTok, Opening Door to Microsoft Bid," *New York Times*, August 3, 2020.
134 **the deal would only be approved:** "Donald Trump: US Treasury Should Get Cut of TikTok Deal," BBC, August 4, 2020.
134 **"It's a little bit like landlord/tenant":** Matt Levine, "Do We Really Have to Talk About TikTok Key Money?," *Bloomberg*, August 4, 2020.
135 **"they don't have any rights unless":** Levine, "Do We Really?"

135 **"to pretend that this is a thing":** Levine, "Do We Really?"
136 **"Oracle is one of the very few":** Navarro, *Taking Back Trump's America*, 178–79.
136 **He wanted the freedom:** Alex Sherman, "Kevin Mayer Talks About His Disappointing Departures at Disney and TikTok, and the Long Decline of Pay TV," CNBC, March 17, 2021.
137 **Yiming wasn't always diligent about including:** "TikTok CEO Kevin Mayer Resigns After Being Excluded from Talks: Source," CNBC, August 27, 2020, https://www.youtube.com/watch?v=o3LJto9je_c.
137 **He was nobody's puppet:** Sherman, "Kevin Mayer Talks About His Disappointing Departures."
137 **still mid-afternoon in California:** Author interviews, October and December 2024.

Chapter 17

138 **In the days directly following:** Author interviews, August 2023, and June 2024.
138 **The executives understood Yiming's words:** Author interviews, August 2023, and June 2024.
138 **made an unusual weekend change:** Paul Mozur, Raymond Zhong, and David McCabe, "TikTok Deal Is Complicated by New Rules from China over Tech Exports," *New York Times*, August 29, 2020.
138 **One described their reaction:** Author interview, August 2023.
139 **V rallied staff behind the idea:** Margaux MacColl, "The Fighter: V Pappas and the Battle for TikTok's Future," *Information*, April 21, 2023.
139 **sued Trump and his staff:** Brian Fung, "TikTok Employee Sues Trump Administration Over 'Unconstitutional' Executive Order," CNN, August 24, 2020.
139 **where key political decision makers lived:** *Katie Ellen Puris v. TikTok Inc., ByteDance Ltd., ByteDance Inc., Douyin Limited, and Lidong Zhang*, Amended Complaint, Civil Case No.: 24 CV 944 (DLC), May 6, 2024.
139 **The other campaign was targeted more broadly:** Author interview, August 2023.
140 **ByteDance and Oracle agreed:** Bobby Allyn, "TikTok Ban Averted: Trump Gives Oracle-Walmart Deal His 'Blessing,'" NPR, September 20, 2020.
140 **ByteDance made a creative argument:** David Shepardson, Alexandra Alper, and Echo Wang, "China's ByteDance Get Trump Nod to Avoid TikTok Shutdown," Reuters, September 21, 2020.
141 **appeared to win the approval:** Jennifer Jacobs, Saleha Mohsin, and Nick Wadhams, "Oracle, ByteDance Accept New Treasury Terms on TikTok," *Bloomberg*, September 17, 2020.
141 **On Thursday the 17th:** Todd Bishop, No, Microsoft Is Not 'Still Involved' in TikTok Discussions, Despite President Trump's Statement," *GeekWire*, September 18, 2020.
141 **the company had published a terse:** "Microsoft Statement on TikTok," Microsoft, last modified September 13, 2020.
141 **his approach alienated potential allies:** Erin Griffith and David McCabe, "'There's No There There': What the TikTok Deal Achieved," *New York Times*, September 20, 2020.
141 **Meanwhile, conservative senators:** "Tillis, Colleagues Raise Significant Concerns to President Trump Regarding Oracle's TikTok Deal," Senator Thom Tillis press release, September 16, 2020; Letter to Treasury Secretary Steven T. Mnuchin from Senator Josh Hawley, September 14, 2020.
142 **one day before the divestment deadline:** "Remarks by President Trump Before Marine One Departure," The White House, September 19, 2020.

346 NOTES

142 **He told the rally audience:** Alexis Benveniste and Jill Disis, "Trump Wants the TikTok Deal to Pour $5 Billion into 'Real History' Education. It's Not That Simple," CNN, September 21 2020.
142 **The *Wall Street Journal* reported:** Aaron Tilley and Stu Woo, "Larry Ellison's TikTok Bid Puts Oracle Chairman Back in the Spotlight," *Wall Street Journal*, October 3, 2020.
142 **Trump's $5 billion idea:** Benveniste and Disis, "Trump Wants the TikTok Deal."
142 **But Trump had expected:** Noah Manskar, Trump Won't Approve TikTok Deal if ByteDance Keeps Control," *New York Post*, September 21, 2020.
143 **The judge took issue:** Cristiano Lima, "Judge Temporarily Halts Trump's TikTok Download Ban," *Politico*, September 27, 2020.
143 **ByteDance won a second victory:** *Marland v. Trump*, 498 F. Supp. 3d 624 (E.D. Pa. 2020), October 30, 2020.
144 **TikTok hadn't heard from the government:** David McCabe, "The Trump Administration Gave TikTok More Time to Reach a Deal," *New York Times*.
144 **"pending further legal developments":** *Marland v. Trump*.
144 **TikTok influencers started selling branded products:** "You Can Now Shop Walmart on the Hottest Place on the Internet—TikTok," Walmart, last modified December 17, 2020.
144 **"Business, entertainment, news, activism":** Taylor Lorenz, "This Is Why You Heard About TikTok So Much in 2020," *New York Times*, December 31, 2020.

Chapter 18

147 **"We intend to become ubiquitous":** Recorded meeting, September 15, 2021, provided by Rob Doe.
148 **By signing their new-hire paperwork:** Puris Amended Complaint at 11 and 20.
149 **TikTok was built on an elaborate pile:** Recorded meetings, September 14–16, 2021; September 27, 2021; January 25, 2022; provided by Rob Doe.
149 **Booz consultants who had also been assigned:** Recorded meetings, September 14–17, 2021; September 23, September 27, September 30, 2021; October 19, 2021; provided by Rob Doe.
150 **On one late September afternoon:** Recorded meeting, September 27, 2021, provided by Rob Doe.
150 **"There are items within the tools":** Recorded meeting, November 2, 2021, provided by Rob Doe.
152 **Project Texas was the brainchild:** Author interviews, October 2024, and January 2025.
152 **could be forced to use that tool:** Rob Doe interviews with author, June 2022.
152 **a hypothetical to illustrate his concerns:** Rob Doe interviews with author, June 2022.

Chapter 19

154 **the company's first Washington, DC, hearing:** "TikTok Testifies on Kids' Online Safety," C-SPAN, October 26, 2021.
154 **Once photographed in $5,000 shoes:** Jeff DuFour and Nevil Martell, "Men of Style," *Modern Luxury DC*, April 1, 2014.

Chapter 20

158 **In fall 2022, a former ByteDance employee:** Albert's story is sourced from a sworn declaration he made to a US court in May 2024; Case 3:23-cv-04910-SI, U.S. District Court for the Northern District of California, May 21, 2024, https://www.documentcloud.org/documents/25148141-3-23-cv-04910-declaration-doc-85-4/.

159 **Ma was known for his pomp and performance:** Stu Woo, "Alibaba Sends Jack Ma Off with Birthday Extravaganza," *Wall Street Journal*, September 10, 2019.

159 **Ant's power alone was staggering:** "Alipay's Worldwide Users Exceed 1 Bln," *Xinhua*, January 9, 2019.

160 **Instead, he gave a set of caveats:** Charlie Campbell, "Where Is Alibaba Founder Jack Ma? What the Saga of One of the World's Richest Men Reveals About China Under Xi Jinping," *Time*, January 4, 2021; Kevin Xu, "Jack Ma's Bund Finance Summit Speech," *Interconnected*, November 9, 2020.

162 **"Retirement has always been a false proposition":** Gong Fangyi, "不做董事长和CEO，黄峥依然控制拼多多," *LatePost*, March 18, 2021.

162 **preached a gospel of mindfulness:** Kevin Xu, "Zhang Yiming's Last Speech: Part I," *Interconnected*, November 8, 2022.

162 **Yiming had met Honnold:** Xu, "Zhang Yiming's Last Speech."

163 **one post from 2010:** According to the blog 老郭种树, Zhang Yiming posted about this on his Weibo account on 2010-05-18 at 13:22. "张一鸣微博 PDF 记录 2286 条完整版下载，另附 231 条精选版日记."

163 **he allegedly praised Mao Yushi:** According to the blog 老郭种树, Zhang Yiming posted about this on his Weibo account on 2011-07-04 at 13:11: "张一鸣微博 PDF 记录 2286 条完整版下载，另附 231 条精选版日记."

163 **he allegedly shared a BBC Chinese interview:** According to the blog 老郭种树, Zhang Yiming posted about this on his Weibo account on 2013-02-03 at 00:53: "张一鸣微博 PDF 记录 2286 条完整版下载，另附 231 条精选版日记."

164 **a perfect blend of East and West:** Ryan Mac and Chang Che, "TikTok's C.E.O. Navigates the Limits of His Power," *New York Times*, September 16, 2022.

164 **In response, Xiaomi had sued:** Laura He, "Xiaomi Wins Temporary Reprieve from US Ban on American Investment," CNN, March 15, 2021.

164 **He lived in a Good Class Bungalow:** Katie Warren, "The CEO of TikTok Is Reportedly in Talks to Buy a $64 Million Bungalow in Singapore—Take a Look at the Street It's On," *Business Insider*, August 2, 2021.

165 **hobnobbing with famous people:** Author interviews, October, November, and December 2024.

165 **perhaps he should buy the restaurant:** Mac and Che, "TikTok's C.E.O. Navigates."

165 **in a tasteful 2,500-square-foot California bungalow:** Author interview, May 2023.

165 **Yiming met with Chinese regulators:** Xie Yu and Liza Lin, "ByteDance Shelved IPO Intentions After Chinese Regulators Warned About Data Security," *Wall Street Journal*, July 12, 2021.

165 **bought a 1 percent stake in the ByteDance subsidiary:** Lingling Wei, "China's New Way to Control Its Biggest Companies: Golden Shares," *Wall Street Journal*, March 8, 2023.

165 **ByteDance and other household names:** Laura He, "China Tells Its Tech Giants to Heed 'Warning' in Alibaba's Record Fine," CNN, April 14, 2021.

165 **It had ordered thirteen firms:** Michelle Toh, "China Orders Tencent and Other Big Tech Firms to Curb Their Finance Businesses," CNN, April 31, 2021.
166 **he would be resigning as the CEO:** "A Letter from Yiming," May 19, 2021, https://web.archive.org/web/20210520021606/https://www.bytedance.com/en/news/60a526af053cc102d640c061.
166 **the idea that he was ready to retire:** Author interview, September 2022.
166 **"nobody thought [his retirement] was real":** Author interview, December 2024.
167 **remained a common fixture:** Mac and Che, "TikTok's C.E.O. Navigates."

Chapter 21

169 **a caricature of a good cop:** Amy Teibel, "CISO Spotlight: Roland Cloutier, CISO," *CISOs Connect*, May 11, 2023.
169 **gave him a rich budget:** Internal ByteDance documents provided by a source.
170 **"What I'm learning right now":** Recorded meeting, September 9, 2021, provided by Rob Doe.
170 **But big swaths of data:** Recorded meetings, September 14–15, 2021; September 20, 2021; provided by Rob Doe.
171 **Biden rolled back Trump's IEEPA order:** "President Issues Executive Order Revoking TikTok and WeChat Executive Orders and Addressing Access by Foreign Adversaries to U.S. Personal Data," Covington, June 10, 2021.
172 **Erich gathered V Pappas:** *TikTok v. Garland*, No. 24–1113, US Court of Appeals for the District of Columbia Circuit, September 16, 2024, 261–356.
172 **"If ByteDance is rendered to a minority position":** *TikTok v. Garland*, 267.
173 **described the algorithm as "a sorting machine":** *TikTok v. Garland*, 320.
173 **But it wasn't until the Obama era:** "The Committee on Foreign Investment in the United States (CFIUS)," Congressional Research Service, last modified February 26, 2020.
175 **government control over the hiring and firing:** *TikTok v. Garland*, 171.
175 **ByteDance was offering to give the US government:** *TikTok v. Garland*, 222.

Chapter 22

179 **When the men met in person:** Author interviews, December 2024; January 2025.
179 **wore a baseball cap to the office:** Author interview, January 2025.
180 **"You guys rely a lot":** Recorded meeting, September 29, 2021, provided by Rob Doe.
180 **"Like, not on the record":** Recorded meeting, January 24, 2022, provided by Rob Doe.
182 **US lawmakers were furious:** "Warner, Rubio Call for Investigation into TikTok in Light of Revelations About Chinese Communist Party's Potential Access to U.S. Data," Senator Mark R. Warner press release, July 5, 2022.
182 **In a September hearing:** "Social Media's Impact on Homeland Security," Homeland Security and Governmental Affairs, US Senate, September 14, 2022.
182 **They declined to answer:** "Social Media's Impact," Homeland Security and Governmental Affairs.
182 **Internal investigators scrambled to determine:** Internal documents provided to author.
183 **They even asked the Lark engineers:** Internal documents provided to author.

Chapter 23

185 **The executive summary of his eventual report:** Internal ByteDance Fraud Risk Assessment (Burness Report) provided to author.
186 **was never shared:** ByteDance/TikTok Statement to *Forbes* found in Emily Baker-White, "TikTok Couldn't Ensure Accurate Responses to Government Inquiries, a ByteDance Risk Assessment Said," *Forbes*, November 28, 2022.
186 **more loyal to people than he was to process:** Author interviews, October and December 2022, May 2023; internal communications provided to author.
186 **advised Rob to "build the bridge":** Author interviews, October and December 2022, May 2023; internal communications provided to author.
187 **built an impressive global security team:** Author interviews, October 2022, May 2023.
187 **ByteDance later sought advice from a law firm:** Memo prepared by lawyers at Baker McKenzie for ByteDance, shared with author.
188 **a system known as the "Green Channel":** Internal ByteDance documents shared with author.
188 **which they believed was an unprofessional "witch hunt":** Internal ByteDance documents shared with author.
188 **responsible for investigating "insider risk":** Author interview, October 2022.
189 **When Chris's investigators began looking:** Internal ByteDance documents shared with author.

Chapter 24

192 **the source showed me the spreadsheet:** Internal documents shared with author.
194 **ByteDance shot back in a thread:** TikTok Comms (@TikTokComms), "1/ @Forbes, reporting about TikTok continues to lack both rigor and journalistic integrity," X, October 20, 2022, https://x.com/TikTokComms/status/1583238906111459328.
195 **Over the next two months:** ByteDance/TikTok acknowledged the Covington investigation and its findings in statements to the *New York Times* and other outlets on December 22, 2022.
196 **called an emergency meeting for the company's communications department:** Author interviews, January 2024; April 2024.
196 **sent all-staff emails explaining:** These were provided to author by a source; they were also later published by *The Verge*. Mitchell Clark and Alex Heath, "TikTok's Parent Company Accessed the Data of US Journalists," *Verge*, December 22, 2022.
198 **In a lengthy letter to lawmakers:** TikTok letter to Chair Cathy McMorris Rodgers, Ranking Member Frank Pallone, Jr., and members of the US House Committee on Energy and Commerce, May 2023.
198 **ByteDance had been served with a subpoena:** Author interview with "Brad," December 2022.
198 **When lawyers advised ByteDance:** Memo prepared by lawyers at Baker McKenzie for ByteDance, shared with author.
199 **Agents interviewed ByteDance employees:** Documents provided to author.
199 **Customs and Border Protection stopped dozens of staffers:** Author interview, January 2023.

Chapter 25

204 **"you heard it here first":** Author correspondence, February 2023.
204 **"He seeks a future":** Mike Gallagher, "Exploding Pagers and the Tech Race with China," *Wall Street Journal*, September 22, 2024.
205 **Wray said in a speech:** Rachel Treisman, "The FBI Alleges TikTok Poses National Security Concerns," NPR, November 17, 2022.
205 **Yellen had called the national security fears:** David Lawder, "U.S. Treasury Yellen: Twitter Should Be Held to Certain Standards for Content," Reuters, November 30, 2022.
205 **The ByteDance C-Suite partially blamed:** Author interviews, October and December 2024.
205 **Michael and his team felt trapped:** Author interview, October 2024.
206 *Politico* **referred to him:** Mike Allen, "SECRET GOP TECH SUMMIT—WOMEN RULE SUMMIT livestream begins 8:20; Bidens at 12:35—OBAMA on Colbert—LISA BARCLAY to Boies, Schiller—B'DAY: Kirsten Gillibrand, Terry Moran," *Politico*, December 9, 2014.
206 **In late 2022, after months of watching:** Jennifer Jacobs and Alex Barinka, "TikTok General Counsel No Longer Oversees US Relations," *Bloomberg Law*, January 27, 2023.
207 **"It was a balloon":** "US-China Tensions: Threat Inflation and Balloon Deflation," *The Problem with Jon Stewart* podcast, February 8, 2023, https://www.youtube.com/watch?v=vzditHqexiQ.
207 **On** *Saturday Night Live*: "Bowen Yang's Chinese Spy Balloon May Be the 'SNL' Star's Best Impression Yet," CNN, February 5, 2023, https://www.cnn.com/videos/media/2023/02/05/snl-chinese-balloon.cnn.
208 **"The trio of cases announced today":** "Principal Deputy Assistant Attorney General David Newman Delivers Remarks Announcing Transnational Repression Cases," US Department of Justice, April 17, 2023.

Chapter 26

209 **Erich suggested to colleagues:** Author interview, October 2024.
209 **In the sleepy week between Christmas and New Year's:** Unless otherwise noted, the following account of TikTok's negotiation with CFIUS is sourced from letters and emails between the parties made public in the appendix to *TikTok v. Garland*.
211 **the only solution that would satisfy the government:** Author interview, February 2025.
211 **started a game of chicken:** Author interview, February 2025.
212 **The company hired SKDK:** Daniel Lippman, "TikTok Hires Biden-Connected Firm as It Finds Itself Under D.C.'s Microscope," *Politico*, March 9, 2023.
212 **It hired Ankit Desai and Jamal Brown:** Karl Evers-Hillstrom, "TikTok Hires Another Former Biden Aide in Push to Avoid US Ban," *Hill*, March 24, 2023.
212 **former Obama campaign masterminds:** Kirsten Grind and Erich Schwartzel, "TikTok's Behind-the-Scenes Help in Washington: Former Obama, Disney Advisers," *Wall Street Journal*, March 30, 2023.
212 **It also tapped Crossroads Strategies:** Lippman, "TikTok Hires Biden-Connected Firm."
213 **"support[ed] two indirect jobs for every internet job":** "The Internet Sector Created 6 Million Jobs, $2.1 Trillion in GDP in 2018, New IA Research Finds," Internet Association, September 26, 2019.

213 **Less than a year before:** "TikTok Executive Speaks to CNN About Security Concern Claims," CNN, July 3, 2022, accessed May 1, 2025.
214 **stand . . . side by side with creators and the TikTok team:** Kaya Yurieff, "TikTok Asks Creators to Help Win Over Lawmakers," *Information*, March 7, 2023.
214 **"Creators" and their plus-ones:** Madison Malone Kircher, "TikTok Stars Go on a D.C. Field Trip," *New York Times*, March 23, 2023.
214 **rooms at the posh Salamander Hotel:** Emily Birnbaum and Sabrina Willmer, "TikTok's Survival Is at Stake in All-Out Fight Against US Ban," *BNN Bloomberg*, July 26, 2024.
214 **covered the wall next to her door with sticky notes:** Photo of the sticky notes at Shuran Huang.
214 **Bowman used his time at the Capitol:** Makena Kelly, "Sen. Rand Paul Becomes Latest Lawmaker Opposing TikTok Ban," *Verge*, March 29, 2023.
215 **Bowman wanted to pass a national data privacy law:** Nicholas Fandos and David McCabe, "Meet the Lonely New York Progressive Defending TikTok," *New York Times*, March 22, 2023.
215 **He also favored algorithmic transparency laws:** "Wyden, Booker and Clarke Introduce Bill to Regulate Use of Artificial Intelligence to Make Critical Decisions like Housing, Employment and Education," Senator Ron Wyden, September 21, 2023.

Chapter 27

217 **playing lawmakers in mock hearings:** Grind and Schwartzel, "TikTok's Behind-the-Scenes Help"; Erin Woo and Juro Osawa, "Inside TikTok CEO's Plan to Play Offense," *Information*, July 26, 2023.
217 **Upton had even given a toast:** Allen, "SECRET GOP TECH SUMMIT."
217 **colleagues described him as a man with a weakness for celebrity:** Author interviews, October and November 2024.
218 **told congressional staffers that TikTok executives:** Author correspondence, March 13, 2023.
218 **reached out to journalists who reported on the company:** Author received such outreach, as did another reporter who wrote in *BuzzFeed News* about receiving it. Chris Stokel-Walker, "Congress Wanted Me to Turn Over a Document About TikTok's Links to China. Here's Why I Refused," *BuzzFeed News*, March 22, 2023.
218 **March 23 was a sunny spring day:** "TikTok: How Congress Can Safeguard American Data Privacy and Protect Children from Online Harms," US House Committee on Energy and Commerce, March 23, 2023.
223 **the limit had a negligible effect on watch time:** Bobby Allyn, Sylvia Goodman, and Dara Kerr, "TikTok Executives Know About App's Effect on Teens, Lawsuit Documents Allege," NPR, October 11, 2024.
223 **The goal of the limit:** Allyn, Goodman, and Kerr, "TikTok Executives Know."

Chapter 28

227 **"I like being in the mix":** Cecilia Kang, "Mark Warner: Tech Millionaire Who Became Tech's Critic in Congress," *New York Times*, October 29, 2017; Jonathan Weisman, "Mark Warner, a 'Business Guy' Democrat, Lands Back in the Fray," *New York Times*, July 15, 2021.
227 **"a creepy low-IQ Chinese plot":** "Tucker: This would give the government terri-

NOTES

228 fying power," *Tucker Carlson Tonight*, March 27, 2023, https://www.youtube.com/watch?v=AZJ-hHxSqkw&t=217s.
228 **Concern over that new power:** Jenna Leventoff, "ACLU Raises Concerns About Senate Bill Aimed at Banning TikTok," ACLU, March 7, 2023.
228 **Some language in the bill:** Megan Loe, "Verifying Claims About the RESTRICT Act and VPN Use for Restricted Apps or Sites," WCNC, April 6, 2023.
228 **described the bill as "garbage":** "Jesse Watters Presses Lindsey Graham on 'RESTRICT Act,'" *Jesse Watters Primetime*, March 29, 2023.
229 **As the RESTRICT Act was imploding:** Author interview with Bijan Koohmaraie, August 28, 2024.
231 **the bill would need to add a provision:** Author interview, January 2025.
231 **insisting that if ByteDance complied:** Evelyn Cheng and Sheila Chiang, "TikTok Wants to Distance Itself from China—but Beijing Is Getting Involved," CNBC, March 24, 2023.
232 **The judge was dismissive of the auditors' arguments:** "SEC Imposes Sanctions Against China-Based Members of Big Four Accounting Networks for Refusing to Produce Documents," US Securities and Exchange Commission, February 6, 2015.
232 **"the Respondents found themselves between a rock and a hard place":** Initial Decision Release No. 553 Administrative Proceeding Files Nos. 3–14872, 3–15116, US Securities and Exchange Commission, January 22, 2014.
214 **"At the end of the day":** Meghan Sullivan, "Sen. Warner on TikTok: Their 1st Loyalty Has to Be to Communist Party," Scripps News, March 22, 2023.

Chapter 29

236 **When Nnete Matima joined ByteDance:** Accounts of Matima and Carter's experiences are sourced from their September 20, 2023, charge filed with the EEOC.
237 **soon bolstered by another complaint:** *Puris v. TikTok Inc.*
237 **$4,000 bonus in "baby cash":** Áine Cain, "11 Insanely Cool Benefits for Facebook Employees," *Inc.*, November 9, 2017.
237 **discourage her reports from hiring women:** Author interview, February 2024.
237 **he "didn't believe in" maternity leave:** Cristina Criddle, "TikTok Shop's Troubled UK Expansion: Staff Exodus and Culture Clash," *Financial Times*, June 7, 2022.
238 **But employees quickly learned:** Patrick Spaulding Ryan, "An Open Letter to IRS Commissioner Werfel on TikTok's Pre-IPO RSU Restrictions," LinkedIn, March 17, 2024.
238 **The platform required employees:** *Puris v. TikTok Inc.*
239 **the company could "claw back" stock granted:** Ryan, "An Open Letter."
239 **a group of security staffers began compiling:** This account is sourced from author interviews in February and April 2024 and from internal ByteDance documents provided to author.
239 **she and hundreds of her colleagues had been trained:** Alexandra S. Levine, "TikTok Moderators Are Being Trained Using Graphic Images of Child Sexual Abuse," *Forbes*, August 4, 2022.
240 **staff also encountered CSAM in Lark chats:** Notes on an internal ByteDance report provided to author.
240 **"No insult to ByteDance":** Audio recording provided to author.
241 **emailing spreadsheets to employees in Beijing:** Alexandra Sternlicht, "Some Ex-TikTok Employees Say the Social Media Service Worked Closely with its China-Based Parent Despite Claims of Independence," *Fortune*, April 15, 2024.
241 **TikTok's corporate Twitter account responded aggressively:** TikTokPolicy

(@TikTokPolicy), "Today's article from @iamsternlicht is factually inaccurate. Facts matter," X, April 15, 2024, https://x.com/TikTokPolicy/status/1779970114252624018.
242 **received at least seven internal complaints:** These violations are sourced from a cache of documents provided to author.

Chapter 30

244 **"Something's changed with TikTok":** Katie Notopoulos, "TikTok Is Kind of Bad Now, Right? The Emphasis on Shopping Really Bums Me Out," *Business Insider*, February 8, 2024.
245 **But tests in the US and Europe flopped:** Cristina Criddle, "TikTok Abandons Ecommerce Expansion in Europe and US," *Financial Times*, July 4, 2022.
245 **started reaching out to creators:** Woo and Osawa, "Inside TikTok CEO's Plan."
246 **Kaytlyn Stewart, a TikToker with more than 2 million followers:** Drama Kween, "Tiktok Shop Has DESTROYED Tiktok," February 15, 2024, YouTube, https://www.youtube.com/watch?v=B1wzElcl3Fk.
246 **In another YouTube video:** Allie Tricaso, "tiktok shop has RUINED tiktok," YouTube, October 23, 2023, https://www.youtube.com/watch?v=i_X_7ARTrgY&pp=ygUJI3Nob3BpZmZ5.
246 **pivoted in a plan known as "Project S":** Cristina Criddle and Qianer Liu, "TikTok Prepares 'Project S' Plan to Break into Online Shopping," *Financial Times*, June 20, 2023.
246 **In early 2023, a journalist and tech critic:** Cory Doctorow, "The 'Enshittification' of TikTok," *Wired*, January 23, 2023.
247 **"The For You used to seem uncanny":** Notopoulos, "TikTok Is Kind of Bad Now, Right?"
247 **"Since representation matters":** V Pappas, "A personal update. I shared this to our TikTok organization over the weekend and wanted to bring visibility here as well." LinkedIn; V also described their decision to come out as nonbinary in this profile: MacColl, "The Fighter."
248 **a model boss for new parents:** MacColl, "The Fighter"; author interview, December 2024.
248 **The happiness and success of the young people:** Woo and Osawa, "Inside TikTok CEO's Plan"; author conversations.

Chapter 31

250 **This set off alarm bells in DC:** Kamala HQ, "lol hey guys," TikTok, February 11, 2024, https://www.tiktok.com/@kamalahq/video/7334529963066019114?lang=en.
250 **tuning in from a wedding in Cancún:** Author interview with Bijan Koohmaraie, August 28, 2024.
251 **In November, a group of young American TikTokers:** Alexandra S. Levine and Emily Baker-White, "TikTok Videos Praising 9/11 Have Exploded, but the Company Denies They're Trending," *Forbes*, November 16, 2023.
251 **colleagues made the final preparations:** Author interview, January 2025.
252 **"If tomorrow, someone tried to buy":** "Capstone: Disrupting Cyber Threats and Protecting U.S. Technology and Data," DVIDS, April 10, 2024.
253 **"we could work behind closed doors freely":** Author interview with Bijan Koohmaraie, August 28, 2024.
253 **The bill "was crafted in secret":** Sapna Maheshwari, David McCabe, and Cecilia Kang, "'Thunder Run': Behind Lawmakers' Secretive Push to Pass the TikTok Bill," *New York Times*, April 24, 2024.

354 NOTES

253 **The companies were so threatened by the potential laws:** Cherri Murphy, "Uber Bought Itself a Law. Here's Why That's Dangerous for Struggling Drivers Like Me," *Guardian*, November 12, 2020; Andrew J. Hawkins, "Uber Is Using Its App to Troll Local Politicians Again," *Verge*, March 10, 2016.

254 **some believed they were locked out of the app:** Sapna Maheshwari and David McCabe, "TikTok Prompts Users to Call Congress to Fight Possible Ban," *New York Times*, March 7, 2024.

254 **"If you ban TikTok, I will find you and shoot you":** Senator Thom Tillis (@SenThomTillis), "This is a voicemail my office received last night. TikTok's misinformation campaign is pushing people to call their members of Congress, and callers like this who communicate threats against elected officials could be committing a federal crime. The Communist-Chinese aligned company is proving just how dangerous their current ownership is. Great work, TikTok," X, March 20, 2024, https://x.com/senthomtillis/status/1770495527508939255.

254 **Capitol Police began investigating the threats:** Redacted Transcript of Classified Energy and Commerce Committee Hearing, *TikTok v. Garland*, 24–1113 (DC Cir.), September 4, 2024.

255 **On the morning of March 7:** Author interview with Bijan Koohmaraie, August 28, 2024.

Chapter 32

259 **Trump made a post on Truth Social:** Todd Spangler, "Donald Trump Opposes TikTok Ban Because It Would Boost Business for Facebook and 'Zuckerschmuck,' a 'True Enemy of the People,'" *Variety*, March 8, 2024.

259 **"I could have banned TikTok":** Robert Farley, "Trump's Partisan Spin on TikTok," *FactCheck*, April 23, 2024.

260 **Trump opposed a TikTok ban:** Lisa Friedman and Sapna Maheshwari, "How Donald Trump Went from Backing a TikTok Ban to Backing Off," *New York Times*, December 28, 2024; Tom Maloney, "Jeff Yass' $15 Billion TikTok Fortune Shines Light on His GOP Clout," *Bloomberg*, March 13, 2024.

260 **The organization's lobbyists also suggested to Republicans:** Author interviews, May and June 2024.

260 **House of Representatives convened to vote:** Kevin Freking, Haleluya Hadero, and Mary Clare Jalonick, "House Passes a Bill That Could Lead to a TikTok Ban If Chinese Owner Refuses to Sell," AP, March 13, 2024.

261 **After the votes were counted:** Author interview with Bijan Koohmaraie, August 28, 2024.

261 **Scalise had a cookie-cake delivered:** Maheshwari, McCabe, and Kang, "Thunder Run."

261 **Representatives from the Chinese embassy:** Hailey Fuchs, "Chinese Diplomats Are Quietly Meeting with Hill Staffers About TikTok," *Politico*, April 17, 2024.

262 **"this so-called reporting doesn't pass the smell test":** Fuchs, "Chinese Diplomats Are Quietly Meeting."

262 **The embassy, however, did not contest *Politico*'s reports:** Fuchs, "Chinese Diplomats Are Quietly Meeting."

262 **They touted a study:** TikTok Economic Impact Report 2024, accessed April 4, 2025.

262 **They distributed a "one-pager" of talking points:** "Nvidia's New Chip Architecture and TikTok's Bill," *Bloomberg Technology*, March 19, 2024.

262 **arrange for fifty TikTokers' stays at the Salamander Hotel:** Emily Birnbaum and

NOTES   355

Sabrina Willmer, "TikTok's Survival Is at Stake in All-Out Fight Against US Ban," *Bloomberg*, July 26, 2024.
262 **Oracle's top lobbyist:** Brian Schwartz, "Oracle Met with Senate Aides About TikTok Data Storage After House Ban Passed," CNBC, April 22, 2024.
262 **After the House vote:** Andrew Desiderio and John Bresnahan, "Cantwell Pans House-Passed TikTok Bill," *Punchbowl News*, April 9, 2024, https://punchbowl.news/article/policy/cantwell-tiktok-bill-guard-act/.
262 **She also suggested holding a public hearing:** David Shepardson, "US Senate Considering Public Hearing on TikTok Crackdown Bill, Committee Chair Says," Reuters, March 20, 2024.
262 **The House would agree to one substantive change:** "Cantwell Statement on Updated House TikTok Bill," US Senate Committee on Commerce, Science, and Transportation, April 17, 2024.
263 **persuading a judge that the Trump administration's actions:** *TikTok Inc. v. Trump*, 507 F. Supp. 3d 92 (D.D.C. 2020).
263 **"The reality—which you know well":** *TikTok v. Garland*, 24–1113 (DC Cir.), Appendix Exhibit N, 413–425.
264 **News of Erich's impending departure:** Jennifer Jacobs, Kurt Wagner, and Alex Barinka, "TikTok to Remove Executive Tasked with Fending Off US Claims," *Bloomberg*, April 21, 2024.
264 **Though his plans were "still in flux":** Internal document shared with author.
265 **"People weren't going to vote against the Ukraine funding package for this":** Author interview with Bijan Koohmaraie, August 28, 2024.
265 **To ByteDance's more than 7,000 US employees:** Internal document shared with author.
265 **On April 20, he added an update:** Internal document shared with author.
266 **One employee mused to a friend:** Record shared with author.
266 **"Isn't it super unethical and unprofessional":** Screenshot from Blind.

Chapter 33

269 **In August 2023, a gaming influencer:** MattKC, "The creators of TikTok caused my website to shut down," YouTube, August 18, 2023, https://www.youtube.com/watch?v=Hi5sd3WEh0c.
270 **quickly became disenchanted with both initiatives:** Juro Osawa, "ByteDance Axes Next VR Headset, in Pullback from Meta Battle," *Information*, December 13, 2023; Juro Osawa, "TikTok Parent's Gaming Stumble Shows Limits of Founder's Vision," *Information*, December 22, 2023.
271 **some companies even scraped entire libraries:** Anna Washenko, "AI Startup Argues Scraping Every Song on the Internet Is 'Fair Use,'" *Engadget*, August 1, 2024; Alex Reisner, "Search LibGen, the Pirated-Books Database That Meta Used to Train AI," *Atlantic*, March 20, 2025.
271 **ByteSpider expanded its crawling:** Kali Hays, "TikTok's Parent Launched a Web Scraper That's Gobbling Up the World's Online Data 25-Times Faster Than OpenAI," *Fortune*, October 3, 2024.
272 **After ChatGPT's late 2022 release:** Coco Feng and Zhou Xin, "AI Takes Priority at TikTok Owner ByteDance, as Sora Disrupts the Future of Video Creation," *South China Morning Post*, February 29, 2024; Alex Heath, "ByteDance Is Secretly Using OpenAI's Tech to Build a Competitor," *Verge*, December 15, 2023.

Chapter 34

273 **"enhance the company's sense of crisis"**: Coco Feng, "ByteDance CEO Wants to Whip Employees Into Shape, as They Lack a 'Sense of Crisis' Amid Fierce Competition at Home and Abroad," *South China Morning Post*, January 30, 2024.

273 **reading OpenAI's technical white papers**: Feng and Xin, "AI Takes Priority."

274 **told suppliers that ByteDance would spend**: Qianer Liu and Juro Osawa, "ByteDance Planned to Spend $7 Billion on Nvidia Chips Next Year," *Information*, December 30, 2024.

274 **the goal of jointly building ByteDance's answer to ChatGPT**: "ByteDance Is Exploring the Combination of Large Models and Hardware," *Pandaily*, September 20, 2024; Juro Osawa, "TikTok Owner ByteDance Elevates Executive Leading AI Development," *The Information*, April 19, 2024.

274 **staffers on Lark discussed how to "whitewash" and "desensitize"**: Heath, "ByteDance Is Secretly."

275 **To roll out Doubao**: Yan Junwen, "2000个"产品经理",帮字节做豆包," *China Entrepreneur*, November 29, 2024.

275 **team dove into other projects**: "ByteDance Is Exploring."

275 **At a ByteDance conference in spring 2024**: Zhang Zipeng, "字节跳动副总裁朱骏：从大模型到用户体验，在做豆包产品时的一点感想," Kejihui New Media, May 15, 2024.

276 **researchers questioned various companies' chatbots**: Ryan McMorrow and Tina Hu, "China Deploys Censors to Create Socialist AI," *Financial Times*, July 17, 2024.

277 **About Tiananmen Square, the bot said**: HIVVIH, "Boox now ships with a Chinese propaganda AI assistant || A broader warning against Chinese electronics," Reddit, December 25, 2024.

277 **Just weeks before the bot's launch**: Ana Swanson, "Biden Administration Clamps Down on China's Access to Chip Technology," *New York Times*, October 7, 2022.

278 **the bot's responses had been prerecorded**: Chang Che and John Liu, "China's Answer to ChatGPT Gets an Artificial Debut and Disappoints," *New York Times*, March 16, 2023.

278 **test models' compliance with "core socialist values"**: McMorrow and Hu, "China Deploys Censors."

278 **Technologists often described the models**: Lou Blouin, "AI's Mysterious 'Black Box' Problem, Explained," *University of Michigan–Dearborn News*, March 6, 2023.

279 **The censors then tested those datasets**: Dominic Paulger, "Navigating Governance Frameworks for Generative AI Systems in the Asia-Pacific," Future of Privacy Forum, May 2024, 53; Daniel Sprick, "Aligning AI with China's Authoritarian Value System," *Diplomat*, February 3, 2025.

279 **The article alleged a "physical link"**: Zen Soo, "Tech Firm Baidu Denies Report That Its Ernie AI Chatbot Is Linked to Chinese Military Research," AP, January 15, 2024.

280 **Baidu strongly denied that it had a relationship**: Sarah Zheng, Jeanny Yu, and Zheping Huang, "Baidu Sinks Most Since 2022 Despite Denying Links to PLA AI," *Bloomberg*, January 15, 2024.

280 **"We have no competing fighting chance"**: Katrina Manson, "US Has Already Lost AI Fight to China, Says Ex-Pentagon Software Chief," *Financial Times*, October 10, 2021.

280 **cited the Baidu incident to underscore the urgency**: Evan Lynch, "U.S. Army Launches Generative AI Platform in Groundbreaking Move," *SIGNAL*, September 10, 2024.

280 **Reuters reported that the Chinese government:** James Pomfret and Jessie Pang, "Exclusive: Chinese Researchers Develop AI Model for Military Use on Back of Meta's Llama," Reuters, November 1, 2024.

Chapter 35

283 **At the conference, Shou was interviewed:** "TikTok CEO Shou Chew and FII Institute CEO Richard Attias at #FII8," Future Investment Initiative, October 29, 2024, https://www.youtube.com/watch?v=1YRAGmFpsiY.
284 **sexually explicit content was common:** Salvatore Romano and Marc Faddoul, "Mapping Ban and Shadow-Ban on TikTok," Digital Methods Initiative, last modified February 10, 2022.
285 **Saudi Arabians began using TikTok:** "TikTok Usage Overtakes Facebook in KSA," *Arab Ad*, February 9, 2022, https://arabadonline.com/en/details/digital/TikTok-usage-overtakes-Facebook-in-KSA.
285 **one advertising agency claimed:** Sonia Majumder, "Saudi Arabia's TikTok Sensation and the Booming Business Behind It," *Middle East Campaign*, November 28, 2023, https://campaignme.com/saudi-arabias-tiktok-sensation-and-the-booming-business-behind-it-2/.
285 **One person targeted by the campaign:** Author interview, October 2024.
285 **condemning the boycott effort:** "TikTok Confirms Its Support for Its Community in Saudi Arabia," TikTok, August 11, 2023, https://newsroom.tiktok.com/ar-mena/tiktok-emphasizes-its-support-for-its-community-in-the-kingdom-of-saudi-arabia.
286 **In the early 2010s:** "Project Raven: How Former White House Veterans and NSA Operatives Turned the UAE into a Hacking Power," Reuters.
286 **The project led to the capture and torture:** "Loujain al-Hathloul: Saudi Woman Activist Jailed for Five Years," BBC, December 28, 2020.
286 **He was also affiliated:** Mark Mazzetti, Nicole Perlroth, and Ronen Bergman, "It Seemed Like a Popular Chat App. It's Secretly a Spy Tool," *New York Times*, December 22, 2019.
287 **G42 had substantial ties to the Chinese state:** Mark Mazzetti and Edward Wong, "Inside U.S. Efforts to Untangle an A.I. Giant's Ties to China," *New York Times*, November 27, 2023.

Chapter 37

294 **On an iPhone-sized screen:** _ovydel_, "bogpr," TikTok, https://www.tiktok.com/@_ovydel_/video/7446030924057152791.
294 **known in Romania as "The King of TikTok":** Adrian Nicolae, "Cine e misteriosul bogătaș BOGPR care a făcut campania independentului Călin Georgescu: Regele TikTok-ului dă sute de mii de € la maneliști și nu vrea să i se dezvăluie chipul. Imagini în premieră absolută!" [Who is BOGPR, the mysterious rich man who funded the campaign of independent candidate Calin Georgescu: the King of TikTok gives hundreds of thousands of euros to manele singers and doesn't want his face revealed. Exclusive premiere images!], *Gandul*, November 25, 2024.
295 **Georgescu won an upset victory in the first round:** Josef Šlerka and Iulia Stănoiu, "How TikTok Almost Won the Presidency for Romania's Far-Right Candidate," *VSquare*, December 19, 2024.

295 **TikTok stars also began receiving offers of cash:** Damien Leloup, Florian Reynaud, and Jean-Baptiste Chastand, "Influencers, Bot Accounts and Illegal Ads: The Troubling Interference Campaign That Annulled Romania's Election," *Le Monde*, December 13, 2024.

295 **The Georgescu campaign had begun several months earlier:** Victoria Olari, "Rise of Unknown Romanian Presidential Candidate Preceded By Telegram and TikTok Engagement Spikes," *DFR Lab*, December 12, 2024.

296 **"Just like Elon Musk supported the Trump campaign":** "Codename: 'Bogpr.' The Mysterious Character Who Dumped Millions of Dollars on TikTok," *Tirana Post*, December 8, 2024.

296 **"My favorite author is Dostoevsky":** "Codename: 'Bogpr.'"; Leloup, Reynaud, and Chastand, "Influencers, Bot Accounts and Illegal Ads."

297 **called on TikTok to testify:** "MEPs Question TikTok About Compliance with EU Digital Rules," European Parliament, December 3, 2024, https://www.youtube.com/watch?v=ZOkfCkt2pq0.

297 **The algorithm, she said, was "the perfect handshake":** Pieter Haeck, "'We Are Getting Fed Up': EU Lawmakers Snap at TikTok Over Romanian Election," *Politico*, December 3, 2024.

298 **"the flimsy suspicions of an intelligence agency":** Christina Lu, "The Speech That Stunned Europe," *Foreign Policy*, February 18, 2025.

299 **ByteDance pointed to the difficulty:** Iain Martin, "TikTok Sets Aside $1 Billion to Cover Future European Data Privacy Fines," *Forbes*, October 11, 2024.

300 **received internal complaints:** Author interview, January 2025.

302 **"To water down First Amendment constraints":** Evelyn Douek, "The Government's Disturbing Rationale for Banning TikTok," *Atlantic*, December 12, 2024.

Chapter 38

306 **"The rush to react to foreign propaganda":** *TikTok, Inc., et al., v. Merrick B. Garland, Attorney General*, Supreme Court 24–656.

306 **In an unprecedented filing:** *TikTok v. Garland*, Supreme Court 24–656, 24–657.

308 **"The government's real target":** *TikTok v. Garland*, Supreme Court 24–656.

310 **The Supreme Court has been hesitant:** Oma Seddiq, "Supreme Court Justices Aren't 'the 9 Greatest Experts on the Internet,' Elena Kagan Said as They Heard a Major Tech Case," *Business Insider*, February 21, 2023.

310 **Kagan's self-effacing line was echoed:** *TikTok v. Garland*, Supreme Court 24–656, 24–657.

311 **Shou Zi Chew posted TikTok's response:** shou.time, "Our response to the Supreme Court decision @TikTok," January 17, 2025, https://www.tiktok.com/@shou.time/video/7460953702673829166?lang=en.

312 **went viral for a post:** Base (@outsoldnation), "Me selecting 'ALLOW' when Rednote asks if I will allow them to track my data 😂 😂," X, January 13, 2025, https://x.com/outsoldnation/status/1879026415771029732.

313 **one friendly animal enthusiast from Sichuan:** Zen Soo, "US TikTok Users Flock to Chinese App Xiaohongshu in Protest with TikTok Ban Looming," AP, January 14, 2025.

313 **A Florida college campus radio station:** Ernest Walker III, "90.5 Hosts TikTok Funeral," January 17, 2025.

313 **hosted a physical mock funeral:** zach.sage, "A Funeral for TikTok," January 19, 2025, https://www.tiktok.com/@zach.sage/video/7461766391574695199.

Chapter 39

315 **After the Supreme Court's ruling:** David McCabe, Adam Liptak, and Sapna Maheshwari, "TikTok Makes Last-Minute Push as Supreme Court Is Poised to Rule on Ban," *New York Times*, January 17, 2025.
316 **"It is a stunt":** David Ingram and Alexandra Marquez, "Trump Says He Will 'Most Likely' Give TikTok a 90-Day Extension to Avoid a Ban," NBC News, January 18, 2025.
317 **As University of Washington researcher:** Mike "looking for research fellowship" Caulfield (@mikecaulfield.bsky.social), "I do think there's something about the Chinese company knowing exactly how to operate in the environment that really brings home where we have arrived." Bluesky, January 18, 2025.
317 **"In agreement with our service providers":** Lauren Feiner, "Trump Says He'll Delay TikTok Ban, but the Platform Must Be Sold," *Verge*, January 19, 2025.
318 **Will Stancil, a left-wing policy researcher:** Will Stancil (@whstancil.bsky.social), "me: 'the reason modern politics has gone insane is that an international class of tech oligarchs and authoritarians have teamed up to create an information environment dominated by social media memes that effectively control public opinion' trump: 'what if tiktok was co-owned by Xi and myself,'" January 19, 2025, https://bsky.app/profile/whstancil.bsky.social/post/3lg47ma53js2n.

Chapter 40

321 **The "Make America Hot Again" party:** Taylor Lorenz, "These Influencers Helped Get Trump Elected. Now They're Ready to Party," *Rolling Stone*, January 20, 2025.
321 **"Now that the law has taken effect":** "Cotton, Ricketts Statement on TikTok Being Removed from App Stores," Senator Tom Cotton, January 19, 2025.
322 **the CEO's presence at the event:** "'Not My Favorite Thing': Hawley Reacts to TikTok's CEO Attending Trump's Inauguration," *Forbes Breaking News*, January 16, 2025, https://www.youtube.com/watch?v=-xuIT8TKHME.
322 **Trump took questions from reporters:** Bobby Allyn, "Trump Signs Executive Order to Pause TikTok Ban, Provide Immunity to Tech Firms," NPR, January 20, 2025.
323 **"TikTok is officially a Trump propaganda platform":** Author screenshot, taken Feb 27, 2025, showing Google Search preview of Krishnamurthy post (since deleted) dated Jan 19, 2025.
323 **"I'm gonna need every single one of you":** Emma Hardesty, "The Not-So-Secret Propaganda of the TikTok Shutdown," *College Heights Herald*, January 20, 2025.
323 **"I literally have such an ick":** Hardesty, "The Not-So-Secret Propaganda."
323 **"At any point, the Trump administration":** Io Dodds, "'It Took the Air Out of Me': How TikTok Creators Reacted to the Chaotic Ban—and Trump's Sudden Reprieve," *Independent*, January 20, 2025.
324 **student journalists called out TikTok's behavior:** Quinn Downing: "Trump Is Not the Savior of Tiktok," *Dickinsonian*, February 6, 2025.
324 **"a thinly veiled tactic for Trump":** Avery Finley, "TikTok and the Future of Social Media Censorship," *Wellesley News*, February 19, 2025.
325 **influencer with more than 35,000 TikTok followers:** Sean Garrette (@seangarrette), "Them even mentioning Trump in that statement makes me not even wanna be back on tiktok when it does come back lol. You get in bed with the dogs, you get fleas," X, January 18, 2025, https://x.com/seangarrette/status/1880820999425560599.
327 **Evelyn Douek, the Stanford professor:** Evelyn Douek (@evelyndouek.bsky.social), "The president holding this much power over one of the major communications plat-

NOTES

forms in this country is very good; very free speechy. Congratulations to everyone involved," Bluesky, April 4, 2025, https://bsky.app/profile/evelyndouek.bsky.social/post/3llyyu52jy22k.

327 **Alan Rozenshtein, a national security lawyer:** Alan Rozenshtein (alanrozenshtein.com), "The TikTok farce continues. Why extend for another 75 days? Why not another 150 or 500? Or until the heat death of the universe? After all, the original 'extension' was lawless Calvinball nonsense. Commit to the bit that laws don't matter and be done with it!" Bluesky, April 4, 2025, https://bsky.app/profile/alanrozenshtein.com/post/3llyyfkas6224.

328 **In an unbuttoned tux and black suede loafers:** "TikTok CEO Shou Zi Chew," hollywoodreporter, TikTok, April 6, 2025, https://www.tiktok.com/@hollywoodreporter/video/7490044507417791787.

328 **his first TikTok in months:** "Hello from LA!," shou.time, TikTok, April 6, 2025, https://www.tiktok.com/@shou.time/video/7490019024907291950.

328 **The next morning, the most popular comment:** Desktop screenshot of Shou's post (cited above) taken by Emily Baker-White on April 6, 2025, at 9:47 a.m.